Who Is an African?

Who Is an African?

Race, Identity, and Destiny in Post-apartheid South Africa

Edited by
Chammah J. Kaunda and
Roderick R. Hewitt

Foreword by
Marshall W. Murphree and
Nobuhle Hlongwa

LEXINGTON BOOKS / FORTRESS ACADEMIC
Lanham • Boulder • New York • London

Published by Lexington Books/Fortress Academic
An imprint of The Rowman & Littlefield Publishing Group, Inc.
4501 Forbes Boulevard, Suite 200, Lanham, Maryland 20706
www.rowman.com

Unit A, Whitacre Mews, 26-34 Stannary Street, London SE11 4AB

British Library Cataloguing in Publication Information Available

Library of Congress Cataloging-in-Publication Data Available

Library of Congress Control Number: 2018952039

ISBN 978-1-978700-54-3 (cloth : alk. paper)
ISBN 978-1-978700-55-0 (electronic)

∞™ The paper used in this publication meets the minimum requirements of American National Standard for Information Sciences—Permanence of Paper for Printed Library Materials, ANSI/NISO Z39.48-1992.

Printed in the United States of America

Contents

List of Figures

List of Tables

Foreword

In supporting the preparation and publication of this book, the administrators of the Maurice Webb Estate have in one dimension followed a well-worn path which has sought to assist efforts to diminish and eliminate ascriptive disadvantage in South African society. Put more simply, the Webb Trust has contributed to the battle against racial, ethnic, gender, and other forms of discrimination in South Africa since Maurice Webb's death in the late 1960s.

From time immemorial, societies have grouped their members on the basis of an ascriptive criteria, i.e., characteristics over which they themselves have had no control—age, race, early socialisation, and gender. Too frequently power elites within societies have assigned these groupings differential status. Herein have lain the roots of discrimination and disadvantage. Humankind's earliest recorded documents chronicle the negative impact of this discrimination on women and conquered peoples. Slavery is another outcome, particularly prominent in the colonial histories of the Americas and the Caribbean. Slavery was, in fact, the most important single component in an extractive system that robbed Africa of much of its wealth during the seventeenth and eighteenth centuries. The area that now constitutes South Africa was subject to relatively little extractive slavery but was subjected to what was in effect internal slavery, with indigenous people being accorded inferior status subordinate to a minority of immigrant whites. Further compounding the racial broth of South Africa at the turn of the twentieth century was the presence of a large number of people from the Indian subcontinent, imported as indentured labor to work in the cane fields.

Such was the South Africa to which Maurice Webb came in 1921. Born in 1889 in London to a Quaker and Fabian family, he left school at the age of fourteen but maintained a lively interest in travel, reading, and music. His questing spirit led him to join a publishing firm in Durban in 1921 at a time when he had no particular interest in race relations or social reform. He was, however, an intensely socially aware individual and before long he became deeply involved in organizations that sought to redress the plight of the underprivileged. Thirty-four such agencies can be identified and it can be noted that he was a cofounder of the South African Institute of Race Relations and chairperson of the Adams College Board of Governors for several years. He died in Bulawayo in 1966, leaving the bulk of his estate for use in studying and eliminating prejudice and discrimination.

Over the fifty years since his death, the administrators of Maurice Webb's estate can reasonably claim to have contributed to this objective. This is generally an age in which discrimination has been discredited, in South Africa notably when it transitioned to a democratic form of government in 1994. Discrimination still exists, however, and we continue to allocate Webb funds to address this. We are also aware of another growing threat to our societal well-being, which is a second component of our program. The crucial element of committed identity is under threat, largely from a pervasive international media complex that offers personal achievement as a sufficient identity goal. Collective identity, if not inexorably linked with status ranking, is a more acceptable thing. Webb found this identity in the divine creation of an undiscriminated humanity. In an oft-quoted comment he said, "I believe that no true society can exist unless there is at the heart of it love of man for man and love of man for God. You cannot love a man and hide him behind a green belt or a ghetto wall. You must know him as a person and see God in his face."[1]

The African continent itself could become a pole for a dynamic and productive identity. Considered by many as the cradle of humanity, ravaged by those from other continents at times in her history, she could become the identity icon of a new age. The path to such a goal is however a contested one, as the chapters of this book show. The search for what one of these chapters calls "liberating identifications," when held within an overarching collective unity, is difficult. This book gives us pointers, and we commend it to all those with an interest in contemporary African identity.

Prof. Marshall W. Murphree
Administrator
The Webb Estate

NOTE

1. Herbert Moyo and R. Simangaliso Kumalo, *The Life and Times of a Man of Faith* (Pietermaritzburg, South Africa: Maurice Webb Memorial Trust, 2012), 8. Gender-exclusive language is admitted in the quoted text.

FOREWORD

South Africa as a rainbow nation continues to experience inequality and this has had severe consequences for the country. Poverty and poor service delivery have resulted in the 2008 and 2015 xenophobic attacks against African migrants in South Africa. It is critical to decipher the root causes of inequality in South Africa. It is true that in South Africa's new dispensation of freedom and democracy there are still unresolved, embedded deep issues of race that are a product of mental colonization and Apartheid. It is crucial to indicate how wealth and education reproduce inequality. Cultural capital reproduces a dominant culture that is embodied in inequalities which, in turn, causes differential service provision. It benefits the dominant class. Local communities are supposed to benefit from social, economic, cultural, and political services, but this requires that they be linked to or be part of the dominant class and this is not happening. The dominant class is keen to maintain its privileged position and has no interest in sharing the fruits of globalization with less dominant classes. In South Africa, the majority of the previously disenfranchised population still lacks the requisite skills and experience to participate meaningfully in the economy and other institutions of public life. It could thus be argued that under conditions of acute economic deprivation, foreign African immigrants who compete with the marginalized black South African population for scarce resources become the easiest and most accessible targets.

Globalization is aimed at reconstructing the international economy and political relations in a way that enhances exploitation. It does not develop the locals and their communities. Instead, the benefit accrues to the private, profit-making enterprises. There are various scholars who have lamented the negative effects of globalization for developing country business. These include: maximization of profit by transnational corporations, leading to underdevelopment of the host country; the tendency of developing countries to lower environmental controls in order to attract foreign investments; and loss of cultural uniqueness and an emergence of a global-culture, which is often the dominant culture. Globalization has eroded the culture of *ubuntu*. Local communities have been marginalized on the basis of the basic human right issues, amongst which is access to information in the language of their choice. Local people in South Africa who are in the majority are being denied the opportunity to use their African languages, thus minoritizing African languages, which is a violation of rights enshrined in the South African Constitution. African languages are marginalized in all spheres, and it is even worse in higher education where universities are generating knowledge.

The contribution by different authors in this book explores strategies for decolonizing Euro-Western knowledge and challenges dominant and colonial mind-set. The authors interrogate questions of African identity in South Africa's dispensation of freedom and democracy. They challenge Afro-phobia, a situation whereby black South Africans who have endured centuries of oppression and of having their lives devalued in turn internalize oppression and hence do not value their own lives as well as the lives of other African nationals. In this case, there is a need to heal the wounds as a matter of social justice in our communities.

A typical example is the so-called "Truth and Reconciliation Commission" chaired by Archbishop Desmond Mpilo Tutu which was seeking to unearth the truth about what happened during the dark days of Apartheid. To a larger extent, the objectives of the commission were met although in other circles it opened up wounds that were healing. The book tackles the question of race and identity within the borders of South Africa with the hope of bringing about peace, reconciliation, and harmony for all.

Prof. Nobuhle Hlongwa
Dean of Teaching and Learning
University of KwaZulu-Natal

Acknowledgments

Many scholars have contributed to making this book a reality. To the executive committee of the Maurice Webb Trust who are well known in South Africa for their work on promoting research on race relations. When the vision to produce this volume evolved in 2015 and they were approached to give support for the publication, their positive response set the stage for this publication.

To Dr. (Mrs.) Mutale M. Kaunda, who served as the editorial administrator of the project while she engaged in her doctoral studies, which she successfully completed.

To the fourteen scholars who have contributed to this volume and tolerated the persistent communication of the editorial team seeking their commitment to the timely submission of their texts and revisions after a rigorous double-blind peer review process.

A special word of thanks goes to Prof. R. Simangaliso Kumalo who is chairperson of the Maurice Webb Trust for his encouragement of this publication.

To Prof. Nobuhle Hlongwa, who had a brief stint as acting dean in the School of Religion, Philosophy and Classics at the University of KwaZulu-Natal, for her support toward seeing the completion of the book.

We end on a note of immeasurable thanksgiving to the *God of Life* for giving us energy and grace to work on this project.

Introduction

Who Is an African?

Chammah J. Kaunda and Roderick R. Hewitt

The eruption of xenophobic attacks against foreigners mostly of black African origins in some communities of KwaZulu-Natal and elsewhere across the country, including Johannesburg, has not only led to negative national and international press coverage, but also had serious ramifications on the social cohesion of South African society.[1] The 2008 and now 2015 xenophobic attacks, especially against African migrants, resulted in threats of retaliation from other African nations whose citizens were being targeted. The deep-seated fears within sections of the society are based upon stereotyping behavioral perceptions about foreigners to the extent that the working-class migrants are called *makwerekwere*, a pejorative term for foreigners. This diverse nation of different ethnic groups has no other choice but to deal with the social cohesion challenge that race and identity politics pose if outcomes of just peace and reconciliation are to be woven into the construct of nation building.

The seriousness of this matter points to the need for in-depth conversation and study that can inform policy development and change in the role of race and ethnic identity within the "rainbow" configuration of nation building. The shift of focus in social and economic development policies necessary to respond to the entrenched challenges of inequality and poverty points to an acknowledgment that there are unresolved structural identity issues bequeathed by the nation's colonial and Apartheid past. This book locates South Africa within the wider construct of the African identity and argues that there is an embedded schizophrenic identity crisis within the society that requires scholarly interrogation. The legacies of South Africa's colonial and Apartheid past have left deep psychological wounds on race that have not been healed since the advent of democratic rule in 1994. The different presentations involve scholarly voices from different ethnic groups that are residents of the nation. Their different social, economic, and political location within the national landscape offers a unique opportunity to examine the central research question of this study: "Who is an African?"

RACE AND IDENTITY

The subject of race and identity is therefore a burning issue that continues to occupy the minds not only of South Africans but the wider residents of the continent of Africa and those who are of African descent who, by force or choice, have become part of the Americas, Europe, Asia, and elsewhere who are identified as Africans in the Diaspora. In the words of the eminent Kenyan writer Ngugi wa-Thiong'o, those who are situated in the diaspora are identified as "Africans-in-exile."[2] Within the South African context, there are many local citizens of differing ethnic backgrounds that refuse to identify themselves as African even though their country is part of the African continent. They are South Africans. Africans are those that live outside of the borders of South Africa within the African continent. To a great extent, their Afro-phobic worldview has been malformed by the residue of fake news, alternate facts, and propaganda from the previous Apartheid-led socialization machinery, contemporary biased media, and other institutions of power that have made it part of their agenda to consistently prescribe a negative portrayal of Africa and its peoples. In the overarching categories of perception, expectation, and representation, Africa receives negative connotations attached to its people who are stereotypically based upon notions of white superiority as the norm, and finally this intentional ideological construct usually results in Africa/ns being misunderstood and mislabeled. The following negative stereotypes are generally associated with Africa/ns: refugees, poverty, ugly, Ebola, HIV/AIDS, corrupt leaders, etc. The impact of these on the psycho-social health of many Africans has resulted in self-hate and shame of one's ethnic identity.

The impact of all this has resulted in people who have demonstrated schizophrenic behavior that mimics values that are meant to devalue their personhood and that of others.[3] The advertising power of the media that stereotypes white as beautiful and black as ugly has resulted in many chemically bleaching their skin to "look fairer" and lots of money being spent by poor black women importing hair from Asia and Brazil to meet their beauty needs. This all points to a serious crisis of identity.[4] The struggles of identity, race, and ethnicity within the society also suggest multiple processes associated with globalization in contemporary society.

WHO IS AN AFRICAN? A SOCIOPOLITICAL DISCOURSE

According to the Freedom Charter (1955) and the South African Constitution (1996), South Africa belongs to all who live in it. However, a clear distinction should be made, on the one hand, between those who can be regarded as being authentically African in South Africa in terms of race and identity, and those who rightfully belong to the body politic based on birth or some other attribute, on the other. The review of the literature on the question of race and identity within the South African context will be made in order to problematize the notion for an ever-changing society. "Who is an African?" constitutes a highly contested question. The University of KwaZulu-Natal's commendable emphasis on being identified as a premier institution of African scholarship for the twenty-first century and beyond demonstrates an intentional, unapologetic statement of commitment to an ideological knowledge discourse that gives priority to African scholarship. This makes the topic of this book, "Who is an African?," intensely relevant.

At a gathering of the Pietermaritzburg Cluster of Theological Institutions held at Seth Mokithini (Methodist) Seminary on June 16 (National Youth Day), 2011, a provocative presentation was made by Charles Villa-Vicencio, professor of systematic theology at the University of Cape Town, author of the final five-volume *Truth and Reconciliation Report* and the director of the Institute for Justice and Reconciliation. He generated intense discussion and debate around this question: "Who is an African?" It was this burning issue that suggested the need for serious and responsible research of the subject.

The structure of the book is divided into three sections that cover issues surrounding the themes of Racism, Xenophobia, and Cultural Identity; Gender, Sexuality and Social Cohesion; and Religion, Protest, and Africanness. In the first theme, seven South Africans and one Zimbabwean interrogated a sub-theme that emerges from the ongoing challenges linked to race and identity. Their different ethnic identity as South African Indian, black, white, and Zimbabwean black offers a powerful scholarly contrast of reading the local landscape on race and racism. These scholars have identified the key issues of: The Changing Salience of Race: Discrimination and Diversity in South Africa; Racism in South Africa Post 1994; The Cause of Afrophobia; Race, Place and Indian Identities in Contemporary South Africa; Being Black Conscious, Being Nonracial, Being African; and *Umuntu Akalahlwa:* An Exploration of an African Ethics. In the second section, the African identity is explored around the sub-theme of gender, sexuality, and social cohesion. The diverse social location of the different scholars linked with this section was intentionally chosen because of the critical discourse that they bring to issues linked to The Role of Indian Women's Movements in Social Transformation; Identity Construction of African Women in the Midst of Land Dispossession; Masculinity and Afrikaner Identity in "Religious" Post-apartheid South Africa; Determinants of LGBTIQ Marginality in South

Africa; and Rituals of Female Solidarity: The Role of *Imbusa* in Promoting Social Cohesion among Married Women in Pietermaritzburg, South Africa. These different issues have exposed the importance of gender, sexualities, and masculinities in the identity construction of South Africans.

The final section covers the sub-theme of Religion, Protest, and Africanness, which pushes the boundaries of African identity to covering issues on Afrikaans Musical Spirituality as rearticulated aspects of the 1978 Afrikaans *Psalm–en Gesangeboek*; Rastafari Perspectives on African identities: Lucky Dube's "Different Colours / One People" in conversation with Peter Tosh's "I Am an African"; Locating Islam and African Muslim Identity within Black/Africana Existential Thought; Urban Immigrant Pentecostal Missiology: The Case of an Immigrant Zambian Pentecostal Pastor in South Africa; and Messianicity and Canonicity within a Postcolonial South African Context. The scholars have focused on some important emerging issues that impact on minority communities within the changing South African sociopolitical and religious landscape

PAN-AFRICAN PERSPECTIVES

This book goes beyond its South African primary identity focus to embrace Pan-African perspectives and argues that Africa's collective and sustainable development lies in the creative and constructive use of its human resources within the continent and beyond. For one thing, this Pan-African vision was so eloquently articulated by pioneering leaders such as Marcus Mosiah Garvey (who declared, "Let Africa be our guiding star: our star of destiny,"[5] and argues that Africa must become the organizing and operating principle for which people of African descent should ensure "consistency and coherence to their way of life"[6]), H. I. M. Haile Selassie, emperor of Ethiopia, President Kwame Nkrumah of Ghana, Jomo Kenyatta of Kenya, and President Nelson Mandela of South Africa, along with many others. Their Afrocentric vision has now been legally entrenched in the Constitutive Act of the African Union in that the act has been amended to make allowance for the direct involvement of the African diaspora in the development agenda of the continent as a whole.

This Pan-African solidarity is politically, culturally, and economically entrenched in the South African rainbow identity that the narrative of reggae artist Lucky Dube describes as: "Many Colours / One People." He employs a Rastafari critique of interrogating the subject of race and ethnicity within the South African context to postulates that it must not become an encumbrance to social and economic progress but a blessing. He postulates, using the voices of those who live on the margins of society, to argue that justice and acceptance of "the other" constitutes the discourse through which South Africa, with its many ethnic differences, can become one people.

This volume therefore constitutes a scholarly attempt to contribute to the ongoing discussion and debate by locating the question of "Who is an African?" within a larger contextual and conceptual framework and by reflecting on the central question of race and identity within and beyond the South African context. This volume also represents an attempt to determine the implications posed by race and identity issues on the contemporary search for nation building that embodies diversity and plurality within its body polity.

NOTES

1. Ashwin Desai, "An Exploratory Critique of the Notion of Social Cohesion in Contemporary South Africa," *Psychology in Society* 49 (2015): 99–113; Sandra Makwembere, "Hallmarks of Irresponsible and Unresponsive Governance: Internal Xenophobic Attacks in South Africa's Municipalities," *TD: Journal for Transdisciplinary Research in Southern Africa*, special edition 11/4 (2015): 118–26.
2. Ngugi wa-Thiong'o, "Writing against Neo-Colonialism," in *Criticism and Ideology*, ed. Kristen Holst Petersen (Stockholm: Nordic Africa Institute, 1988), 92–103.
3. See V. S. Naipaul, *The Mimic Men* (London: Penguin Random House, 2001). Naipaul describes a colonial experience of mimicking in a postcolonial world.
4. Naipaul, *The Mimic Men*.
5. Amy Jacques-Garvey, ed., "Philosophy and Opinions of Marcus Garvey," *Journal of Pan African Studies* (eBook, 2009), <https://archive.org/stream/ThePhilosophyOpinionsOfMarcusGarveyOrAfricaForThe Africans/EbookPhilAndOpinions_djvu.txt/> [Accessed: June 15, 2017].
6. Noel Leo Erskine, *From Garvey to Marley-Rastafari Theology* (Gainesville, FL: University Press of Florida, 2005), 44.

I

RACISM, XENOPHOBIA, AND CULTURAL IDENTITY

ONE

The Changing Salience of Race

Discrimination and Diversity in South Africa[1]

Jeremy Seekings

INTRODUCTION

In a world in which racial labeling and discrimination are regrettably commonplace, the South African system of Apartheid stood out as an extreme attempt to order a society explicitly and systematically according to racial categories. Many aspects of Apartheid were not unique to South Africa. What made Apartheid unique was its systematic depth and breadth, as the powers of a modern state were deployed to order society along "racial" lines, going far beyond racism and racial discrimination to generalized social engineering around state-sanctioned racial ideology and legislation. It would therefore be astonishing if post-apartheid South African society was not shaped profoundly by the experience of Apartheid, remaining distinctive in terms of the social, political, or economic roles played by "race." Despite the rhetorical commitment to nonracialism of the African National Congress (ANC), the abolition of Apartheid-era racial legislation and the adoption of a widely lauded constitution, race remains ever present in contemporary South Africa. To a large extent, this is due to a deep-rooted and enduring consciousness of race in society. To some extent, it is due to factors that reflect choices made by post-apartheid political elites: the use of the race card in public life, including in politics, and new policies of racial discrimination involving, especially, affirmative action in employment and contracting, with the stated objective of redressing the disadvantages experienced by nonwhite South Africans (either collectively or individually) under Apartheid.

Racial discrimination in economic life against black[2] people has been largely ended in South Africa. Some lingering discrimination by white employers against black people no doubt persists, but it is probably more than offset by the effects of affirmative action. Persistent racial inequalities reflect class stratification rather than racial discrimination, as we have argued at length elsewhere.[3] Income is distributed within the African population almost as unequally as within the population as a whole, as opportunities have expanded rapidly for many African/black people to move into better-paid occupations at the same time as many others languish in poverty because of poor schooling and chronic unemployment. Yet society remains highly racialized. Interracial contact, let alone marriage, remains very limited.

This continuing salience of race is surprising in several respects. First, the deracialization of citizenship and public policy (with the minor exception of affirmative action and black economic empowerment) removed the impetus to racial identities that many scholars emphasized when discussing the South African past.[4] Second, the precise salience of race in South Africa stands in sharp contrast to other societies with which South Africa is often compared. Telles shows how important race is in contemporary Brazil, but in *some*, rather than all respects. Contrary to the Brazilian ideology of "racial democracy," racial discrimination seems significant in economic life. Yet in terms of identities and social interactions, Brazilians are remarkably nonracial.[5] Telles distinguishes between vertical relationships, in which race is important, and horizontal ones, in which it is not. Post-apartheid South Africa appears to be the opposite of this. The vertical dimension of racism appears to have been largely eliminated (or perhaps even reversed), but the horizontal dimension appears resilient (or perhaps has even increased, as racial differences within the increasingly multiracial middle class have grown and become more visible). In this chapter, I examine some of the reasons for the continuing salience in South Africa of what Telles calls the horizontal dimension of racism.

RACIAL CLASSIFICATION AND IDENTITY

The foundation of Apartheid was the system of racial categorization enshrined in law by the 1950 Population Registration Act (and subsequent amendments). The act provided for all South Africans to be classified into one of three basic racial categories:

> A white person is one who in appearance is, or who is generally accepted as, a white person, but does not include a person who, although in appearance obviously a white person, is generally accepted as a Colored person. A native is a person who is in fact or is generally accepted as a member of any aboriginal race or tribe of Africa. A Colored person is a person who is neither a white person nor a native.

Later, a fourth category—Indian—was added, for people of South Asian descent, the label "native" was replaced by the labels "Bantu" and "black." Racial classification was recorded in official identity documentation. From 1970 the "black" category was further subdivided into ethnic or linguistic groups[6] (such as Zulu and Xhosa).

This racial categorization was largely "commonsensical" and consensual, based on agreed and broadly coterminus factors (descent, language or culture, and appearance). In difficult or contested cases, classification was not based on either descent or purely biological markers. Instead, the cultural markers of "appearance" and "general acceptance" were most important. While informal "rules" about appearance—including about skin color or hair—were used by white officials and lay people alike, they were used inconsistently, and appearance was generally interpreted in terms of social standing or class. Overall, judgments about social standing (friends, work, name, dress, deportment, tastes) were most important in contested cases.[7] Culture was more important than descent among black South Africans also. ANC leader Walter Sisulu was therefore (generally) accepted as African even though his father was white. Ambiguous and contested cases generally involved the very small minority of "Colored" people. "Colored" was a composite and diverse category including the descendants of relationships between white and black people, the descendants of "Malay" slaves brought from Southeast Asia and (after 1970) descendants of the indigenous Khoi and San who inhabited the Western Cape prior to the arrival of either white or African/black people and did not speak Bantu languages. Segregating white and Colored people was a primary objective of the Apartheid state.

The abolition of the Population Registration Act in 1991 promised the end of official racial classification. This was not to be. The existing racial classifications of South Africans born before then remained recorded in a population register and the official forms used to register births continued to require information on the parents' "race." As Maré[8] shows, racial classification (including self-classification) has remained routine in bureaucratic forms decades after the supposed end of Apartheid. This continuing classification goes far beyond the requirements of new legislation that provides for racial discrimination in favor of black, and especially African, people).

Whether because or independently of this historic and continuing official classification, South Africans tend to see their society in racialized terms. Asked about racial identities, only a tiny proportion of South Africans aver the Apartheid-era categories of "African" (replacing, in official use, the former label "black"), white, Colored, and Indian. How people categorize themselves also accords closely with how (they say) other people see them. In other words, there remains a close correlation between official Apartheid-era and post-Apartheid racial classifications, post-Apartheid self-classification (or identity) and post-Apartheid classification (or labeling) by other people.[9] This does not mean, however, that these racial identities are the only identities that South Africans have. Asked who they are, South Africans will often say they are South African, and that they are proud of this.[10] Increasingly, they are likely also to employ class identities (working class, middle class, poor, etc). And many also use nonracial cultural identities, including religious ones (Christian, Muslim) or ethnic ones (Xhosa, Zulu, Afrikaans).

Racial categories themselves mean different things to different people. Asked for reasons for their racial self-classification, white South Africans typically refer to their physical appearance or descent. African and Colored South Africans do not refer to physical appearance or descent, but instead emphasize "culture" (and, in the case of Colored people, the categorization of the Apartheid period). There is little difference in the distribution of self-assessed skin color among African and Colored people, but white people see their skin color as distinctly paler.[11] While almost all South Africans use racial categorization in everyday life, it seems to be white South Africans who hold onto biological conceptions of race.

This is in part because white South Africans—as with white people in many other contexts—take their culture for granted. Culturally, whiteness is invisible to most white people.[12] African people are much more conscious of their cultural distinctiveness. Speaking different languages at home, often attending different churches, and perhaps above all retaining distinctive beliefs about, for example, ancestors and witchcraft[13] and family.[14] The end of Apartheid has also been accompanied by a resurgence of "Colored" identity. Under Apartheid, Colored identity was defined by the intermediate status of Colored people in the racial hierarchy: aspirations to assimilation into white society and fears of relegation to the status of African people combined with widespread feelings of shame as well as marginality. Following the Apartheid era, a racialized conception of "Colored-ness" grew stronger, with renewed affinities to whiteness and deepened racism toward African people.[15]

In recognition of cultural diversity, post-Apartheid nation building in South Africa employed the discourse of the multicultural "rainbow nation" rather than building a common nonracial South African national identity. The National Anthem thus combined elements of both the hymn associated with the liberation movements and the Apartheid-era anthem, and is sung in four major languages. Official multiculturalism serves, however, to reproduce the culturally based racial identities of the past.

In 1998 the then deputy president, Thabo Mbeki, emphasized racial inequality in a controversial speech in which he described South Africa as comprising "two nations, the one black and the other white":

> One of these nations is white, relatively prosperous, regardless of gender or geographical dispersal. It has ready access to a developed economic, physical, educational, communication and other infrastructure. This enables it to argue that, except for the persistence of gender discrimination against women, all members of this nation have the possibility of exercising their right to equal opportunity, and the development opportunities to which the Constitution of 1993 committed our country. The second and larger nation of South Africa is black and poor, with the worst-affected being women in rural areas, the black rural population in general and the disabled. This nation lives under conditions of grossly underdeveloped economic, physical, educational, communication and other infrastructure. It has virtually no possibility of exercising what in reality amounts to a theoretical right to equal opportunity, that right being equal within the black nation only to the extent that it is equally incapable of realisation.[16]

Mbeki here was drawing on a tradition of referring to "two nations" that originated in the mid-nineteenth century, class-divided Britain (in the writings of Benjamin Disraeli[17]) and was popularized in still race-divided United States of America in the late twentieth century.

For Mbeki, the project of nation building in South Africa entailed bridging the divides between the racially defined "nations" above. "Nation building is the construction of the reality and the sense of common nationhood which would result from the abolition of disparities in the quality of life among South Africans based on the racial, gender and geographic inequalities we all inherited from the past," he said in 1998.[18] Note that there is no mention here of class inequalities. The implication is that the "national question"—defined in racial terms—has precedence above the social question of class-based inequalities. Programs of race-based affirmative action are to have precedence over pro-poor or interclass redistribution.

On average, white South Africans remain privileged after Apartheid, and most African people remain poor. But data on the average person within racial categories ignores the rapid increase in inequality within those categories, especially within the African population. The rapid growth of the African elite and middle class, at the same time as unemployment locks many other African people into chronic poverty, has resulted in incomes (and opportunities) within the African population being distributed nearly as unequally as in South Africa as a whole, and this inequality is as extreme as anywhere in the world. It would be more appropriate to view South Africa economically in terms of three "nations": the almost entirely African poor, the mostly African working classes, and the multiracial middle classes and elites.[19] Culturally, however, Mbeki might be closer to the mark, insofar as cultural differences persist. Even here, however, there has been massive change.

The growth of the African middle class has been the result primarily of the deracialization of education and of the labor market, and secondly of discriminatory post-Apartheid policies of affirmative action.[20] The public service implemented affirmative action policies rapidly after 1994. The 1998 Employment Equity Act required midsized and large private employers to set targets for the transformation of their workforce and to report on their progress in achieving these targets. The growth of African elites has been the result primarily of discriminatory policies of black economic empowerment in business. The 2003 Black Economic Empowerment Act set in motion a massive redistribution of corporate ownership from the old white elite to the emerging black elite and indirectly expanded opportunities for black managers, professionals, and entrepreneurs. The African middle class and elite are the primary agents of a reinvention of African culture: "African" names and dress are adopted, and supposedly traditional rituals are practiced with newfound fervor.

Post-Apartheid South Africa is thus characterized by a paradoxical combination of features. Race is no longer coterminous with class, with opportunities for upward mobility opening rapidly for some African people while opportunities remain limited for many others. Class is increasingly important. Racism has almost certainly declined. Yet race retains its central position in identities and culture, and political parties can and do continue to play the race card. The priority attached to the rhetoric and policies of affirmative action suggests that the national question takes precedence over the social question, but at the same time African elites rhetorically recommit themselves to nonracialism and a concern for the poor.

Maré has wondered how far the "ordinariness" of racial consciousness (or "race-thinking") in post-Apartheid South Africa is the consequence of post-Apartheid policies of racial categorization:

> To meet with the requirements of the Employment Equity Act, to gain admission to universities, to claim travel allowances, to play in sports teams, to provide information for tax purposes, to ask the National Research Foundation for funding, to register births and so on, each requires a statement of race belonging. . . . There is no opportunity in these forms to avoid the issue. At every level there is an official, from the government minister responsible to the company personnel officer or employment equity manager, to monitor adherence or compliance or progress. No provision is made for alternatives to the basic "Four races" of Apartheid South Africa, or to reject such classification. Leaving the space blank, which remarkably few seem to do, means that someone else is required to complete it to balance the books.[21]

Even if the state was to abandon any such administrative categorization, it is hard to imagine that South Africans' acute consciousness of race would vanish. South Africans' racialized identities and perceptions of others have strong roots in civil society. "Race-thinking" persists uneasily alongside a strong commitment to transcending the racial divisions of Apartheid. It is the deep-rootedness of race-thinking (among African as much as if not more than white people) that makes debates over, especially, affirmative action, so complex and invidious.

RACISM AND RACE RELATIONS

The study of interracial attitudes and interactions (or what was formerly called "race relations") has exploded in post-Apartheid South Africa, after a period of dormancy in the final decades of Apartheid. Research has diversified despite the facts that most people continue to live in residential areas that are, in practice, racially segregated, and most children continue to attend schools with children of the same "race." Indeed, one of the most striking findings of post-Apartheid survey research is how few South Africans enjoy much interracial contact. In a survey conducted in 2000–2001 by James Gibson,[22] white, Colored, and Indian respondents were asked a series of questions about African people, and African people the same questions about white people. Only 16 percent of the respondents, weighted appropriately, reported having "a great deal" of contact at work with members of the designated group, while only 6 percent reported having "a great deal" of such contact outside work. Another 13 percent reported having "some" such contact at work and another 13 percent reported having some such contact outside of work. Just 8 percent said they ate meals "quite often" with members of the designated group. A tiny 4 percent said they had "quite a number" of friends in the designated group, with another 20 percent saying they had "only a small number" of such friends. Overall, one in three South Africans reported any of the above; two out of three South Africans said that they had little or no contact with members of the designated group.

Subsequent research in Cape Town—which has distinctive demographics, with African and white minorities alongside a Colored near-majority—found what appear initially to be rather higher levels of cross-racial contact.[23] Only 40 percent of African and Colored respondents said that all of their five closest friends were from the same racial group as them, and only about 20 percent of white respondents said the same. For sure, large majorities of respondents in all three racial groups said that all or most of their closest friends were from the same racial group, but the data suggest that, in Cape Town at least, only a minority of the adult population moves in entirely mono-racial social circles. Even smaller proportions of working people say that they work in mono-racial working environments.

The apparently higher level of interracial contact in Cape Town probably reflects two factors. The first is methodological: The 2005 survey did not ask white and Colored respondents about their interaction with African people specifically, nor did it ask African people about their interaction with white people specifically. It is likely that much "cross-racial" contact is between with white and Colored people, or between African and Colored people, neither of which would have shown up in Gibson's earlier study.[24] Second, it is likely that there are higher levels of cross-racial contact in urban than in rural areas. There are certainly many more opportunities for such contact in urban areas.

Perhaps unsurprisingly, given the general lack of contact, Gibson[25] found evidence of interracial suspicion and distrust on the part of non-African respondents toward African people and among African respondents to white people. The bars in figure 1.1 show the proportion of the weighted sample who agreed (or agreed strongly) with each of seven statements about the designated group. Almost one in five South Africans agreed that South Africa would be a better place without the designated racial group. Almost half agreed that they do not believe what members of the designated racial group said, that they feel uncomfortable around them, and that they find it hard to imagine ever being friends with one of them. Almost two out of three South Africans agreed that it is difficult

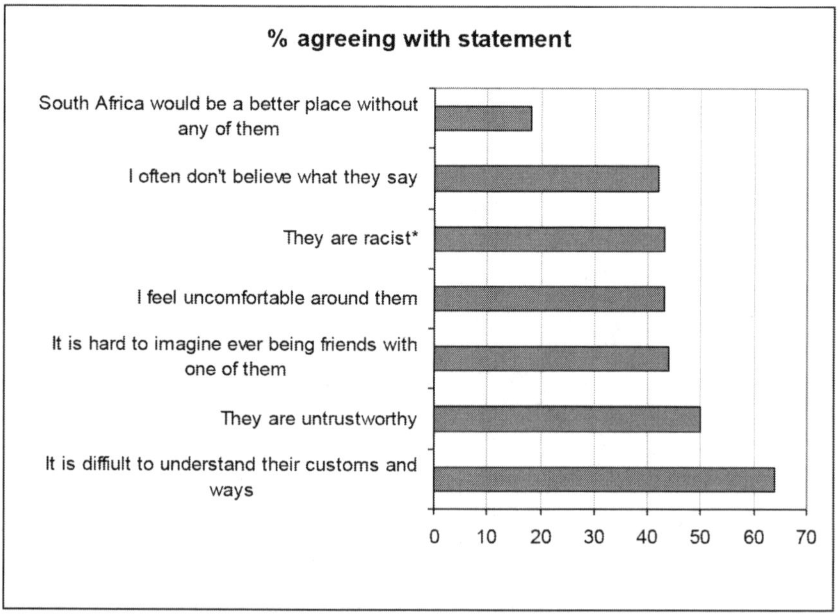

Figure 1.1. The limits to social de racialization, 2000–01.

to understand the customs and ways of the designated group. Without exception, larger proportions of African respondents agreed with these statements about white people than did white, Colored, or Indian respondents when asked about African people.[26] The 2003 South African Social Attitudes Survey (SASAS) similarly found that large minorities of every racial group agreed that most members of their own racial group were racist. A large majority of African people thought that most white people were racist. Large majorities of white and Colored people thought that most African people were racist.[27]

Gibson[28] shows that there is an inverse correlation between most forms of interracial contact and racial *dis*trust: The more contact that respondents report with members of the designated group, the less likely they are to agree with statements indicating prejudice or wariness. The exception to this is contact at work, which has no significant effect on interracial attitudes. Gibson shows that contact is especially important to white, Colored, and Indian respondents.[29] Subsequent research tended to corroborate this.[30]

Limited social de-racialization does not mean that there has been no perceived improvement in race relations. A series of surveys have found that South Africans believe that race relations have improved since the end of Apartheid. According to Gibson's 2001 survey, 16 percent said that race relations had improved a great deal, and a further 45 percent said that race relations had improved somewhat. In 2003 a survey conducted by the Kaiser Family Foundation, the *Washington Post*, and Harvard University found that as many as 68 percent of South Africans believed that race relations were better than they had been under Apartheid, and as many expected that race relations would continue to improve over the next five years.[31] The 2003 SASAS also found that most African, Colored, and Indian people (but less than half of white people) said that race relations had improved since 1994.[32] But the same surveys found evidence that *improved* race relations did not mean *good* race relations. Race relations remains a pressing problem for 49 percent of Gibson's respondents and a further 33 percent described them as important.[33]

In Cape Town, where there appears to be a higher level of interracial interaction than in South Africa as a whole, there is less discomfort about racial interaction. Survey data from 2005 show that only one in five African adults, one in six Colored adults, and hardly any white adults said that they felt uncomfortable around people who were not the same race as them. Similarly, small or very small proportions said that they could not imagine being friends with people of different races.[34] Much of this openness to interracial interaction might be between only two of the three "racial" groups in Cape Town: It is possible that white people in Cape Town feel comfortable with and can imagine being friendly with Colored people (and vice versa), but not with African people (and vice versa). Nonetheless, the data suggests a degree of de-racialization.

At the same time, however, there is striking evidence that racial differences are highly salient in some social situations. In the Cape Town survey, only a minority of respondents said that they had actually socialized with people from other racial groups in the past seven days. Respondents also discriminated routinely with respect to their attitudes toward cross-racial marriage. While very few respondents articulated explicit prejudice against cross-racial marriage, almost all were very much more positive about marriages to members of their own racial group than they were to inter-racial marriage (see above figures). African respondents, for example, were not at all opposed to kin marrying African people, but were relatively hostile to kin marrying white, Colored, or Indian people.

Without longitudinal data, it is hard to assess just how much attitudes have changed over time. Largely anecdotal evidence suggests that explicit and overt racism has declined. But it seems likely that a consciousness of racial difference has been resilient, and this is reflected in specific contexts such as attitudes toward cross-racial marriage.

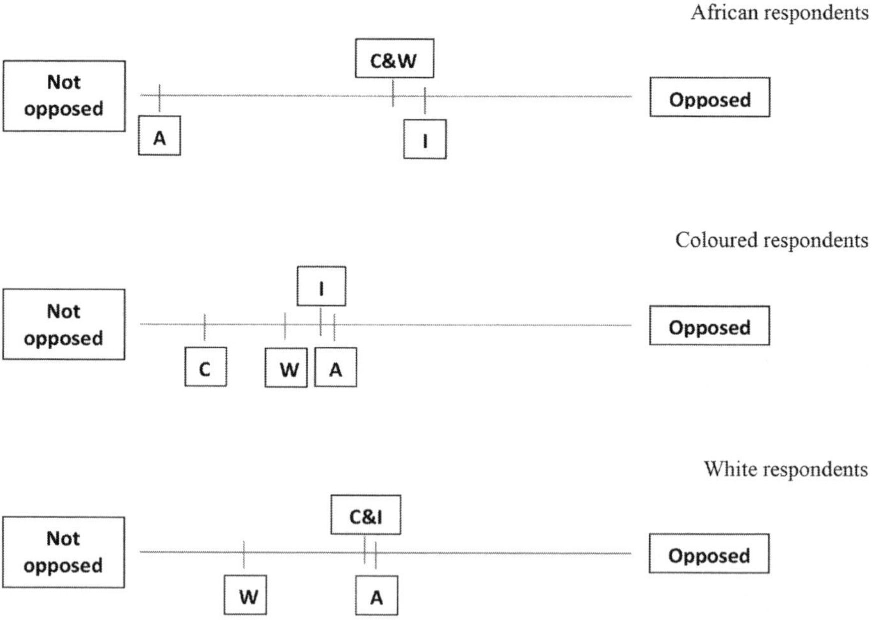

Figure 1.2. Attitude toward a family member marrying someone, according to race of respondent and of the prospective spouse (A for African, C for Coloured, I for Indian, W for white).

INTERRACIAL INTEGRATION AND INTERACTION

Patterns of residential segregation have not broken down to any great extent since the transition to democracy. Analyzing data from successive population censuses, Christopher showed that South African towns and cities began to desegregate racially in the 1990s.[35] White segregation levels (as measured by a standard segregation index) peaked in Cape Town in the 1991 census (and in South Africa's other major cities in either the 1985 or 1991 censuses). Segregation levels for all racial groups declined between the 1991 and 1996 censuses. But the pace of desegregation was very slow indeed. Christopher updated his analysis using 2001 census data.[36] Slow desegregation continues, but "the vast majority of the urban population continues to live in highly segregated suburbs."[37] More recent research using 2011 census data shows that desegregation continued in both Cape Town and Johannesburg, but both cities remain highly segregated.[38]

Indeed most new housing areas established after the end of Apartheid are as segregated as the older neighborhoods established (or remade) under the Apartheid Group Areas Act. "Choices" about where to live are, of course, severely limited by economic inequalities. Prices of housing and land make it almost impossible for low-income African or Colored households to move into middle-class suburbs. In the absence of detailed studies about "residential choice," however, it remains unclear how important are social networks (i.e., in what other areas do households that might move have connections or friends) or social preferences (i.e., to what extent do people prefer to live in neighborhoods with other people sharing a similar culture, which is to some extent coterminous with former racial classifications). People may have been forced to move under Apartheid but now might be making choices that perpetuate residential segregation. In Cape Town, many African or Colored households with rising incomes choose to live in mono-racial neighborhoods. Cape Town is far more racially segregated than would be the case if income and wealth were the sole determinants of residential choice.

Not all neighborhoods are mono-racial. Some neighborhoods have moved from being mono-racial to mixed racial through a process of desegregation. In some cases, such desegregation has been transitory. In some inner-city areas (such as, most famously, Hillbrow in Johannesburg), desegregation prompted total "white flight" which resulted in the areas becoming mono-racial again.[39]

This process presumably hardens rather than dissipate racial animosity or ambivalence. Some other neighborhoods have desegregated more sustainably, for example, in Cape Town, in the formerly poor white area of Ruyterwacht and the mixed-income, formerly white Muizenberg. In

Ruyterwacht—which was the site of racialized and possibly racist protests in the early 1990s, low housing prices made it attractive for upwardly mobile Colored households. The nonwhite population rose from almost zero in the 1980s to an estimated 40 percent by 2000. Most of the new residents were young Colored families with small children. They were better educated and had higher incomes than most of the existing white residents, and their houses were noticeable for their newly built garages, second stories, swimming pools, and satellite dishes. Many of the new residents were Muslim, which might be expected to add another element of discord in a neighborhood that was hitherto exclusively Christian. But a typical comment from their white neighbors was that "here, our Coloreds are good"—expressing both an engagement with post-Apartheid realities and an inability to discard entirely the racial discourses of the past. Faced with two incidents of rape, white and Colored neighbors joined in a neighborhood watch. In Teppo's account, "hierarchist" white residents and their new Colored neighbours "embrace one another across racial lines, perhaps reluctantly at times, but knowing full well it is the only choice for both groups if they wish to keep their suburb secure."[40]

Muizenberg, on the False Bay coast, shows equally dramatic transformation.[41] Between the 1996 and 2001 censuses, the white share of the population fell from three-quarters to only just over one-third. Muizenberg became an extraordinarily mixed area, with very similar proportions of white, Colored, and African (including immigrant African) residents—although racial desegregation has been concentrated in the less expensive sections. In Muizenberg, however, racial desegregation did not lead to social interaction and integration. Most white families sent their children to nonlocal schools further down the peninsula, used their cars to shop outside the area, and tended to socialize elsewhere. The long-standing richer white residents viewed local facilities as deteriorating as a result of racial and class desegregation. Churches provided rare sites for racial interaction, although cross-racial membership might not have meant that there was much interracial interaction.

The second category of residential "desegregation" entailed new neighborhoods that were integrated from the outset. In Cape Town the first such area was Summer Greens. Summer Greens became home to a lower middle class that combined both upwardly mobile African and Colored families, and downwardly mobile white ones.[42] By 2000 about one half of the suburb's residents were Colored, one-third white, and the rest African. The developers encouraged a "village atmosphere" and sense of community: Residents were not allowed to build high walls (instead the entire suburb is walled), and the streets were designed to be public spaces rather than just transport routes. Residents, especially those who moved here from Colored or African areas, were very positive about security, but few had close contact with their neighbors. White residents complained about "low-class behavior" by people who "aren't very sophisticated, you know," as well as of cultural differences. One white man did not want his children to play with African children, because of the risk of AIDS. There were few facilities in the suburb that could facilitate interracial interaction. The most positive interpretation is that racial integration is a slow process, especially in middle-class suburbs where people emphasize their own privacy and have limited interaction with any neighbors. The experience of other newly built middle-class and elite neighborhoods seems similar: Racially mixed neighborhoods, whether gated or not, are often not significantly integrated, as is evident in case studies from around Johannesburg.[43] In elite neighborhoods, there is often little or no contact between neighbors regardless of race. The alienation of new black residents is well illustrated in novels such as *Coconut*.[44]

The picture in low-income areas is a little more encouraging. While a large number of new Reconstruction and Development Programme (RDP) houses have been built by the state since 1994, almost all have been allocated in ways that ensure that the new neighborhoods are monoracial. In Cape Town, for example, the state generally avoided allocating houses in the same settlement to poor Colored and poor African people. There have been a handful of exceptions, especially Delft South. There, Colored and African residents were generally very suspicious of each other at the outset, but the breadth and depth of cross-racial interactions slowly improved.[45]

A third category of partial desegregation entailed low-income housing development in middle-class suburbs, where land prices are high. These have attracted considerable publicity and controversy. Examples of this in Cape Town include Imizamo Yethu in Hout Bay, Masiphumelele in Noordhoek, Westlake near Muizenberg, and Marconi Beam in Milnerton. In each case, the low-income settlements grew far faster than planned, exacerbating the difficulties of providing services and infrastructure. The residents of these new low-income areas rarely share transport with their middle-class neighbors (the former using public transport, the latter private) or even shops (with different supermarkets catering for different groups of consumers), and almost never interact socially. Typically, race and class differences overlap and reinforce each other.

Overall, very few South Africans live in racially integrated neighborhoods, and few of those that do so live in neighborhoods that can be described as meaningfully integrated across racial lines. Even when the market or the state throws people from different racial groups together in a neighborhood, there is little interaction, and racial othering and prejudice remain commonplace.

A minority of schools have desegregated, not primarily because of residential desegregation but rather because of the absence of zoning restrictions which means that large numbers of young people undergo lengthy commutes to attend schools that are distant from their homes. Most schools remain mono-racial, because they are in mono-racial areas, but a minority of children—including many white, Indian, and Colored children, together with a small minority of African children—do undergo the experience of attending a multiracial school. The pioneering study by Dolby of the racial desegregation of a public school was based on research in a Durban high school in 1996.[46] Dolby's subject school had been a white school in a lower-income white residential area. By 1996 two-thirds of the students were black. The one-third that were white were typically poor-performing students from poorer homes who could not escape to better, more expensive schools. Almost all of the teachers, however, were white, and they sought to preserve the school's "white" identity through, for example, compelling boys to play rugby and wear the school blazer. Students grouped along racial lines on the school field. Racial epithets were common in the corridors. The combination of threatened or resentful white teachers and students, and a growing majority of black students, made for an explosive mix.

The environment at Dolby's school was very highly racialized, but school pupils did not simply reproduce an Apartheid-style conception of race in terms of biology, history, or past culture. Rather, they renegotiated race around the dynamics of taste (especially clothes, music, and clubs). African pupils defined blackness not in terms of Zulu tradition ("This is the [19]90s," one girl protested to a white teacher who anachronistically imagines that Zulu-speaking girls attend the traditional Zulu reed dance) but in terms of global African American culture (and icons such as Michael Jackson, Michael Jordan, Whitney Houston, and top rap artists). But Colored students also drew on African American fashion in defining their cultural identity: Levi jeans, Dickies chino pants, baseball warm-up jackets. White students drew on different global influences: more sexy clothing, techno music, and so on. Black, Indian, Colored, and white students valued different clothes, listened to different music, played different sports, and went to different clubs. Deviants—such as an African girl who wore clothing perceived as "white"—were humiliated or ostracized. By policing the adopted cultural markers of race, the students themselves actively reproduced racial difference and division, at the same time as they renegotiated their own racialized identities.

Similar research was subsequently conducted in schools elsewhere in the country. A series of studies in Cape Town[47] showed how similarity and difference were rarely based on race per se, but rather on gender, lifestyle, class, religion, moral values, and language. But race remained ever present in adolescents' thoughts and language, and underlay many of the other cultural dimensions. The students at all-African, all-Colored, and all-white schools had quite distinct tastes with respect to music and media. At mixed schools, the differences were less stark, and there was more overlap, but preferences remained broadly racialized.

In a world of segregated neighborhoods and schools, malls have become an important site of interracial interaction. Nkuna described how young people of all races tried to construct a new multiracial identity in The Zone, an upmarket mall in Johannesburg, on the basis of overlapping tastes in clothing (specific labels/brands), music, and other markers of fashion (hair, body piercing).[48] This is, however, a very middle-class world. Almost half of the young people at The Zone consist of students in higher education, and almost all attended private schools or formerly white schools in the suburbs. Very few attended township schools. The culture is not only consumerist, but embraces American styles while rejecting "parochial" South African fashions (i.e., kwaito music). In southern Cape Town, the less elitist Longbeach Mall provided a shared space in which adolescents from the segregated neighborhoods of Fish Hoek, Ocean Vie and Masiphumelele could interact, although the interactions were too modest to constitute substantive "integration."[49]

A series of studies by Dixon, Tredoux, and others show that there is often little interracial interaction even in social spaces that appear to be integrated, such as public beaches,[50] the dining halls of integrated universities,[51] nightclubs.[52] The "lived experience of contact often led to the reestablishment of racial boundaries."[53]

Survey data suggest that the workplace is an important site of interracial interaction and is probably the *most* important site for most people. In Cape Town, according to a 2005 survey, very small minorities of each race group said that they worked in mono-racial environments. Unfortunately, there is little published research on the everyday reality of interracial interactions in the post-Apartheid workplace. Bezuidenhout[54] describes four engineering factories, where the basic racial hierarchy has barely changed with the transition from Apartheid to democracy, although it is no longer maintained through violence. He points to the racialized perception among African workers that they were still discriminated against, even though this discrimination was now based on seniority within the company rather than (explicitly) race. In his study of a car-manufacturing plant, Masondo found that "ordinary workers" felt "more comfortable" in mono-racial social groups, especially because of linguistic barriers. But black and white salaried staff did interact: They were "always together during lunch hours."[55] Black workers complained that the new black managers "treat us the same way as the white managers did. They shout at us as if we are their children."[56] Racial interactions in the workplace clearly warrant further research. To what extent, or in what ways, or how often, do interracial interactions transcend workplace hierarchies? What are the consequences of racialized hierarchy (or its erosion) in the workplace for the reproduction (or erosion) of race-thinking?

DISCRIMINATORY ATTITUDES AND EXPERIENCES

Ethnographic research in neighborhoods and schools suggests that racial differences and divisions remain pronounced, but finds little evidence of the kind of brutal racism associated with white South Africans in the early Apartheid period. Experimental research on behavior and survey-based research on attitudes tends to support this assessment. Experimental research on race has been pioneered in South Africa by Justine Burns. In one of Burns's experiments, secondary school students in Cape Town played the "dictator game," in which players are given real money and then choose how much to pass onto anonymous "partners," whose photo they have seen but otherwise know nothing about. Using a photo allowed Burns to test for the effect of the partners' race, or at least race in terms of physical appearance. Burns found that there was no direct race effect, i.e., that players did not discriminate against partners who appeared to be racially different. This behavior appeared to be motivated by an aversion to inherited inequality, and racial appearance was taken as a proxy for inherited inequality.[57] In more complex "trust games," students exhibited complex patterns of racial interaction—but for the most part did not exhibit the "in-group" bias that might be expected.[58]

The participants in Burns's experiments knew that they were in an experiment, and this might affect their behavior. The participants did not know, however, that interracial interaction is the focus of the research. In surveys, respondents might also select responses in the knowledge that they are being researched, but the use of "vignettes" can help to disguise the focus of the research. Respondents can be presented with one or more vignettes describing a situation, followed by a question or series of questions related to the situation. Sniderman and Piazza[59] used vignettes to examine "modern" forms of racism in the United States. In their "laid-off worker" vignette, respondents were presented with a scenario in which a person (or subject) is retrenched, and are then invited to suggest how much (if any) financial assistance that person should receive from the government while looking for work. The scenario varies insofar as the subject (or retrenched person) is given different characteristics: white or black, male or female, younger or older, single or married, with or without children, and dependable or not dependable. A variant of this vignette was used in surveys conducted in Cape Town in 2003 and 2005 to probe the effects of race on perceptions of distributive justice. By including a range of characteristics for each subject, the respondent's attention is being diverted in part at least from the racial characteristic.

Questions about distributive justice are a telling test of one dimension of racial attitudes because the official ideology of Apartheid emphasized that each racial group (and each ethnic group within the African population) should look after its own: White South Africans were not responsible for the poverty of black South Africans; rich South Africans were only responsible for poor South Africans if they were members of the same racially demarcated "community." One might expect that the overriding racialization of society under Apartheid and the continuing salience of race have resulted in a close correlation between race and attitudes toward distribution or distributive justice. The government, ANC, and the media frequently accuse white South Africans of being opposed to "transformation", i.e., to redistributive social and economic policies. If this was the case, then we would expect to find that South Africans will assess the desert of other members of their own racial group (i.e., "insiders") more favorably or positively than that of members of other racial groups (i.e., "outsiders").

The results of the vignette-based survey experiments in Cape Town in 2003 and 2005 suggested that the race of the respondent and the race of the subject were of little import in whether a respondent considered a subject deserving. For example, white respondents did not discriminate significantly against African or Colored subjects. In the 2003 survey, there were clear (and counterintuitive) race effects on the amount that the respondent said that the subject should receive per month from the government: White respondents were more generous, perhaps because they had a more inflated view of what constituted a "minimum" income; more curiously, black and Colored respondents as well as white respondents suggested that larger grants be made to white than to African or Colored subjects.[60] The 2005 data showed also that white respondents were a lot more generous in the sums they "awarded" to the fictional subject, but in contrast to 2003 there was no indication that respondents were more generous to white subjects. Overall, in this dimension of social attitudes, race seemed to play little effect, and there was little or no evidence of racism or racial discrimination. These findings from survey vignettes were not dissimilar to Burns's findings using data from field experiments.

White South Africans have no qualms, however, in expressing opposition to race-based policies, such as affirmative action and Black Economic Empowerment (BEE). Several studies suggest that there is wide and strong support for government interventions to help the poor, but only among African people is there a majority in favor of race-based affirmative action (in employment), black economic empowerment, or redistribution of land.[61]

Survey data suggest that most South Africans believe that "race relations" have improved since the end of Apartheid, and neither surveys nor field experiments provide evidence of significant racial discrimination in attitudes or experimental behavior. But discrimination might persist in other domains, and it is even more likely that discrimination is *perceived* as continuing.

The 2005 Cape Area Study asked about recent experiences of discrimination. Respondents were asked whether, in the five years since 2000, they had "been treated worse than other people or benefited" because of their race. Very few respondents said that they had experienced negative racial discrimination. Most African respondents said that they had benefited because they were black, while most Colored and white respondents said that they had neither benefited nor been treated worse.

This was followed by a series of questions about experiences in specific settings (see figure 1.3). Almost all African respondents reported that they had been watched or followed in shops, compared to a minority of Colored respondents and very few white respondents. Larger proportions of African respondents than Colored or white respondents reported experiencing each of the other four situations (being treated with less respect, being treated worse in restaurants and shops, being treated by people as if they were afraid of you, and being treated by other people as if they were better than you). But in these other four situations the proportions of African, Colored, and white respondents who reported that they had had the experience were not massively different. For example, just over one-half of African respondents reported being treated with less respect, compared to over one-third of Colored and white respondents.

These results are broadly consistent with the findings of countrywide surveys. Most South Africans report that they never feel that they are being discriminated against. A larger minority of white and Indian people report experiencing discrimination than among African or Colored people. Discrimination is perceived as occurring primarily at work (especially by African people), when applying for jobs (especially among white and Colored people), and in shops (especially among white people, curiously).[62]

One study that did find evidence of discrimination was a field experiment testing whether politicians were more likely to respond favorably to same-race constituents than to constituents from other racial groups, controlling for other factors (including co-partisanship).[63] South Africans do discriminate, in some contexts, but not in all contexts, and not in some contexts where we would anticipate discrimination, given the country's history.

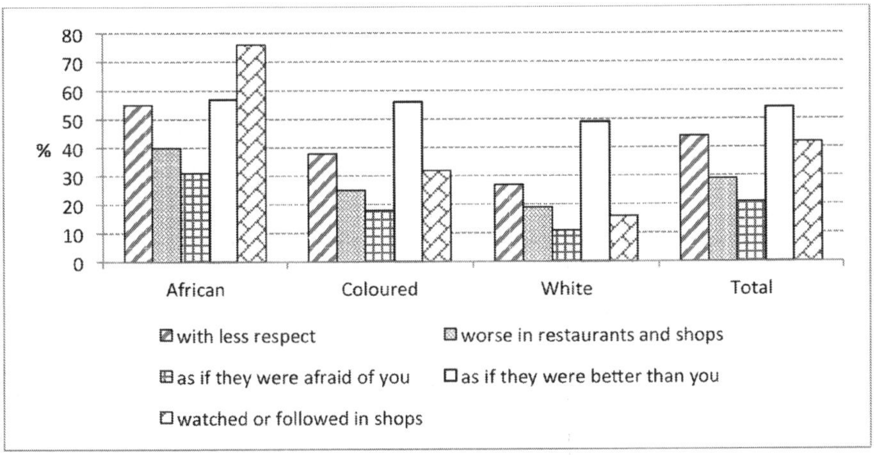

Figure 1.3. Experiences of discrimination, Cape Town, 2005. Respondents who reported that they have often or sometimes been treated . . .

DISCRIMINATION AND DISADVANTAGE

As the South African economy came to revolve more and more around wage labor, so the most important economic manifestation of racism was access to employment and hence earnings. From the 1920s to the 1970s, racial discrimination confined most African people to low-paid occupations. When African and white people were in the same occupation—for example, teachers and police—white employees were paid more than their African counterparts. This picture began to change dramatically from the 1970s.[64] Moll[65] showed that the share of inequality in the distribution of wages that was accounted for by *inter*racial differences declined from 65 percent in 1980 to 42 percent in 1993, while the share accounted for by *intra*racial differences rose from 35 percent to 58 percent. The racial wage gap declined but still remained large, with median earnings for African workers only about one-quarter of the median for white workers, in 1995.[66] But a series of studies demonstrated that this persistent racial wage gap was due primarily to differences in education, skill, location (urban/rural), and economic sector, rather than to racial discrimination per se. Moll[67] also found that racial discrimination amounted to 20 percent of mean African wage in 1980 but just 12 percent in 1993.

It is difficult to assess changes in racial discrimination in the labor market since the end of Apartheid. Burger and Jafta examined survey data from 1995 to 2004 to assess changes over time in the part of the racial gap in both employment and (formal sector) wages that could not be explained in terms of other readily measured variables such as years of schooling and location.[68] They find that there had been a narrowing of the racial wage gap since 1994 at the top end of the wage distribution, but not overall. The unexplained element remained, i.e., white workers apparently continued to earn a premium in the labor market, essentially because they earned higher returns on their education than did Indian, Colored, or, especially, African people. In later work using data to 2011, Burger, Jafta, and von Fintel[69] found that both the racial employment gap and the "unexplained" part of this gap declined in the 2000s, presumably reflecting pressure for affirmative action. Neither the racial wage gap nor the unexplained part of it declined however. Better-qualified black men did benefit in terms of both employment and wages.

As most of these econometric studies emphasize, returns to education surely continue to vary by race in part because of the enormous but unmeasured differences in both the quality of education and social capital (i.e., the contacts that people have). Taking such factors into account would surely reduce considerably the "unexplained" component of the racial wage gap, and reduce further the importance of racial discrimination relative to other factors such as inequalities in real skills and useful contacts.

Burger and Jafta's work points to the importance of distinguishing between different sections of the labor market. Unlike in (say) Brazil or the United States, there are few unskilled white workers competing with black workers for low-paid employment (and of the small number of unskilled white workers, some might have hidden class advantages, for example, young people with part-time jobs as waitresses). It is at the top end of the labor market that the effects of persistent racial discrimination against African people or affirmative action in their benefit would be concentrated. There are unfortunately few studies of the top end of the labor market, especially among young entrants. But some data suggests that, in some sectors, patterns of discrimination have changed markedly over very short periods of time. In the late 1990s, the public sector was the primary venue for affirmative action. The proportion of public sector managers who were African rose from 30 percent in 1995 to 51 percent in 2001. The proportion of senior managers who were African rose from 33 percent to 43 percent.[70] As many as 70 percent of all African graduates get their first job in the public sector.[71] In the early 2000s, legislation has pushed larger private-sector employers to similar shifts in employment patterns. This led to a marked decline in the racial wage gap among managers.[72]

A second, complicating factor in the analysis of racial discrimination in labor market outcomes (i.e., employment and wages) using cross-sectional data is that substantial numbers of younger white people have emigrated, or are at least outside of the country for long periods of time. While they might be outside the South African labor market, their choice is probably not entirely exogenous to conditions in the labor market. I am unaware of any studies that examine the real effects of affirmative action legislation on the labor market for school-leavers or, especially, university graduates, but there is no shortage of anecdotal evidence that young white men and women believe that affirmative action policies and practices are foreclosing opportunities for employment, and that this perception influences decisions about emigration. If it was true that white graduates are emigrating to avoid unemployment (perhaps because they would "choose" unemployment over employment in occupations that are inferior to those to which they aspired), then emigration would cause analyses of cross-sectional data to underestimate the effects of affirmative action.

Unfortunately, there is no experimental research in South Africa similar to the work assessing the extent and patterns of racial (or other) discrimination in the labor market. If such research was conducted, however, it is likely that it would find that in occupations in which they are applicants from all racial groups (i.e., excluding unskilled employment), racial discrimination is practiced in favor of black applicants through affirmative action and BEE policies. Panel studies (such as the National Income Dynamics Study [NIDS]) offer another promising way forward for the empirical analysis of patterns and dynamics of advantage and disadvantage in post-Apartheid South Africa. Analysis of panel data is likely to confirm the following: Most children from poor neighborhoods—almost all of whom are African—grow up in home environments that are unconducive to educational success, and attend schools where the quality of education is very poor. Many remain in school until their late teens, but are unable to acquire many skills. Their ability to find employment is constrained by their lack of skills and experience, their location far from most job opportunities, and their lack of contacts that could help them find employment. Many move into the underclass of the chronically unemployed, with intermittent short spells of unskilled work. On the other hand, children from middle-class neighborhoods—who comprise rapidly rising numbers of African as well as Indian and white children—attend better schools, enjoy the benefits of middle-class home environments, and gain work experience through part-time jobs (especially in school holidays). They move into higher education and then into the labor market. White middle-class children enjoy the relative benefits of wider and deeper social networks, but have the disadvantage of being white in an affirmative-action environment.

CONCLUSION

The available evidence suggests that race remains of enormous social and cultural importance despite a decline in economic importance. Earnings and incomes reflect race far more than class. This raises questions, however, about the meaning of class in the South African context. In its intellectual seedbed in northwest Europe during the Industrial Revolution, there was generally a close relationship between "objective" class positions (in terms of relationships to the means of production) and everyday cultures. As E. P. Thompson famously argued, the working class was made culturally as well as through changes in the form and shape of capitalism. In South Africa, "race"—understood as a social and cultural phenomenon, not biologically—has shaped profoundly cultural change, interacting complexly with the growth of a modern state and a capitalist economy. While the social question predominated in Britain and most of northwest Europe, the national question retains an everyday salience in South Africa.

Insofar as this is the case, then South Africa would appear to be the opposite to Brazil, where race is of limited cultural and even social importance but of continuing economic significance. In the terms used by Telles,[73] in Brazil there is racism in terms of vertical relations but not of horizontal relations, while in South Africa there is "racism"—or at least the acknowledgment of racial difference—in terms of horizontal relations but not of vertical relations. In Brazil, interracial marriage and racial discrimination in employment are both common. In South Africa, after Apartheid (and subject to caution with respect to the extent and effect of affirmative action), neither is common.

Race remains relevant in South Africa for primarily cultural reasons. Most South Africans have clear racial identities (although they might not be their most important identities) and readily view others in racial terms (although not only in such terms). This is not simply a lingering manifestation of racism. Indeed, experimental and other research suggests that there is remarkably little racism in terms of racial discrimination in assessments of (for example) trustworthiness or desert. Rather, it reflects the persistence of racism in a softer sense, which is in terms of social preferences. South Africans may not be hostile to racialized others but prefer to live and generally socialize with culturally similar neighbors and for their kin to marry within racial (i.e., cultural) groups rather than outside them. As Maré[74] (2014)—and, before him, Neville Alexander—has warned, however, the use of racial categories can never be innocent, and obviously facilitates hostility to the "other" or outgroup.

The available evidence on post-Apartheid South Africa is sadly and surprisingly limited. Little progress has been made yet with respect to two key kinds of study. First, data from panel studies is yet to be used to explore precisely how and why "race" shapes progress through school and into the labor market. Second, there are still too few studies of how race, class, and culture are made and understood in the lived experience of South Africans, at home, in neighborhoods, in schools, and in workplaces. In addition, there is a dearth of empirical research on how employers and others comply with official requirements to categorize people, and on the extent or effects of pro-African racial discrimination (i.e., affirmative action) in employment. South Africans often assert that their own experiences of racial discrimination are inconsistent with the picture that emerges from academic studies such as the ones reviewed in this chapter. Understanding how and why personal experiences relate to measured trends and patterns is a major challenge. In South Africa, as in Brazil, we are only beginning to unravel the complicated interactions of race, class, and culture in the contemporary context.

APPENDIX

Table 1.1. Attitudes Toward Interracial Marriage within Family, by Race of Respondent and Race of Prospective Spouse

Apartheid-era Racial Classification of Respondent		*Race of Prospective Spouse*			
		Black/African	*Colored*	*Indian*	*White*
African	Mean	1.75	–0.15	–0.49	–0.16
	sd	0.75	1.49	1.44	1.47
	N	408	408	408	408
Colored	Mean	0.55	1.26	0.63	0.78
	sd	1.21	0.96	1.17	1.13
	N	478	478	478	478
White	Mean	–0.25	–0.02	–0.12	0.87
	sd	1.08	1.05	1.03	1.02
	N	252	252	252	252
Other	Mean	0.68	0.64	–0.28	0.61
	sd	1.52	1.33	1.52	1.35
	n	35	35	35	35

Note: possible scores range from -2 to +2; negative scores indicate disapproval, positive scores approval. sd: standard deviation.
Source: Cape Area Study, 2005

NOTES

1. An earlier version of this essay was published as: Jeremy Seekings, "The Continuing Salience of Race: Discrimination and Diversity in South Africa," *Journal of Contemporary African Studies* 26/1 (2008): 1–25.

2. It is not possible to write about race in South Africa without using racial categories. This essay refers to "white," "Colored," "Indian," and "African" people, according to official and predominant popular usage, and uses "black" to refer to African, Colored, and Indian people collectively. These are all socially and culturally constructed categories.

3. Jeremy Seekings and Nicoli Nattrass, *Class, Race and Inequality in South Africa* (New Haven, CT: Yale University Press, 2005); Jeremy Seekings and Nicoli Nattrass, *Policy, Politics and Poverty in South Africa* (London: Palgrave Macmillan, 2015), also published as *Poverty, Policy and Politics in South Africa* (Cape Town: Jacana, 2016).

4. For example: Michael MacDonald, *Why Race Matters in South Africa* (Cambridge, MA: Harvard University Press, 2005).

5. Edward Telles, *Race in Another America: The Significance of Skin Color in Brazil* (Princeton, NJ: Princeton University Press, 2005).

6. Anthony J. Christopher, "'To define the Indefinable': Population Classification and the Census in South Africa," *Area* 34/4 (2002): 401–8. See also Tom A. Moultrie and Rob E. Dorrington, "Used for Ill; Used for Good: A Century of Collecting Data on Race in South Africa," *Ethnic and Racial Studies* 35/8 (2015): 1447–65.

7. Deborah Posel, "What's in a Name? Racial Categorizations under Apartheid and Their Afterlife," *Transformation* 47 (2001): 59–82. See also Deborah Posel, "Race and Common Sense: Racial Classification in Twentieth-Century South Africa," *African Studies Review* 44/2 (2001): 87–113.

8. Gerhard Maré, *De-classified: Moving beyond the Dead End of Race in South Africa* (Johannesburg: Jacana, 2014).

9. Seekings and Nattrass, *Class, Race and Inequality in South Africa*.

10. See Arlene Grossberg, Jaré Struwig, and Udesh Pillay, "Multicultural National Identity and Pride," in *South African Social Attitudes: Changing Times, Diverse Voices*, ed. Udesh Pillay, Ben Roberts, and Stephen Rule (Pretoria: Human Sciences Research Council, 2006), 54–76.

11. Seekings and Nattrass, *Class, Race and Inequality in South Africa*.

12. Melissa Steyn, *Whiteness Just Isn't What It Used to Be: White Identity in a Changing South Africa* (Albany, NY: SUNY Press, 2001).

13. See Adam Ashforth, *Witchcraft, Violence and Democracy in South Africa* (Chicago, IL: University of Chicago Press, 2005).

14. Margo Russell, "Are Urban Black Families Nuclear? A Comparative Study of Black and White South African Family Norms," *Social Dynamics* 29/2 (2003): 153–76.

15. Mohamed Adhikari, *Not White Enough, Not Black Enough: Racial Identity in the South African Colored Community* (Cape Town and Athens, OH: Double Storey and Ohio University Press, 2005).

16. Government Communications (GCIS), "Statement of Deputy President Thabo Mbeki at the Opening of the Debate in the National Assembly, on 'Reconciliation and Nation Building,' National Assembly Cape Town, May 29, 1998," <http://www.dirco.gov.za/docs/speeches/1998/mbek0529.htm/> [Accessed February 23, 2017].

17. See Benjamin Disraeli, *An Inquiry into the Plans, Progress, and Policy of the American Mining Companies* (London: John Murray, 1825); Benjamin Disraeli, *England and France; Or a Cure for the Ministerial Gallomania* (London: John Murray, 1832).

18. Marlene Roefs, "Identity and Race Relations," in *South African Social Attitudes: Changing Times, Diverse Voices*, ed. Udesh Pillay, Ben Roberts, and Stephen Rule (Pretoria: Human Sciences Research Council, 2006), 77.

19. Seekings and Nattrass, *Class, Race and Inequality in South Africa*; Seekings and Nattrass, *Policy, Politics and Poverty in South Africa*.

20. See Roger Southall, *The New Black Middle Class in South Africa* (Johannesburg: Jacana, 2016).

21. Gerhard Maré, "Race Counts in Contemporary South Africa: 'An Illusion of Ordinariness,'" *Transformation* 47 (2001): 75–93. See also Maré, *De-classified*.

22. James Gibson, *Overcoming Apartheid: Can Truth Reconcile a Divided Nation?* (Pretoria: Human Sciences Research Council Press, 2004).

23. Seekings and Nattrass, *Class, Race and Inequality in South Africa*.

24. Gibson, *Overcoming Apartheid*.

25. Gibson, *Overcoming Apartheid*.

26. Gibson, *Overcoming Apartheid*, 123–24.

27. Roefs, "Identity and Race Relations," 88–90.

28. Gibson, *Overcoming Apartheid*.

29. Gibson, *Overcoming Apartheid*, 139–42.

30. James Gibson and Christopher Claassen, "Racial Reconciliation in South Africa: Interracial Contact and Changes Over Time," *Journal of Social Issues* 66/2 (2010): 255–72.

31. Elizabeth Hamel, Mollyann Brodie, and Richard Morin, "A Survey of South Africa Ten Years into the New Democracy," paper presented at the 59th Annual Conference of the American Association for Public Opinion Research, Phoenix, Arizona, May 2004.

32. Roefs, "Identity and Race Relations," 90–91.

33. Gibson, *Overcoming Apartheid*.

34. Seekings and Nattrass, *Class, Race and Inequality in South Africa*, 32.

35. Anthony J. Christopher, "Urban Segregation in Post-Apartheid South Africa," *Urban Studies* 38/3 (2001): 449–66.

36. Anthony J. Christopher, "Further Progress in the Desegregation of South African Towns and Cities, 1996–2001," *Development Southern Africa* 22/2 (2005): 267–76.

37. Christopher, "Further Progress," 267.

38. Kevin Parry and Amanda Van Eeden, "Measuring Racial Residential Segregation at Different Geographic Scales in Cape Town and Johannesburg," *South African Geographical Journal* 97/1 (2015): 31–49.

39. Alan Morris, *Bleakness and Light: Inner-City Transition in Hillbrow, Johannesburg* (Johannesburg: Witwatersrand University Press, 1999).

40. Annika Teppo, "The Making of a Good White: A Historical Ethnography of the Rehabilitation of Poor Whites in a Suburb of Cape Town" (unpublished PhD diss., University of Helsinki, 2004), 231.

41. Charlotte Lemanski, "Desegregation and Integration as Linked or Distinct? Evidence from a Previously 'White' Suburb in post-Apartheid Cape Town," *International Journal of Urban and Regional Research* 30/3 (2006): 564-586.

42. Helen Broadbridge, "Negotiating Post-Apartheid Boundaries and Identities: An Anthropological Study of the Creation of a Cape Town Suburb" (unpublished PhD diss., Stellenbosch University, 2001).

43. Ivor Chipkin "Middle Classing in Roodepoort: Capitalism and Social Change in South Africa," *PARI Long Essays* No. 2 (Johannesburg: Public Affairs

Research Institute, University of Johannesburg, 2012). See also Federica Duca, "Left Outside or Trapped in the Visible and Invisible Gate: Insights into the Continuities and Discontinuities in the Creation of Good and Just Living in Open and Gated Suburbs of Johannesburg" (unpublished PhD diss., University of Trento, Public Affairs Research Institute, 2014).

44. Kopano Matlwa, *Coconut* (Johannesburg: Jacana, 2007).

45. Singumbe Muyeba and Jeremy Seekings, "Race, Attitudes and Behavior in Racially-mixed, Low-income Neighbourhoods in Cape Town, South Africa," *Current Sociology* 59/5 (2011): 655–71. See also Charlotte Lemanski, "Spaces of Exclusivity or Connection: Linkages between a Gated Community and Its Poorer Neighbour in a Cape Town Master Plan Development," *Urban Studies* 43/2 (2006): 397–402.

46. Nadine Dolby, *Constructing Race: Youth, Identity and Popular Culture in South Africa* (Albany, NY: SUNY Press, 2001).

47. Crain Soudien, '"We Know Why We're Here': The Experiences of African Children in a 'Colored' School in Cape Town," *Race, Ethnicity and Education* 1/1 (1998): 7–29; Crain Soudien, "Constituting the Class: An Analysis of the Process of Integration in South African Schools," in *Changing Class: Education and Social Change in Post-Apartheid South Africa*, ed. Linda Chisholm (Pretoria: HSRC Press, 2004); Crain Soudien, "The Reconstitution of Privilege: Integration in Former White Schools in South Africa," *Journal of Social Issues* 66/2 (2010): 352–66; Imke Gooskens, "Boundaries and Crossing Points: Children, Geography and Identity in the Fish Hoek Valley," *Social Dynamics* 32/1 (2006): 135–68; Rachel Bray, Imke Gooskens, Lauren Kahn, Sue Moses, and Jeremy Seekings, *Growing Up in the New South Africa: Childhood and Adolescence in the New South Africa* (Cape Town: Human Sciences Research Council Press, 2010).

48. Lucert Nkuna, '"Fitting-In' to a 'Classy Place': The Zone and Youth Identity," in *Globalisation and New Identities: A View from the Middle*, ed. Peter Alexander, Marcelle Dawson, and Meera Ichharam (Johannesburg: Jacana, 2006), 261–74.

49. Racialized patterns of conspicuous consumption are not limited to young people. See Wolfhard Kaus, "Conspicuous Consumption and 'Race': Evidence from South Africa," *Journal of Development Economics* 199 (2013): 63–73.

50. John Dixon and Kevin Durrheim, "Contact and the Ecology of Racial Division: Some Varieties of Informal Segregation," *British Journal of Social Psychology* 42 (2003): 1–23.

51. Leigh Schrieff, Colin Tredoux, John Dixon, and Gillian Finchilescu, "Patterns of Racial Segregation in University Residence Dining-Halls," *South African Journal of Psychology* 35 (2005): 433–43; Leigh Scherieff, Gillian Finchilescu, and John Dixon, "Understanding the Seating Patterns in a Residence-Dining Hall: A Longitudinal Study of Intergroup Contact," *South African Journal of Psychology* 40/1 (April 2005): 5–17.

52. Colin Tredoux and John Dixon, "Mapping the Multiple Contexts of Racial Isolation: The Case of Long Street, Cape Town," *Urban Studies* 46/4 (2009): 761–77.

53. John Dixon and Colin Tredoux, "Beyond the Optimal Contact Strategy: A Reality Check for the Contact Hypothesis," *American Psychologist* 60/7 (2005): 697–711; John Dixon, Colin Tredoux, Kevin Durrheim, Gillian Finchilescu, and Beverley Clack, '"The Inner Citadels of the Color Line': Mapping the Micro-

ecology of Segregation in Everyday Life Spaces," *Personality & Social Psychology Compass* 2 (2008): 1–23.

54. Andries Bezuidenhout, "Post-colonial Workplace Regimes in the Engineering Industry in South Africa," in *Beyond the Apartheid Workplace: Studies in Transition,* ed. Edward Webster and Karl von Holdt (Pietermaritzburg, South Africa: University of KwaZulu-Natal Press, 2005), 73–96.

55. David Masondo, "Trade Liberalisation and Work Restructuring in Post-Apartheid South Africa: A Case-Study of BMW," in *Beyond the Apartheid Workplace: Studies in Transition,* ed. Edward Webster and Karl von Holdt (Pietermaritzburg, South Africa: University of KwaZulu-Natal Press, 2005), 165.

56. Masondo, "Trade Liberalisation and Work Restructuring," 168.

57. Justine Burns, "Inequality Aversion and Group Identity in a Segmented Society," (unpublished paper, University of Cape Town, 2004).

58. Justine Burns, "Racial Stereotypes, Stigma and Trust in Post-Apartheid South Africa," *Economic Modelling* 23 (2006): 805–21.

59. Paul Sniderman and Thomas Piazza, *The Scar of Race* (Cambridge, MA: Belknap Press, 1993).

60. Jeremy Seekings, "The Continuing Salience of Race: Discrimination and Diversity in South Africa," *Journal of Contemporary African Studies* 26/1 (2008): 1–26; Jeremy Seekings, "'Just Deserts': Race, Class and Distributive Justice in Post-Apartheid South Africa," *Journal of Southern African Studies* 34/1 (2008): 39–60.

61. ILO, *Economic Security for a Better World* (Geneva: International Labour Office, 2004); Ben Roberts, "The Happy Transition? Attitudes to Poverty and Inequality after a Decade of Democracy," in *South African Social Attitudes: Changing Times, Diverse Voices,* ed. Udesh Pillay, Ben Roberts, and Stephen Rule (Pretoria: Human Sciences Research Council, 2004), 101–130.

62. Roefs, "Identity and Race Relations," 88–89.

63. Gwyneth H. McClendon, "Race and Responsiveness: An Experiment with South African Politicians," *Journal of Experimental Political Science* 3/1 (2016): 60–74.

64. Owen Crankshaw, *Race, Class and the Changing Division of Labour under Apartheid* (London: Routledge, 1997).

65. Peter Moll, "Discrimination Is Declining in South Africa but Inequality Is Not," *Journal for Studies in Economics & Econometrics* 24/3 (2000): 91–108.

66. Haroon Bhorat and Murray Leibbrandt, "Correlates of Vulnerability in the South African Labour Market," in *Fighting Poverty: Labour Markets and Inequality in South Africa,* ed. Haroon Bhorat, Murray Leibbrandt, Muzi Maziya, Servaas van der Berg, and Ingrid Woolard, (Cape Town: University of Cape Town Press, 2001), 83. See also Rulof Burger and Rachel Jafta, "Returns to Race: Labour Market Discrimination in Post-Apartheid South Africa," (working paper No. 04/06, University of Stellenbosch, 2006): 19.

67. Moll, "Discrimination Is Declining in South Africa."

68. Burger and Jafta, "Returns to Race."

69. Rulof Burger, Rachel Jafta, and Dieter von Fintel, "Affirmative Action Policies and the Evolution of Post-Apartheid South Africa's Racial Wage Gap" (working paper no. 2016/66, UNU-WIDER, Helsinki, 2016).

70. Keith Thompson and Ingrid Woolard, "Achieving Employment Equity in the Public Service: A Study of Changes between 1995 and 2001" (working paper no. 02/61, Development Policy Research Unit, 2002).

71. Cited in Miriam Altman, "Wage Determination in South Africa: What Do We Know?" *Transformation* 60 (2005): 58–89.

72. Cited in Altman, "Wage Determination in South Africa."

73. Telles, *Race in Another America.*

74. Maré, *De-classified.*

Two

Cracking the Skull of Racism in South Africa Post-1994

Vuyani S. Vellem

INTRODUCTION

With limitation, this chapter examines the problem of racism at root level in the context of Empire.[1] Black Theology of Liberation (BTL) is not merely rearticulated and reasserted here, rather it is presented and reinterpreted to illustrate not its sterility as such, but the dangers of its perpetual "castration"[2]—the "castration" of its goals and the agency of a black interlocutor by canons of Eurocentric knowledge and culture, whose self-proclaimed superiority continue to reign supreme in the twenty-first century.

"Under the aegis of globalisation, totalising ambitions are no longer limited to intra-societal domination but have acquired global or planetary dimensions."[3] Fred Dallmayr affirms our argument that in this context of the hegemonic, totalizing ambitions of Western domination are worrying symptoms of racism, illustrated by numerous examples in South Africa whose racial history is well-known in the world. The discussion of racism in this context might seem a repetition of the debates associated generally with the BTL paradigm, but it is not! This chapter proposes to tackle racism within the aegis of globalization and to critique Eurocentric modernity, the latter which according to Nelson Maldonado-Torres is constitutive of racial logic itself.[4] Maldonado-Torres says, "Racism, then, is from this point of view a central element in the formation of the modern/colonial world."[5] The prevalent "race-blind"[6] approaches and the "normative invisibility"[7] of whiteness amidst these repugnant racial epiphanies in South Africa therefore either hide or deny that "race constitutes the transversal dividing line that cuts across multiple power relations such as class, sexual and gender at a global scale"[8] as in our local context, South Africa. In yet another work by Stanley Arnowitz and Heather Gauntney, an assertion is made that since 9/11 the rise of fundamentalism and the obsession of the United States with security has coincided with xenophobia with the "ugly politics of race" also rising.[9]

This fetishized idea of racism in the totalizing *macht* of the West, explicable through numerous examples since the encounter between black and white in South Africa is mirrored in these epiphanies of racism in post-1994 South Africa. More so, it simply suggests that others have assumed "that might, or success, does in fact make right in the sense that it establishes merit in the form of intellectual and cultural superiority."[10] So, this disease is too deep, it is hidden somewhere, it is cunning and slippery at core. BTL as a school cannot be but petrified by this, especially in post-1994 South Africa, where an impression of triumph against racism has been falsely created.

Dare we avoid the question about how "fraudulent"[11] BTL has been? James Cone's recent work makes one tremble at the doubt he casts on Reinhold Niebuhr's grasp of the question of racism, especially during the lynching of black bodies in the United States.[12] This doubt, about the capacity of the beneficiaries of racism to grasp the magnitude of its damage to the black bodies, is best expressed by Zakes Mda when he says, *the white man never learns.*[13] While there is almost adequate work on racism in the different epochs of our history of the struggle in South Africa, the vexing question of the proneness of race analysis to "fraudulence" and an elusive grasp of this problem by those whose experience is different from that of the victims probably suggests that we should diagnose this problem elsewhere—even deeply so.

Our approach in reflecting on these questions, the fraudulent, race-blind, normative invisibility and elusiveness of race, doubt, and the extent to which all of this castrate the goals and agency of black Africans against this problem, is ipso facto analectic: "Analectics designates a method "which begins from the Other as free, as one beyond the system of totality; which begins, then, from the Other's word, from the revelation of the Other, and which, trusting the Other's word, labours, works, serves, and creates."[14]

Fred Dallmayr further explains that "analectics does not end in a bland consensualism but respects the gap or difference (*dia*) between self and other, between oppressor and oppressed, shunning the temptation of a totalising synthesis."[15] For how long will the trust, labor, work, service, and creation of a black person by centuries of racism be systemically denied?

Empire provides such a methodological engagement with this subject, an historical entry point for us, as it points to the *long durée* of a civilization fraught with forms of killing that started at least five hundred years ago, or even beyond, suffered by the black. At least a case for the original sin of racism as constitutive of modernity—its metamorphosis and its current epiphanies—could be traceable to slavery in the lived experiences of the black African people.

By Empire:

> we refer not so much to the political and economic mechanisms that shape what we characterise as Empire, although that cannot be excluded, but rather to an *ethos*, a way of thinking and doing, a *Weltanschauung*, and even a certain theology that demonstrates the imperial spirit, which is innate to the form of social organisation that we visualise as Empire.[16]

Racism in our times is thus an ethos, an imperial spirit, innate to the sociopolitical, ecclesial organization and institutions of management and learning in our society. For this reason, Manning Marable, who argues that blacks are recognized in America even though they have never been "members of the American family,"[17]affirms this *long durée* of racist oppression. Jim Wallis's argument that the original sin of America is racism signifies the same.[18] We could argue that blacks are "recognized" in South Africa, but they have never been members of the Eurocentric conversations, philosophical and historical partners, thus "full members" of Eurocentric modernity.[19] Strangely though, harrowingly so, blacks have constantly been treated as strangers in their own motherland and forced to live within an ethos foreign to them and whose assumptions are constantly propelled as superior. Even most piercing is the willingness of a black person to be a stranger in his/her motherland.

It should be clear, right from the very onset, that blackness as a starting point of analysis within the framework of the methodology elucidated, is not a plea for "family membership" in Western tools of knowledge, but the locus of enunciation within the philosophy and ethics of liberation. Percy More says, "For black people in an anti-black world there is never a moment in their lives when their blackness is not an issue such that it can be treated as irrelevant to their existence."[20] This chapter first makes a call for the departure from the prejudice paradigm as it diffuses alertness to the toxic progression of racism, especially when its links with modernity are made, the next point this chapter makes.

The long history of racism, its proto-foundational acts, traced to Eurocentric modernity, inevitably prompts the irruption of the memory of the miserable, arguably seen in the growing viscerality of politics in South Africa. Moving to the next point, this chapter attempts to debunk the deployment of culture as a concealing mechanism to enhance the misrecognition of the inherent intent to obliterate others, and then the incapacity of the Cartesian Ego to tackle and confront the conquering mind-set that provides ground to Eurocentric epistemology. While intended as a tentative subject of the conversation, the *long durée* of brokenness, the chapter illustrates, cannot be unrelated to the drift into visceral politics that is taking place in South Africa and in the context of Empire that shapes our conversation on racism.

BEYOND THE PREJUDICE PARADIGM

Let us begin this section with a broad rendition of prejudice in relations to the discussion of racism by Percy More:

> The usual defence of a racist white person is to call the black victim of racism racist. This is what Lewis Gordon appropriately calls "equal-opportunity racism" and is expressed in statements we frequently hear: "Blacks are also racist." This means if everyone is a racist, then either no one is a racist or racism is a natural human phenomenon and no one can really be blamed for being human.[21]

The starting point of BTL has never been based on racism as a natural human phenomenon, but the historical justification of racism, the structural domination, violent oppression, and the denial of the humanity of black people, all of which create anthropological pauperization, impoverishment, and the cultural annihilation of the black person—the death of a black person—to mention but a few. White power structure, à la Steve Biko—the core of racism—is the crux of the response of Black Consciousness and, ipso facto, BTL. Racism, while related to prejudice is more than prejudice itself, it is structural, it is an ethos built on prejudice that creates legal, philosophical, theological, economic, and cultural structures undergirded by a concealed spirit of the superiority of the white race. It creates an utterly unjust ethos, historically preceded by genocide, epistemicide, and spiritualicide to attain its filthy goals. Its ethos and spirit continue to reign long after its explicit claims and scientific validations have disappeared. It is a mind-set that is structurally manifested in our sociopolitical and ecclesial organizations.

For this reason, as is the case in South Africa post-1994, the "recognition" of blacks in a white ethos and power structure does not equate to their status as full members and, ipso facto, the absence of racism itself. It is exactly because blacks are "recognized" that discourses of "ignorance," "innocence," "arrogance," sheer obstinacy, and fascism to defend racism are deployed as strategies to perpetuate this demon that continues to designate a black person as stranger in her/his polis.

Illustratively, Allan Boesak[22] debunked pseudo-innocence as one feature that characterized white response to racism and black acceptance of this order. Later on, Boesak appropriates the same thesis, namely, the claim to innocence and ignorance by many whites and the acceptance of inferiority by blacks, in a work that critiques the relationship of this propensity with globalization, especially the current systems of economic management. More recently, J. N. J. (Klippes) Kritzinger[23] employs Boesak's thesis, "Farewell to Innocence," and adds other categories, "Farewell to Ignorance," "Farewell to Arrogance" too, if we are to succeed in dealing with "deep-seated attitudes and approaches that keep on bedevilling relationships between black and white people in this country."[24] The preacher who is the subject of Kritzinger's critique lives in Sandton. Sandton is among the wealthiest suburbs of South Africa, a stone's throw away from Alexander Township. While there are blacks who live in Sandton, it is seriously doubtful they are "recognized" as members of the "Sandton" community. Metaphorically and historically "Sandton" cannot continue to exist without "Alexander."

With the creation of a white city and the black locations popularly known as townships in South Africa, the white world and the black world have existed in a bifurcated sociopolitical order within the colonial and Apartheid power structures.[25] Blacks have never been accorded citizenship in a civilized space that was racialized and bifurcated.[26] Ignorance, innocence, arrogance, obstinacy and racist fascism are evidently symptoms of sophistication, to sustain this question: "Where is racism if blacks are recognized so much and have political liberation in South Africa post-1994?" "What more do they want?" The underlying assumption is that the recognition and presence of blacks in white structures of power signifies the absence of racism.

That Apartheid was a dominant ideology, following on Gramscian analysis, an autocratic system of ideas intended to totally separate the races, influence every facet of daily life, and ensure non-European compliance with white domination is a prime example of a Eurocentric modernist project and, thus, the refutation of the treatment of racism as prejudice. "As an aspect of political culture, it was based on race and ethnicity, political expedience, and biblical authority, and popularised by traditional intellectuals working through such ruling institutions as the church, State, and educational system."[27] This chapter is built on this interpretation and understanding of BTL whose analysis of race cannot be diffused to the analysis of racism as a natural human phenomenon in the face of a progressive trajectory of racism even to fascist levels of its denial today. It is thus important to move our conversation to the toxic relationship of racism with modernity, already alluded to above.

RACISM AND EUROCENTRIC MODERNITY

The relationship of racism with forms of imperialism is almost a fact that is difficult to dispute. Arnowitz and Gautney argue that the fifteenth- and sixteenth-century voyages of the discovery of the "new" world were strictly speaking motivated by the search for raw materials and the slave trade. However, for the first time in human history—a time that coincided with these voyages—the enslaver did not call the enslaved "dog" or "beast" merely metaphorically. On account of skin color, it was presumed that black Africans were as "race unlike any other"—a race whose enslavement, regardless of class or caste, was considered "scientifically" valid.[28] Apartheid thus has to be interpreted as part of this order that began with voyages, this order of the missions of civilization and slavery justified by racial logic. In other words, the specter[29] of racial violence in South Africa post-1994 is not unrelated to this long history, *long durée* of racism.

A number of incidents in 2016 South Africa inevitably prompt the memory of a black African nonperson not as a dog or beast metaphorically, but a scientifically valid object, dog, beast, for the economic, political, theological, and cultural satiation of a superior race. Anamnestic ethics provides us with a prism to examine this matter in conjunction with an analectic view of this memory—the call to transcend or struggle against it. Anamnestic ethics thus does not allow us to view memory as a cognitive concept—a forte of Eurocentric rationality, it is not "memorialisation" according to Judith Butler—but rather memory as the past that flashes right now, the flashes of the bodies broken, excruciated, violated, and dismembered but now! Bénézet Bujo explains that a "morality of memoria" is central to an understanding of African ethics and anamnesis.[30] He states:

> African ethics is articulated in the framework of community, which involves remembering one's ancestors. As a narrative community, fellowship here on earth renews the existence of the community of the ancestors. This re-establishing (poiēsis) in turn implies the praxis which efficiently continues the remembrance of the ancestors and gives a new dynamism to earthly fellowship. Consequently, ethical behaviour in the Black African context always involves re-establishing the presence of one's ancestors; for one who takes the anamnesis seriously is challenged to confront the ethical rules drawn up by ancestors, in order to actualise anew the "protological foundational act" which first called the clan fellowship into life.

There are two ways to apply Bénézet Bujo's sentiments, at least for this chapter. First, the specter of these racist epiphanies actualizes anew the protological foundational acts of racism and Eurocentric modernity—the reestablishment of the ancestral presence of racism—those actions that first moved from calling blacks "dogs" or "beasts" metaphorically to scientifically and theologically justifying their doubt as human beings. Second, this specter reestablishes the memory of Queen Nzinga, Amilcar Cabral, Oscar Romero, Tiyo Soga, Steve Biko, and others, the protological foundational acts of resistance, by lives lived and killed in the ubiquitous zones of racism. The memory of racism is too deep to forget! The past of racism flashes right now, its violence on the underside of history and the dungeons of modernity are reestablished by epiphanies of racial bigotry in South Africa. This specter of racial epiphanies in the present instantiates a remembering, reliving and reestablishment of *memoria miserabilis*. The ghost of colonial conquest, a Europeanized object, legitimized by a Christianizing spirit of the Europeanization of the world, comes back to haunt us and will continue to do so if its core remains untouched. To the extent that one who has ever been, and is, a victim of racism will ever grasp its rationality—racism ruptures the imaginary of a victim as simply difficult to understand, harrowingly incomprehensible, and irrational. Therefore, the cognitive resources of the West, with their foundations in this ugly order, become so unhelpful if not toxic to the memory of the victims. But what is the rationality of this problem and its antics? To this we must now turn.

ON THE CUNNING OF RACISM

To recapitulate, we have attempted to argue that racism should be examined through the lenses of Empire and that these rampant epiphanies of racism that defy and continue to undermine the work that has been done in analyzing and resisting this problem ostensibly reestablish the memory of the miserable, irrupting from the proto-foundational acts of racism in its long relationship with Eurocentric modernity. Now we need to further examine its cunning antics to finally nail it, to crack its skull. How does it hide its head?

The title of the article by Pierre Bourdieu and Loïc Waquant, "On the Cunning of Imperialist Reason," inspires the subtitle of this section more than its content. Bourdieu's and Wacquant's statement suggests the following: "Cultural Imperialism rests on the power to universalise particularities linked to a singular historical tradition by causing them to be misrecognised as such."[31] The power behind the misrecognition of the rationality, the cognitive resources of imperial power, ipso facto, Empire, is the universalization of what is essentially the particularity of a culture. Empire has an imperial spirit. This spirit is doggy and is misrecognized.

BTL is on record in its critique of universalities associated with the canons of Western knowledge. Itumeleng Mosala[32] is one example, hermeneutically speaking, that dealt Western universality a blow by stating that BTL in its early developments began to apply its mind to the "concern for a cultureless and culture-bound, classless and class-based, raceless and race-oriented Jesus."[33] Culture is the issue here—the myth of cultural universalism derived from one particularity among cultures employs strategies to veil its particularity and thus perpetuates the misrecognition of the core rationality and logic of Western modernity. Enrique Dussel critiques this myth in this manner:

> "Eurocentrism" is precisely characterised by the assumption that historical expressions of European particularity in fact constitute moments of *abstract human universality in general.* This reflects the singularity of European particularity as the first such identity that *in fact* became global, as the first concrete human expression of universality. *Modern* European culture, civilisation, philosophy, subjectivity, and so on thereby became identified as equivalent to the human universal abstractions of culture, civilisation, philosophy, and subjectivity in general, *without further qualification.*[34]

The arrogance of Eurocentric canons of knowledge is unprecedented.[35] The misrecognition of Eurocentric particularities is concealed in what the same knowledge system elevates as abstract human universality, while the representation of this universal humanity is singularly equated to its own anthropological assumptions. Furthermore, as Dussel argues, European culture, inter alia, does not need explication, interrogation, or critique by others save on its own terms—it is final!

It is the defense of this myth that particularly fascinates us. Itumeleng Mosala cites Amilcar Cabral to argue that Christianity was spread at gunpoint in South Africa:

> When Goebbels, the brain behind the Nazi propaganda, heard the word "culture," he reached for his pistol. This shows that the Nazis—who were and are the most tragic expression of imperialism and of its thirst for domination—even if they were all degenerates like Hitler, had a clear idea of the value of culture as a factor of resistance to foreign domination.[36]

Mosala argues that the essence of conflict between Africans and the West is the clash of cultures. Kathryn Tanner presents a history of the word "culture" and according to her "the word *Kultur* applied to social groups."[37] She says, "Germans had first to secure a sense of themselves as a distinct people through the notion of *Kultur*."[38] The idea of the purity of their culture, must have led the Germans to be aware of its value to resist foreign domination as Mosala implies, and thus "Goebbels' gun" was necessary for domination and the protection of this culture. Linda Alcoff puts it this way: "The progressive teleology of Europe which sanctions its expansion by a belief in its own superiority is not the natural by-product of a culture on the rise, but the result of false narratives, occluded histories, burned books and murdered scholars."[39] In the absence of "Goebbels' gun," in the context of democracy in South Africa, these false narratives, occluded histories and her-stories, the burning of books and the murdering of scholars continue in a different manner. Accordingly, "The Clausewitzian slogan that war is the continuation of politics by other means—which entailed that politics is the continuation of war by other means,"[40] suggests that politics and its ethos do continue the project of the obliteration of others. Ramon Grosfoguel asks: "How is it possible that the canon of thought in all the disciplines of the Social Sciences and humanities in the Westernised university . . . is based on the knowledge produced by a few men from five countries in Western Europe?"[41]

In the absence of guns, to propel the canons of thought produced by few men from five countries, to dismantle the culture of black African people, Eurocentric epistemology deploys its cunning antics of misrecognition to wage the continuation of war through culture.

Jesse Mugambi says, "Culture is the total manifestation of a people's self-understanding and self-expression, through politics, economics, ethics, aesthetics, kin-ship and religion."[42] As a totality, Charles Kraft's[43] view that culture is made up of forms, patterns, and processes, illuminates this point even further. Kraft alerts us to the fact that there are "component entities of culture and the purposes they serve."[44] These component entities of culture occupy different levels and combined together they suggest that "a person's culture then is designed to serve the basic functions that all humanity needs to have provided for." Yet there are differences too as there are "constants that originate within culture as well."[45] Kraft continues, "Among these are things that are common to all human experience, such as culture itself." [46] Here lies the paradox, the fact that all human beings are immersed in one culture or another clearly suggests that culture itself is a constant including other categories of constants that originate from within common to all cultures. Culture, according to Amilcar Cabral, is an important element—constant—of a people's history with its roots plunged into the material conditions of a people.[47] For this reason, "the anthropological notion of culture discourages the snap judgements of a complacent ethnocentrism."[48] Stated otherwise, cultures have a core and that core is culture itself, consequently leaving no room for ethnocentrism, the erosion of the history of others and the disintegration of the component entities of one particular culture.

Following this, there are outer levels, components, of culture moving out from its core or moving in to its core. If the cultural core—constant—of the black African person is destroyed, dismantled, and crushed, no matter how much the outer levels of the core fancy black African expression, the compatibility between the outer levels and the inner core of culture is not attained; there is disharmony. To suck out the core—the constant of culture—is to kill. "Things fall apart," à la Chinua Achebe. Gustavo Gutierrez says:

> In the ultimate analysis, poverty means death—first, physical death, because poor people are dying of sicknesses that can often be easily cured by medical science today but not in poor countries. Second, in addition to this physical as well as economic death from poverty, there is a cultural side, a cultural

> death. Anthropologists say that "culture is life." When we despise a culture, a religion, a race, a gender, an ethnic group, we are killing persons—culturally speaking—belonging to that sector of humanity.[49]

With this understanding of culture, especially as deployed for the continuation of war by other means, the misrecognition of the nucleus—the core, or constant—of racial superiority and supremacy is one strategy, intended for the same purpose, the *long durée* of the fundamental doubt of the humanity of a black person. The sucking of the core of the cultural system is another strategy of cultural obliteration. These two are driven through universality and the hidden but assumed finality of the epistemological canons of the West in the absence of physical war. As the destroyer of black African culture, the West has attacked the core of the culture of the black African physically, but continues this destruction by quintessentially creating incompatibility between the outer levels of black African culture and its inner core, thus the complete annihilation of the spirituality, the religiosity of a black person. Explicitly stated, no two cultures in the world, for example, can have similar expressions of Christian faith. Western epistemology cannot speak for or about African culture.[50] If it does, it can do so only with African epistemology. Without African epistemology and culture, it continues to kill by sucking out the brain of a black person, the brain of black African culture.

CARTESIAN EGO: THE ETHICAL WORM OF EMPIRE

If *ubuntu* is the core of black African philosophy and ethics, what then constitutes the core of the philosophy and ethics of Eurocentric modernity? The naturalization of violence, killing, conquest, universality, arrogance, ignorance, and finality against the existence the black? The reason why the lives of others are easily sacrificed—conquered—for the security of some, is this the core of this culture? The relationship between modernity and the Cartesian Ego might shed some light in this regard. Maldonado-Torres says one of the features of the spirit of European culture is "an attitude characterised by a permanent suspicion,"[51] subtle at most, an attitude of permanent suspicion of the humanity of a black person. He says, "Misanthropic scepticism provides the basis for the *preferential option for the ego conquiro*,"[52] the "I conquer, therefore I am." He goes on: "The *imperial attitude* promotes a fundamentally genocidal attitude in respect to the colonised and racialised people."[53] This "worm," the Manichean misanthropic skepticism, is at the heart of the subtle and hiddenness of the canons of Eurocentric knowledge, quintessentially against the life of a colonized and racialized self. Maldonado-Torres says:

> This means that the significance of the Cartesian *cogito* for modern European identity has to be understood against the backdrop of an unquestioned ideal of self-expressed in the notion of the *ego conquiro*. The certainty of the self as a conqueror, of its tasks and missions, preceded Descartes's certainty about the self as a thinking substance (*res cogitans*) and provided a way to interpret it. I am suggesting that the practical conquering self and the theoretical thinking substance are parallel in terms of their certainty. The *ego conquiro* is not questioned, but rather provides the ground for the articulation of the *ego cogito*. Dussel suggests as much: "The 'barbarian' was the obligatory context of all reflection on subjectivity, reason, the *cogito*."[54]

The preferential option for the self that conquers, which puts the humanity of the black person on permanent doubt, provides the ground, the interstice for the expression of the Cartesian Ego. Following Maldonado-Torres, this is the imperial attitude that defines the modern man.

Now, "spirit as power,"[55] to employ Mosala's insights, the Spirit of God that transcends institutional power, the Spirit of God that creates, is experienced by blacks as a conquering spirit that severely and permanently doubts the humanity of a black person whose life affirmation is perpetually suppressed by a Eurocentric Christianity. The capacity of racist logic to be misrecognized whenever there is no possibility to assume physical violence in order to destroy and dismantle the cultural dispensation of the black African, the incapacity of the imperial spirit of racial supremacy and superiority to question conquest, despite its destruction everywhere and anywhere being seen, experienced, and felt even by the whole of creation today, is the fusion of the "spirit as power" in Western culture and the bondage of Western Eurocentric epistemology with the conquest of the world. Such a "spirit as power" that penetrates the core of the spirituality or religiosity of a black African, by sucking the very core of African culture, is the ultimate destruction of a black person. Linda Alcoff explains:

> Western philosophy passes itself off as universal and disembodied, without cultural roots or limitations. This is its own self-deception, for which the concept of modernity provided the alibi. Philosophies born elsewhere, from the underside of modernity, are rewriting this historical self-understanding of European philosophy as well as the telos of global thought.[56]

The "wretched of the earth," who are not what being is in the West, a being that is not there, disembodied and without root, are kept in this state in Western philosophy, due to its incapacity to question conquest.[57] According to Grosfoguel, ontological dualism assumes that the mind is distanced from the body. The mind is undetermined and unconditioned by the body. To sustain this mind, only the body of the wretched should be a being that is not there. The Cartesian ego is based on this ontological dualism of the mind and the body. The "I think, therefore I am" is sustainable only if the "I" is elevated and seen as a category that is undetermined by the body, otherwise the dismantlement of this dualist ontology would naturally bring the mind back to where it belongs, namely, the body. Abstract knowledge, that is, knowledge that is assumed to be without a body, has been the constant point of agitation among students of the liberation paradigm.

There is another deeper problem. How does knowledge that is driven by the isolated "I" get to be validated? It is an internal monologue of the subject of knowing—it is solipsistic. Solipsism grants certitude to knowledge, meaning that self-certified forms of knowledge are a feature of Eurocentric canons of knowledge. It is essentially epistemic solipsism that is dangerously hiding racism. A further point still needs to be made. Does this mean that there is no dialogue in the West? Can we argue that theirs is simply a monologue based on ontological dualism and solipsistic validation of knowledge? Not necessarily.[58] The exponents of the Eurocentric canons can speak for themselves. Simply, from our perspective, especially from the perspective of black Africa, anamnestic ethics with its analectic starting point of crushed knowledge based on "I am because we are," a struggle for the liberation of the wretched is waged. The discussion of this other alternative form of knowledge construction is beyond the scope of this essay but one thing only: The exclusion of this other alternative model of knowledge construction on matters that matter to black African lives, and more importantly the violent destruction of this alternative as a viable starting point, is a matter of justice. Enrique Dussel's point sums this up for us: "This is why Boesak's "the courage to be" is immensely important. Not only as negation of the negation involved in oppression, but also as affirmation of Black, African actuality, the dignity of being a historic people with its own traditions, heroes, art, and religion."[59]

But there is even more: the "I" of "I think therefore I am" dethrones God as only God should have finality in any epistemological and cultural dispute among civilizations. In this sense therefore, liberation, the courage to be, the negation of the negation of the doubt of the humanity of a black person, the negation of the imperial attitude of the West, is a project of life for the black.

VISCERAL POLITICS AND RACISM POST-1994

Visceral politics offers a tentative proposal for a symptomatic analysis and interpretation of the thesis argued in this chapter. In the context of Empire, power configurations that cover politics, economics, and the "lifeworld," or to put it differently, the fusion of culture with faith, politics, economics, and culture, violently defended in our current world, implies that the victims are harrowingly throttled.

The militarization of politics, economics, and culture, the whole of life as "The Accra Confession" suggests, threatens the whole of life by sustaining a killing civilization. The bonds that convivially affirm the whole constellation of life are ruptured. How then can the victims express their grievance against such a *long durée* of powerful, dastardly recycling machinery, the cunning of racism, the spirit that has the capacity to hide with its incapacity to confront the evils of conquest? Linda Alcoff takes this insight from Dussel: "The obviousness of the modernist fallacies manifest, Dussel interestingly suggests, a bad conscience . . . a restless conscience toward the injustice committed."[60] It is the desperation of guilt unacknowledged that forces the vanquished, the conquered, to accept irrational claims and to escape the daily hauntings of the *memoria miserabilis*. The concoction, derivative of the toxic mix of the core of black African spirituality with logic intended to obliterate the very core existence of a black, is a mixture of genocidal spirit, epistemic solipsism with inexplicable damage to the Spirit as Power for a black.

Is this not what the *#RhodesMustFall* indicates? When human excretion was poured onto Cecil John Rhodes's bronze statue in 2015, a new epoch that marked a moment of decolonization in South Africa was born. If the very core of this war against blacks—the unrelenting innate genocidal spirit, the tactics of misrecognition, the unbaiting, pervasive, and permanent doubt of the humanity of a black in post-1994 describe this order—what other language remains for the victims to express the *long durée* of this pain? Can you smell it? Visceral politics by the powerless suggests that racism, as in the smell of the excretion, continues to exist! The soul, which comprises reason, spirit, and desire, is ruptured at core in a restless conscience of the perpetrator against the injustices committed but perpetually denied to the point of dethroning God, the legitimate authority for our finality to affirm to humanity of the victims.

It cannot be easy to deny that the perpetuation of the cultural values of the dominant and hegemonic groups in South Africa continues as symptomized by the Fallist and Decolonising movement. The epistemic violence pervasive in all sectors of our public life given for now propagation of hegemony and the ability of institutions such as the church and others that do not use coercive power to create cultural values that perpetuate the domination of the black persons creates unpredictability of response by the victims.

Racism stinks! It is a thick stench firstly of the millions of bodies lying down the seabed of the Atlantic Ocean if not ceaselessly floating around with the currents of the seas and oceans of this earth. It stinks in the Elmina dungeons of transatlantic slavery; it stinks everywhere in the United States,

Brazil, Cuba, and fills the air in South Africa. While the victims smell and feel it, racism is said to be no longer there. Racism is bestial and the inhalation of air polluted with this disease is truly the air inhaled by children who grow up at Thabo Mbeki village, the squatter camps, and many other informal settlements where even toilets are difficult to build just for the recognition of the dignity of a black person. In Mamelodi, on the informal settlement called Stoffel Park, sewage is a challenge as in many areas that have been revealed during the current election campaign for local elections in South Africa. If we cannot theorize racism, visceral politics symptomize it.

CONCLUSION

This essay argued that BTL, the courage to be of the wretched, the negation of the negation of the humanity of the blacks in the *long durée* of the machinery of Eurocentric modernity, its tactics and its logic, exuding in the spirit of Empire remains fragile if the skull of racism is not cracked. One might say the title suggests violence. Not at all, Africans speak about beating something on its head, like a snake if you need to finally kill it. Sucking out the software of racism, its tactics, it restlessness, is to refuse and reject the finality of modernity, universality of this project, at least, to reject as killing the validation of incoherent and false narratives of the West in the context of Empire.

NOTES

1. The theme of Empire is widely discussed and numerous works on it have been published. For example, the publication of "The Accra Confession" in 2004, whose text uses and critiques the concept of Empire as a particular configuration of power, led to discussions of this concept extensively within the Reformed family.
2. See Frantz Fanon, *Black Skin, White Masks*, Kobo ed., trans. Richard Philcox (New York: Grove Press, 1967), 24.
3. Fred Dallmayr, "The Underside of Modernity: Adorno, Heidegger, and Dussel," *Constellations* 11 (2004): 112.
4. Some scholars discuss racism within the broad world-systemic view of modernity such as Maldonado-Torres, "AAR Centennial Roundtable: Religion, Conquest, and Race in the Foundations of the Modern/Colonial World," *Journal of the American Academy of Religion* 82 (September, 2014): 636–65. See also Ramon Grosfoguel, "What Is Racism," *Journal of World Systems Research* 22 (2016): 9–15.
5. Maldonado-Torres, "Religion, Conquest, and Race," 653.
6. Siphiwe I. Dube, "Race, Whiteness and Transformation in the Promise Keepers America and the Mighty Men Conference: A Comparative Analysis," *HTS Teologies Studies/Theological Studies* 72/1 (2016): 5–7, DOI: 10.4102/hts.v72i1.3476.

7. Dube, "Race, Whiteness," 5–7.

8. Grosfoguel, "What Is Racism," 11.

9. See Stanley Arnowitz and Heather Gauntney, *Implicating Empire: Globalisation and Resistance in the 21st Century World Order* (New York: Basic Books, 2013), xviii–xix.

10. Linda Martin Alcoff, "Philosophy, the Conquest, and the Meaning of Modernity: A Commentary on 'Anti-Cartesian Meditations: On the Origin of the Philosophical Anti-Discourse of Modernity' by Enrique Dussel," *Human Architecture: Journal of the Sociology of Self-Knowledge* 11/1, article 6. Available at <http://scholarworks.umb.edu/humanarchitecture/vol11/iss1/6/> [Accessed: June 17, 2017].

11. Tinyiko S. Maluleke and Sarojini Nadar, "Alien Fraudsters in the White Academy: Agency in Gendered Colour," *Journal of Theology for Southern Africa* 120 (2004): 5–17.

12. See James H. Cone, *The Cross and the Lynching Tree* (Maryknoll, NY: Orbis, 2011), 30–64.

13. Zakes Mda, *Little Suns* (Cape Town: Umuzi, 2015), 51.

14. Dallmayr, "The Underside of Modernity,"114.

15. Dallmayr, "The Underside of Modernity,"114.

16. Néstor Míguez, Joerg Rieger, and Jung Mo Sung, *Beyond the Spirit of Empire* (London: SCM Press, 2009), 1.

17. Manning Marable, "Racism in a Time of Terror," in *Implicating Empire: Globalisation & Resistance in the 21st Century World Order*, ed. Stanley Arnowitz and Heather Gautney (New York: Basic Books, 2003), 11.

18. Jim Wallis, *America's Original Sin: Racism, White Privilege, and the Bridge to a New America* (Grand Rapids, MI: Brazos Press, 2016).

19. The current brawl in the Philosophy Society in South Africa is but a crystal-clear example of this problem. Black scholars have reportedly left this body on the grounds of protracted experiences of racism, and Percy More's article, cited below, reflects on this problem.

20. Percy M. More, "Isn't Identity Informed by Experience?" *Mail & Guardian* (February 24–March 2, 2017), 25.

21. More, "Isn't Identity Informed by Experience?"

22. Allan A. Boesak, *Farewell to Innocence: A Social-Ethical Study of Black Theology and Black Power* (Johannesburg: Raven Press, 1977).

23. J.N.J. Kritzinger, "Response to Pastor André Olivier of Rivers Church, Sandton," <https://www.kathradafoundation.org/news/response-pastor-andre-olivier-rivers-church-sandton/> [Accessed: June 12, 2016].

24. Kritzinger, "Response to Pastor André Olivier," 1.

25. Mahmood Mamdani, *Citizen and Subject: Contemporary Africa and the Legacy of Late Colonialism*, Princeton Studies in Culture/Power/History (Kampala, Uganda: Fountain, 1996).

26. It is not worth repeating this elaborately in this essay because there are so many other works that have given this exposition. Instead, our purpose will be to illustrate that racism cannot be viewed as a problem that ended with the demise of Apartheid in South Africa.

27. Rupe Simms, "Black Theology, A Weapon in the Struggle for Freedom: A Gramscian Analysis," *Race & Society* 2/2 (2000): 175.

28. Emmanuel Chukwudi Eze, "Double Consciousness and the Democratic Ideal," in *Colonialism and Its Legacies*, ed. Jacob T Levy with Iris Marion Young (Lanham, MD: Lexington Books, 2011): 224.

29. Eight days into the new year in 2016, Penny Sparrow, a Durban-based estate agent, was apparently so infuriated by the "crowding" of the beaches by black people that she vented her disgust on the social media platform Facebook, in which she called black people "monkeys" that crowd the beaches. Later in the year, on the Twitter social media platform, Chris Hart, a popular television journalist who comments on economic issues, stated that the "majority" appear to be "angry" and think that they are "entitled." Later in the same year, Judge Mable Jansen explicitly stated that rape was culture among black people. There have also been many reported incidents of racial rage. In one restaurant, a black person wrote on the receipt for a waitress, that he would not pay any tips before the land is returned to black people. Those of us who have lived in Johannesburg for some years have become familiar with incidents of racial road rage. Another racial incident captured on a cell phone video toward the end of 2016 involved two white assailants who forced Victor Rethabile Mlotshwa into a coffin while threatening to set him alight. There are many such incidents reported in the press. This chapter attempts to examine the core, without essentializing the matter, and represents more than a simple reflection on the upsurge of these incidents through the prism of anamnestic ethics.

30. Bénézet Bujo, *Foundations of an African Ethic: Beyond the Universal Claims of Western Morality* (Nairobi: Paulines, 2003), 56–57.

31. Pierre Bourdieu and Loïc Wacquant, "On the Cunning of Imperialist Reason," *Theory Culture & Society* 16/1 (February 1999): 41–58.

32. Itumeleng J. Mosala, *Biblical Hermeneutics and Black Theology in South Africa* (Grand Rapids, MI: Eerdmans, 1989), 21–24.

33. Mosala, *Biblical Hermeneutics*, 21.

34. Enrique Dussel, *Beyond Philosophy: Ethics, History, Marxism and Liberation Theology* (Landham, MD: Rowman & Littlefield, 2003), 42–43.

35. See Vuyani S. Vellem, "Black Theology of Liberation: A Theology of Life in the Context of Empire," *Verbum et Ecclesia* 36/3, article 1470, <http://verbumetecclesia.org.za/index.php/VE/article/view /1470/> [Accessed: June 17, 2017]. Here, Vellem argues for the symbiosis of racism and capitalism. See also Vuyani S. Vellem, "Black Theology of Liberation and the Economy of Life," *Ecumenical Review* 67 (2015), in which the racial justification of slavery is discussed.

36. Itumeleng J. Mosala, "Spirituality and Struggle: African and Black Theologies," in *One Nation: A Festschrift for Beyers Naude*, ed. Charles Villa-Vicencio and Carl Niehaus (Cape Town: Human & Rousseau, 1995), 83.

37. Kathryn Tanner, *Theories of Culture: A New Agenda for Theology* (Minneapolis, MN: Fortress Press, 1997), 9.

38. Tanner, *Theories of Culture*, 9.

39. Alcoff, "Philosophy, the Conquest, and the Meaning of Modernity," 60.

40. Eduardo Mendieta, foreword to "The Liberation of Politics: Alterity, Solidarity and Liberation," in Enrique Dussel, *Twenty Theses on Politics* (Durham, NC: Duke University Press, 2008), 12.

41. Ramon Grosfoguel, "The Structure of Knowledge in Westernised Universities: Epistemic Racism/Sexism and the Four Genocides/Epistemicides of the Long 16th Century," *Human Architecture: Journal of the Sociology of Knowledge* 11 (2013): 74.
42. Jesse N. K. Mugambi, *Christian Theology and Social Reconstruction* (Nairobi: Acton, 2003), 119.
43. Charles H. Kraft, *Christianity in Culture: A Study in Dynamic Biblical Theologising in Cross-Cultural Perspective* (Maryknoll, NY: Orbis, 1979), 64–77.
44. Kraft, *Christianity in Culture,* 64.
45. Kraft, *Christianity in Culture,* 95.
46. Kraft, *Christianity in Culture,* 95.
47. Cf. Mosala, "Spirituality and Struggle," 84.
48. Tanner, *Theories of Culture,* 37.
49. Gustavo Gutierrez, "Liberation Theology for the Twenty-First Century," in *Romero's Legacy: The Call to Peace and Justice,* ed. Pilar Hogan Closkey and John P. Hogan (2007), 11.
50. Percy More appeals to Linda Alcoff's question: "Who has the authority to speak for others?" This same question is similar to Spivak's: "Can the Subaltern Speak?" The deployment of Western epistemology to speak for others is a known discourse of paternalism and patronizing aspects of the whites in the least of their relationship with blacks. Without farewell to arrogance, the argument in this chapter is that this is not only about patronage and paternalism; it is about killing, epistemicide by sucking out the core constants of black African culture.
51. Nelson Maldonado-Torres, "On the Coloniality of Being: Contributions on the Development of a Concept," *Cultural Studies* 21/2-3 (2007): 46.
52. Maldonado-Torres, "On the Coloniality of Being," 246.
53. Maldonado-Torres, "On the Coloniality of Being," 246.
54. Maldonado-Torres, "On the Coloniality of Being," 245.
55. Mosala, "Spirituality and Struggle," 85.
56. Linda Martin Alcoff and Eduardo Mendieta, introduction to *Thinking from the Underside of Modernity* (Lanham, MD: Rowman & Littlefield, 2000), 3.
57. Cf. Maldonado-Torres, "On the Coloniality of Being," 253.
58. There are many examples of internal critique of modernity.
59. Dussel, *Beyond Philosophy,* 15.
60. Alcoff, "Philosophy, the Conquest, and the Meaning of Modernity," 61.

THREE

Black Solidarity Impaled

The Cause of Afrophobia

Bernard Matolino

INTRODUCTION

I aim to achieve two things in this chapter. First, I will seek to offer an analysis of how mistaken the view that there is something fundamentally black or African[1] that ties people of this race together is. Second, I will seek to argue that black or African people are open to the possibility of conflict just like any other people. From these two considerations, I will seek to draw the conclusion that the incidents of xenophobia that South Africa has intermittently witnessed, since it was admitted to the association of free nations, can be explained in very simple terms of competition for material resources amongst the most vulnerable and disadvantaged people of the continent. In the course of making my second point, I will seek to show that the ethical basis on which traditional African society, which would have made the socio-ethical values associated with black people work, have largely disappeared on an African continent that has become largely predatory.

AFRICAN SOLIDARITY

African solidarity as a political idea has been around for quite a while. Its most able exponents were nationalists or socialists who doubled as theorists and politicians and ultimately played a leading role in the fight for Africa's independence. These thinkers and politicians, in responding to colonialism and racism that had victimized black people, sought to find a collective and cohesive point to rally black people together in attempts to defeat the twin evils of colonialism and racism. Two detailed approaches, which were replicated to varying degrees, were advanced in Kwame Nkrumah's notion of the African personality and Léopold Sédar Senghor's negritude. The idea of negritude was not only an attempt at articulating the beauty and equality of the black person in the face of racist colonialism, but it also sought to underscore the collective identity of black persons. In Aimé Césaire's[2] poem, first published in 1939, the celebration of the black man's characteristics, which are seen as a testimony of her inferiority by the white race, are extolled as virtues that characterize black people everywhere. Accordingly, Senghor advances this celebration to be a mark of characteristics that black people everywhere share. The idea of African personality that both Nkrumah[3] and Senghor[4] advance seeks to give an ample declaration to the basic way in which African people approach reality. Their view of reality is one that is communitarian. In advancing a communitarian view, they argue that Africans had always led a life that essentially encompassed a great degree of identifying with the other, sharing in the other's fate, and caring for the other's welfare. The basis of this orientation was found in highly communalistic and highly dependent traditional societies. This dependency, the ethic of community, where the individual prioritizes the reality of the community over her own, becomes the guiding principle of making sense of the reality of self, others, and the world at large. It becomes both an ethic and politics that guides how the individual interacts with others and deliberately fashions her own relations as well as her social institutions.

Thus, from the nationalists' perspective, what sponsored the idea of the possibility of black solidarity or black unity was a sense of two shared realities amongst all black people. The first reality is that of oppression, racism, and exclusion. Blacks had been targeted and had received this unfair treatment largely because they were black. Rationalization had been offered either to show that blacks were naturally inferior to whites, hence in need of civilization, or they were simply objects of trade that could be used to affect the economic success of the expanding nations of conquest. The second reality that sponsored the possibility of black solidarity or unity was the fundamental interpretation of the black worldview which Senghor and Nkrumah saw as the African personality. These communitarian aspects of the sociality of the self, both politically and ethically, were seen as defining characteristics that were commonly shared amongst all black people. If there was something that would distinguish black people from the rest of humanity, it was to be found in the communitarian ethos of care, cooperation, and strong identity with the community, and a shared collectivist interpretation of life. For Senghor, what made Africans to be Africans was their innate heightened use of emotion as a tool of understanding, analyzing, and making sense of the world. This use of emotion was in opposition to the white person's rationalistic approach which tended to emphasize discursive knowledge as a mode of coming to terms with the reality of the world. Senghor sees the white person's manner of formulating knowledge as cold and distanced whereas the African's way of knowledge is not only warmer but brings the subject that knows (the person) and the object to be known very close to each other. Hence, the difference between the black person and the white person is well established in their basic attitudes toward interpreting the reality of the world.

Although there are many valid objections to Senghor and Nkrumah's mapping of the informants of the African view of life and politics, the important point that they make is that there are distinguishing characteristics that identify black people and set them apart. These characteristics make black people more amenable to the idea of a shared communitarian ethos of caring for each other and being present to each other's fate such that they ultimately become participants in a totality of life that is communally grounded. With the understanding that life is shared and communitarian in nature, the individual and political ethos that is developed is one that is firmly grounded, not only on the individual contributing to the good of the community, but finding her/his own identity in the good of that very community.[5] The ideal political arrangement of society is one that also primarily emphasizes the discovery and animation of a shared good.[6] That shared good is one that is responsible for the realization of shared goals, a shared life, and shared sense of purpose.

Thus, the class of scholars, cited immediately above, that came on the heels of nationalists sought, unwittingly, to give credence to what nationalists had argued for. Although they did not necessarily approve of the nationalist political view, which they correctly criticized for turning into one-party dictatorships, they shared the basic view with nationalists that there was an African orientation to life that was grounded on the importance of community. The importance of the community imposed on all individuals the obligation to behave in ways that promoted harmony.[7] In the precise promotion of harmony, all interests of individuals could be collapsed into one reality that individuals could easily find once ignorance or misperception of their real interests[8] had been removed. However, a new class of scholars has expressed some serious doubt about the viability of such a communitarian outlook. Questions about the status of individuals' rights[9] have been raised in the light of the exaggeration of the status of the all-engulfing importance of the community.

Yet the idea of an ethic that prioritizes the reality of the community remains very much alive, though cast in different forms as exemplified in Metz[10] and Ramose. The appeal to the idea of the community as a guiding principle both for the manner in which the individual conducts herself as well as the sociopolitical structures that must be developed to guide individual behavior remains popular on the continent. In the various ways in which the ethic and politics of communitarianism is stated, its underlying principle is one that seeks to enjoin the individual to the reality of the community by not only identifying with the communal mores but also practically living them out. What is at the heart of the communitarian ethic is care for the other; this care is extended to all people who are members of that community. The care given to the individual member of the community is also in some ways extended to the stranger. For example, it is taken to be the case that when two strangers meet, they would seek to establish possible ways in which they are related and if they are able to establish that possibility, then they would behave toward each other as if they were related in that manner. While it is not entirely accurate to claim that everyone is related to everyone, the communitarian ethic sees the interdependence that exists among people as one that creates a special type of rights and duties which are properly exercised or claimed within the ambit of the community. Metz captures this broad idea well when he notes:

> These and many other construals of communing or living harmoniously with others suggest two recurrent themes. Notice that they are ways in which individuals can relate to one another; communion is not the same as what a sociologist might associate with talk of "community," which to many ears will suggest something corporatist such as a group or society.
>
> On the one hand, part of relating communally is what I call "identifying with others," a matter of being close, belonging and participating, experiencing life as bound up with others, and considering oneself a part of the group. On the other hand, one finds reference to being sympathetic, being committed to others, responding to others' needs, and acting for others' good, which I call "exhibiting solidarity."
>
> More carefully, it is revealing to understand identifying with another (or being close, belonging, etc.) to be the combination of exhibiting certain psychological attitudes of "we-ness" and cooperative behaviour. The psychological attitudes include a tendency to think of oneself as a member of a group with the other and to refer to oneself as a "we" (rather than an "I"), a disposition to feel pride or shame in what the other or one's group does, and, at a higher level of intensity, an emotional appreciation of the other's nature and value. The cooperative behaviours include being transparent about the terms of interaction, allowing others to make voluntary choices, acting on the basis of trust, adopting common goals, and, at the extreme end, choosing for the reason that "this is who we are."[11]

From the above extended quote, I find two points worthy of emphasis. The first is that the notion of community is not seen in mere corporatist arrangements. On the contrary, the community is seen as something that one is deeply associated with, that she ultimately shares either in the pride or the shame of that community. This way one's sense of identity or ethic is derivative from the community. The second point is that there is a sense in which community members feel not only as belonging together but fundamentally identify with each other that their sense of "I" dissipates into a collective "we" which is seen as the organizing principle around which the identity of each member of the community is derived. It is from this idea of a collective we that each individual sees herself as obligated to be of a particular predisposition toward the other. The predisposition is one of consideration and care for the other because the individual is implicated in the reality of the other as they both contribute to the collective "we."

As a political tool, African solidarity has been expressed in the politics of African unity. The idea of unity was premised principally on the mission to fight colonialism and free Africans. Nkrumah refused to accept that Ghana was free until all of Africa had been freed. By this stance, he was committing himself to the idea that Africans shared both a painful reality of oppression but also a future and hope of shared freedom and progress. Yet, at the level of the intended political programs that were designed to be truly African, the most prominent being socialism and consensus, it has been argued that there is a shared approach to life among Africans that makes these political programs possible. The shared view that exists amongst Africans is one that, as Metz points above, prioritizes the creation of a collective "we" and attendant feelings of solidarity and care for the other.

In the fight for political freedom, African countries cooperated with each other. Those countries that had gained their freedom first started offering material and emotional support to those that were still engaged in the fight for freedom. As the struggle continued, the collective sense of Africans as being bound together in some fundamental way and the need for African unity was truly emphasized. The formation of the Organisation of African Unity (OAU) was principally aimed at ensuring the achievement of total freedom of all Africans by eliminating colonialism as well as promotion of African unity.[12] It was from this collaboration during the fight for independence that common goals, views of indebtedness, and interdependence were created at the beginning of each country's journey as a free political entity. As South Africa was the last country to attain political freedom, together with the fact that when it opened up to the rest of the continent, it presented itself as a sophisticated economy with many possibilities for those Africans that could see them, much was expected of it. Not only was it expected to play its part as the most sophisticated country on the continent with world-class infrastructure, it was also expected to open its doors to fellow African brothers and sisters.

THE SURPRISE OF XENOPHOBIA

From media reports, when the first acts of xenophobia[13] occurred, they caught local authorities and the continent by surprise. What was even more galling about the violence was the manner in which perpetrators of that violence, in local communities, made it very clear that they did not wish to have foreigners in their presence and actively saw them as partially responsible for the breeding of local misery. The trite and oft-repeated accusation that foreigners were responsible for stealing locals' jobs[14] lacked merit but most importantly sought to dehumanize the foreigner as one who was not suitable to occupy any job or to have a meaningful and fulfilling relationship with any member of the local community. In catching observers and supporters of African unity by surprise, the xenophobes had succeeded in undermining the supposed most important principle that guides African attitudes and life. In condemning the xenophobic outbreak of 2015, the South African cabinet expressed both regret and outrage when it stated:

> Cabinet condemns in the strongest terms the recent acts of violence against foreign nationals. At this point, Cabinet would like to extend its heartfelt condolences to the families of those who lost their lives and a speedy recovery to those who are injured. No amount of frustration or anger can justify these attacks and looting of shops. While noting the issues raised by communities, violence toward another fellow human being can never solve these issues. Rather, it reflects badly on us as a people, going against the very ideals and foundations of our democracy. South Africa fought against colonialism and Apartheid alongside fellow Africans so that all humanity in our continent should be respected and treated with dignity.
>
> Today, South Africa enjoys a free country, which was attained through the contribution of a number of the African Countries. Our own late icon, President Oliver Tambo was accommodated for close to thirty years in Zambia and many other South Africans that lived in exile. Fellow African countries, did not only host our people, they also contributed resources and some paid the ultimate price and lost their own citizens in the course of South Africa attaining democracy. South Africa will never be derailed from pursuing the Pan African vision as encapsulated in AU Agenda 2063, which was since pursued by our forefathers Kwame Nkruma, Azikiwe, Mualimu Julius Nyerere and Nelson Mandela.[15]

But was this act of locals turning on their neighbors really surprising? Was it the case that there was something fundamentally un-African in the xenophobes' attitude toward their so-called neighbors? While a case may be made, following Metz and supporters of the communitarian ethic and polity, that all members of the community are enjoined to contribute to the maintenance and sustenance of the community both as a normative and structural mode that an individual identifies with, I am not convinced that friends of communitarianism are entirely always frank in their analysis of how communities are constituted. Communities come about as a result of deliberate conjectures by people who are situated in a particular way. I intentionally identify communities to be a result of deliberate conjectures since I believe that human activity that results in the constitution of structures that we call communities is not only deliberately fashioned by individual agency but is also ultimately reliant on basic assumptions that people make about themselves and their world. If we combine these two facts then what we have is that the community is a result of some contingencies that combine in particular ways to give rise to the ethic and reality of communitarianism. However, this outcome should not lead to the assumption that the community is an enduring reality that all individuals will consistently seek to identify with. On the contrary, what the reality I have just described suggests is that the idea of community is one that is continually open to the shaping power of contingencies of human agency and their interpretation of the world. As a result of that agency, in the interpretation of the world, individuals come to fashion their reality in ways that we may think of as communitarian in the fundamental kind of way that communitarians have tended to. But if we take the route that I suggest here, we will see that there is nothing so fundamental about the idea of community or its founding principles. There is nothing fundamental about any sense of the community; it is all accidental and whatever people construct is in relation and in response to their specific interpretation of their surroundings. When people claim to have a sense of a collective "we," that claim directly proceeds from their interpretation of their surroundings and how they see reality.

It follows that there is no basis for thinking of an African reality as something that is strictly grounded in Nkrumah and Senghor's views on what the African personality is. Such a personality is representative only of a particular moment of the entire history of African people. A single moment of history, no matter how highly we think of it, is but only a single moment. Nkrumah and Senghor's African personality is not an eternal reality of the African person and her view of life. Neither does it follow that there is an ethic of a "we" that is fundamentally founded on some collectivist outlook on the essence of life. Such a view is consistent with a particularized moment of a people's existence.

Any political outlook that seeks to prioritize the notion of a community as a collective of individuals who are something more than an aggregate could be correct only for a specific epoch. Metz's argument above, for example, which is representative of standard communitarian frameworks, erroneously insists on the timelessness of the particular interpretation of community that he gives. But factors and structures that shape ordinary and everyday life in Africa are recognizably different from the structures and forces that were behind the ethos as so described by Metz.

The Africa of today is recognizably different from traditional African societies in that both the pressure to modernize and for individuals to lead more or less atomistic lives have become a real feature of the African setting. Added to this are the realities of Africa's political failures that have come in the form of military dictatorships, one-man rule, the failure to democratize, unbridled misrule, and fearless kleptocracies. These realities have effectively contributed to the creation of sociopolitical structures that are highly predatory and dangerous. These political structures treat ordinary citizens like prey as they render ordinary citizens' lives unsustainable.

THE MARGINALIZED AFRICAN

While cursory commentary into the events around xenophobia has tended to lament the lack of *ubuntu*[16] on the part of perpetrators, and the commentators have taken opportunity to reemphasize the need for the revitalization or return to the ethic and politics of *ubuntu*,[17] such commentary has crucially ignored an important aspect. While it is commonly known and accepted that incidents of xenophobia tend to occur in areas that are seriously underprivileged both materially and intellectually, little has ever been said about how those conditions are a factor that contributes to a dehumanized view of life. When people live on the margins of the society's prosperity and progress, when they are effectively left out of all processes and structures that affirm their dignity and humanity, it might just be unrealistic to expect that they will behave in ways that affirm others' dignity and humanity, so I argue.

With the communitarian ethic, which includes *ubuntu*, the understanding is that the individual contributes to the common good. In that common good s/he is recognized as someone who has a standing and capability to contribute meaningfully to the common good that s/he shares with fellow human beings. If s/he is going to claim any benefit or right from that common good, it is because s/he recognizes her/his own input as something that matters. The community, in turn, by giving to the individual equally recognizes her input as worthy of a return of favor. As a consequence, there exists mutual recognition between the individual and the community. However, this situation only obtains where individuals are not marginalized by the same community. For mutual recognition to be there, the individual must have a clear and distinct sense of membership in the community and her standing must be approximately the same as that of any other individual in the community.

In situations where the individual exists at the margins of the community or where the community renders the individual's contribution meaningless, in a world or situation where the individual does not understand her/himself to be any meaningful part of the happenings in community, s/he cannot exhibit ethos that are consistent with the community's mores. If communitarianism is built on the understanding that the individual has a role to play in the community and that role contributes to her/his identity as well as to the construction of some notion of shared good, if s/he is deprived of the opportunity to play that meaningful role, then s/he has been deprived of all his/her identity and all the resources that make him/her a member of the community. As a marginalized individual s/he will play by the rules of his/her marginalization, and sometimes her/his actions are a protest to the norms of community that s/he is not allowed to be effectively a member of and an equal participant in.

Thus the very basis of the communitarian ethos, the community, has either been so radically transformed or has been severely compromised such that it can no longer be a necessary and sufficient condition for the realization of communitarianism. The particular breaking point in this analysis is the inability of the community to treat all members of the community in a fair and justifiable manner. Communities in Africa today can hardly justify their influence and contribution on individual behavior. This is particularly so in the case where individuals have been cast aside by the forces present in communities or by structures of inequality that now constitute the reality of the African community.

Present-day South Africa is one of the most unequal societies in the world. The difference that exists between those who have it and those who have nothing is as vast as any difference can be. Immigrants who have become part of these disenfranchised, dehumanized, and marginalized human settlements in South Africa are victims of the very same processes and systems of marginalization in their own countries of birth. When they move to South Africa with the hope of finding opportunities, they are naturally and automatically cast with their fellow Africans in marginalization and disenfranchisement. In that uncomfortable coexistence, the brute reality and final outcome of marginalization comes to the fore in the form of dehumanizing behavior toward the perceived other. But what effectively is at play is the reality of what it means and what it is for some members of the human community to exist at the fringes of that very human community. When people are stripped of all dignity and hope, when they feel that they are no longer a part of the greater community but are now a subset of that greater community, they will develop alternative interpretations of life.

Effectively, what has disappeared are the so-called ties that bind Africans together toward a search for the common good that is shared by all members of the community. What has replaced those ties is the brute competition for resources and modes of surviving which make the notion of unity and solidarity a mirage. In the midst of the competition for resources, which is scantily acknowledged by the cabinet's statement, the same sort of inhumanity that characterizes such competition in mainstream society is expressed as hostility against the foreigner in less sophisticated communities. While such an analysis can be restricted to the reality of South Africa as a country, the same problem presents itself in different ways in other countries. What we now have are governments that have failed at their work of creating the economic and political infrastructure that can guarantee the basic conditions under which ordinary people can lead their lives with dignity and the assurance that they are full members of communities that matter.

Since conditions of full membership to the community cannot be guaranteed for everyone, there is no sense in which we could talk of the communitarian ethos as equally applicable to all humans who now happen to share the same geographical space. The continued acts and structures of dehumanization that are widespread across the continent, and the deliberate marginalization of people that comes with it, effectively clamp any notion of unity between people and any notion of shared characteristics that are to be found, naturally, among the people of this continent.

CONCLUSION

The prognosis is grim. If the dehumanization of ordinary people continues to be authored at various levels of their existence by structures that marginalize them and reduce their existence to an inhuman station, we will increasingly witness outbreaks of behavior that is hardly recognizable. While politicians and academics may bemoan the death of a communitarian ethos, the people bemoan the death of decency, service provision, being cared for, and being made to be an effective member of one's larger community. As long as those who have the power and ability to reduce levels of poverty and desperation on the continent are unable to do so, the very poor, disenfranchised, marginalized, and ostracized will have an unusual interpretation of life that will never be African or human. It will be an interpretation of life as informed by extreme poverty. Solidarity and unity do not flow naturally from Africans, rather they are established by the sorts of institutions that are created to cater for everyday and very basic needs of securing a dignified human existence for all Africans. Once those basic needs are not taken care of in a way that suggests the humanness of those who exist within particular societies, the competition for the little available resources will become ever more brutal and unforgiving.

NOTES

1. By black or African, I refer to the dominant racial group on the continent or the indigenous racial group on the African continent.

2. Aimé Césaire, *A Return to My Native Land* (Harmondsworth, UK: Penguin Books, 1969).

3. Kwame Nkrumah, *Consciencism: Philosophy and Ideology for Decolonisation and Development with Particular Reference to the African Revolution* (London: Heinemann, 1964).

4. Léopold Sédar Senghor, *On African Socialism* (London: Paul Mall Press, 1964).

5. Ifeanyi Menkiti, "Person and Community in African Traditional Thought," in *African Philosophy: An Introduction*, ed. Richard A. Wright (Lanham, MD: University Press of America, 2009), 171–81; Kwame Gyekye, *Tradition and Modernity: Philosophical Reflections on the African Experience* (New York: Oxford University Press, 1997), 3; Bénézet Bujo, *The Ethical Dimension of Community: The African Model and the Dialogue between North and South* (Nairobi: Paulines Publications Africa, 1998).

6. Kwasi Wiredu, "Democracy and Consensus in African Traditional Politics: A Plea for a Non-party Polity," in *Postcolonial African Philosophy: A Critical Reader*, ed. Emmanuel Chukwudi Eze (Oxford: Blackwell, 1997), 303–12; Mogobe B. Ramose, *African Philosophy through Ubuntu* (Harare: Mond Books, 2002).

7. Thaddeus Metz, "Just the Beginning for Ubuntu: Reply to Matolino and Kwindingwi," *South African Journal of Philosophy* 33/1 (2014): 65–72.

8. Wiredu, "Democracy and Consensus."

9. J. O. Famakinwa, "The Moderate Communitarian Individual and Primacy of Duties," *Theoria* 76/2 (2010): 152–66; Nkiruka Ahiazu, "On the Normative Aspects of Globalisation," <http://www.ojs.mona.uwi.educ/idex.php/cjp/article/viewfiel/284/184/> [Accessed: February 2, 2011].

10. I will use Thaddeus Metz as an example of the sort of solidarity that I am opposed to.

11. Thaddeus Metz, "An Ubuntu-based Evaluation of the South African State's Response to Marikana: Where's the Reconciliation?" *Politikon* 44/2 (2017): 287–303.

12. Andrew Okem, Lucky Asuelime, and Raquel Adekoye, "Re-visiting Xenophobia in South Africa and Its Impact on Africa's Integration," *Africa Insight* 45/2 (2015): 75–85.

13. I use xenophobia and Afrophobia interchangeably, since the former in South Africa is expressed specifically as the latter.

14. Paulin Mbecke, "Anti-Afrophobia Policy Shortfall and Dilemma in the New Partnership for Africa's Development and South Africa," *TD: Journal for Transdisciplinary Research in Southern Africa* 11/4 (2015): 71–82.

15. South African Cabinet Statement, <http://www.dfa.gov.za/docs/2015/cabinet0415.htm/> [Accessed: June 1, 2016].

16. As an ethic of caring for the other.

17. This idea of the ethic of care precludes bringing harm to the other.

FOUR

Race, Place, and Indian Identities in Contemporary South Africa

Goolam Vahed and Ashwin Desai

INTRODUCTION

Narendra Modi visited South Africa in July 2016 as part of a four-nation tour of Africa that included Tanzania, Mozambique, and Kenya. In advance of Modi's proposed two-day visit on July 8-9, a "South Africa Welcomes Modi Committee" was formed. It was chaired by businessman Raman Dhawan, with Mukesh Patel from the Swaminarayan Hindi Mission as vice chairperson. The committee described itself as: "A volunteer-based organisation promoting SA-India relations for communities, by communities. It pays tribute to the deep ties between India and SA, highlighting the formidable contribution made by members of the Indian diaspora in all walks of life in the continent of Africa."[1]

While former Indian prime minister Inder Kumar Gujral, former presidents Abdul Kamal and Pratibha Patel and president of the Indian National Congress, Sonia Gandhi, had visited South Africa in the post-Apartheid period, Dhawan stated that never before had an Indian head of state "addressed a public gathering of this magnitude on South African soil."[2] Modi's visit would bring together one of India's oldest diasporas and the broader South African community. This bond, Dhawan said, spanned five generations and it was appropriate that the meeting was taking place in South Africa where Mohandas K. Gandhi and former South African president Nelson Mandela had given birth to new ideals of freedom and democracy.[3]

During his South African visit, Modi held meetings with President Jacob Zuma and leading political figures, and visited Johannesburg, Pietermaritzburg, and Durban. The latter is home to the largest concentration of Indians outside of India. A reception at the Durban City Hall hosted by the city's mayor was attended by Zulu King Goodwill Zwelithini, Kwa-Zulu-Natal premier Willies Mchunu, and other local dignitaries, with entertainment by local dance troupes. Modi's visit included a train trip in Pietermaritzburg to mark Gandhi's famous 1893 journey that ended with him being thrown off a train for refusing to move out of a coach reserved for whites. Local Pietermaritzburg resident Prabhanu Das was thrilled by the experience. He said that he had waited nearly four hours for Modi's visit. "In India, I never got a chance to meet him. Today, I got within touching distance."[4]

The high point of the visit was what the welcoming committee described as a "grand welcoming event," a public reception at the Ticketpro Dome in Johannesburg. A portal launched for the public to register for the event resulted in ten thousand people signing up within a short time. According to Dhawan, the cultural program aimed to "reflect a fusion of colour and rhythm that weaves the rich tapestry of Africa and India into a new harmony for both continents, [creating] a rich cultural experience that is unique and unmatched in the world."[5] Jayasperi Moopen, a South African Indian choreographer who coordinated the entertainment for the cultural evening, said that South Africa and India were:

> Intertwined through a sense of cultural kinship and affinity and of course our shared history. This shared history and heritage has created unique dance forms in the 156-year history of Indian South Africans, where classical movements of Bharatanatyam and Kathak have fused with the traditional rhythms of African dance, bringing together synergies of these rich heritages.[6]

At the Ticketpro event, Modi wore a "Madiba" shirt to identify with former South African president and anti-Apartheid icon, Nelson Mandela. This prompted some ironic, even hilarious, comments from readers of the *Indian Express* in India following an article on Modi's Johannesburg speech in the July 10, 2016, edition:

- Satwinder Singh—ironically the shirt was probably made in India using child labour
- Subbu—Shame on you Feku. Don't behave like a clown
- Land Eng—Mera naam joker—Mera naam feku, mera Kaam daku[7]
- Chandramukhee—This shirt is associated with Nelson Mandela, and our Prime Minister reminds us of him, let us respect Narendra Modiji for his great respect for that leader.
- RAVI L—Fekus past is criminal no wonder his old age activities are signs of Alzheimer's disease
- Parth Garg—Remember Subra Swamy's comment on BJP ministers visiting foreign countries look like "waiters." He will now change it to "drummers."

- bitterhoney—Every year, July 10th will be celebrated all over the world as Joker Day

Notwithstanding such reactions, Modi's aim, of course, was to identify with Africa sartorially. However, the event was overwhelmingly "Indian" and Modi himself stated, "Today, after what I am witnessing here, people in India must be thinking that maybe the event is taking place in India." He hailed the Indian diaspora in South Africa as "proud sons and daughters of Indian heritage" who had sacrificed their lives in the anti-Apartheid struggle:

> We may live on distant shores; in different time zones; and on different hemispheres; Our ancestors may have been separated in history; Our nationalities may be different; and Our support may be for different cricket teams. But, our common cultural, religious and spiritual heritage ensured that we remain close and connected. Both, in our hearts and our minds. . . . Your ancestors were one of the first to leave the shores of India. Their sacrifice, their determination to preserve their cultural roots, and will to succeed against all odds not only shaped the generations of South African Indians. It also impacted, influenced and guided the mind-set of Indian diaspora the world over. In many ways, what Indian diaspora stands for all over the world today is because of what your forefathers were able to achieve despite all adversity. . . . You are the proud sons and daughters of the Indian heritage. You are the hardworking and loyal citizens of South Africa. You are also a part of the flourishing global Indian family. . . . You are a window to India's heritage, to our ethos and to our values. And, you form an important life line for our ties with this land. In conclusion, let me say that your achievements, your contributions and your success make us all proud. It has been a privilege for me to connect with you.[8]

Mukesh Patel was buoyed that there was no resistance to the visit; "only enthusiasm and encouragement from every walk of life. . . . [The] coming together of the Indian diaspora as well as South Africans sees an unprecedented enthusiasm for a new vision of unity and friendship."[9] As we illustrate, this is not a reflection of relations on the ground as social relations between Indian and African South Africans are tense, while Modi's visit brought to the surface Hindu/Muslims divisions.

Modi's visit was marked by symbolism, with the figure of Gandhi looming large. The Indian leader described his visit as a "pilgrimage." "I am getting the opportunity to visit three places that are significant to Indian history and Mahatma Gandhi's life. This is the place where the seed was laid for Mohandas to start the journey of the Mahatma." Modi also visited the Phoenix Settlement that Gandhi established in 1904 and Constitution Hill in Johannesburg. He said in his Johannesburg speech, "It was here that Mahatma Gandhi conceptualised his politics. This is the birthplace of *Satyagraha*. South Africa transformed Mohandas into a Mahatma."[10]

Many Indian South Africans were upset that they failed to get a glimpse of Modi in the flesh. Dhayalan Moodley and Kamini Prakash, amongst others, called for the tour to be broadcast on television. Prakash wrote in a letter to the *Daily News*:

> The SABC (South African Broadcasting Corporation) should have live coverage of the visit. . . . I bemoan the fact that most of us will not be privileged to hear Modi speak. Whether it has been in war-torn Jaffna in Sri Lanka, Malaysia, Europe, the Middle East, the US, Canada, Australia, Mexico, or UK, Modiji has been greeted with wild adulation by members of the Indian community. As Lord Paul Swaraj said last year, Indians are "proud of Narendra Modi. He has raised the profile of India and Indians all over the world." May he succeed in his endeavours.[11]

Observers of South African Indian politics were keen to note how former anti-Apartheid activists would react to the visit. Few raised any protests against Modi, despite the fact that he was chief minister during the 2002 Gujarat massacres and was accused of complicity in them. One who did speak out was Ismail Vadi, member of the Gauteng Provincial Government and board member of the Ahmed Kathrada Foundation. Writing in his personal capacity, Vadi stated that South Africans were:

> Still haunted by the ghosts of Gujarat. The deaths, injuries, mayhem and destruction of property that followed the fateful burning on February 27, 2002 of the train in Godhra (Gujarat) will remain a bloody blot on India's history. . . . India's governing elite cannot escape moral culpability for the gross violations of human rights and acts of genocide that occurred in those horrifying three weeks.[12]

Vadi was referring to the 2002 Gujarat riots or pogrom that followed the deaths of fifty-eight Hindus when a train caught on fire on February 22, 2002. Without proof, Narendra Modi, then chief minister of Gujarat state, declared that the attack was an act of terrorism by Muslims. What followed was an attack by Hindus against Muslims on February 28, resulting in over two thousand deaths.[13] Vadi felt that Modi's brand of Hindu nationalism was at odds with the "expansionist, humanistic vision" of Jawaharlal Nehru, India's first prime minister, and that of Nelson Mandela. He was confident that South African Indians "born in our country have no aspirations to return to India. . . . We make bold to say that our destiny is inextricably linked to the majority of South Africans, and not with India."[14] Naeem Jeenah of the Africa Middle East Centre, likewise, urged South African Indian Muslims to identify wholly with South Africa and not to show affinity with any other nation. He appealed to them not to apply for Overseas Citizen of India (OCI) cards.[15]

While the historic relationship of the African National Congress (ANC) was with the Congress Party of India and not with Modi's Bharatiya Janata Party (BJP), as prime minister of the powerhouse that is present-day India, Modi had the red carpet eagerly rolled out for him. While at one level it might be easy to read the differences between the BJP as a party of the Hindu right and the ANC as a movement of all-embracing nationalism, the ANC shares some awkward similarities with the BJP. It has its own massacre to deal with: Marikana, where thirty-four miners were murdered by police in 2012 in an operation laden with political subtexts. Like India, South Africa has opened its doors to global capitalism while implementing a conservative macroeconomic program domestically which has nurtured a small number of black millionaires and billionaires, while poverty and inequality is rising, alongside corruption scandals, much like India. In words reminiscent of the BJP's Hindu nationalism, the ANC is increasingly prone to a language of racial nationalism.[16]

In any event, Vadi's was a minority voice. Ahmed Kathrada, who was sentenced to life imprisonment on Robben Island with Mandela in 1963, and his foundation met with Modi, who immediately put a photograph of himself and Kathrada on his twitter account. *Muslim Views* reporter Mahmood Sanglay wrote that Kathrada's foundation, usually "diligently responds to human rights issues." As a nongovernmental organization, "the foundation did not have to observe the protocols and formalities expected from state institutions. . . . The foundation opted to accommodate instead of speaking truth to power."[17] Following Modi's visit, the Indian government contributed R2 million to the Ahmed Kathrada Foundation. The donation was announced by Indian High Commissioner Ruchi Ghanashyam at a banquet in Johannesburg on Heritage Day, September 24, 2016.[18]

There was great interest in whether Ela Gandhi, granddaughter of the Mahatma, would be present to welcome Modi to the Phoenix Settlement. Ela Gandhi, who chairs the Gandhi Salt March Committee and the Gandhi Development Trust, and produces *Satyagraha*, a monthly newspaper, was, in her words, looking "forward to hosting the Indian leader. . . .The Indian government always supported the anti-Apartheid struggle—both the Congress Party and the BJP when they were in power."[19] Following the visit, Indian Ministry of External Affairs spokesperson Vikas Swarup tweeted: "A sapling for sarvodaya. PM @narendramodi plants a pepper and bark tree at the Phoenix Settlement. Ela Gandhi with him."[20] Shiv Visvanathan, a professor at the Jindal School of Law, wrote in response to Modi's visit to Phoenix:

> On Sunday newspapers blandly inserted a front-page picture of PM Narendra Modi enacting one of the great moments of history, the alchemical

> moment when Gandhi the young lawyer, was ejected out of the train for travelling in the first class. I looked closely at the picture. Modi sits wooden as if he is posing for a Tussauds wax portrait. No newspaper had any reaction. I guess most people saw it as normal, a PM playing tourist with history.
>
> I was appalled and agitated when I saw Ela Gandhi welcome him to Phoenix Farm. I was reminded of a comment by a historian who said, "today every party rewrites history." . . . The Right, especially the RSS, was opposed to Gandhi and had little to do with the national movement. There was an even greater irony in Modi's trip as the RSS, of which he was a *pracharak* (full-time worker), was opposed to Gandhi. I do not know what Modi thought while he sat in the wood planked train. But, I was wondering whether at that moment the RSS and its ilk thought of apologising to Gandhi and the nation for the assassination. I was for one moment expecting an apology for the 2002 riots. An apology would have made history doubly alchemic, if he had used his sense of the truth commission to offer a new sense of reconciliation in Gujarat. It would have made the train ride another turning point in history. Yet, Modi is not moved enough. . . . As he and Jacob Zuma step out one becomes worried for two legacies—the legacy of Mandela now cannibalised by Zuma and the ANC and the lessons of Gandhi which a majoritarian BJP/RSS regime has quickly sidestepped.
>
> I am afraid of the new sense of normalcy I see around me. It is as if a whitewashing of history has taken place. . . . The RSS has begun sanitising its role in history, while isolating the Congress from its great genealogies. Beyond the political economy of such acts, there is a wiser question of memory itself. Memory today seems bits and nuggets of data without context. It seems to lack the density of the value frames of the earlier era. I remember my old friend and teacher, Ramachandra Gandhi. During Emergency Indira Gandhi had gone to Rajghat to pay respects to the Mahatma. Ramu met her and quietly with folded hands asked her not to insult the memory of his grandfather. Ramu believed that for Mrs Gandhi to declare Emergency and seek solace in Gandhi was obscene. It was not a question only of insulting history, but showing a disrespect to the value frame, the everyday ethics of the Gandhi era. Watching him, no one in the crowd felt Ramu had done anything wrong. There was despite initial consternation an acceptance. Each accepted the call of their respective roles. But one senses a different travesty of history today.[21]

Support for Modi and the BJP among local Indians was evident in the way some turned any criticism of Modi into a Hindu/Muslim communal divide. Imraan Buccus wrote a mildly critical column about Modi's visit in his weekly column for a local newspaper.[22] In a letter to the editor, Keshuba Naidoo saw Buccus's intervention as a way to "promote anti-Hindu sentiment, albeit behind a veil of education. . . . Try doing this in some countries that Buccus is more familiar with and risk being beheaded."[23] Buccus is immediately identified as a Muslim and therefore anti-Hindu and by implication anti-India. There is also an assumption that as a Muslim, Buccus should be "more familiar" with presumably Muslim-ruled countries.

In responding to Jeenah's criticism of Modi, Nirode Bramdaw prefaces his article with a story from the 2003 cricket World Cup match between India and Australia, during which a group of Muslim spectators were supporting Australia. One wore a T-shirt that read, "Stop the War in Iraq." When Bramdaw questioned the men, they were not aware that Australia was the third country to send troops to Iraq, after the United States and Britain. His point was that it was hypocritical of them to support Australia. Bramdaw concludes his article by comparing Jeenah's call to the "moron wearing a 'Stop the War in Iraq' T-Shirt, waving an Australian flag." Read in this context, it appears, in Bramdaw's view, Jeenah's call was "moronic."[24]

Like Naidoo, Bramdaw is quick to draw the implication that to be critical of Modi is to be anti-Hindu and anti-India. Under Apartheid and in present-day South Africa, all four, Buccus, Naidoo, Bramdaw and Jeenah, would be defined as Indian but this clearly fractures when it comes to global politics. To balance this out it would be fair to also argue that more and more Indian Muslims, rather than identifying with India, see themselves as part of the global *ummah*.

The Modi visit brought to the fore Hindu/Muslim tensions and also the ways in which local anti-Apartheid activists chose to respond. Some, like Vadi, wanted a boycott of Modi. Others, like Ela Gandhi, embraced him and in personally receiving him at the Phoenix Settlement legitimized Modi's attempt to appropriate Gandhi. A fracturing along religious lines was exactly what academic and social commentator Brij Maharaj warned against in the lead-up to Modi's visit.[25]

A less obvious but no less crucial issue that the Modi visit brought to the fore is local Indians' relationship to the "motherland."

"MOTHERLAND": INDIA IN THE IMAGINATION

The scrapping of the Population Registration Act in 1990 ended the legal regime separating Indians from other "race" groups in South Africa. At the time, a key issue for Indians was whether they would become part of a color-blind South Africa or whether "Indianness" would be perpetuated in new ways and by new forces. One impulse was at a global level. In the period from 1927 to 1946, Indian South African affairs were mediated by an Indian agent general who evolved into a high commissioner. That special office closed when the Indian government withdrew its representative in response to racist land legislation against Indians (the "Ghetto Act" of 1946) and India took up the South African Indian question at the United Nations.[26]

During the Apartheid era, India led the international boycott of South Africa and was a close supporter of the ANC. One of the unintended consequences was that Indian South Africans became increasingly cutoff from India as the boycott restricted cultural, sporting, and religious ties between the countries. Immigration from India had, of course, ended with the Smuts-Gandhi Agreement of 1914. A negligible number of Indians traveled to South Africa during the Apartheid years but there were no direct flights to India and goods from that country were routed via a third country. The last attempt to organize a tour to India by South African Indian footballers in 1953 was scuppered when the South African government refused passports to the players. It also banned the entry of Indian wives into South Africa and forced India to shut down its high commissioner's office in 1954.[27]

The years following the end of Apartheid coincided with the rise of India as a global economic and political force. Bollywood served as the advance guard of India's global cultural reach while its cricket board has all but usurped England and Australia as the preeminent financial power in world cricket. Post-Apartheid South Africans met India at a time when the country was swamped by "a rising tide of self-congratulation."[28] How have Indian South Africans reacted to the country of their forefathers?

Many have reached out to the "motherland," with the extent of that connection dependent on individual personal circumstances. It is decidedly easier for a middle-class individual to buttress an imagined connection to the motherland through visits, trade, and satellite television than it is for a poor person.

One aspect in particular that has come to the fore, perhaps surprisingly in a post-Apartheid, globalization era, is a quest for political, cultural, and consumer identity linked to individuals' "roots." Connecting one's personal biography to ever narrower and more specific historical developments is at the heart of early twenty-first century identity politics. Among South African Indians, this has included writing autobiographies and memoirs, and tracing family histories to tiny villages in different parts of India. Most South African Indians are linked directly to India but there are also instances of people whose ancestors came to South Africa via places such as Mauritius, Trinidad, and Fiji. The demand for ancestral knowledge is such that agencies have been established to conduct investigations on behalf of individuals.[29]

Some have made the journey to India, despite in many cases being uncertain as to where their ancestors originated from. Many searches have been unproductive. School principal Jay Naidoo, for example, related how he traced his roots back to the village of his great-grandfather, who arrived in Natal as an indentured worker. When Naidoo eventually reached the village of Godyattam in Tamil Naidu in 2007 and asked for the "Chetty family," he learnt that all five hundred families in the village had the name Chetty, which was a caste designation.[30] For many others, the search and visit end on a happier note and they find the experience satisfying and gratifying.

A more successful search was that by the family of M. L. Sultan, who arrived as an indentured worker in 1890, took up farming after completing his indenture, and at the time of his death in the 1950s left a substantial portion of his estate to education. The M. L. Sultan Technikon was built with this money and now forms part of the Durban University of Technology. A search over several decades eventually bore fruit when the Sultan family located their relatives in Collam, a small village in Kerala, South India. They made contact with a relative, Mohammed Ajum Shamshudeen, and found a series of letters that were exchanged between Shamshuden and Sultan. A family reunion of 250 members of the Sultan family was held in Durban in November 2015 and at the end of March 2016, six members of the Sultan family, who are now based in different parts of the world, visited the ancestral village for a face-to-face meeting with relatives after a break of 125 years.[31]

Many Indians are searching for their roots as "security" against feelings of anxiety produced at the current conjuncture by factors such as South Africa's affirmative-action policies and increasing anti-Indian sentiments vocalized locally; the national tertiary sector boycotts by students, which are creating a feeling amongst many that the country is on the verge of imploding; and threats by credit rating agency Standard & Poor's that South Africa sovereign foreign currency rating faces being downgraded to junk status. Hansen has referred to this feeling amongst Indians as the "melancholia of freedom."[32]

In this context, many Indians are motivated to acquire Persons of Indian Origin (PIO) or OCI status. The Indian government inaugurated the category of nonresident Indian (NRI) for both economic and political reasons in 1973. The Hindu nationalist BJP then extended NRIs by introducing the PIO card in 1998 which made it easier to maintain relations with India and extend that affective link to a material one.[33] For the Indian government, this also held an economic benefit as it raised foreign exchange while politically being part of a wider "effort by the BJP government to create a 'global Indian family.'"[34] The target group was not the old indentured diaspora, nor was it the poorer migrants to the Gulf regions, but the affluent Hindu professional class settling in the United States and Western European countries.[35]

This broadening of who constitutes an Indian national seeks to cultivate allegiance to a form of global Indian citizenship that transcends the nation-state. This association has been formalized through the Global Organisation of People of Indian Origin (GOPIO). GOPIO's website explains its mission:

> GOPIO was founded at the First Global Convention of People of Indian Origin in New York in 1989. The initial thrust of GOPIO was fighting human rights violation of people of Indian origin. Although this has been improved in the last one decade, human rights violations continue to be a major issue for PIOs living outside India. GOPIO has now set its priorities in pooling our resources, both financial and professional, for the benefit of PIOs, the countries they come from and India.[36]

This project runs counter to what Vadi argues above about Indian loyalty to the South African nation and, within that, a subsumption under the rubric of a black identity. The Indian government's project has a race and class bias. Working-class Indian South Africans will find it difficult to travel to India or otherwise take advantage of the sense of diaspora that the Indian government is seeking to foster. The cost of searching for one's roots and the application fee is prohibitive for most Indians. South Africa continues to determine their citizenship, mobility, and labor-market opportunities. Ironically, under difficult economic conditions and with a stagnant or shrinking economy, the ideological construct of race as applied by African nationalists and the preferential treatment meted out to Africans and Coloreds legislatively confines poorer Indians to their "place" in South Africa, very much as would belonging to a caste in India.

For the more affluent in the community, bonding with the motherland includes other aspects; "spiritual" tourism to Hindu and Muslim religious shrines; medical tourism; Indian satellite television and Bollywood movies. Indian fashion is also keenly consumed by South African Indians with disposable income. South African Indian support for India's cricket team is another sign of this connectedness. When India (and Pakistan) tour South Africa, thousands of South African Indians don Indian shirts and wave Indian flags. This irks many non-Indian South Africans who see it as further evidence that Indians can never be "real" South Africans as they have one eye on the subcontinent.[37]

The close relationship between Indian capital in the form of the Gupta family and President Zuma and his family has added to negative perceptions of Indians, as it confirms the stereotype of the nefarious Indian trader using money to buy influence with the rulers of the day and to advance business interests.

We would suggest, however, that while many Indian South Africans have an emotional attachment to India, and despite current economic and political problems, the majority of Indians continue to regard South Africa as "home." The working classes are rooted here because their class position makes mobility difficult while the middle classes look to more lucrative alternatives like Dubai, Australia, and the United Kingdom. They display what Mishra describes as "imaginary homelands from the space of distance."[38]

THE FADING RAINBOW

South Africa's first nonracial election in 1994 promised a move away from the sealed boundaries of Apartheid's racial identities. Common citizenship would glue all into a South African "nation." In the words of ANC stalwart Govan Mbeki, whose son, Thabo Mbeki, would become South Africa's second president, nonracialism would allow South Africans "to forge one nation, a non-racial democracy in a unitary state."[39] Archbishop Desmond Tutu spoke of "rainbowism," in which the four "nations" in South Africa could maintain their boundaries but also come together to forge a nation.[40] And in his inaugural address in 1994, Mandela said that South Africans would work "to build the society in which all South Africans, black and white, will be able to walk tall, without any fear in their hearts, assured of their inalienable right to human dignity—a rainbow nation at peace with itself and the world."

The concept of "rainbowism" held the promise that South Africans would recreate themselves within particular racial, religious, and ethnic milieus, and come together as equals in celebration of unity through diversity in a nonracial state. The last Apartheid head of state, F. W. de Klerk, anticipated this when he stated in 1990 that in the evolving South Africa, the various "people and communities [could] remain themselves and be able to preserve the values that are precious to them—so that the Zulus, the Xhosas, the Sothos and the whites can feel secure in their distinctiveness."[41] Or as Hansen put it, "Nonracialism became an injunction to find an authentic expression within the multicultural nation: now that you are free, define yourself as you truly are, define your own culture and your own history."[42]

The danger, of course, is that in a context of competition for limited resources, racial and ethnic identities can strengthen and become valorized. Despite the struggle against a common foe, the minority white government, many Indians voted for the former white ruling party in 1994. This was especially the case for working-class Indians, who felt marginalized and feared majority rule. The (then) predominantly white

Democratic Party (DP), led by Tony Leon, played on these fears in the 1990s. Ferree's study analyses how voting patterns have been politically engineered in South Africa. With regard to Indians in the 1990s, Ferree points out that the:

> Democratic Party (DP) made particularly vigorous efforts in the Indian communities of Chatsworth and Phoenix. . . . The party emphasised that ANC affirmative action policies were adversely affecting Indians and painted itself as the most able adversary to the dominant party. . . . The DP adopted a negative slant towards the state, a pugilistic stance towards the ruling party, attempting to polarise Indian and Coloured relations with Africans.[43]

Race-based access to resources is a topic of intense discussion amongst Indians. In the initial post-Apartheid period, quotas were on the basis of "white" and "black," but the 1970s Black Consciousness designation of black as including Africans, Indians, and Coloreds is unraveling into its component parts: African, Colored, and Indian. The concerns of Indians are dependent on class. While middle-class Indians may be concerned with obtaining places at tertiary institutions or promotion at work, for many working-class Indians the struggle is about bare survival. Political scientist Sanusha Naidu stated in an unpublished report to the ANC in 1999 that working-class Indians were reluctant to support the ANC because they felt that the party was "preserving the interests and needs of the African people vis-à-vis the Indian worker."[44]

Education has historically been key to the upward mobility of Indian South Africans. The current situation provides little optimism. The children of affluent parents are sent to private schools where the annual fee per child is often more than most working-class families can expect to earn per annum, and this is supplemented with tuition at prohibitive costs to ensure that children get the best possible academic grounding.[45] In contrast, working-class Indians attend schools in townships that are the victims of inadequate state resources.

An example from the Medical School at the University of KwaZulu-Natal (UKZN) is pertinent to the argument of knowing one's place in society and seeking creative ways to circumvent constraints. In June 2016 the weekly *Sunday Tribune* newspaper led with the following banner headline: FOR SALE; A place in med school; UKZN probes syndicate enrolling Indian students as Coloured. The report stated:

> In 2015 and 2016 Indian South Africans needed to score a minimum of 90.83 percent overall in matric to study medicine at UKZN. For the same period Coloured pupils needed a score of 65 percent. It is believed the syndicate allowed Indian South Africans to pass themselves off as Coloureds and gain entry to the medical school. It is further alleged that this was done for a sum

> of money. The guidelines for the selection of first year students states that the university should take 69 percent African students, 19 percent Indian, nine percent Coloured, two percent white and one percent other.[46]

In response to these allegations, UKZN spokesperson Lesiba Seshoka told the newspaper:

> This could be a flaw in the system. If the allegations are found to be true then this means that the students would have lied about their ethnicity to cheat the system. This could be a method that is being used to get into medical school. If we investigate and find out that the students are Indian South Africans and they lied, they will be removed from the university.[47]

The report mentioned that considerable amounts of money changed hands; in the region of R250,000. This episode illustrates that twenty-two years into South Africa's democracy, Apartheid race categories are alive and well and applied with the same zealousness as by the former ruling National Party, though for different reasons. One wonders how the university would prove that a person is not Colored? What would be the litmus test? During Apartheid, "Colored" came to be defined by what you were not. According to the Population Registration Act of 1950:

> A white person is one who in appearance is, or who is generally accepted as, a white person, but does not include a person who, although in appearance is obviously a white person, is generally accepted as a Coloured person. A native is a person who is in fact or is generally accepted as a member of any aboriginal race or tribe of Africa. A Coloured person is a person who is not a white person or a native.[48]

Famously, if informally, to distinguish a Colored person from a white person during the Apartheid era, there was something called the "pencil test." If a pencil passed through one's hair without effort, one could be reclassified white. In the absence of a Racial Classification Board and with the demise of residential and school segregation, it would be interesting to see how KwaZulu-Natal would expose someone defining themselves as Colored as actually being Indian. Names would not help either. Thousands of Indian South Africans have adopted Pentecostalism and "Christian" names. Would Colored have to mean the ethnicity of a person going back a few generations? If an Indian and white couple had children, would that offspring be Colored? If so, this would make a mockery of the supposed rationale for the perpetuation of racial categorization: the attempt to mitigate privilege.

Working-class Indians would not be able to afford such creative ways of circumventing the law. They also have limited job options as the occupations that were once their preserve in KwaZulu-Natal, even low-paying ones in factories and the municipality, are perceived to be reserved for Africans. This is a function of the fact that employers must meet employment quotas that mirror South Africa's demographics where Africans constitute over 80 percent of the population. In a shrinking economy, this often means a de facto freeze on hiring Indians. The effects on township communities such as Chatsworth are devastating. As Desai and Vahed point out, "The shedding of jobs since the early 1990s has created a host of socio-economic problems with women often bearing the brunt of the burden."[49] There is a growing stratum of young men who are alienated and find solace in gangs and drugs which are "a temporal refuge from a bleak reality in which they feel they do not have a future."[50] While levels of unemployment are as high, or even higher, among Africans and Coloreds, Indians see their plight as related to affirmative action.

The irony of race-based affirmative action is that a poverty-stricken Indian resident of Chatsworth and an affluent one from Umhlanga are categorized under the all-inclusive label "Indian." Poor Indians compete with their advantaged counterparts for limited university places and on the job market where race quotas apply.[51] Working-class Indians laboring under the rubric of "Indian" in the new South Africa are tending to congeal under the shelter of Indianness. This is a well-known sociological phenomenon, a form of defensive communitarianism. Some cross-race neighborliness is developing in working-class areas like Chatsworth, where Africans have moved in, but these instances are limited.[52]

Recent developments at the national broadcaster, the South African Broadcasting Corporation (SABC) confirmed for many Indians that they were being marginalized. Under then CEO, Hlaudi Motsoeneng, the SABC imposed a 90 percent local content quota on all its radio stations. This posed a problem for Lotus FM, which caters specifically for Indians. The South African Hindu Maha Sabha (SAHMS) wrote to the SABC that this requirement would have serious repercussions for Lotus FM in procuring content and would threaten the station's viability. Motsoeneng responded on a news channel that "in India they don't play South African music." He found it "shocking that people who stay in SA, we regard them as Indian, SA Indian. They don't want diversity music. We are not going to allow that. We are not a banana republic here."[53] Jazz musician Don Laka, an associate of Motsoeneng and described as being influential in the decision, wrote on his Facebook page that Lotus FM cannot expect to be "excluded [from the requirement] by wanting to play Bollywood. We stopped the outflow of monies to the US and UK and now you think that should go to India? We say NOOOOOOOOOO! You need to play SA music, integrate with other cultures of SA, as his [Hlaudi's] fight was not about bringing about through the back door, but to kill anything related." In response to threats from listeners that they would boycott the station,

Laka said, "Please toe the line and stop with your threats or we will campaign for a total shutdown."[54]

Indian fears were reflected in support for minority parties, particularly for Amichand Rajbansi, whose electoral appeal was based on highlighting concerns such as housing, jobs, and affirmative action.[55] Scorned by those who supported the anti-Apartheid struggle and who were against ethnic organizations, Rajbansi skillfully entered into an alliance with the ANC after 1994. The ANC initially needed him to secure a majority in the KwaZulu-Natal provincial legislature and later saw him as someone who could contest the Democratic Alliance's monopoly of Indian voters in a context where Indians were reluctant to vote for the ANC. In an environment where whites held economic power and Africans political power, Rajbansi was seen by many Indians as willing to stand up for their rights. As he told reporters at the 150-year commemoration of Indians in South Africa in 2010, Indians were "still being side-lined and marginalised by the ANC government. We are treated as second class citizens. People are opening their eyes to the inequality Indians face in this country."[56] Many Indians concurred and it is not surprising that some have a nostalgic yearning for the Apartheid past.

Tensions between Indians and Africans have been a persistent feature of the South African political landscape. A central reason for this was the way they were positioned in competition with each other in the colonial economy. Despite the ANC embracing the figure of Mohandas K. Gandhi as an icon of the liberation struggle, the historical record shows that Gandhi kept his social and political distance from Africans.[57] Haunting Indian memory, if not already folklore, are the explosive three-day racial riots in 1949, where pogroms against Indians were carried out by Africans in Durban,[58] with the connivance, many believe, of the white burgesses, and a further outbreak of racial riots in Inanda in 1985.[59] These incidents constituted the Indian as a scapegoat par excellence, upon whom economic and social stresses may be taken out.

The stereotype of Indian South Africans as exploitative traders remains strong. When Indians commemorated 150 years in South Africa in 2010, influential media columnist Fred Khumalo used his *Sunday Times* column to portray Indians as exerting undue influence on politicians, including Nelson Mandela. If "such a powerful, reputable darkie-with-political-power could have his Indians," could not others do likewise, he asked?[60] Relations between Indians and Africans remain delicately balanced. At the launch of the ANC's local government manifesto in June 2016, a Hindu leader, Advocate Ranjiv Nirgun of the Hindu Maha Sabha religious group, was asked to lead prayers for the event. Local media reported that while praying, "ANC supporters mocked . . . laughed and made disparaging comments."[61] This is not the first reported instance where religious leaders have been jeered. At an anti-xenophobia rally organized by King Zwelithini in 2016, "a Muslim priest who spoke in Zulu, was also booed."[62]

Recent protests against Indians as a race group have taken a more concrete form with the formation of the Mazibuye African Forum. Key members are Phumlani Mfeka and his cousin Zweli Sangweni, who told the *City Press* newspaper that they were members of the ANC's Ward 41 Branch, which covered areas north of Durban, such as Newlands East, Siyanda, and KwaMashu D Section. They denied being anti-Indian or that their agenda was racist, stating that they were merely addressing the "economic marginalisation of Africans."[63]According to Sangweni, Indians "benefited through colonialism and Apartheid. . . . We do not regard them as Africans but . . . [as] Indians in the diaspora."[64]

Two decades into post-Apartheid South Africa, tensions persist around the need for social cohesion and social and economic redress. The failure of the ANC government to achieve this balance has allowed a new political party, the Economic Freedom Fighters under the leadership of former ANC Youth League leader Julius Malema, to gain substantial support in a short space of time. It is proving difficult to forge a common South African citizenship and the social fabric is decidedly fraying around race. These tensions can also be profitably exploited to gain electoral support. In its worst form, periodic xenophobic pogroms have exploded, mainly directed against migrants from Africa and the Asian subcontinent.[65]

LAAGERS WITHIN *LAAGERS*

While we live in an era of the greatest movement in human history, with millions of people on the move, we also have people withdrawing into various *laagers* of identity. At the time of writing (October 2016), the UK had voted to withdraw from the European Union, widely seen as a rejection of transnational identities in favor of British sovereignty. In post-Apartheid South Africa, too, various racial, ethnic, class, regional, religious, and other identities are being asserted. This is often shorn up by the legal distinctions discussed above where South African citizens remain divided into racial categories, viz., black African, white, Colored, and Indian/Asian.

Since their arrival in South Africa, Indians have undergone significant social, cultural, religious, and political transformation. The 2011 census reflected that over 95 percent of South African Indians regard English as their first language. The census also showed that a quarter of South Africa's Indians have converted, mainly from Hinduism to Pentecostal Christianity. This percentage is likely considerably higher now but the last census, in 2011, did not count for religion. Despite these changes, South African Indians remain legally defined as Indian in various pieces of legislation and also remain so in the eyes of fellow South Africans. Their status and life opportunities are influenced by their class position as well as their language, education levels, and religion.

Distinctive religious and cultural identities are embraced at the same time that identification with a global diaspora or, in the case of Muslims, global *ummah*, is strengthened. Tensions exist between belonging to South Africa, belonging to the rainbow nation, belonging to one's race group, or belonging more narrowly to a religious, ethnic, or language group. While being "Indian" matters in relations with others (whites, African, Coloreds), it does not constitute a homogenous bloc and is being disaggregated on a multitude of levels, such as language, regional origins, ethnicity, education, and class. Due to constraints of space, we focus on religion here.

There is increasing conversion of mainly South Indian Hindus to Pentecostal Christianity. Whereas traditional churches, despite providing schools, hospitals, and other material benefits, have failed historically to make significant inroads among Hindus, Pentecostal Christianity, mainly as result of the work of Pastor J. F. Rowlands who adapted Christianity to the specific needs of the Indian community, has made huge inroads. From the 1930s onwards, Rowlands established a solid foundation, making significant inroads among Indians, the rate of conversion probably being even higher in the past three decades.[66]

Conversion is impacting on social identity. In the formative period, many Hindu converts to Christianity were descendants of Indian municipal workers who were mainly working class. Kumar argues that one consequence is the sense among Hindus that those who converted were socially inferior. This has to do with remnants of "caste consciousness that prevails even after its formal demise as a social unit."[67] More recently, however, many converts are upwardly mobile, and church membership may include worshippers from other race groups, thus widening identity in a way that remaining Hindu could not, since membership remains predominantly Indian. It helps that there is an ideology that permeates some churches that to be affluent is to be closer to God, with many pastors leading by example.

The rapid strides that Pentecostals made amongst Hindus yielded a response. During the 1970s and 1980s newspapers were filled with letters criticizing evangelical activities, pointing to the contradiction of Indians embracing a religion that formed the basis of the Apartheid regime, and even accusing converts of cultural betrayal.[68] But Hindus have also responded by examining their own faith. The past few decades have seen neo-Hindu reformist movements such as the Arya Samaj, the Ramakrishna

Centre, and the Divine Life Society, which moved from ritual Hinduism to a more philosophical and enlightened understanding, make their mark. Neoconservative movements reject such practices as the worship of multiple gods in temples.[69]

Linguistic-based organizations continue to see themselves as synonymous with Hinduism. Telegu speakers are represented by the Andra Maha Sabha (AMS), whose website states that the organization was formed "to cater for all the Social, Cultural, Spiritual and Educational needs of the Telugu-speaking peoples of South Africa. It is the only National body representing the Andhra people." Yet the website also states that the aim of the organization is "to encourage the study of Hinduism and the philosophy of our religion."[70]

The South African Tamil Federation (SATF), formed in 1967, has as its aim "to improve the quality of life, to inculcate strong leadership and to secure the empowerment of the Tamil community of South Africa." While specifically Tamil in orientation, the sun on the emblem "symbolises Lord Nadaraja [The Lord of Dance] in his pulsating cosmic dance. If Lord Nadaraja stops dancing everything will cease to exist."[71]

While both the AMS and SATF are linguistically based, they are inherently Hindu in orientation. "The result," Kumar writes, "is that they keep Christians of the same linguistic background on the periphery." Tamils and Telegus consequently suffer cultural alienation and "find social identity elsewhere, which is to affirm a Christian identity."[72] This is likely the case in most cultures of the world. The point is that a change in religious allegiance changes group dynamics. Those who convert forge a new identity outside of the primary group because religion is such a powerful force in their lives and the marker of difference between them and others. Conversion is thus impacting on the identity of being Indian.

Among Indian Muslims, too, one discerns a tendency to shed the so-called Indian aspects of their Islam. Muslims have lived mostly as "Indians" since their arrival in South Africa. The past two decades have been witness to Muslim males embracing the beard, women wearing the veil, men and women wearing "Islamic" dress, Muslims shunning television, going on regular pilgrimage, attending Islamic schools, and so on. Through such behavior, boundaries are being constructed between Muslims and non-Muslims within the supposed Indian community. This is not to suggest that Muslims constitute a homogenous group but that they are reinforcing religio-cultural identity as part of a broader process of religious revival that has clearly marked them off from other Indians.[73] Indeed differences among Muslims run the gamut from how to pray to when to observe Eid to what food is permissible, and these are often played out in the public and are vitriolic.

It is worth pausing to consider the disaggregation of the category "Indian" as it manifested around the visit of Indian Prime Minister Modi. Although by no means exclusively so, it is notable that the, albeit limited, opposition to the Indian government's attempt to convene a diaspora came mainly from Indian Muslims in South Africa. More crucially, when these voices of protest were raised, the response was that they were anti-Hindu. As for the Muslim critique, the question arises whether this represents a rejection in being interpellated or positioned as Indians per se, or whether it is in fact the assertion of an identity that is peculiarly Muslim. While sub-continental politics have rarely manifested within the Indian community in South Africa, it is safe to say that any survey asking for the informed opinions of Hindu and Christian Indians on the one hand, and Muslim Indians on the other, would register marked differences on issues such as Gujarat 2002, Kashmir, and Palestine, to mention but a few.

SOME CONCLUDING REMARKS

Through the long twentieth century, Indians refused to know their place. Many strained against racial boundaries (finding innovative ways to circumvent the Group Areas Act that are now part of urban legend), joined in the Congress Alliance of the 1950s, or redefined themselves as black in the 1970s. Indeed, excluded from the Orange Free State under Apartheid, some Indians sought to reclassify themselves as Colored; Singh, for example, became Sing. Echoes of this can be found in the example of medical students seeking entry at the University of KwaZulu-Natal as Colored.

As much as Indians have hung on to an identity, they have also "played" with identity under conditions that sought to imprison them in it. It would be shortsighted intellectually to simply respond to those Indians who think of themselves as part of a bigger diaspora or those Indian Muslims who favor being part of a global *umma* as backward looking. In both cases they are stretching identity over and across national boundaries. In this context, the phrase "knowing one's place" follows John Western's usage which beckons possibility. As he puts it, knowing one's place, by: "Its witting ambiguity also implies that there is some pregnant meshing of the two meanings, and that from this meaning can arise a third meaning: to 'know one's place' can imply an appreciation of its possibilities, to know its potential creativity for social action."[74] If the medical school vignette exposes the way in which many Indian South Africans are struggling against a new form of racialization in South Africa, however valid the policy may be, the visit of Indian Prime Minister Narendra Modi to South Africa during July 2016 illustrates the way in which the demise of Apartheid has liberated an idea of "Indianness" that transcends national boundaries, and in its own way, shores it up. The rise of India as a global power and offers of limited citizenship by the Indian state have initiated a certain pride in the notion of India as the ancestral home, all the more attractive given the way in which life opportunities are laid out in South Africa.

This has a historical lineage. In the early 1900s, some Indians sought to use the term "British born" to claim their rights under Empire in a country bent on seeing them as temporary sojourners. In the 1930s there was an attempt on the part of the South African government to repatriate them to places like Borneo and British Guiana. And when the National Party election platform of 1948 promised repatriation and refused them citizenship, they made common cause with the movements for African majority rule and claimed their rights as South Africans, a right that the National Party government finally conceded in 1961.

The current conjuncture, despite its promise of nonracialism, imposes racial boundedness in ways reminiscent of Apartheid.[75]

While there are those who simply accept this imposed identity, there are others who are straining, mocking, juggling with identity. Race remains, but as this essay has sought to show, there are those who are stretching it at the edges, giving one a sense of a cricket pitch that hardens and crumbles at the same time. Some Indians choose to bat with caution, padding up behind ethnic *laagers*, while others appear as pinch hitters, smashing boundaries.

NOTES

1. Fareed-ud-deen Chaitoo, "Launch of the SAwelcomesModi Organizing Committee at the SWAD Restaurant at the Killarney," LENZINFO, June 17, 2016, <http://www.lenzinfo.co.za/?p=18542/> [Accessed: June 17, 2017].
2. *The Indian Express*, June 30, 2016.
3. Faizel Patel, "Indian Prime Minister Narendra Modi to Visit South Africa, June 17, 2016, <http://www.radioislam.org.za/a/index.php/latest-news/18705-indian-prime-minister-narenda-modi-to-visit -south-africa.html/> [Accessed: July 6, 2016].
4. Mervyn Naidoo, "Modi visits KZN," July 10, 2016, <http://www.iol.co.za/news/politics/modi-visits-kzn-2043665/> [Accessed: August 10, 201].
5. *The Indian Express*, June 30, 2016.
6. *The Indian Express*, June 30, 2016.
7. "My name is Joker, my name is Feku, my work is banditry."
8. *The Hindu*, July 9, 2016.
9. Patel, "Indian Prime Minister Narendra Modi."
10. *The Hindu*, July 9, 2016.
11. *Daily News*, July 7, 2016.

12. Ismail Vadi, "Ghosts May Haunt Modi's Visit to SA," *City Press*, July 5, 2016, <http: / / city-press.news24.com / News / ghosts-may-haunt-modis-visit-to -sa-20160702 / > [Accessed: August 1, 2016].

13. See Christoph Jaffrelot, "Communal Riots in Gujarat: The State at Risk?" *Heidelberg Papers in South Asian & Comparative Politics* no. 17 (South Asia Institute, University of Heidelberg, 2003). DOI: 10.11588 / heidok.00004127.

14. Vadi, "Ghosts May Haunt."

15. Cited in Nirode Bramdaw, "Modi Is the Most Voted for Leader in the World," *Sunday Tribune*, July 17, 2016, 20.

16. See John S. Saul and Patrick Bond, *The Present as History: From Mrs Ples to Mandela and Marikana* (Johannesburg: Jacana, 2014).

17. Mahmood Sanglay, "The Indian with Blood on His Hands," *Muslim Views*, July 2016, 11.

18. Fareed-ud-deen Chaitoo, "Indian Government Donates R2m to Ahmed Kathrada Foundation," LENZINFO (September 27, 2016), <http: / / www.lenzinfo .co.za / ?p=19828 / > [Accessed: October 5, 2016].

19. Shannon Ebrahim, "Much Anticipated Modi Visit Not Welcomed by All," *Independent Online*, July 7, 2016), <http: / / www.iol.co.za / news / politics / much-an ticipated-modi-visit-not-welcomed-by-all-2042669 / > [Accessed: August 12, 2016].

20. *The Indian Express*, July 9, 2016, <http: / / indianexpress.com / article / in-dia / india-news-india / pm-narendra-modi-south-africa-durban-mahatma-gandhi -phoenix-settlement-2903714 / > [Accessed: September 10, 2016].

21. Shiv Visvanathan, "How PM Modi Rewrote History by Tampering with It in Durban's Phoenix Settlement," *Mail Online India*, July 23, 2016, http: / / www.dailymail.co.uk / indiahome / indianews / article-3705080 / How-PM-Modi-rewrote-history-tampering-Durban-s-Phoenix-settlement.html / [Accessed: October 4, 2016].

22. *Mercury*, July 14, 2016.

23. *Mercury*,(July 20, 2016.

24. Cited in Bramdaw, "Modi is the Most Voted-for Leader," 20.

25. Brij Maharaj, "Modi Visit May Be Divisive," *Post*, June 22, 2016, 16.

26. Goolam Vahed, "Nehru Is 'Just Another Coolie': India and South Africa at the United Nations, 1946–1955," *Alternation*, special edition no. 15 (2015): 58.

27. Vahed, "Nehru Is 'Just Another Coolie,'" 75–78.

28. Ramachandra Guha, *India after Gandhi* (London: Pan Books, 2007), 719.

29. See Thembisa Waetjen and Goolam Vahed, "Passages of Ink: Decoding the Natal Indentured Records into the Digital Age," *Kronos* 40 / 3 (2014): 45–73.

30. *Sunday Times Extra*, November 21, 2010.

31. Farook Khan, "Finding Sultan's Family Roots in India," *Post*, February 24–28, 2016, 5.

32. Thomas Blom Hansen, *Melancholia of Freedom: Social Life in an Indian Township in South Africa* (Princeton, NJ: Princeton University Press, 2012).

33. Judith M. Brown, *Global South Asians: Introducing the Modern Diaspora* (Cambridge: Cambridge University Press, 2006), 159.

34. Thomas Blom Hansen and Finn, introduction to *Sovereign Bodies: Citizens, Migrants, and States in the Postcolonial World*, ed. Thomas Blom Hansen and Finn Stepputat (Princeton, NJ: Princeton University Press, 2005), 34.

35. Peter van der Veer, "Virtual India: Indian IT Labour and the Nation-State," in *Sovereign Bodies: Citizens, Migrants, and States in the Postcolonial World*, ed. Thomas Blom Hansen and Finn Stepputat (Princeton, NJ: Princeton University Press, 2005), 285.

36. See "Global Organisation of People of Indian Origin," http://www.gopio.net/ [Accessed: October 1, 2016).

37. Ashwin Desai and Goolam Vahed, "Identity and Belonging in Post-Apartheid South Africa: The Case of Indian South Africans," *Journal of Social Sciences*, special issue no. 11 (2010): 10.

38. Vijay Mishra, *The Literature of the Indian Diaspora: Theorising the Diasporic Imaginary* (London: Routledge, 2007), 16.

39. Govan Mbeki, *The Struggle for Liberation in South Africa: A Short History* (Cape Town: David Philip, 1992), 26.

40. J. M. Coetzee, "Retrospect: The World Cup of Rugby," *Southern African Review of Books*, July-August 1995, <http//web.archive.org/web/20001001002444/www.uniulm.de/~rturrell/anthro4html/CoetzeeJ. html/> [Accessed: September 10, 2016].

41. Alistair Sparks, *Tomorrow Is Another Country: The Inside Story of South Africa's Negotiated Settlement* (Johannesburg: Struik, 1994), 128.

42. Hansen, *Melancholia of Freedom*, 8.

43. Karen E. Ferree, *Framing the Race in South Africa: The Political Origins of Racial Census Elections* (Cambridge: Cambridge University Press, 2010), 94.

44. Ashwin Desai and Brij Maharaj, "The Making and (Re)making of Ethnic Identity: The Case of Indian South Africans," *Oriental Anthropologist* (2007): 83.

45. Goolam Vahed and Thembisa Waetjen, *Schooling Muslims in Natal: Identity, State and the Orient Islamic Educational Institute* (Pietermaritzburg, South Africa: University of KwaZulu-Natal Press, 2015), 335–40.

46. *Sunday Tribune*, June 26, 2016.

47. *Sunday Tribune*, June 26, 2016.

48. Richard T. Schaefer, *Encyclopedia of Race, Ethnicity, and Society* (London: Sage, 2008), 81.

49. Ashwin Desai and Goolam Vahed, introduction to *Chatsworth: The Making of a South African* Township, ed. Ashwin Desai and Goolam Vahed (Pietermaritzburg, South Africa: University of KwaZulu-Natal Press, 2013), 13.

50. Desai and Vahed, *Chatsworth*, 14. See also Desai and Vahed, *Chatsworth*, 234–41; 276–91; 292–304; 305–18.

51. Vahed and Waetjen, *Schooling Muslims in Natal*, 335–40.

52. Thembisa Waetjen, "*Bathola Ikhaya*: Two African Women Come to Chatsworth," in *Chatsworth: The Making of a South African Township*, ed. Ashwin Desai and Goolam Vahed, (Pietermaritzburg, South Africa: University of KwaZulu-Natal Press, 2013), 200–233.

53. Maharaj, "Modi Visit May Be Divisive," 16.

54. Kyle Zeeman, "Don Laka Hits Out at Lotus FM over 90% Boycott 'Threats,'" *Times LIVE*, May 25, 2016, <http://www.timeslive.co.za/entertainment/2016/05/25/Don-Laka-hits-out-at-Lotus-FM-over-90-boycott-threats/> [Accessed: October 25, 2016].

55. Desai and Vahed, "Identity and Belonging in Post-Apartheid South Africa," 11.

56. *Daily News*, December 6, 2010.

57. See Ashwin Desai and Goolam Vahed, *The South African Gandhi: Stretcher-Bearer of Empire* (Stanford, CA: Stanford University Press / New Delhi: Navayana, 2016).

58. Goolam Vahed, "The Making of Indianness: Indian Politics in South Africa during the 1930s and 1940s," *Journal of Natal & Zulu History* 17 (1997): 28–33.

59. Heather Hughes, "Violence in Inanda, August 1985," *Journal of Southern African Studies* 13/3 (1987): 331–54.

60. *Sunday Times*, October 24, 2010.

61. Maharaj, "Modi Visit May Be Divisive," 16.

62. Maharaj, "Modi Visit May Be Divisive," 16.

63. *City Press*, January 19, 2014.

64. *Daily News*, July 16, 2013.

65. See Ashwin Desai and Goolam Vahed, "Non-Governmental Organisations and Xenophobia in South Africa: A Case Study of the Gift of the Givers (GOTG)," *Alternation* 20/7 (2013): 24–66.

66. See Gerald Pillay, "Community Service and Conversion," in *Christianity in South Africa: A Political, Social, and Cultural History*, ed. Richard Elphick (Los Angeles, CA: University of California Press, 1997), 286–96.

67. Pratab Kumar, "Behind the God-Swapping in the South African Indian Community," pt. 2, *The Conversation*, June 27, 2016, <http://theconversation.com/behind-the-god-swapping-in-the-south-african-indian-community-part-2-61051/> [Accessed: July 9, 2016].

68. Pillay, "Community Service and Conversion," 295.

69. Pratab Kumar, "Behind the God-Swapping in the South African Indian Community," pt. 1, *The Conversation*, June 26, 2016, <http://theconversation.com/behind-the-god-swapping-in-the-south-african-indian-community-part-1-60954/> [Accessed: July 9, 2016].

70. "Andra Maha Sabha," <http://www.amssa1931.org.za/> [Accessed: July 20, 2016].

71. "South African Tamil Federation," <http://satamilfed.org.za/#about.us/> [Accessed: July 20, 2016].

72. Kumar, "Behind the God-Swapping," pt. 2.

73. See Goolam Vahed, "Indian Muslims in South Africa: Continuity, Change and Disjuncture, 1860–2000," *Alternation* 7/2 (2000): 67–98.

74. John Western, *Outcast Cape Town* (Minneapolis, MN: University of Minnesota Press, 1981), 8.

75. See Maré, *De-classified.*

FIVE

Liberating Identifications

Being Black Conscious, Being Nonracial, Being African

Nico Botha

INTRODUCTION: DIFFERENT CONSCIOUSNESS IN DISCOURSE WITH THEOLOGY

The thesis of this chapter[1] is that in a nonessentialist[2] approach to identity, the simultaneity of diverse types of consciousness is plausible. The study, however, is not aimed at advancing a theoretical argument, but rather revealing the liberating potential of these types of consciousness if they are mediated by praxis. Indeed, in a creative tension between Black Consciousness, nonracialism, and an African consciousness, deep and lasting liberation is possible. As sociohistorical constructs these three are not mutually exclusive, neither could they be neatly categorized or classified into chronological phases. As a tribute to Jakes Gerwel (January 18, 1946—November 28, 2012), a South African academic and anti-Apartheid activist, the article draws from the struggle pedigree of John James Issel (August 17, 1946—January 23, 2011) and Cecyl Esau to show the embodiment of the simultaneity of Black Consciousness, nonracialism, and an African consciousness. Rector Jakes Gerwel made the University of the Western Cape (UWC) an "intellectual home of the left," with attention to social and political issues. The university attracted increasing numbers of students from disadvantaged communities. Apart from Colored people, more and more black students enrolled. Gerwel was succeeded in 1995 by Cecil Abrahams, who was succeeded by Brian O'Connell in 2001. UWC retained the status of an autonomous university during the education restructuring of 2002.[3] A short summary of Johnny Issel's life is in order:

> During his final year at Western Cape University, Issel joined the Black Consciousness student movement, the South African Student Organisation

(SASO), and was elected its first chairperson in the Western Cape. On being denied the right to study for an honours degree and after being expelled from the university, he was appointed the first regional secretary of SASO in the Western Cape.

In 1973 Issel . . . was issued with his first five-year banning order. Two more were to follow.

From 1974 until 1986, he was imprisoned many times . . . often in solitary confinement, including Athlone, Pollsmoor, Victor Verster and Kensington. . . . After six months in Pretoria Central he was released but the torture he endured, including electric shock, scarred him emotionally for life. In 1980, he was appointed the first organiser for the broad-based community newspaper, Grassroots. Eight months after Grassroots was launched, he was banned. Issel played a leading role in the establishment of the UDF in 1983 and the subsequent formation of UDF structures within the Western Cape. After the unbanning of the African National Congress (ANC) in 1990, Issel was appointed to the interim provincial committee and became its first full-time regional organiser. He then left the Provincial Legislature and went into business and thereafter went to Europe for a few years.

On April 24, 2007, President Mbeki conferred the Companion of the Order of Luthuli in Bronze to Issel. He was a member of the uMkhonto we Sizwe Military Veterans' Association (MKMVA).

Issel passed away on January 23, 2011.[4]

The following is also a short historical statement on Cecyl Esau:

> As organiser of the United Democratic Front (UDF) in the late 1970s, he made huge contributions: Esau was member of the African National Congress (ANC) and its uMkhonto we Sizwe military wing. He worked in student politics in the University of the Western Cape.[5]

Of course, they were in the search of a nonracist, nonsexist democratic dispensation, while the emphasis might have been more on the one than on the other. For Gerwel, Issel, and Esau, issues of the Bible, faith, church, and theology were not foreign. Informed by this knowledge, an attempt was made in the study to bring the three types of consciousness of being black, being nonracial, and being African into discourse with the discipline of theology, albeit in a rather limited fashion at the closure.

THE ORGANIZATION OF THE CONTENTS

The chapter is structured and organized in the following manner: First, a few narratives and/or anecdotes pass the revue in an attempt to illustrate that, more often than not, consciousness is not a question of absorbing substantial theory, but has as its source an incident, a story, or an anecdote. Put differently, the calling into service of stories and anecdotes is aimed at showing that consciousness is most of the time mediated by praxis. This will be shown by drawing explicitly from the life narratives of Gerwel, Issel, and Esau. Second, the pertinent concept of liberating identifications has been explored. Third, the meaning of Black Consciousness has been dealt with, not so much by recycling the literature, but by briefly engaging the question: Can or should anyone still be maintaining Black Consciousness in South Africa today? As far as the literature is concerned, Biko's *I Write What I Like* is the most obvious exception. Any discussion about Black Consciousness that excludes Biko's writings would make very little sense. Fourth, the notion of nonracialism has been looked at in the light of new appearances of fragmentation and division on an ethnic, racial, or racist basis. Fifth, African consciousness has been introduced as a rather new mode of consciousness needed in South Africa. Finally, these three types of consciousness are enlightened, albeit briefly, by the Gospel of Christ and brought to their climax in this theological framework.

CONSCIOUSNESS AS NARRATIVE OR ANECDOTE

Jerry Modisane

Students at UWC, or "Bush College," as it was identified to draw attention to the fact that this was a product of Apartheid structured for those who were classified as Colored, were heavily exposed to Black Consciousness during the 1970s. Apart from adherents of Black Consciousness at UWC, high-profile speakers from the movement were lined up to address students at mass meetings. One such speaker was Jerry Modisane, who came to enlighten UWC students about the meaning of Black Consciousness, and particularly about the role of SASO. The issue, which remained quite vividly in the minds of some who were enrolled at UWC at the time, is that Modisane was detained by the Special Branch shortly after having visited UWC, just as he was about to board a train at Bellville station. For some who have had a chance to listen to Modisane and have witnessed the very gentle way in which he expressed very important issues related to the philosophical understanding of Black Consciousness and SASO as a potent vehicle in taking the movement forward, this came as a shock. The argument raised by some could be formulated approximately as follows: If someone like Modisane could be seen by the Apartheid regime as dangerous and revolutionary, then surely there must be something vital in the philosophy that he was expounding. UWC students, who were uncertain about this new political philosophy by thinking that Black Consciousness amounted to racism in reverse, changed their minds and started embracing Black Consciousness. Some elaboration about this narrative is needed, but for now, it would be safe to suggest that the turn in UWC students was informed more by praxis than a solid intellectual or theoretical position.

William "Bloke" Modisane was born on August 28, 1923. He grew up in Sophiatown, a multiracial suburb in Johannesburg. His father was murdered and sister died from malnutrition at a very young age. His mother resorted to running a shebeen to provide the family with livelihood means.

Modisane started working at Vanguard bookshop, which was owned by a former trade unionist. He later joined the Drum magazine at the time when the magazine was known for its investigative journalism that exposed the prison and farm conditions in the 1950s. He was part of a team of writers that included Henry Nxumalo, Can Themba, Es'kia Mphahlele, and Lewis Nkosi, all with high literary writing skills. He also worked as a jazz critic for the Golden City Post, the Johannesburg weekly tabloid and Drum's sister publication. It was from the Leslie Charteris thriller novels featuring the Saint that he got his nickname "Bloke." While working for Drum he used his position to advance the objectives of the nonracial Union of South Africa Artists and the Arts Federation.

His short stories, *The Dignity of Begging* and *The Respectable Pickpocket* (1954), were first published by Drum in 1951. *The Situation*, published by Black Orpheus, was about an African who was situated above his people and finds he did not fit in neatly anywhere. This formed part of the African Theatre Workshop.

In 1959, Modisane left South Africa for England. There in 1963 he published *Blame Me on History*. The book is like Themba's short story, *Requiem for Sophiatown*, a township that was destroyed in the late 1950s. It was an examination of what Apartheid did to the character and self-esteem of the educated black man. The book was banned in South Africa in 1966. In exile, he worked as a writer, actor, and broadcaster and starred in *The Blacks* at the Royal Court Theatre drama.

He died in Dortmund, West Germany, in 1986 at the age of 63. He was one of South Africa's finest writers and intellectuals. A striking book was, *Blame Me on History*, (1963).[6]

Themba Sono

Another high-profile visitor from the Black Consciousness movement to UWC in the 1970s was Themba Sono. The encounter with Sono in a mass meeting of students at UWC is remembered not so much for his ideas on Black Consciousness, but for a very interesting perspective on a portion from the Bible. In what could be seen as a contextual reading of Luke 4:18–19, with its dimensions of good news to the poor, healing, and liberation as a type of manifesto for the redemptive mission of Jesus, Sono's inference was that if Jesus were to live in Apartheid South Africa of the 1970s, he would side with the black racially oppressed and economically exploited. This was the essence of black theology that emanated from Black Consciousness. Sono's contextual hermeneutic made a lasting impression on some since this was the kind of interpretation that would not be heard in any of the South African churches at the time. Once again, as in the case of Modisane, this mediation of Scripture through praxis went much further in winning over students than grand theories and philosophies.

Themba Sono was president of SASO from 1971 until July 3, 1972, when he was expelled from the organization (see extract). He was also a cofounder of the Black People's Convention (BPC) in 1971 with the aim to encourage adult participation and promotion.[7]

> After his expulsion from SASO and completion of his degree, Sono received a scholarship to study abroad and he lived overseas in the USA for twenty years. After completing his studies, he joined the academic world and became a renowned liberal scholar.
>
> In 1998, he was appointed president of the South African Institute for Race Relations, which is a reputed liberal think tank. He served in this position until 2003. He was also president of the Free Market Foundation from 1997 to 2000. He joined the Democratic Party and became an active member. After complaining about poor race relations within the party he left it for a new party, founded by Patricia De Lille, Independent Democrats. He is now a Member of Parliament for Gauteng Legislature and National Deputy President of the Independent Democrats.
>
> Prof. Sono has written widely on free market policies and transformation. One of Sono's books is titled, *Reflections on the Origins of Black Consciousness*.[8]

BEING BLACK CONSCIOUS, BEING NONRACIAL: GERWEL, ISSEL, AND ESAU

The brief narratives about Modisane and Sono center on Black Consciousness and speak to a very specific phase in the struggle against Apartheid. The term "phase," however, is not used in the sense that it is over and done with. As we proceed now to look at personalities who have embodied both Black Consciousness and nonracialism, the point needs to be made from the onset that the embodiment of both by some illustrates almost perfectly that Black Consciousness and nonracialism are not mutually exclusive intellectual paradigms, but that they overlap.

The three personalities to pass the revue are Gerwel, Issel, and Esau. Gerwel is included particularly as a tribute to someone who has brought together in his mind and praxis Black Consciousness and nonracialism, perhaps more consistently than others.

The attempt at showing that these three embodied both Black Consciousness and nonracialism confronts a very complex matter: How is such dialectic to be defined? How does one develop a discourse that can clinically, in a watertight fashion, tell what the meaning of the embodiment of Black Consciousness and nonracialism is? I had a rather informal discussion with Tinyiko Maluleke, former deputy registrar at University of South Africa (UNISA) and former vice principal, Students and International Affairs, at the University of Johannesburg (currently special advisor to the vice chancellor and principal at the University of Pretoria). He made the very sharp observation with reference to the question, "Who is an African?" that we have not yet arrived at a definition, but live as Africans every day. He went on to argue that the issue is perhaps more about being African than breaking our heads about definitions. It is an ontological matter, i.e., if he was correctly understood, a matter of who we are in our daily lives more than who we are in terms of a modernist definition.

One shall look in vain for lengthy discourses with any of Gerwel, Issel, and Esau on Black Consciousness or nonracialism. Their lives and their praxis are the texts that reveal their radical consciousness on both aspects. Further research is needed into their life stories, to reconstruct them as best as they could and then tell us what kind of epistemology, the theory of knowledge, it would be that would emanate from a praxis of liberation based on Black Consciousness and nonracialism.

As reconstructions of the intellectual history of Gerwel and Issel have started only now after both have passed on, what is beginning to emerge quite clearly is that they were at ease with both Black Consciousness and nonracialism. Gerwel seems to have turned to Black Consciousness in the late 1960s and it is recorded that he had been an educational advisor to the SASO. It is clear, however, from an anecdote that he understood the limited nature of Black Consciousness as a political philosophy or intellectual tradition.[9] In Willemse's memory, Gerwel was wary of viewing Black Consciousness as the be-all and end-all of race views. Gerwel's turn to nonracialism could be traced back arguably to his taking the witness stand in the famous Delmas trial where Lekota and others were charged by the Apartheid state. Much as Lekota himself was a strong proponent of Black Consciousness, he had by then quite clearly embraced nonracialism. In the late 1980s, when Gerwel became vice chancellor and principal of UWC, he worked progressively toward transforming a bush college into a people's university, or in his own understanding, the academic or intellectual home of the political left. There are analyses and interpretations suggesting that this introduced a new level of consciousness for him, since "left" in the context of the Cape at the time would include Black

Consciousness, nonracialism, and tendencies related to Lenin, Stalin, Trotsky, Marx, and Gramsci, to name these specifically. Indeed, as suggested by the current vice chancellor and principal of UWC, O'Connell, "left" for Gerwel "meant opposition to the regime, which played itself out in different ways." In the early 1990s, i.e., before the revolution of 1994, his intellectual and ideological choices became more clear-cut with his election to the Western Cape regional committee of the African National Congress (ANC), culminating in his appointment as director general in the new democratic presidency under Mandela in 1994.[10] This was perhaps the clearest indication of his option for a nonracist, nonsexist democracy, by joining in office the custodian *par excellence* of the struggle for an inclusive just and democratic dispensation.

Turning to Issel now, the following anecdote is called into service to illustrate in simple terms his option for Black Consciousness. In standing in the elections at UWC for the Student Representative Council (SRC) in the 1970s, he cited the well-known expression: "You can play the black notes on the piano and you can play the white notes, but for harmony you have to play both the black and the white." His manifesto was clearly informed by Black Consciousness and, yet, in a somewhat ironic manner, he was also addressing himself to nonracialism, if such an interpretation would not be too far-fetched. What is well recorded was that Issel met with leaders of the Black Consciousness Movement like Biko and was appointed regional secretary of SASO in the Western Cape. It would be safe to assume that Issel's journey with nonracialism started around the time that he became organizer for the community newspaper *Grassroots*. Further demonstrating his revolutionary organizing skills was his rich involvement in diverse organizations of a political, community, or para-church nature. These organizations range from the Cape Youth Congress, which he was instrumental in founding, the Rocklands Ratepayers Association, the Cape Areas Housing Action Committee, the Clothing Workers Union, the End Conscription Campaign, and the Church Urban Planning Committee.

In the context of this chapter there is a need to make the following critical note: Issel's wide-ranging and rich involvement on different levels reinforced the argument that the issue of consciousness was not so much a matter of abstract theory, but of praxis, much as he was well-versed in texts. His turn to nonracialism would ultimately be consolidated by his involvement in the UDF. In fact, it was revealed later that Issel was one of the main movers for the creation of the UDF with a slogan that captured in a simple way the ideal of nonracialism: APARTHEID DIVIDES, UDF UNITES. Such was his commitment and his revolutionary élan that it was ironic that he could not be present at the launch of the UDF in August 1983 due to a banning order.

The third personality to qualify as someone who has profoundly embraced and embodied Black Consciousness and nonracialism is Esau. In a short interview with Scott, who himself was steeped in the Cape underground during the struggle against Apartheid as an MK cadre, his immediate response to the question, "Who in his understanding has dialectically brought together Black Consciousness and nonracialism in his or her life of struggle," was Cecyl Esau. His own story, which is captured in his statement in court, showed a rich reflection of his political journey up to the period shortly before the 1994 revolution in South Africa. His story started as follows:

> During the first elections for the Coloured Representative Council (CRC) in 1969 my father canvassed for the Labour Party candidate on the platform, "A vote for Labour is a vote against Apartheid." When "pamphleteering," he took me along. At that time, I did not grasp everything, but found the activities, for example, going to political meetings, very stimulating.

In addition, the story revealed further evolvement of political consciousness at secondary school in his home town, Worcester, where he formed a discussion group with peers. He was particularly influenced by exposure to students from UWC who in 1973 attempted to close the institution by staging a "walk off." An issue that would have had a lasting influence on his political life was the encounter with Ferrus. According to Esau's narration, it happened as follows:

> During my final year at school, 1974, I met John Marinus Ferrus, commonly called Hennie. At that time, he was still a banned person. During the 1960s he was an active member of the Congress Movement and served a couple of years on Robben Island for offences against the state. He commanded widespread support in Worcester and surrounding areas for his uncompromising stand against Apartheid which caused untold suffering. Also, he kept the flame of the Congress alive. One important truism he taught me was that there were many things one wanted to do, but could not do, and one often failed to do the things which one could. In short, this meant to me, however, lofty and inspiring dreams might be that one should at all times be pragmatic in tackling the problems of the day. Furthermore, his shining example as a people's leader who was always at the forefront in confronting injustice, despite continued police harassment, made a lasting impression on me. He also awakened my interest in the political history of Worcester and surrounding towns.[11]

Later on, of course, when Esau himself enrolled at UWC to study law, he shifted from supporting the move to close down the university to a very sophisticated understanding of strategy and tactics in terms of which the institution was to become an indispensable base for mobilization, training and organization. Esau himself became general secretary of the Student Representative Council at UWC and was on campus during the turbulent 1976. The fact that he was detained three times during 1976 bears testimony, more than anything else, to his deep commitment to the struggle for national liberation. Later, in 1980, he spent five and a half months in "preventative detention." In 1983 Esau helped establish the Cape Youth Congress as perhaps the clearest indication of his decisive option for congress movement and for nonracialism. A very important part of his political journey had been the studying of texts on liberation struggles in Latin America, Southern Africa, and Vietnam.

Perhaps there are a few issues still that form an important part of his political pedigree but have not necessarily been captured in his statement in court. One such matter is his turning to Black Consciousness, which was nowhere shown more clearly than in the emergence of the Worcester Student Organisation (WSO) in the aftermath of the student uprisings of 1976. Two of the leaders in WSO, inter alia, Esau and Johnson, were briefly detained and questioned by the Special Branch. Esau and Johnson were particularly questioned on why they wanted to learn IsiXhosa. In an ironic fashion, the engagement with the Special Branch on the matter of learning one of the African languages has reinforced the resolve to embrace Black Consciousness. Esau's turn to nonracialism would later in the 1980s be clearly demonstrated by his involvement in the UDF, where he emerged as one of the leading activists, mainly responsible for mobilization and organization in rural areas. He had suffered numerous detentions in solitary confinement and was ultimately sentenced to twelve years' imprisonment on Robben Island for furthering the aims of a banned organization and for being an MK cadre.

Before concluding this part of the study, an allusion should be made to the reality that both Issel and Esau had a deep affinity with religion. Issel, for example, was tipped to become a priest and Esau was a very active member of the African Methodist Episcopal (AME) church in Worcester. Both worked in and through the church's Urban Planning Commission (CUPC) in Cape Town, and had good connections with ecumenical bodies, for example, the Western Province Council of Churches, and of course the South African Council of Churches, and almost naturally with personalities and bodies in the Cape Islam, too many to mention here. In his work in the rural areas, Esau was known to have connected particularly with pastors who have studied at UWC.

It is of paramount importance to mention the affinity with religion and in particular the church, not because this provides legitimacy to the struggle, as it was a just "struggle in itself," but in the context of this chapter, it reinforces the argument that most of the time there was not only one "consciousness," but a combination. The respect for religion, and the strategic understanding of faith-based organizations (FBOs) as important agents in the struggle for justice, came to the fore as indispensable sources in the struggle narratives of Issel and Esau.

Whether one interprets the gravitation of the three persons from Black Consciousness to nonracialism as discontinuous, or whether one accepts a measure of overlapping between the two, the thesis of this chapter remains the following: One and the same individual had the capacity to embrace both and, more than that, to embody or stand for both. These were liberating identifications if they are not forced into the mold of essentialist identities. Indeed, as Gerwel suggested regarding Black Consciousness, they were not everything. A further issue, which has been alluded to, is that the stories of Gerwel, Issel, and Esau, however inadequately told, revealed that consciousness cannot be unpacked in terms of meta-discourses, but it is mediated by praxis, i.e., an ongoing struggle for liberation and justice.

LIBERATING IDENTIFICATIONS

The Ontological Turn

The brief narratives of consciousness and struggles of Gerwel, Issel, and Esau may perhaps be interpreted as follows: The espousing of Black Consciousness and nonracialism in the struggle for national liberation constituted an ontological, practical break in their lives, i.e., a turning from the imposition of slave and racist identities by Apartheid to liberating identifications. There are three concepts coming to the fore that need to be unpacked briefly, not in terms of watertight definitions, but in relation to the praxis of liberation as embodied by those under discussion here: First, there is the notion of an ontological turn borrowed from[12] an educationist from the United Kingdom. In broad terms, following Wheelahan's interpretation, Barnett's call for an ontological turn is a call away from a focus on knowledge and skills to the "pedagogy for the human being." He goes on to describe this mode of being as "being-for-uncertainty,"[13] which does not know much about the world, nor have at its disposal a raft of skills to deploy in and on the world. Being-for-uncertainty stands in certain kinds of relationships to the world. It is disposed in certain kinds of ways. It is characterized, therefore, by certain kinds of dispositions. Among such dispositions are carefulness, thoughtfulness, humility, a critical approach, receptiveness, resilience, courage, and stillness.[14]

In a different context and in appropriating Barnett's ontological turn as being-for-uncertainty to Black Consciousness and nonracialism under Apartheid, the suggestion here is that the consciousness embodied by Gerwel, Issel, and Esau in the struggle against the virulence of the Apartheid system could equally be typified as being-black conscious-for-uncertainty and being-nonracial-for-uncertainty. The outcomes of the struggle were never guaranteed, and the onslaught of the regime in detaining thousands, banning some, driving some into exile, killing others through cross-border raids created great uncertainty about where the struggle was going. It was only the *being-for-uncertainty* that has kept the freedom fighters going. Indeed, the age of struggle in South Africa was an age of carefulness, thoughtfulness, humility, a critical attitude, receptiveness, resilience, courage, and stillness. Perhaps Wheelahan is right in contending that these attributes are "less likely to result if the only enduring orientation available is the market, which values competitiveness, entrepreneurship and the commodification of knowledge,"[15] yet, in South Africa, once again, these are the only attributes that can potentially, and perhaps only slightly so, offset the devastation of neoliberal capitalism on humans and the environment.

Liberating…

Second, liberation is an important element in this chapter. In the interconnectivity between liberation and Black Consciousness, for example, J.N.J. Kritzinger asserts that "the praxis of Black Consciousness aims at holistic liberation. It is concerned not only with liberating black people from personal inferiority feelings, but from the whole system of racist oppression."[16] In taking his cue from the Black Theology Resolution, he differentiates between internal and external liberation which is understood to signify liberation from "circumstances of internal bondage" and "from circumstances of external enslavement."[17] The internal liberation alluded to has to do with forms of psychological or spiritual liberation where black people undergo a deep conversion in self-image, rediscovering themselves as human beings in their own right.[18] An important feature of this self-rediscovery is the shedding of impositions, stereotypes, and caricatures, or to speak with Gerwel, the "destruction" by whites. As far as external liberation is concerned, it is interesting to note that in terms of Black Consciousness, it has to do, first and foremost, with self-reliance and solidarity as sources of identity and power.[19]

Twenty years into democracy in South Africa the issues of self-reliance and solidarity remain as relevant as in the heyday of the Black Consciousness Movement, though in an entirely different political context. Of course, self-reliance in a democratic South Africa cannot mean the establishment of Black People's Convention–type projects, but it could mean a different understanding of access to resources that is not aimed at self-enrichment. Self-reliance in a democratic state could also mean a greater confidence in homegrown strategies for poverty alleviation and job creation, which in turn may necessitate a different engagement with neoliberal capitalism and the institutions that drive it. It is in particular the matter of solidarity that prevails in a situation where the discourse on inequality, poverty, and unemployment suggests an ever-widening gap between the "haves" and the predominantly black "have-nots."

Identifications

Third, the concept "identifications," is called into service rather than identity or identities. Seemingly, as suggested by van Erasmus van Niekerk, the idea of speaking of identifications rather than identities originated with the University of Stellenbosch philosopher Johan Degenaar, who argued that the concept identifications is a manner of indicating that a person can embrace more than one type of identification simultaneously.[20] The concept seems to transcend the narrow, reductionist, and essentialist understanding of identity that has caused political and socioeconomic havoc in South Africa. It opens the way and liberates people to be comfortable with hybridity in the mode of multiple or shifting identities. In appropriating this to the struggle narratives of Gerwel, Issel, and Esau, the argument would be that the embodiment of diverse identifications could be quite a liberating experience. It is a matter of being more rather than having more.

ONCE MORE: LIBERATING IDENTIFICATIONS

To locate the notions of an ontological turn and liberating identifications in the struggle narratives of Gerwel, Issel, and Esau is to attempt at making the following construction: In turning from the "destructions" of Apartheid, i.e., the imposed "ontological" identities and classifications of Apartheid to Black Consciousness and nonracialism, they have chosen liberating identifications. A further issue, once again, is that in so doing, they have shown the capacity of human beings to embody more than one type of identification. In fact, this chapter does not reflect on the leaning of all three to Marx or Gramsci, which would have reinforced the thesis on the embodiment of diverse types of consciousness, ideologies, or intellectual paradigms by individuals.

ON BEING BLACK CONSCIOUS

This section commences by inducing a very personal story: Before mentioning the account, a note needs to be made about the reference to Modisane and Sono elsewhere in the chapter. In a real sense, the two stories or anecdotes form part of my own journey with diverse types of identifications. There are two elements to the story called into service here as metaphors of my journey with Black Consciousness, nonracialism, and here and there Marxism, and in particular, in terms of Gramsci's political and economic historiography.

Yellow, Yet Black Conscious

The first story is about the hugely challenging encounter with a sixteen-year-old secondary schoolboy in the city of East London in the Eastern Cape. In visiting the city in 1976, Leon Meyer, who was to become my brother-in-law later, spoke about his affinity with Black Consciousness and his respect and admiration for Biko, Pityana, and Modisane, three of the foremost leaders in the Black Consciousness Movement at the time. He introduced me to the publication of the Black Consciousness publication *Black Review*, and challenged me to reflect on the ideas expressed in the journal. What was the issue here? In simple terms, here he was, Leon, a "yellowish" sixteen-year-old boy who was as into Black Consciousness as could be. Henceforth, the matter for me was quite clear: There should be something in Black Consciousness that required my serious consideration.

Leon went on to matriculate in 1978 and before the results were released he had skipped the country to join the MK in Lesotho. Based on his intellectual prowess, which caused the Special Branch to hunt him down at a young age, accusing him of spreading socialist ideas amongst his peers at school, he mobilized himself upwardly in the MK structures. He went for training in countries like Cuba, the former Czechoslovakia, and the German Democratic Republic, and afterwards was appointed as political commissar to the MK. Those in the Cape underground during the days of the struggle, for example, Aneez Salie, Shirley Gunn, Leon Scott, and the late Johnny Issel, have testified to his political skill and bravery. Once again, therefore, the very story of Leon Meyer revealed the capacity to embody different modes of consciousness, ideologies, political paradigms, and philosophies. Leon was believed to have gravitated radically toward Marxism-Leninism, before being assassinated by the "Eugene de Kock hit squad" in Maseru in December 1985.

"More Griqua Than Myself"

The other story is traced back to the late 1970s, during my ministry in the rural town of Vanrhynsdorp in the Northern Cape; it must have been in 1979, to be slightly more accurate. Out of the blue I received a visit from a complete stranger, whose name I do not know up to today, except that I have a fairly good recollection of the place where he came from, namely, a settlement in the proximity of Vanrhynsdorp called Beeswater.

His mission was to go around in search of the Griquas, to mobilize, organizes, and to unite the Griquas. In response, I told him a little bit about my own ancestry with particular reference to the matrilineal roots that were to be traced back to an area call Leeukuil just outside Griquatown in the Northern Cape. The reaction of the visitor was quite astonishing, because, almost as if to jump in the air, he repeatedly shouted in great excitement, "You are more of a Griqua than myself." Painstakingly, I had to clarify a few issues. First, that there was no way that I would ever deny my roots. I shared with him some childhood memories, going back to the first three years at the Berlin Mission School in Douglas in the Northern Cape, about a hundred kilometers from the diamond city of Kimberley. In particular, I shared the war cry with him, chanted by learners during athletics, competing against schools from neighboring towns, for example, De Aar. I also shared with the visitor the songs we knew as children, which were sung during the festive season, in particular, a New Year's song that phonetically sounded like "*elele kuhuhu*," sung to celebrate the arrival of the New Year. These were my roots and these I would always cherish. I also tried to explain to the man from Beeswater, however, why in "Apartheid South Africa" I was wary of striving toward essentialist identities, and why I was never really interested to research my genealogy.

Furthermore, I tried to clarify why some of us were more in favor of black conscious than Griqua conscious. I attempted in vain to engage him discursively in the unifying nature of Black Consciousness, if "black" is understood not to refer to skin pigmentation but rather as an expression of the solidarity of the racially oppressed and economically exploited. He left, not in anger, but in friendship as we agreed to disagree.

In Brief: Black Consciousness

In a rather fragmentary way some elements of Black Consciousness were emerging in the two aforegoing stories; for example, that the "black" in Black Consciousness has got absolutely nothing to do with skin pigmentation, but as a political philosophy, Black Consciousness refers to a state of solidarity between oppressed people. This will now be worked out in the following paragraphs.

Opposition to white domination in South Africa was not an invention of the Black Consciousness Movement that emerged in the late 1960s. According to Kritzinger, who has done extensive research into Black Consciousness and Black Theology, those students who started the Black Consciousness Movement were painfully and respectfully aware "that many had gone before them and had even given their lives in that struggle."[21] Since 1652 there was an awareness of being embedded in the history of resistance against oppression. In fact, the very history of resistance revealed that "black" has never been a question of skin color, since it is inclusive of the Khoi struggles.

In the understanding of the *auctor intellectualis* of South African Black Consciousness, Steve Biko, it was a mental attitude that causes black persons to refuse to be subservient beings. It was a refusal to run away from themselves and to emulate others. Way into the new South Africa there was still a need to deal seriously with the typical pathologies Biko's Black Consciousness tried to address, for example, alienation, self-rejection, and indeed forms of internalized racism and oppression.[22] It is accepted too easily, for example, that amassing wealth by hook or by crook is evidence of the advancement from Apartheid to democracy, without posing the critical question, whose value is this? On a different, but not unrelated level, the continuous violent nature of South African society and, in particular, the murder statistics, suggests strongly that life has become cheap. Beyond a revitalization of Black Consciousness are there new modes of dealing with new feelings of inferiority, new forms of alienation and self-rejection?

In Biko's Black Consciousness there was a proposal for a "true humanity." In calling into service Hegel's construct of describing the thesis-antithesis-synthesis model, without using the specific concepts, Biko argued that the thesis under Apartheid was white racism with the concomitant racial oppression and economic exploitation, the antithesis the black struggle against oppression, and as future music or synthesis there was the quest for a true humanity. The pertinent question to be asked is whether the search is still on in the best-case scenario, or whether it has started at all in the worst-case scenario.

Let us accept that the democratic revolution of 1994 was supposed to set in motion the search for the new human being in South Africa. Let us also accept that indeed this was a major breakthrough, which was supposed to be the launching pad for a qualitatively new dispensation.

Perhaps one of the biggest impediments for making decisive advances toward the true humanity, envisaged by Biko, was and still is the prevailing racial capitalism, a construction of Black Consciousness, thinking to analyze the uniquely South African economic system.

In concluding, the following disclaimer needs to be made about this small portion of Black Consciousness. The reference to Biko only for a basic understanding of Black Consciousness relates to the fact that the study is not on the movement in terms of its different phases, but as far as Black Consciousness is concerned the assumption that the three differentiations under discussion fit the profile of Black Consciousness as expounded by Biko. It would be fair to suggest that all three embraced the Black Consciousness of Biko, much as they encountered Marxist ideology (which is very much part of the second phase of the Black Consciousness Movement) in the struggle against Apartheid, espousing it to a greater or lesser extent.

ON BEING NONRACIAL

Once again, like the section on Black Consciousness, the discussion on nonracialism starts with a personal narrative: My journey with nonracialism began in the church in the late 1990s, in joining a confessing movement of the black Dutch Reformed Churches called the Belydende Kring (BK). The objectives of the BK were to struggle against Apartheid in church and society in general and, in particular, to work for the unity of the ethnically and racially divided members of the Dutch Reformed family of churches. The BK became an important location for cutting one's teeth on nonracialism in bringing together, across the Apartheid divide, black and white, male and female.

My most decisive option for nonracialism arose with the inception of the UDF with the honor bestowed upon me of becoming the first chairperson of the West Coast UDF, mobilizing and organizing it in towns like Saldanha Bay, Vredenburg, Laaiplek-Velddrift, Hopefield, and further afield. I was then pastor of the former Dutch Reformed Mission Church (DRMC) in Laaiplek-Velddrift. There was a very strong bond among activists in Atlantis where "revolutionaries," for example, Noel Williams and Karl Cloete, emerged. During the time of the run-up to the founding of the UDF in Rocklands, Mitchel's Plain in the Cape, August 20, 1983, and thereafter, workshops were held as far afield as my home town, Worcester, for political schooling. I remember having attended such a workshop where Cronin provided excellent input on the Freedom Charter. The most remarkable experience for me was the interaction with some working-class people of the West Coast who were mainly members of the Food and Canning Workers Union of Oscar Mpetha, who had once worked at a fishing factory in Laaiplek-Velddrift.

Quite vividly in memory was the deep political understanding of workers who accepted at the time that the struggle against Apartheid and for national liberation was more important than short-term victories on the shop floor. The UDF praxis of the West Coast has proven beyond a shadow of a doubt that the dichotomy between the bread-and-butter issues of the working class and national ideological struggles could be overcome; also that partnerships between the trade unions, a political front, for example, the UDF and churches, or faith-based organizations, were feasible. This reality was brilliantly demonstrated in a rally at Saldanha Bay in the run-up to the elections for the tricameral parliament. As a strategic move to mobilize against the tricameral parliament, Boesak, Carolus, Mpetha, and Nissen were brought to the rally as speakers. What needs to be mentioned specifically is that this was the exact time of the emergence of the "Confession of Belhar" in the DRMC, which contradicted Apartheid in the strongest theological terms by witnessing to unity, reconciliation, and justice. I was privileged to attend, as a young minister, the 1982 synod of the DRMC where the draft "Confession of Belhar" was adopted with great emotion. I was equally privileged to work with colleagues, for example, Lizette and Leonardo Appies for the establishment of the West Coast Council of Churches (WCCC) as an affiliate of the SACC. The inauguration of the WCCC took place in Hopefield during 1985 and was done by the then secretary general of the SACC, Beyers Naudé. Yet another honor for me was to be part of the process for the construction of the Kairos Document, of which I became a signatory. The mentioning of both the "Confession of Belhar" and the "Kairos Document" is to indicate the affinity with different modes of liberation theology at the time. The strong leaning toward black theology and Latin American liberation theology, as well as brands of liberation theology from Asia, such as Minjung from Korea and Dalit from India, provided wonderful equipment for the church's struggle against Apartheid.

Controversies around Nonracialism

The concept nonracial or nonracialism gave rise to a few controversies. First, some argued that nonracialism is impracticable and, consequently, constituted an impossibility. The argument here was that the concept nonracialism suggested the ultimate nonexistence of races, which in South Africa is improbable. There is a hunch that the argument will be advanced mostly by those who do not appreciate the history of the concept in relation to the praxis of liberation. This is said not to detract from the simple reality that technically those who object to the use of the term are perhaps correct in absence of racism.

Second, there was a difference of opinion on whether what was meant by nonracial or nonracialism was not really antiracist or nonracist. Once again, it appeared to be technically more apt to speak of antiracism or nonracism than nonracial or nonracialism. There was a proviso, however, which was that whether one spoke of nonracialism or anti- or nonracism, the issue was not merely about a reaction to particular forms of racism, but the entire South African life. To respond with indignation to the racist incident at the University of the Free State, but then to remain unaffected by the gross inequalities, poverty, and unemployment in the country was to have a hugely reductionist understanding of nonracialism or antiracism.

Third, there seems to have been a growing number of South Africans revealing a newly found bliss of "color blindness." The treacherous nature of the argument on color blindness is that the history of racism and racist rule gets negated completely in an attempt to conceal the material gain that accrued from it. That explains why affirmative action, fraught as it might have been with contradiction, was summarily rejected as a strategy for redress.

Fourth, a controversy was to use nonracialism and multiracialism interchangeably, overlooking the difference between a philosophical-ideological concept aimed at creating a new society and a statement of fact that is still tainted by racialism.

No attempt would be undertaken to trace the historical roots of nonracialism. Instead, a cursory look was taken at attempts within the congress movement to give new impetus to nonracialism during the past decade or so. In broad terms, the most basic understanding of nonracialism was enshrined in the 1955 Freedom Charter by the wording, "South Africa belongs to all those who live in it." The statement could of course be easily subverted from a historical perspective, as indeed happened at the conference, where the presentation was made on which this chapter is based. The question is simply whether almost sixty years down the line the statement was not entirely meaningless in the light of the division of land in South Africa. Yet this was exactly the issue with nonracialism whereby the situation was unbearable in the light of inequality, poverty, and unemployment. Nonracialism is a strategic, ideological concept contending that things cannot continue as they are now. In the light of new appearances of race-based fragmentation and division, it is hoped that the quest for nonracialism will unite South Africans in striving for a more egalitarian society. Nonracialism was of course also one of the founding values of the constitution.

Further, in drawing from the "Strategy and Tactics" document of 2007[23] and "Deepening of Nonracialism in South Africa" of 2010, the following seemed to be emerging as unavoidable in the discourse on nonracialism: First, that the debate on nonracialism is about finding "discursive spaces where everyone can debate . . . without being pigeon-holed by race—nor ignored." As a progressively democratic approach, nonracialism is different from "color blindness" in terms of which race does not matter. It is different in the sense that race is not ignored, but located properly in the context of the real existing political and socioeconomic power relationships.

Second, that nonracialism is not aimed at creating "one thing" out of all South Africans, but rather feeds into diversity, multiple identities, and tolerance.

Third, the advancement of nonracialism is strategically aimed at dealing with dichotomies, showing up in post-Apartheid South Africa. There are, inter alia, three such dichotomies: Race-conscious policy making in the country reinforces and mobilizes identities based on race. Prime examples are the Labour Relations Act and the persistent practices at institutions and in the labor market to require people to identify themselves in terms of ethnicity and race. A further very serious example is the irony of post-Apartheid South Africa where black political power and white economic power prevail. In the context of neoliberal capitalism and the uniquely South African character of the economic system, this constitutes a serious contradiction resulting in perpetual inequality. Without fear of contradiction it could be claimed that those bearing the brunt of such inequality are women. Consequently, it is important to keep nonracialism, the class issue, and non-sexism in a creative, discursive relationship to one another.

ON BEING AFRICAN

To introduce African consciousness as the third member of the triad under discussion in this chapter is to argue strongly for the inculcation of a new consciousness that goes beyond Black Consciousness and nonracialism. It is precisely for that reason, however, that this concept is much more complex than the other two. Part of the complexity has to do with the vastness of the continent and the huge diversity between and within regions and countries. There is the matter that is constantly raised in discussions on the difference between the Arabic North African countries and sub-Saharan Africa, to use a rather problematic description. A breakdown of issues like culture and language renders the situation even more complex.

At tertiary institutions, where the need for the Africanization of the curriculum is identified, the project is delayed more, quite often than not, since "definitions" that cover everybody are virtually unachievable. The hint to gravitate from Eurocentrism to Afrocentrism is most of the time not helpful since the exercise required is much more complex than simply cleansing Africa from everything European or Western. What is even more cumbersome than a shift from Eurocentrism to Afrocentrism is the attempt at ethnographic reconstruction.

In the space available here, a tentative proposal is offered on what *being African* might mean if the notion of identification is applied rather than trying to achieve an essentialist definition of African identity. Elsewhere in the article, there is an allusion to the wise interpretation of Maluleke when he argues that the issue is much more about *being African*, i.e., how we live our lives daily in Africa rather than constructing watertight definitions on who is an African. In rhetorical terms, we might say that we did not yet know who an African was and is, but practically we live as Africans. Such an understanding is much more liberating than to attempt to satisfy the modernist need for little secluded boxes.

Yet, for purposes of constructing a proposal on *being African*, Thabo Mbeki's essay "I Am an African"[24] is called into service. If the metaphor of identification is appropriated to the text, at least three categories of identification emerge: First, in terms of a richly poetic construction on the flora and fauna of the continent, one could speak of an *ecological identification* which suggests that *being African* is to identify with the living environment, ecosystems, natural resources, and indeed all that is on offer in the created and inhabited Africa.

Second, to be African is to own up to all manner of *woes* that have become part of the continent since colonialism, Apartheid, and the ever-new manifestations of war, civil war, refugees, poverty, famine, natural disasters, corruption, undemocratic practices, and of course the scourge of HIV and AIDS. An African is someone who does not shy nor run away from the serious challenges that confront the continent.

Third, *being African* is to manifest positively about the opportunities on offer in the continent. Africans should be wary of interpreting opportunities, however, only to mean the opportunities for economic growth as is indeed witnessed in quite a few countries currently and, therefore, the opportunities for personal advancement in socioeconomic terms. Opportunities are not merely technocratic objects for the material progress of Africans. The greatest opportunity on offer to Africans is to advance progressively by returning to *ubuntu*. The past two decades have seen a growing body of literature on the meaning of *ubuntu* and its appropriation to diverse contexts. What must suffice here is a brief allusion to the liberating potential of *ubuntu*. In the context of the article, an interpretation of Tutu's *ubuntu* theology by Michael Battle appears to be quite relevant. In a chapter on "*Ubuntu*'s Liberation," Battle writes: "In Tutu's hands, *ubuntu* represents the claim that human identities are uniquely made to be cooperative more than competitive."[25]

CONCLUSION: CHRISTIAN FAITH BEING THE HEART OF LIBERATION, BLACK CONSCIOUSNESS, NONRACIALISM, AND AFRICANISM

To be able to substantiate the thesis that liberating praxis is possible if a mediating tension is achieved between Black Consciousness, nonracialism, and Africanism, we would have to comprehend each of these methods of resistance by taking into account the role Christian faith played in the overcoming of exploitation, domination, and discrimination of Apartheid.

Black Consciousness as the Nitty-Gritty of Freedom

The background of these methods of resistance and the merging of the three approaches was as follows: First, the overall transcending of Black Consciousness regarding oppression has to be appreciated. During the 1960's a vacuum ensued after the banning of the ANC and the PAC and their leaders. This political void was quickly filled with a new movement toward political consciousness of the grassroots people, to be called Black Consciousness.

Christianity was the basis of Black Consciousness: Archbishop Taylor of the Anglican Church convened a meeting that led to the formation of the University Christian Movement,[26] which became the instrument and mouthpiece of Black Consciousness, the Black Consciousness Movement (BCM). At first, this philosophy or way of life caused dissention, but soon great harmony came about between different groups of resistance—this became the spear point of constructive advancement to resist Apartheid in general.[27]

The BCM was a rejection of whites in general, even those of liberal ilk: "If the white man wants to help, he can go home and free his own people" (Stokely Carmichael aka Kwame Ture). Because of the Black Consciousness philosophy, the whites, especially white liberals, were rejected for the first time in South Africa, as they were seen to maintain traditional "white" values, which were condescending.[28] The slogan, especially maintained by Steve Biko, "Black man you're on your own," created a new attitude in the dominated people, providing a temporary approach to reach inner development toward independence.[29] They realized that to become free, first they have to take responsibility for their own lives and become philosophically free as a way of life, and psychologically liberated to stand on their own feet. This attitude created a new situation in South Africa that was extremely difficult to control, as the white dominating structures could not subjugate this exuberant spirit. The consequence and the approach of the system was simply to clamp down with force, which resulted in the death of some of the leaders of the BCM—for example, Steve Biko, Black Consciousness—but was, however, the beginning of the end of Apartheid in principle, as it would create free and proud human beings, an inner freedom that could not be enslaved from outside anymore.

Black Consciousness formed the backbone of inner and outer liberation and created a nonessentialist freedom of identity where people were in command of their own lives—for the first time with self-respect and dignity as human beings. Black Consciousness laid the foundation for new strategies that could come about in the struggle against exploitation and domination, for example, an attitude of nonracialism as a strategy of cooperation, and Africanism as a method of unity.

The inner and outer power of Black Consciousness was overwhelming in many lives and countered, for example, reverse racism, revenge, and hatred through nonracialism and Africanism.

In the new democratic South Africa, many of the problems and disasters came about because of the shortcut many people in political control and with responsibility for society and access to vast amounts of funds took. They did not go through the inner liberation by means of Black Consciousness to be proud to be fully human beings with all the responsibility and dignity that go with it. The consequences were calamitous, as egoism, racism, and reverse racism, for example, were not conquered. Truly liberated human beings are proud to be simply what they are, with the necessary self-respect and respect for others.

Nonracialism as Awareness of Being Human Together with all other Human Beings

Awareness is a synonym of *consciousness* which arises from the experiences people have of themselves and their society. This means that awareness or consciousness is paradoxically beyond understanding: Personal experiences can be described as a view from inside and therefore unique and, consequently, indefinable in terms of everything else—the individual is, as it were, inside of what is happening: a uniquely personal experience.[30]

What is nonracialism? It is simply the awareness of treating other people as merely other human beings, regardless of race, skin color and culture; this is a *nonracial attitude* and it is one of these indefinable approaches. This, however, is extremely difficult to comprehend as we in South Africa grew up with a color consciousness that went beyond all boundaries and limitations in our personal lives and infiltrated us completely from childhood. We grew up, enslaved by the concept of race, with the consequence that we transgressed all borders psychologically and automatically in our attitude toward others, attacking others with racial prejudice. This affected the so-called "whites," as well as the so-called "blacks," "Coloreds" and "Indians," who, on the other hand, reacting to the white dominating and exploiting structures.

This racial and racist attitude had consequences in all spheres of life, in economics, politics, education, culture, etc. We had to be liberated completely from inside, regarding our action to see and treat other persons as merely other human beings in all spheres. This is the core of nonracialism, which, however, seldom springs from inner renewal and freedom. This approach of nonracialism is the key to understand Steve Biko's Black Consciousness together with his strong feelings for nonracialism: His famous saying was that *blackness is not a skin color, but a mode of life*; and so, we can repeat that also for "Coloreds," "Europeans," "Chinese," "Indians," etc. We are agents of our lives and not objects of other people. One of the world's main problems is that most people in the world are controlled by a small minority—one of capitalism's criticisms is that it divides people into the dehumanizing "exploiting" and "exploited"; whereas most accept capitalism as the natural way of life, but that is another story.

Africanism Identifies People in Their Own Right over Others

People normally grow up with pride of their land of birth, or perhaps[31] one person reacts to another person's identity negatively out of the need caused by pain and defense, whereas the person with a healthy attitude reacts out of a positive identity in such a way that new relationships could form out of different but African identities in such a way that new potential is activated toward cooperation.

The first step toward the Africanism of all who live in Africa is to acknowledge that black people and white people have lost their "humanity," and one way to reach true emancipation is to go through a new awareness of consciousness, and follow a genuine liberated nonracialism toward brotherhood and sisterhood of Africans.

The power of this approach is the gospel of Christ, claiming that human beings were made in the image of God and that the differences between us as human beings are far less and comprehensively weaker than the overwhelming similarities—if we follow Christ our Savior we are "one," bound by the love of God in his service to build the kingdom of God in this world in justice, and serve one another by washing the other's feet—especially regarding economic equality and political freedom from divisive structures.

NOTES

1. The essay was presented at an interdisciplinary conference on "Brown" Identity at the Beyers Naudé Centre for Public Theology, Faculty of Theology, Stellenbosch University, November 30–December 1, 2012.

2. Essentialism indicates that things have an essence or ideal nature that is independent of, and prior to, their existence. Philosophically, this would signify that the nature or existence of something is fixed, determined, and controlled by its "essence."

3. "Professor Gert 'Jakes' Johannes Gerwel," South African History Online, <http://www.sahistory.org.za/people/professor-gert-jakes-johannes-gerwel/> [Accessed: June 17, 2017].

4. "John James Issel," South African History Online, <http://www.sahistory.org.za/people/john-james-issel/> [Accessed: June 17, 2017].

5. "Esau Cecyl," South African History Online, <http://www.sahistory.org.za/people/esau-cecyl#sthash.IXuMzVHO.dpuf/> [Accessed: June 17, 2017].

6. "William 'Bloke' Modisane," South African History Online, <http://www.sahistory. org.za/people/william-bloke-modisane/> [Accessed: June 17, 2017].

7. "Black People's Convention (BPC)," South African History Online, <http://www.sahistory.org.za/ topic/black-people%E2%80%99s-convention-bpc/> [Accessed: June 17, 2017].

8. "Professor Themba Sono," South African History Online, <http://www.sahistory.org.za/people/professor-themba-sono/> [Accessed: June 17, 2017].

9. M. J. Willemse, <http://archivedpublicwebsite,up,ac.za/sitefiles/files/46/349/Huldeblyk%20prof/ %20 Gerwel/> [Accessed: October 13, 2013].

10. Rebecca Davis, "Remembering Jakes Gerwel," *Daily Maverick*, November 29, 2012.

11. Cecyl Esau, "Memories of a Political Prisoner on Robben Island, 1987–1991," *Kronos* 34/1 (2008): 41–65.

12. Ronald Barnett, "Learning for an Unknown Future," *Higher Education Research & Development* 23/3 (2004): 247–60.

13. Elizabeth Leesa Wheelahan, "How Markets Distort Decisions to Undertake Education, Vocational Knowledge, Provision and Qualifications," proceedings of the 4th International Conference of Researching: Work and Learning, 2005.

14. Barnett, "Learning for an Unknown Future," 258.

15. Wheelahan, "How Markets Distort Decisions," 6.

16. J.N.J. Kritzinger, *South African Black Theology*, study guide 2 for MSB301-F: Mission as Liberation: Third World Theologies (Pretoria: University of South Africa, 1989), 24.

17. "SASO Resolution on Black Theology, 1971," <http://www.blackpast.org/saso-resolution-black-theology-1971/> [Accessed: March 10, 2017); Hendrik Wvan der Merwe, Nancy C. J. Charton, D. A. Kotze, and Ake Magnusson, eds., *African Perspectives in South Africa* (Stanford, CA: Hoover Institution Press, 1978).

18. Kritzinger, *South African Black Theology*, 25.

19. "Jakes Gerwel," Wikipedia, <https://en.wikipedia.org/wiki/Jakes_Gerwel/> [Accessed: June 17, 2017]; "The Life of Jakes Gerwel," <http://www.news24.com/SouthAfrica/News/The-life-of-Jakes-Gerwel-20121128/> [Accessed: June 17, 2017].

20. In a conversation with Erasmus van Niekerk on how South Africans tackle the question of identity, taken as we are with an obsession with essentialist identities, he mentioned how Johan Degenaar, the University of Stellenbosch philosopher, would consistently speak of identifications rather than identity. The conversation took place in August 2015 at the University of South Africa.

21. Kritzinger, *South African Black Theology*, 4.

22. Steve Bantu Biko, *I Write What I Like: A Selection of His Writings*, ed. Aelred Stubbs C. R (Johannesburg: Picador Africa, 2002).

23. African National Congress, "Unity in Action towards Socio-Economic Freedom," December 2012, <http://www.anc.org.za/docs/pol/2013/strategyp.pdf/> [Accessed: June 17, 2017].

24. Thabo Mbeki, "I Am an African," speech delivered by Thabo Mbeki on behalf of the African National Congress, Cape Town, May 8, 1996, <http://www.soweto.co.za/html/i_am-an-african.htm/> [Accessed: October 13, 2016].

25. Michael J. Battle, "A Theology of Community: The Ubuntu Theology of Desmond Tutu Interpretation," *Journal of Bible & Theology* 54/2 (1995): 172–82.

26. "University Christian Movement (UCM)," South African History Online, <http://www.sahistory.org.za/topic/university-christian-movement-ucm/> [Accessed: June 28, 2016].

27. "Black Consciousness Movement," South African History Online, <http://www.sahistory.org.za/article/black-consciousness-movement/> [Accessed: June 28, 2016].

28. Horst Kleinschmidt, *White Liberation: A Collection of Essays* (Johannesburg: Ravan Press, 1972), 1.

29. Biko, *I Write What I Like*, 1.

30. Kleinschmidt, *White Liberation*, 9.

31. Kleinschmidt, *White Liberation*, 11.

Six

Umuntu Akalahlwa

An Exploration of an African Ethics

Sibusiso Masondo

INTRODUCTION

One of the leading figures in the study of African traditional religion (ATR) and African theology, Professor John S. Mbiti, pointed out that ATR does not seek converts or to proselytize but people are born into it.[1] Historian of religion Kofi Asare Opoku took the point further by saying that ATR is an open and plural system.[2] It has no closed cannon. It is open to other interpretations of reality and respects the rights of those who hold and advocate them. Other interpretations of reality are respected and allowed to flourish and those who adhere to these beliefs are never discouraged. Since ATR does not engage in proselytization, that is, does not actively seek converts, there is no need to convert anyone. This worldview possesses resources that can be very useful in our quest to find solutions to African problems.

Church historian Ogbu Kalu, in his work on worldview, ecology, and development in West Africa, stated that, "Indigenous cultures are underpinned by worldviews which serve as reservoirs of knowledge."[3] Kwesi Kwaa Prah made a very good case for Africans to value their heritage by saying that "if Africa is to join the march to economic prosperity and the social and economic empowerment of its humanity, it must establish its efforts on its own cultural usages away from the smothering and suffocating embrace of western economic hegemony and cultural effacement. The cultivation and development of African languages are crucial to this."[4] Furthermore, the tendency to ignore or undermine African heritage is exacerbated by an African elite that is trapped in colonialism. They insist on using colonial languages and according them higher status than indigenous languages. Therefore, there is a need to unearth gems from African languages as part of this project. Language is a reservoir of knowledge and wisdom.

This chapter will draw on one such IsiZulu phrase as a way of thinking about some of the moral and ethical concerns confronting the continent of Africa in the twenty-first century, especially the victimization of the African poor by being made into refugees in places like Ethiopia, Somalia, Sudan, the Congo, Rwanda, and Burundi. The 2008 and 2015 outbreaks of xenophobic violence in South Africa will be the focal point. This is not definitive by any means but it provides an entry point to thinking about personhood and human rights. This project is part of what Oyekan Owomoyela calls "the task of reclaiming African humanity which is a significant part of the process of decolonisation."[5] Most discussions of African personhood start off by recalling the dictum *umuntu ngumuntu ngabanye abantu* (lit., "a person is a through other people"). These ideas are encapsulated in the idea of *ubuntu,* which is a theory of being or becoming in the world.

CONSTRUCTING *UMUNTU*: BEING OR BECOMING

The social and cultural anthropologists John L. and Jean Comaroff, in their study of personhood among the southern Tswana during the late colonial era, concluded that personhood was perceived as becoming rather than being.[6] Being implied social stasis, stagnation, or social death. A person was constantly developing and making progress toward reaching her/his potential. They move from the premise that in the southern interior, among the Tswana in particular, personhood was a social construct. In fact, this happened in two ways: "First nobody existed or could be known except in relation and with reference to, even as part of, a wide array of significant others, and second, the identity of each and every one was forged, cumulatively, by an infinite, ongoing series of practical activities."[7] Furthermore, "selfhood was not ascribed: status and role were determined by factors other than birth or genealogy, although social standing was typically represented in genealogical terms."[8] The Tswana society, for example, is said to be at once highly communal and also highly individuated.

The African concept of personhood is, therefore, enmeshed in community. The individual depends on the community for self-identification. The humanity of each individual is validated in the community. The individual depends on the community to become—to fully realize her/his potential. The idea of "becoming" is consistent with African thought where knowledge is constantly changing. People move through different developmental stages in life until they reach a state of being part of the "communion of ancestors." Within the "communion of ancestors" there is development and growth as well.

John S. Mbiti coined the dictum: "I am because we are and, since we are, therefore I am," meaning "I participate, therefore, I am" to capture the essence of participation for an African person.[9] Participation in community life is the duty of every person. Each person is endowed with gifts and talents. These gifts are given by the ancestors so that they can benefit the whole community. No one is expected to be a loner—*inkomo edla yodwa* (lit., "a cow that grazes on its own"). An individual can never be self-sufficient, she/he will always need support, guidance, help, communion, solidarity, etc., from other people. There are dangers associated with cutting oneself off from the rest of the community. People are gifted differently. There are people who have gifts that you do not have, and they use them to benefit you and others in the community. A certain degree of balance is created, thus maintaining order. There is no space for people who are self-absorbed or selfish. Such people cut themselves from the community. Usually, such people are the ones who are accused of witchcraft because they put their narrow personal interests above those of the community. Some go as far as to appropriate supernatural powers to achieve their goals. For anthropologists Diane Ciekawy and Peter Geschiere, witchcraft, "epitomises the frightening realisation that there is jealousy and aggression within the intimate circle of the family where only solidarity and trust should reign."[10]

Witchcraft accusations emanate from situations where an individual is perceived to be pursuing narrow personal interests at the expense of the community. There is a clear link between witchcraft accusation and dehumanization. When one is deemed a witch, it means that they are not human but subhuman or superhuman because of the powers they possess. In fact, "some of the abominations that are sometimes attributed to witches, like bestiality and cannibalism, suggest that witchcraft accusations involve the demonization of fellow human beings."[11] The theory of witchcraft gives us a window through which to understand competing interests in African communities.

The process of acquiring one's personhood is an active one. The person actively participated in the process of "building themselves up." John L. and Jean Comaroff raise a crucial point that is often overlooked in some studies, that there are obstacles and opportunities in the process of identity construction.[12] They burst the bubble of the myth of harmonious African society by pointing out that there were social tensions that manifested in rivalries and eventually witchcraft accusations. The onus was on adults, especially males, given the prevalence of patriarchy in many parts of Africa, to build themselves up and protect themselves from being eaten up by their enemies.

Personhood can never be in a state of "being." A state of "being" assumes that something is static, fixed, unmoving, and unchanging. No living self could be static as stasis meant social death. A state of "becoming," on the other hand, refers to something dynamic, vibrant, full of life, and active. As long as the person is alive, they never stop "becoming." Layer upon layer of who they are keeps on being revealed—assuming that there are many facets to a person. Only the powerful and antisocial agents are capable of stopping a person from "becoming." In some cases, it is a question of being derailed or distracted but one gets on the road again with the help of sacred specialists. This deviant behavior is frowned upon, yet at the same time it is feared. Deviant behavior of any kind disturbs societal relations and relations between humans and divinities. This disturbance creates a state of disequilibrium and chaos ensues. Chaos can take the form of illness, tension as a result of rape, death, and other misfortunes. Traditionally, there were societal sanctions against deviant behavior—depending on the severity of the action.

There are external factors that stop a person from becoming. These are the factors that disable one from reaching their full potential. *Ukukhinyabeza* is an active process that frustrates or even stops an individual from becoming. It is a process that actually disables, disempowers, and incapacitates an individual, which in turn affects the community. It stops an individual from realizing their full potential and by extension robs the community of the benefits of their potential. This concept is key in discourses on witchcraft. Bewitchment includes acts that cripple others—*ukukhinyabeza*—not allowing others to "become." The antisocial agent actively plays a role in making the other not to become. Becoming is about maximizing the potential that each person is endowed with. Actions of witches are crippling. Actions of other antisocial agencies like colonial governments, multinational companies, government policies, etc., could be analyzed through the theory of witchcraft. These agencies have contributed a lot to the state of despair among the African poor in the continent.

UMUNTU AKALAHLWA

The IsiZulu phrase *umuntu akalahlwa* deals with two related aspects, that is, (a) the responsibility that one has to others, and (b) dealing with deviance. *Umuntu akalahlwa* (lit., "a person cannot be thrown away") means that a human person is not disposable. The implication of this statement is that there is intrinsic value in each person. There is a sense that regardless of what had happened there is always a possibility for rehabilitation. There is also the implicit acknowledgment that in each person there is a struggle between good and evil. It is premised on the belief that human beings have a huge potential to change and become better and more sociable. The widely held belief is that good always triumphs over evil. Evil is broadly perceived as antisocial activities and behavior. Anyone who engages in such activities is said to be engaged in witchcraft.

Each person is endowed with gifts and talents from conception to make positive contribution to society. These gifts are meant to be used for the benefit and development of the community. One is meant to be one's brother's keeper. Every person is created for a purpose and they need to spend their lives fulfilling it. People are meant to use these gifts, especially for the benefit of others, otherwise they do not deserve to be alive. In the case of ancestral calling to become a traditional healer, it is believed that a person cannot refuse it. If an individual does refuse the call s/he is threatened with death, misfortune, or some other catastrophe. Such is a call to serve others and refusing to accept it means that people in the community will be deprived of the benefits of the ancestral investment in this person.

The IsiZulu term *umuntu* is a constructed entity through societal machinery, i.e., socialization. In fact, an individual is "essentially a relational being who gets significance and pertinence by his or her integration in a given human community."[13] Society, through its social code of behavior, morality, and ethics, expects individuals to meet certain expectations. All the socializing agencies introduce a person to the patterns of life and expected responses in the community. In his identification of the moral foundations of an African culture, Kwasi Wiredu stated that:

> And the way in which a sense of communal belonging fostered in the individual is through the concentrated stress on kinship identity already adumbrated in our earlier allusions to the Akan concept of person. Not only is there what might perhaps be called an ontological basis for this identity in terms of the constituent parts of personhood, but there is also a distinct normative layer of a profound social significance in that concept. Thus conceived, a human person is essentially the centre of a thick set of concentric circles of obligations and responsibilities matched by rights and privileges revolving round levels of relationships irradiating from consanguinity of household kith and kin, through the "blood" ties of lineage and clan, to the wider circumference of human family hood based on the common possession of the divine spark.[14]

In the phrase *umuntu akalahlwa* there are two crucial aspects that promote human welfare and compassion, that is, caring for others and dealing with deviance. There is an ethical imperative to care for others, especially those in distress. It makes the attacks on foreigners a serious ethical problem because of their vulnerability. First, it critiques the promotion of self-interest at the expense of others. According to Harvey Sindima, African thought "respects individuality but abhors individualism."[15] Individualism is singled out as the major problem in community building as it puts self-interest before that of the community. Furthermore, "the African concept of community encourages teamwork and communalism, while at the same time creating and offering possibilities for self-awareness, sense of responsibility, and development of one's potential. All activity is oriented toward fostering community life."[16] There are proverbs and sayings from different groups across the continent that speak to the importance of an individual being part of a community.

Second, it encourages generosity toward the poor and strangers in one's community. African theologian Gabriel Setiloane,[17] in developing an African theology, invoked a Sotho-Tswana phrase stating, *modidi ke moloi* (lit., "a poor person is a witch"). It means that those who have should not knowingly let the poor go hungry. If they did, they risked having the wrath of the ancestors fall upon them. Ancestors ensure communal prosperity, order, and authority.[18] The role of the ancestors in this worldview is to reward goodness and punish badness. Since the ancestors derive their authority from the Supreme Being, they are perceived to be just and fair. The ancestors are understood to be guardians of morality and social order. They reward the good and condemn evil. Third, there is an imperative to be hospitable to strangers. There is an IsiZulu phrase that says: *isisu somhambi asingakanani singangenso yenyoni* (lit., "the stomach of a traveler is as small as a bird's kidney"), meaning that by giving hospitality to a stranger a person will not lose anything. Instead, that act of generosity acknowledges the humanity of the traveler and the fact that in a similar situation one would also appreciate hospitality. There is also an ethical imperative on the stranger to graciously accept hospitality. It is a way of affirming the humanity of the one who offers. This point is aptly made by Chirevo Kwenda in his argument that giving and receiving are equally important in African thought.[19]

Deviance is when an individual undermines, violates, dismisses, abuses, or even rejects societal norms and values. It upsets a sense of balance and harmony, which is an important aspect of communal life in Africa. In fact, "the wellspring of morality and ethics in African societies is the pursuit of a balance of individual, with communal wellbeing."[20] *Inswelaboya* (criminal), through her/his actions, disqualified her/him from the category human. Their deviance or criminal act made them the undesirable "other." It is a process of self-excommunication. Antisocial behavior dehumanizes both the perpetrator as well as the victim. This point is aptly made by Archbishop Desmond Tutu in his book *No Future without Forgiveness*, when he states, "To dehumanise another inexorably means that one is dehumanised as well."[21] This kind of behavior is perceived as both evil and immoral. Societal balance and harmony are disturbed by such acts. Such acts are disruptive to social order. They cause distress and anxiety among members of the community. Healing is meant to reinstate harmony and restore balance. Some of the healing rituals play reinstatement and restorative roles. Ideally, the individual who violated the ethical code would go through disciplinary procedures and the guilt would be pronounced by a competent court. The individual has to confess her/his guilt. S/he would have to pay their debt to society (reparation) before their reintegration. There is a sense of justice in this formulation. The individual is given another chance to make a contribution to society. The South African government took a decision to apply the principle of restorative justice when dealing with certain categories of offenders. The Department of Justice and Correctional Services have developed a policy of rehabilitation of certain categories of offenders with a view to reintegration back into their communities. To show their commitment to this concept, they even named one of the correctional facilities at Empangeni, Qalakabusha (lit., "start afresh or anew").

The African philosopher Kwasi Wiredu, in thinking about the moral foundations of an African culture, stated that "the sense of human solidarity which we have been discussing works particularly to the advantage of foreigners, who, in the deeply felt opinion of the Akans, are doubly deserving of sympathy; on grounds, first, of their common humanity and second, of being, at any rate, from emotional and material support of their kinship environment."[22] As noted earlier, hospitality to strangers is an important ethical imperative among AmaZulu and other African groups. There is a discourse that has othered two groups of people in South Africa, that is, *amakwerekwere* (African immigrants, the "undesirable other") and *abelungu* (lit., "white people," the "desirable other"). African migration into South Africa has been part of life especially since the discovery of gold in Johannesburg and diamonds in Kimberley. For a long time, African immigrants had never been perceived as a direct threat. This point is made very well by Banda that "these migrants were not necessarily a threat since South Africans themselves were shunning mine work. Furthermore, these migrants occupied the lowest strata of the jobs available in the mines."[23] Since 1994, with the large influx of people from different countries in Africa as a result of wars, repression, or economic collapse in their countries, they have increasingly been seen as a threat, especially by those at the margins of the economy. The 2008 and 2015 attacks came after a process of dehumanization of African immigrants. In order to justify these attacks, those responsible accused foreign nationals of engaging in activities that are antisocial. They were accused of "job stealing," "bringing drugs and corruption to our country," and "taking our women."[24] They were not just made into strangers, but they were made into an "undesirable other." The dehumanization of the African self by other Africans can be explained as having resulted from colonial racism which "succeeded in alienating many Africans from their own culture."[25] The colonial mentality "makes a formerly colonised person to overvalue things coming from his erstwhile colonial master."[26] It is this mentality that led to the devaluing of the African self and the demonization and vilification of African foreign nationals.

DEHUMANIZATION OF THE AFRICAN SELF

Pictures are beamed around the world of people from the African continent who have been displaced from their homes, carrying everything they could retrieve from their homes in small bags. The majority of these are women and children. The United Nations Refugee Agency has estimated that there are over eighteen million displaced people in sub-Saharan Africa.[27] These people are accommodated in camps with limited facilities relying on the goodwill of aid agencies for their survival. There are a number of reasons why they find themselves in such situations. For some, it is the outbreak of civil wars in their countries, which has been a prominent feature of postcolonial Africa. Some are economic refugees because economies in their countries have collapsed and they need to find a place where they can make a living. There is a sense of desperation that one observes from these people because they cannot imagine any future for themselves and their children. Over the years there had been an influx of jobseekers from Mozambique, Zimbabwe, and other southern African countries into South Africa.

In 2008 South Africa witnessed unprecedented attacks on African foreign nationals by locals. There was a repeat of this phenomenon in 2015. There is a consensus of opinion that these attacks took a racial form as the focus was on African people.[28] For Sibusiso Tshabalala:

> At the heart of South Africa's complex problem with xenophobia is the loaded meaning of the term "foreigner." Pejoratively, the term "foreigner" in South Africa usually refers to African and Asian non-nationals. "Other" foreigners—particularly those from the Americas and Europe go unnoticed—they are often lumped up with "tourists," or even better, referred to as "expats."[29]

The focus of these attacks was on the poor foreign nationals who lived among the locals in the townships and informal settlements. Businesses belonging to Somalis and other foreign nationals were looted and sometimes burned down. There were cases where some people were beaten up and some even killed.

Such violence and violation of human rights and human dignity did not only affect foreign nationals but South African women who are married to some of these men and their children, thus the formation of wives' clubs as support networks like the United Nigerian Wives in South Africa. "The United Nigerian Wives in South Africa (UNWISA) club was set up two years ago to support wives who tell of being shunned by family and friends for falling in love with Africans from outside South Africa."[30] In fact, Gavaza Maluleke, writing on the construction of the xenophobia narrative in South Africa, pointed out that "for many local women married to foreign nationals, xenophobia is a daily experience in which they worry about their foreign partners as they go off to work because the attacks can occur at any time. One woman taking her sick children to hospital was asked by the female nurses, "Why are you giving these people residence papers?," which she felt was intended to degrade and discredit her choice of partner.[31] In the July 15, 2010, issue of the *Daily Maverick*, Tanya Pampalone introduced her readers to real people whose lives were ruined by these attacks.[32] These are people who had come to South Africa to make a living for themselves and their families but they watched all that going up in smoke.

HUMANIZATION OF WHITENESS

On the other hand, *Umlungu* ("white") is an interesting character. This character is associated with affluence, success, wealth, technological innovation, and modernity (*isimodeni*). In the South African context, this view is a legacy of colonialism and Apartheid.[33] In fact, "whiteness in South Africa seems to possess almost magical powers, continuing to determine and mark privilege and, connectedly yet distinctively, desirability."[34] Even though whites are implicated in the oppression and deprivation of black people in South Africa, they are the "desirable other." There are instances when a reference is made to *lomlungu unobuntu* (lit., "this white person has *ubuntu*"). In other words, there are some redeeming features in this alien. The idea of *umlungu* as a desirable other is promoted through advertising. The preference for whiteness and white imagery is even reflected in the advertising of condoms in Uganda. In fact, "the most popular images associated with condom commercials are; baggy jeans, Coca-Cola, rap music, and pale skin—not an 'ordinary' African life—but a certain 'it feels good' culture more typical of American MTV."[35]

Witchcraft discourse is a mechanism to smooth the tension between ethical ideals and reality. It is very useful in giving us a good understanding of the processes involved in including and excluding people. It explains why certain people are excluded. Evil, in African thought, does not live off and in itself, it is always embodied. It needs a body of a human or animal or witch familiar. The activities of witches stop people from becoming. Witches are said to operate in secret to plot against innocent members of society. They are perceived to have extraordinary powers to harm others. The impact of corruption, political instability, and economic collapse can be perceived the same way as that of the activities of the witches.

CONCLUSION

The IsiZulu phrase *umuntu akalahlwa* is a further explication of the ideal contained in *ubuntu*. A human person is said to have intrinsic value. Each person is endowed with a basket of gifts meant for the benefit of the community. Individualism is discouraged as it leads one to social isolation. The community is where a person fully realizes who they are. Archbishop Tutu referred to a person with *ubuntu* as someone who is open and always ready to affirm others. The community gives an individual all the social skills necessary for successfully realizing their potential. A person according to this ideal cannot be thrown out or disposed. Given all the good qualities that the person is endowed with, the person can be rehabilitated. According to this view, a human person cannot be ostracized or removed from society. However, South African communities systematically excluded foreign immigrants from their communities, thus opening a way for their attack.

Umuntu akalahlwa provides us with a useful framework for understanding and critiquing the xenophobic violence meted out to African foreign nationals by sections of the South African population in 2008 and 2015. In terms of African ethics and what is contained in *umuntu akalahlwa*, a human being should not cause the other pain and suffering. The only time where people are harmed is when they have been dehumanized, in other words, their *ubuntu* or humanity has been revoked. Such is done systematically to deny the other humanness. In the case of African foreign nationals living in South Africa, the violence was directed to the poorest of the poor, job seekers, small-business owners, and many others who found themselves situated down the socioeconomic ladder. The accusations leveled against them were meant to take away their humanity and blame most of the social ills, as well as the desperate condition of the South African poor, on them. Some of the accusations that were leveled are that they brought crime, drugs, and stole women or simply turned children into wives. All these accusations were meant to demonize African nationals and then provide "reasons" or justification for taking action against them. When the attacks occurred, the assailants were not attacking fellow human beings, but "demons" or inhuman subjects who were responsible for their desperate condition. The brutality with which the attacks were carried out bears testimony to the fact that they were "removing" a cancer that was destroying their communities.

The curious aspect of these attacks was that they were mainly directed at foreign African nationals. Reflecting on the xenophobic attacks in South Africa and the general displacement of people across the African continent, one is left with the question: "What happened to the ideals of *ubuntu* and pan-Africanism?" One of the ideals of pan-Africanism was to "contain rampant ethnic fissures"[36] in order to advance African unity. The incidents of xenophobia in South Africa, the Rwandan genocide, events in Darfur, and many others indicate the loss of humanity and a descent to the subhuman category. Children are recruited to become soldiers and are made to commit acts of terror against other people. *Umuntu akalahlwa* speaks to this situation very clearly. In Rwanda, neighbors turned on each other—the same was reported in some cases in South Africa. People who lived in the same place suddenly became strangers. The blame cannot be carried by people on the ground only, but some of the leaders across the continent have made things difficult for citizens. They acted in ways that stopped people from becoming.

NOTES

1. John S. Mbiti, *Introduction to African Religion* (London: Heinemann Educational Books, 1991).
2. Kofi Asare Opoku, "African Traditional Religion: An Enduring Heritage," in *Religious Plurality in Africa: Essays in Honour of John S. Mbiti*, ed. Jacob Olupona and Sulayman Nyang (New York: Mourton De Gruyter, 1993), 67–82.
3. Ogbu U. Kalu, "The Sacred Egg: Worldview, Ecology and Development in West Africa," in *Indigenous Traditions and Ecology*, ed. John A. Grim (Cambridge, MA: Harvard University Press, 2001), 228. See also Ogbu Kalu, *African Pentecostalism: An Introduction* (Oxford: Oxford University Press, 2008).
4. Kwesi Kwaa Prah, *Beyond the Colour Line: Pan-Africanist Disputations: Selected Sketches, Letters, Papers, and Reviews* (Trenton, NJ: Africa World Press, 1998), 69.
5. Oyekan Owomoyela, "With Friends like These . . . A Critique of Pervasive Anti-Africanisms in Current African Studies Epistemology and Methodology," *African Studies Review* 37/3 (1994): 78.
6. John L. Comaroff and Jean Comaroff, "On Personhood: Anthropological Perspectives from Africa," *Social Identities* 7/2 (2001): 267–83.
7. Comaroff and Comaroff, "On Personhood," 268.
8. Comaroff and Comaroff, "On Personhood," 268.
9. John S. Mbiti, *African Religions and Philosophy* (London: Heinemann, 1969).
10. Diane Ciekawy and Peter Geschiere, "Containing Witchcraft: Conflict Scenarios in Postcolonial Africa," *African Studies Review* 41/3 (1998): 5.

11. Gerrit Brand, "Witchcraft and Spirit Beliefs in African Christian Theology," *Exchange* 31/1 (2002): 44.

12. Comaroff and Comaroff, "On Personhood," 269.

13. Owomoyela, "With Friends like These," 88.

14. Kwasi Wiredu, "The Moral Foundations of an African Culture," in *Philosophy from Africa: A Text with Readings*, ed. P. H. Coetzee and A.P.J. Roux (New York: Routledge, 2002), 291.

15. Harvey Sindima, "Liberalism and African Culture," *Journal of Black Studies* 21/2 (1990): 190.

16. Sindima, "Liberalism and African Culture," 199.

17. Gabriel M. Setiloane, *African Theology: An Introduction* (Johannesburg: Skotaville, 1986).

18. Robin Horton, "On Rationality of Conversion," *Africa* 45/3 (1975): 231.

19. Chirevo V. Kwenda, "Beyond Patronage: Giving and Receiving in the Construction of Civil Society," in *Sameness and Difference: Problems and Potentials in South African Civil Society*, ed. James R. Cochrane and Bastienne Klein (Washington, DC: Council for Research in Values and Philosophy, 2000), 243–68.

20. John Oyotunde Isola Bewaji, "Ethics and Morality in Yoruba Culture," *A Companion to African Philosophy*, ed. Kwasi Wiredu (Malden, MA: Blackwell, 2004), 396.

21. Desmond Mpilo Tutu, *No Future without Forgiveness* (New York: Image Doubleday, 2000), 35.

22. Wiredu, "The Moral Foundations of an African Culture," 294.

23. Harvey C. Chidoba Banda, "Xenophobia as a Form of Human Insecurity: The Plight of Malawian Migrants in South Africa," *Southern African Peace & Security Studies* 2/2 (2013): 35.

24. "South African Xenophobia: Why Is There So Much Hatred of Foreigners?" *The Week*, <http://www.theweek.co.uk/63378/south-african-xenophobia-why-is-there-so-much-hatred-of-foreigners/> [Accessed: June 17, 2017].

25. Kwasi Wiredu, "Problems in Africa's Self-Definition in the Contemporary World," in *Person and Community: Ghanaian Philosophical Studies*, ed. Kwasi Wiredu and Kwame Gyekye (Washington, DC: Council for Research in Values and Philosophy, 1992), 59.

26. Wiredu, "Problems in Africa's Self-Definition," 62.

27. UNHCR, "Africa," <http://www.unhcr.org/africa.html/> [Accessed: June 17, 2017].

28. Hussein Solomon and Hitomi Kosaka, "Xenophobia in South Africa: Reflections, Narratives and Recommendations," *Southern African Peace & Security Studies* 2/2 (2013): 8.

29. Sibusiso Tshabalala, "Why Black South Africans Are Attacking Foreign Africans but Not Foreign Whites," April 15, 2015, <http://qz.com/384041/why-black-south-africans-are-only-attacking-foreign-africans-but-not-foreign-whites/> [Accessed: June 17, 2017].

30. "Wives' Club Fights South African Xenophobia after Attacks," *Times Alive*, April 30, 2015 <http://www.timeslive.co.za/local/article14643947.ece/>, [Accessed: June 17, 2017].

31. Gavaza Maluleke, "Women and the Xenophobia Narrative in South Africa," *OpenDemocracy*, August 20, 2015, <https://www.opendemocracy.net/gavaza-maluleke/women-and-xenophobia-narrative-in-south-africa/> [Accessed: June 17, 2017].

32. Tanya Pampalone, "Faces of Xenophobia: The Victims of 2008 Attacks," pt. 2, *Daily Maverick*, July 15, 2010, <https://www.dailymaverick.co.za/article/2010-07-15-faces-of-xenophobia-the-victims-part-2/#.WUU-o1X19hF/> , [Accessed: June 17, 2017].

33. African Men and Masculinities, "Are White Women Still the Epitome of Beauty in Post-Apartheid South Africa?" April 21, 2013, <https://newafricanmen.wordpress.com/2013/04/21/are-white-women-still-represented-as-the-epitome-of-beauty-in-post-Apartheid-south-africa-still/> [Accessed: June 17, 2017].

34. Kopano Ratele and Leswin Laubscher, "Making White Lives: Neglected Meanings of Whiteness from Apartheid South Africa," *Psychology in Society* 40 (2010): 84.

35. Emmanuel Katongole, "Postmodern Illusions and the Challenges of African Theology: The Ecclesial Tactics of Resistance," *Modern Theology* 16/2 (2000): 247.

36. Prah, *Beyond the Colour Line*, 86.

II

GENDER, SEXUALITY, AND SOCIAL COHESION

Seven

"I Am Born of a People Who Would Not Tolerate Oppression"[1]

The Role of Indian Women's Movements in Social Transformation

Rowanne Sarojini Marie

INTRODUCTION

In 1946 the poet B. D. Lalla wrote about the Indian female hawker drawing attention to the disliked label "Coolie Mary."[2] A verse of the poem reads:

> To thy door each bitter morning
> Cold or hot or wind a-storming
> Comes she with her breath a-panting[3]

The "Coolie Marys" of South African society have made huge contributions to the democracy that we enjoy as a rainbow notion. However, it has become evident that such documented histories of Indian women are few and far between or they were subsumed within broader histories. But these narratives carry a rich heritage and if they are lost altogether, then some critical principles of social transformation could potentially be buried with these hidden histories. Numerous narratives of the role of Indian women have gone untold or remain undocumented simply because it is taken for granted that these are covered within the greater historical annals. For the few that are recorded, this is done so within the cultural wrappings of the male encounter and experience. The depravation and lack of the female voice in these historical annals leave us, particularly Indian women, poorer for not having broader acquaintance to these remarkable narratives. As I excavate through these histories of the heroes of the struggle, brave women who were not prepared to be subjected to a life of oppression, I invite you to journey with me.

HISTORICAL BACKGROUND

Indian women, who arrived in South Africa in 1860 as indentured laborers to work on the sugarcane estates, mainly in Natal, came with the hope of finding a better life. On the contrary, historical records tell us that they entered into a life of physical torture, hardship, pain, slavery, and were subjected to oppression.[4] "In search for their fortune, they had not only found themselves indentured but they had transgressed fundamental cultural and social codes. Shame, disappointment, and dishonour weighed too heavily on the immigrants to allow them to keep in touch with their families, fraternities and villagers."[5] Having arrived in South Africa under such diverse and trying circumstances, the Indian community found itself at a point of no return, and was thus faced with the challenges of making a life in a land of broken promises and reformulating an identity as "settlers" in South Africa.[6]

The colonial oppression, traditional bondages, and patriarchal attitudes in which many Indian women found themselves had kept them limited to the domestic sphere, with a number of them engaging in hawking and market gardening, selling predominantly fresh fruit, vegetables, and flowers.[7] Around the 1920s in Natal, a number of Indian women had also become involved in weaving baskets which they sold either door-to-door or along the roadside.[8] By then, all Indian females gained the name "Coolie Mary," which was used by whites, since they had difficulty pronouncing Indian names.[9]

Unfortunately, women were restricted in the opportunities offered to them, and they were mainly confined to the sugar estate because of their skill and ability in the plantations, or alternatively, they were employed as domestic workers.[10] This often meant that the quality of food given to them was inferior compared to that of their male counterparts who found employment elsewhere, and they received only half the wages for the same amount of work done by men.[11]

For Indian women of that period, market gardening and hawking became a small, yet significant, source of income.[12] They were driven to these domestic means of income as a way to survive economically as many of them were living below the poverty line.[13] Walker highlights that between 1943 and 1944, a comparative assessment revealed that 70.6 percent of the Indians in Natal were living below the poverty line.[14] These poverty-stricken situations were confirmed by prominent political activist and medical practitioner Dr. Goonam, who vividly describes the extent of poverty amongst the Indian community, particularly felt by the women, as leaving them feeling helpless against such poverty.[15] Hence, it was such desperate situations that compelled Indian women to look for means of survival. Since formal work was not generally available to Indian women in South Africa, and also because many women did not have necessary skills for formal employment, they had no option but to resort to domestic labor for income and survival.

Alleyn Diesel,[16] who traces the stories of Indian women in South Africa, points out that many Indian women have interesting and sometimes compelling stories to tell and that they are remarkably articulate in telling these stories, which demonstrates their strength and determination in the face of adversity. She also argues that in recent years the documented stories of people in the so-called "previously disadvantaged" communities in South Africa have almost completely overlooked the experiences of Indian women.[17] Diesel is very cautious of the fact that some feminists believe that "privileged" white women should not write or "speak for" those women whose voices have been silenced by their oppressive circumstances.[18] However, this reservation is met only with enthusiasm and encouragement from Indian women themselves, hence she is encouraged to have such experiences documented.[19]

Indian women may have been dubbed "Coolie Mary," but they were under no circumstances prepared to remain with such an identity that kept them in subjugation. Instead, they began to rally together in resistance against such oppressive identities and sought ways to recraft their identities. The term "coolie" was used by colonialists for indentured laborers. It was derived from the Tamil word *kuli*, which referred to payment for menial work for persons without customary rights and who were at the lowest level in the industrial market. The term later transformed from *kuli* into *coolie*.[20]

Presently, we find that Indian women have begun to make great strides in education and the various fields of the economic sector. The Indian community recently celebrated 150 years since their arrival in South Africa, and it is remarkable to note that their story had progressed from arriving with a little suitcase on board the SS *Truro*, speaking very little or no English, to having made national impacts in all spheres of the country's livelihood. Indian women in South Africa have excelled in the fields of education, medicine, health care, business, science, religion, and theology as well as many other areas, but this was not without its challenges. The benefits enjoyed by contemporary women can be attributed to brave and courageous women of the indentured community who mustered together in the struggle.

INDIAN WOMEN'S RESISTANCE

Although Indian women were confined and docile, they were acutely aware of the oppression surrounding them. Desai notes that there were many of them who, contrary to tradition and culture, saw the need for women to be educated.[21] As an emblem of defiance against oppression, as early as 1907 Indian women formed the first movement called the Indian Women's Association (IWA), which was initiated by Tamil Christian women and was soon joined by women of other religious affiliations. "The IWA met monthly, with talks by women that aimed to provide 'moral and intellectual education.'"[22] Contrary to popular belief, these women were not meeting to drink chai and eat chapatti!

Unfortunately, the names of many of these women were not known, simply because the cultural practice was to address them by the names of their husbands.[23] Yet again, credit for the sterling work that Indian women had been involved in was sapped by those they were married to. Despite that, the IWA continued to grow and impact many women who were caught within cultural limitations and stereotypes, very often challenging these cultural limitations. Desai states:

> In the first year of existence, the IWA petitioned the education department to provide education for girls, the Colonial Secretary to repeal the "iniquitous" £3 tax[24] on women, started sewing classes. . . . The IWA considered it discriminatory to single out women. Members realised that they had "unbounded" work to perform in elevating the present position of women, therefore the support of all true sons and daughters of India is necessary.[25]

The impact of the IWA spilled off onto yet another form of mass action on October 21, 1913, where Transvaal Indian women *satyagrahis* began defiance activities by hawking without licenses in Vereeniging. They were not arrested. They crossed the Natal border and encouraged the miners in Newcastle to join this resistance campaign.[26] In addition to the unjust taxation, a fresh grievance came to light which worked as a catalyst to this mass action. In March 1913, the Cape Supreme Court ruled that all marriages not performed according to Christian rites were illegal. This meant that most Indian marriages were regarded as invalid, thus, making their children illegitimate and depriving them of inheritance.[27] Naturally, this deeply agitated the women.

On November 6, 1913, at 0630, Mohandas Karamchand (MK) Gandhi leads the Great March, which includes 127 women. In this group was sixteen-year-old Valliamma Mudaliar, who was arrested along with others and sentenced to three months rigorous imprisonment in Pietermaritzburg jail. Since Mudaliar is young and cannot not cope with the rigors of prison life, (which includes inhuman treatment at the hands of the jailors), she falls seriously ill and becomes bedridden. Gandhi secures Valliamma Mudaliar's release before the expiry of her jail term. But by then her life is hanging by a thread. On February 22, 1914, sixteen-year-old Valliamma Mudaliar dies in her house in Johannesburg of a fever contracted in prison.[28]

The South African Indian Congress (SAIC) was unofficially formed in 1919 to support the interests of the Indian community. It became an official organ in 1923 and a women's movement emerged out of this. This was necessary in view of the upsurge of anti-Indian agitation in the European community and moves to enact legislation to segregate Indians.

In each of these movements and events of resistance were prominent "propellers" who were at the forefront of steering such activities of defiance and promoted women's rights, in particular, their rights to education. For example, there was Dr. Kesaveloo Goonam Naidoo, a Tamil woman who was the first Indian woman doctor in South Africa. She was unfortunately not allowed to study medicine in South Africa and as a twenty-two-year-old woman, she took a flight to the United Kingdom and headed for Scotland to study medicine. She returned to South Africa, and when she had applied to practice at government hospitals was turned down with the response that white nurses would not take instructions from a black doctor. She then set up her medical practice in 1936. Dr. Goonam, in her autobiography *Coolie Doctor*, relates the hardships endured by Indian women who wanted to educate themselves.[29]

Education has always been very important to Indians.[30] It was seen as the major route to upward social mobility to attain better jobs in industry and the professions. However, the tradition of not educating female children was quite strong in the initial years of the arrival of indentured Indians. Ebr-Vally gives an account of one of the first schools, St. Aidan's Mission Springfield School, around 1900, where there was a record of only one female pupil.[31] One of the greatest fears that elderly traditional Indian folk in South Africa often expressed was that education would influence Indian girls to work and that in turn would lead them "astray," hence it was better for them to remain domesticated. But strong, brave women like Dr. Goonam were not prepared to remain within such cultural repression and transitioned from being "Coolie Mary" to being "Coolie Doctor." Goonam constantly declared that the lot of Indian women was not just to remain in domestic spheres as "Coolie Mary" and she inspired Indian women in South Africa to be motivated by the example of women in India who were in the vanguard of the freedom struggle. Being at the forefront of the resistance movement, she herself was imprisoned seventeen times, together with a number of other comrades.[32]

Interestingly, when Dr. Goonam approached the Natal Indian Congress to seek representation for women within the organization, she was told that Indian women were not sufficiently advanced to receive representation.[33] Clearly, as already noted, the oppression and enslavement suffered by these women were a result of the internal cultural practices, as well as external factors, which excluded them from social life. Ela Gandhi asserts that women's struggles take place on two fronts, the first being the stepping out of cultural and traditional understandings of gender roles, while the second deals with institutional power in various spheres.[34] Hence these were the types of factors that drove Indian women to formulate their own movements.

By the 1950s other emerging Indian women leaders and activists such as Fatima Meer, Zainab Asvat, and Amina Pahad joined the nonracial Federation of South African Women in their struggle for democracy for all.[35] As the decades have gone by, we have found that Indian women were at the forefront of such political activity because of the oppressive circumstances they found themselves in.[36] These women were not prepared to settle for an identity that kept them suppressed and in servitude, nor were they prepared to remain as basket women. Their plight to resist an oppressive identity and to recraft their own identities was what drove and motivated them to rally into women's movements.

THE ROLE OF RELIGION IN MOBILIZING WOMEN

Religion, in particular Christianity, was an important factor in bringing women together and served as a unifying force amongst them. By its very nature, church structures created forums and opened spaces where women met as large gatherings.[37] Even though the Bible and Christianity are seen as legitimizing the exclusion that women encounter due to patriarchal interpretations, it is also recognized as having the potential to liberate women.[38] Say Pa asserts that Indian women often find fresh ways of reading the Bible that can release them from such marginalization and exclusion.[39] Biblical anecdotes depict themes such as freedom, liberation, equality: "one body in Christ," "there is neither Jew nor Gentile," "there is neither male nor female in Christ"; such clichés offered women the bravery to resist oppression of all forms.

The church has also cradled the most prolific African women's organization, namely, the *Manyano*.[40] Although this is not within the scope of this chapter, one cannot speak of Christian women's movements without acknowledging the dynamic role played by the Manyano.

But to keep faithful to a homogenous group, this chapter focuses specifically on the resistance initiated by Indian women. It must be noted that South African experience points to women of various class and religious affiliations who were actively involved in the struggle against oppression of all sorts. Women did not necessarily gather as religious groups, but religion itself, e.g., Christianity, offered a platform for women to assemble together. Each of these religious groups would require a dedicated chapter in itself in order to do justice to the dynamic role played by various religious groups. However, for the purpose of this chapter, the role of Christianity in particular will be briefly addressed.

As mentioned above, the IWA, which was formed in 1907, was started by Tamil Christian women. The work of Joy Brain (1983) was one of the earlier historical and statistical accounts of Christian Indians in Natal from the period 1860 to 1911. Brain records that of the 152,184 Indian immigrants between 1860 and 1911, 2,150, i.e., 1.4 percent were identified as being Christian.[41] Desai notes that the SS *Truro*, which carried 340 indentured laborers, brought with it an estimated eighty-seven Christians.[42] The historical account of Brain asserts that the first ten to disembark from the Truro and set foot on Natal soil constituted two Christian families.[43] Although Indian women were supposedly confined and docile, there were many who, contrary to tradition and culture, saw the need for women to be educated. Desai attributes this to Christian families who were at the forefront of the drive to educate women.[44] He illustrates this with the example of Miss Stephens, who was the first Indian nurse in Durban in 1914, and the Lawrence sisters, all of whom qualified in various fields such as education and music. It was Sylvia Lawrence who became a lecturer at Springfield Teachers Training College and introduced music education to Indian schools.[45]

The individual stories of Indian women have been subsumed within the larger narrative of oppression. It is for this purpose that scholars like Govinden[46] intentionally trace the histories of these women who have left an imprint on the generations to follow. One such woman that Govinden traces is Kunwarani Lady Gunwati Maharaj Singh, an Anglican woman who is said to have made an important contribution to the development of women in colonial Natal.[47] Inasmuch as the Kunwarani[48] made such significant contributions toward mobilizing women to improve their oppressive conditions, not much of this has been documented. She is generally mentioned in the written records of her illustrious husband, Kunwar Sir Maharaj Singh, who came as an agent general to South Africa in 1932. One could only imagine that all that was mentioned of her was that she was the wife of the Kunwar, without giving details of her involvement and tireless work to champion the cause of Indian women in colonial Natal. However, upon quarrying further, one finds that for a woman of her time, where the education of girls was not actively promoted, the Kunwarani came from an exceptional educational background. She completed her teacher's diploma at the University of London in 1917, and unlike the women of her time, she married at the age of twenty-nine. She also lectured in history and literature at the Isabella Thoburn College, which was attached to the University of Allahabad.[49] In addition, she wrote a number of research papers on women, some for which she received awards. Her role in South Africa was not just for the social uplift of women, but also greatly impacted on the Anglican Church (particularly St. Paul's Anglican Church in Durban, where she and her husband were members). She worked tirelessly to promote women's visibility in her attempts to improve their status and to expand conceptual spaces for them. She also saw the need to address social and religious barriers and began to focus on the mission of the church during a time when women played a subordinate role in church and society. Coming from another continent, but deeply understanding colonial oppression, the Kunwarani became part of a body of women who shared in a common sisterhood and experienced a common faith.

Other heroes such as Phyllis Naidoo, born into a strong Methodist home in 1928, added colossal value to the active role of Indian women. From her early formative years, her experiences did not allow her to simply take things for granted. When she was just ten years old, her father, Simon David, a school principal, took her to an Institute of Race Relations conference in Pietermaritzburg, at which she was to serve tea.[50] At this conference she became acutely aware of the evils of racism, and began to mobilize a number of women's associations, awakening women to the ills of oppression. Even though she was sent to Robben Island and was in exile in some seven different countries, this did not stop her from her role of activism propelling social transformation. She published seven books and wrote several papers.

Such remains the context of many other Indian women, whose contributions and active involvement become muffled within the wrappings of "his-story." Other such narratives of influential Indian women often go untold or undocumented simply because it is taken for granted that these are covered within the greater historical annals. What does get recorded is the male encounter and experience. The depravation and lack of female voices in these historical annals leave us, particularly Indian women, the poorer for not having full exposure to these amazing narratives. However, we find that through up-and-coming female scholars, more intentional research is being done and there is a concerted effort to document the experiences of Indian women in South Africa.

From this background, one understands that when Indian women make strides and take the risk of breaking beyond the barriers of culture, this marks a victory. Indian women were fearlessly venturing into terrain where they were once considered inferior. As we see the numbers increasing in terms of Indian Christian women involved in the education and health sectors, various forms of church ministry, those who are ordained as full-time priests, as well as those who are becoming more involved in theological studies, it serves as a reminder that those who have gone ahead have created space for those who follow.

INTERESTS AND NEEDS?

When Indian women formed movements such as the IWA, they not were just meeting as a social group but they came together for a greater purpose and with particular "needs" and "interests." This is what gender planners now term Strategic Gender Interests and Practical Gender Needs. Hence, as early as 1907, these women were strategically engaging in gender planning and addressing critical issues related to interests and needs, though they may not have termed it as such. Moser succinctly argues that gender planning is not an end in itself but "a means by which women, through a process of empowerment, can emancipate themselves."[51] Practical gender needs relate to physical conditions and immediate needs: food, shelter, work, water, and so forth. These needs relate to access. Strategic gender interests relate to status in society—for instance in terms of access to employment, inheritance, mobility, political or social participation—based on gender. These needs relate to control.

It was Maxine Molyneux who developed the notion of "interests" within the WID (Women in Development) era.[52] She argued that the planning for low-income women in the Third World must be based on their interests—in other words, their prioritized concerns.[53] Molyneux differentiated amongst three specific interests, thus developing a threefold conceptualization, namely, women's interests, strategic gender interests, and practical gender interests. Having identified the different interests of women, Molyneux argued that it is possible to translate them into planning needs; in other words, the means by which their concerns may be satisfied. Molyneux described gender interests as "those that women may develop by virtue of their social positioning through gender attributes."[54] Gender interests can be either practical and/or strategic, each being derived in a different way and each involving different implications for women's subjectivity.

Almost a decade later, Caroline Moser developed the notion of Practical Gender Needs (PGNs) and Strategic Gender Interests (SGIs) by referring predominantly to PGNs and SGNs with the rationale that an interest defined as "prioritised concern" translates into a need.[55] Moser differentiated clearly between gender planning, which focused on the power relationships, and gender-conscious planning, which primarily takes account of women's problems and leaves the existing planning methods relatively untouched.[56] An underlying rationale to clearly demarcating these interests and needs is that men and women not only play various and different roles in society with distinct levels of control over their resources, but also that they often have different needs.

As such, PGNs are those needs that have been identified by women within their socially defined roles as a response to an immediate perceived necessity (e.g., inadequacies in their living conditions such as the provision and accessibility of water, health care, and employment). In contrast, SGIs vary by context and are identified by women as a result of their subordinate social status. They tend to challenge gender divisions of labor, power, and control, as well as traditionally defined norms and roles (e.g., legal rights, domestic violence, equal wages, and women's control over their bodies).

PGNs are those formulated from the concrete, tangible conditions women experience, and they are usually in response to immediate perceived necessity identified by women within a particular context. Practical gender needs are determined inductively, are seen as a direct reaction to problems and interests that are perceived as being immediate, and they are based on social conventions such as the gender-specific division of labor and the roles it allocates to women. Although some may argue that no one agrees on how to define the notion of women's interests given the interactions of race, class, and other objective and subjective interests, there are common threads that bind their narratives together emerging out of their lived experiences.

What does become clear is that as early as 1907, Indian women were conscious of their "needs" and "interests" and used these movements as a vehicle to address what we today would call practical gender needs and strategic gender interests. In addition to considering their immediate practical needs evident by their impoverished situations, these women were also engaging critically on issues of women's land rights, access to education, employment opportunities, political representation, health issues, and to a large extent gender roles, as well as cultural stereotypes, which, for example, did not encourage females to be educated.

WHAT INSPIRED WOMEN'S RESISTANCE?

One of the early movements was the IWA, which was initiated by Tamil Christian women. The Christian religion itself created structures for such mass gatherings of women, which became a forum for women to rally together. Many of these women were deeply inspired and impacted by Gandhi and his teachings. Women could not have asked for a better champion than Gandhi since he was "sensitive to their imposed indignity, and conscious of their worth, he wove women's needs into the fabric of the fight for freedom."[57] It was mainly Gandhi's philosophy of *Satyagraha*[58] that inspired Indian women. *The reason that Satyagraha* was said to have *found favor among the Indians was that it marshaled their innermost resources, thereby giving them the dignity that their legal disabilities sought to deny.*

The notion of *Satyagraha* conveys that "physical force is forbidden even in the most favourable circumstances."[59] Gandhi officially used the term *Satyagraha* for the first time in South Africa at the beginning 1907. This was when he organized opposition to the Asiatic Registration Law (the Black Act), requiring that all Indians, young and old, men and women, get fingerprinted and keep registration documents on them at all times. Gandhi advised the Indian community to refuse to submit to this indignity even if this meant them being imprisoned for "defying the law."[60] Interestingly, the term *Satyagraha* is very often used as a synonym of "passive resistance," but Gandhi himself clarifies this and states that there is a distinction between the two. He writes the following is a letter:

> I have drawn the distinction between passive resistance as understood and practised in the West and *Satyagraha* before I had evolved the doctrine of the latter to its full logical and spiritual extent. I often used "passive resistance" and "satyagraha" as synonymous terms: but as the doctrine of *Satyagraha* developed, the expression "passive resistance" ceases even to be synonymous.[61]

Gandhi shows in his writings that "passive resistance" by its very nature has defects that are seen in every movement that passes by that name. But he also asserts that at times the term passive resistance has been mismatched, citing the example Jesus Christ, who has indeed been acclaimed as the prince of passive resisters. He submits that in the case of Jesus Christ, passive resistance must mean *Satyagraha* and *Satyagraha* alone. There are not many cases in history of passive resistance in that sense. The phrase passive resistance was not employed to denote the patient suffering of oppression by thousands of devout Christians in the early days of Christianity. Gandhi asserts that he would therefore class them as *Satyagrahis*.[62] And if their conduct is described as passive resistance, passive resistance in that case becomes synonymous with *Satyagraha*. But Gandhi's object was to show that *Satyagraha* is essentially different from what people generally mean in English by the phrase passive resistance.[63] He further clarifies that:

1. Passive resistance has admitted of violence as in the case of the suffragettes[64] and has been universally acknowledged to be a weapon of the weak.
2. Moreover, passive resistance does not necessarily involve complete adherence to truth under every circumstance.

3. Therefore, it is different from *Satyagraha* in three essentials: *Satyagraha* is a weapon of the strong; *Satyagraha* admits of no violence under any circumstance whatsoever; and it ever insists upon truth.

Gandhi rejected the idea that injustice should, or even could, be fought against "by any means necessary"—if you use violent, coercive, unjust means, whatever ends you produce will necessarily embed that injustice. The theory of *Satyagraha* sees means and ends as inseparable. The means used to obtain an end are wrapped up in and attached to that end. Therefore, it is contradictory to try to use unjust means to obtain justice or to try to use violence to obtain peace.[65] Gandhi, who was deeply inspired by the life and teachings of Christ, became a catalyst of and laid a strong foundation for women's resistance.

CONCLUSION

As we unearth the hidden histories of Indian women in South Africa, we discover brave women who had an innate tenacity to reject oppression. Through the role of individual women, various Indian women's movements were propelled that played a crucial role in transforming the lives of women. It transformed them from being "Coolie Mary" into new identities that expressed their worth and significance as women. When women were energized into such critical masses, they came together with a clear and definite purpose, and were not congregating as a social group.

Religion and Christianity, in particular, played a very significant role, creating the platform and offering fearlessness for women to gather as mass movements. Although these were not politically driven at that stage, it gave room for women to address their needs and interests. These movements were transformative and life giving, and were largely instituted on the principles of *Satyagraha*. Whereas Gandhi served as a catalyst, there were many brave, unsung woman heroes of the struggle who remained unwavering to the cause despite the harsh and despotic conditions that they encountered. Much of the freedoms and access that all South African women enjoy today can be attributed to such brave women who mobilized mass action.

While many of the narratives of these brave women who mobilized such movements remain hidden histories, they have left us with three important principles worth revisiting in our ongoing plight to transform communities, namely, "truth," "strength" and "nonviolence." As contemporary women of a rainbow nation, we pay tribute to resilient yet unsung Indian women who carved an inscription in the historical chronicles of social transformation.

NOTES

1. Title borrowed from Thabo Mbeki's "I Am an African" speech.
2. Rehana Ebr-Vally, *Kala Pani: Caste and Colour in South Africa* (Cape Town: Kwela Books, 2001), 51.
3. Ebr-Vally, *Kala Pani*, 51.
4. Rowanne Marie, "Across the Kala Pani: Untold Stories of Indian Christian Women in South Africa," *Oral History Journal of South Africa* 2/1 (2014): 89–101.
5. Ebr-Vally, *Kala Pani*, 138.
6. Nesen Pillay, ed., *The Indian South Africans* (Pinetown, South Africa: Owen Burgess, 1989), 148.
7. Kalpana Hiralal, "Docile Indian Women Protest—We Shall Resist: Passive Resistance in South Africa 1946–1948," *Journal of Social Science* 22/3 (2010): 153–62.
8. Ebr-Vally, *Kala Pani*, 150.
9. Ebr-Vally, *Kala Pani*, 150.
10. Uma Dhupelia-Mesthrie, *From Cane Fields to Freedom: A Chronicle of Indian South African Life* (Cape Town: Kwela Books, 2000), 8.
11. Dhupelia-Mesthrie, *From Cane Fields to Freedom*, 14.
12. Ebr-Vally, *Kala Pani*, 52.
13. Ebr-Vally, *Kala Pani*, 52.
14. Cherryl Walker, *Women and Resistance in South Africa* (Cape Town: David Philip, 1991), 71.
15. Kesaveloo Goonaruthnum Naidoo, *Coolie Doctor: An Autobiography* (Durban: Madiba Publishers, 1991), 155.
16. Alleyn Diesel is not Indian but examines the experiences of Indian women in South Africa, particularly those in KwaZulu-Natal.
17. Alleyn Diesel, *Shakti: Stories of Indian Women in South Africa* (Johannesburg: University of the Witwatersrand, 2007), 5.
18. Diesel, *Shakti*, 5.
19. Diesel, *Shakti*, 5.
20. Ashwin Desai, *Inside Indian Indenture: A South Africa Story, 1860–1914,* (Cape Town: HSRC Press, 2010), 78.
21. Desai, *Inside Indian Indenture*, 227.
22. Desai, *Inside Indian Indenture*, 278.
23. Desai, *Inside Indian Indenture*, 278.
24. Up to 1913 a compulsory annual tax was imposed on every Indian male of sixteen years and over and every Indian female of thirteen years and over who failed to reindenture or to return to India. See Y. S. Meer, *Documents of Indentured Labour: Natal 1851–1917* (Durban: Institute of Black Research, 1980).
25. Desai, *Inside Indian Indenture*, 278.
26. S.A.I. Tirmizi, *Indian Sources for African History* (New Delhi: Manohar, 1989), 9.
27. Ashwin Desai, "The 1946–1948 Passive Resistance Campaign in Natal, South Africa: Origins and Results," in *1913, Satyagraha: Passive Resistance and Its Legacy,* ed. Devarakshanam Betty Govinden and Kalpana Hiralal (New Delhi: Manohar, 2015), 85–103.

28. "Valliamma Munuswamy Mudaliar, SA Political Activist Dies from a Fever," South African History Online, <http://www.sahistory.org.za/dated-event/valliamma-munuswamy-mudaliar-sa-political-activist-dies-fever/> [Accessed: June 18, 2017].

29. Naidoo, *Coolie Doctor*, 102.

30. Ebr-Vally, *Kala Pani*, 185.

31. Ebr-Vally, *Kala Pani*, 158.

32. Naidoo, *Coolie Doctor*, 113.

33. Naidoo, *Coolie Doctor*, 100.

34. Ela Gandhi, "The 1913 Women's Marches: Learning from the Past," in *1913, Satyagraha: Passive Resistance and Its Legacy*, ed. Devarakshanam Betty Govinden and Kalpana Hiralal (New Delhi: Manohar, 2015), 259–73.

35. Shireen Hassim, *Women's Organisations and Democracy in South Africa: Contesting Authority* (Madison, WI: University of Wisconsin Press, 2006).

36. Under the tutelage of her father, Zainab Asvat became politically active at a very young age. On June 13, 1946, resisters set up camp on the plot at the corner of Umbilo Road and Gale Street, waiting to be arrested—these included Zainab Asvat, Zohra Bhayat, Amina Pahad, Zubeida Patel of Johannesburg and Mrs. Lakshmi Govender and Mrs. Veeramah Pather. "Zainab Asvat," South African History Online, <http://www.sahistory.org.za/people/zainab-asvat/> [Accessed: June 18, 2017].

37. For example, the first recorded meeting of the Methodist Women in the Transvaal Province (Gauteng) was held in Berea in 1907 concerning the possibility of organizing the work of women in the various Methodist churches. The outcome of a similar Pretoria 1908 meeting resulted in a united organization of isolated branches called the Transvaal Methodist Women's Association. "Women's Association," <https://www.methodist.org.za/organisations/womens-association/> [Accessed: June 18, 2017].

38. Anna May Say Pa, "Reading Ruth 3:1–5 from an Asian Women's Perspective," in *Engaging the Bible in a Gendered World: An Introduction to Feminist Biblical Interpretation in Honour of Katharine Doob Sakenfeld*, ed. Linda Day and Carolyn Pressler (Louisville, KY: Westminster John Knox Press, 2006), 47–59.

39. Say Pa, "Reading Ruth," 48.

40. Fatima Meer, "Women in the Apartheid Society," <http://www.anc.org.za/content/women-apartheid-society/> [Accessed: June 18, 2017].

41. Joy Brain, *Christian Indians in Natal 1860–1911* (Cape Town: Oxford University Press, 1983), 247.

42. Desai, *Inside Indian Indenture*, 278.

43. Brain, *Christian Indians in Natal*, 12.

44. Desai, *Inside Indian Indenture*, 227.

45. Desai, *Inside Indian Indenture*, 277.

46. Devarakshanam Betty Govinden, 2002. "Out of the Purdah Club: The Contribution of Kunwarani Lady Gunwati Maharaj Singh in Colonial Natal," in *Her-Stories: Hidden Histories of Women of Faith in Africa*, ed. Isabel Apawo Phiri, Sarojini Nadar, and Devarakshanam Betty Govinden (Pietermaritzburg, South Africa: Cluster Publications, 2002), 262–78.

47. Govinden, "Out of the Purdah Club," 262.

48. According to Govinden, the titles Kunwar and Kunwarani are equivalent to "The Honorable," and came to be used for this agent general and his wife. Govinden, "Out of the Purdah Club," 277.

49. Govinden, "Out of the Purdah Club," 267.

50. "Phyllis Naidoo," South African History Online, <http://www.sahistory.org.za/people/phyllis-naidoo/> [Accessed: June 18, 2017].

51. Caroline Moser, *Gender Planning and Development: Theory, Practice and Training* (London: Routledge, 1993), 190.

52. Maxine Molyneux, "Mobilisation without Emancipation? Women's Interests, State and Revolution in Nicaragua," *Feminist Studies* 11 (1985): 227–54.

53. Molyneux, "Mobilisation without Emancipation," 232.

54. Molyneux, "Mobilisation without Emancipation," 232.

55. Moser, *Gender Planning and Development*, 37.

56. Moser, *Gender Planning and Development*, 37.

57. Lynn Norvell, "Gandhi and the Indian Women's Movement," *British Library Journal* 23/1 (1997): 12–27.

58. *Satyagraha* was a movement started by Mohandas K. Gandhi; the word derives from the Sanskrit language and loosely translates as "insistence on truth" (*satya*, "truth"; *agraha*, "insistence" or "holding firmly to") or holding onto truth or truth force. At times, Gandhi also referred to it as love-force or soul-force. The term *satyagraha* was coined and developed by Gandhi (1869–1948).

59. Mohandas K. Gandhi, *Satyagraha in South Africa*, trans. from Gujarati by V. G. Desai (Ahmedabad, India: Navajivan, 1928), 96–98.

60. "Mohandas Karamchand Gandhi," South African History Online, <http://www.sahistory.org.za/people/mohandas-karamchand-gandhi/> [Accessed: June 18, 2017].

61. "05. The Science of Satyagraha," *Selected Works of Mahatma Gandhi*, vol. XVI, p. 509, 25-1-1920, <http://www.mkgandhi.org/selectedletters/05science_of_satyagraha.html/> [Accessed: June 18, 2017].

62. A *Satyagrahi* (a person using *Satyagraha*) would resist the injustice by refusing to follow an unjust law. In doing so, he would not be angry, would put up freely with physical assaults to his person and the confiscation of his property, and would not use foul language to smear his opponent. A practitioner of *Satyagraha* also would never take advantage of an opponent's problems. "Mohandas Karamchand Gandhi," South African History Online, <http://www.sahistory.org.za/people/mohandas-karamchand-gandhi/> [Accessed: June 18, 2017].

63. "44. Gandhi Explains 'Satyagraha,'" South African History Online, <http://www.sahistory.org.za/archive/44-gandhi-explains-satyagraha/> [Accessed: June 18, 2017].

64. Suffragettes were members of women's organizations in the UK in the late nineteenth and early twentieth centuries that advocated the extension of the franchise, or the right to vote in public elections, to women. The movement became militant and radical with much property damage.

65. Scott Couper, "But Let Us Remember Him Then and Never Forget," in 1913, *Satyagraha: Passive Resistance and Its Legacy*, ed. Devarakshanam Betty Govinden and Kalpana Hiralal (New Delhi: Manohar, 2015), 139–79.

EIGHT

Identity Construction of African Women in the Midst of Land Dispossession

Maserole Kgari-Masondo

INTRODUCTION

Central development in South Africa's past has pivoted on issues surrounding land and identity. There have been active attempts to dispossess the conquered from their land, to reshape it, and to describe or imagine the land in the mental paradigm of the white settlers, and this in the process affected peoples' identity, especially African women.[1] African women were the ones hit hard by forced removals because their livelihood depended on working the land. Losing land meant that they lost their identity and had to reconstruct it in the new area. White groups used land appropriation as a weapon of control and as a means to improve their society at the expense of the dispossessed. The term "African" in this essay refers to all indigenous people of South Africa i.e., Sotho-Tswana, Nguni, Tsonga, Venda, and the Khoi-San.[2]

This chapter addresses the land dispossession and its ramification to the identity of the Sotho-Tswana women of Ga-Rankuwa who were displaced from Lady Selborne in the 1960s. Lady Selborne, currently known as Suideberg, was located in Pretoria, founded in 1905, and destroyed by Group Areas legislation in the 1960s. As Carruthers has shown, the township was unusual in the history of South African urbanization in being an area in which Africans could hold title to land through the Urban Areas Act of 1923 and the Native Areas Amendment Act of 1937.[3] The Sotho-Tswana women of Lady Selborne who were resettled in Ga-Rankuwa, as with all other victims of forced removals, have a painful history that ripped apart their community spirit, attachment to the environment, identity, and their self-esteem.[4] In this instance, forced removals were anti-African women, anti-indigenous knowledge process, and bolstered the European political, economic, environmental, and cultural identities.

In this chapter, identity refers to how women view themselves and how others view them. Identity is a basic component of human social relations—to each other and the environment. The literature shows that, although forced removals and land alienation have received historiographical attention, they have received little analysis through the socio-environmental lens and identity domain in relation to African women. The environmental, indigenous approach and identity dimension has been lacking in such investigations and this chapter will contribute to filling that academic gap. This is part of the socio-environmental history and indigenous knowledge initiative that is growing in historiographical weight in South Africa. This chapter seeks to contribute by its investigation of changing perceptions of social identity of the women of Lady Selborne who were relocated in Ga-Rankuwa in the 1960s.[5]

METHOD AND APPROACH

The study draws on social identity theory which derives group membership and its implications to identity formation.[6] Tajfel argues that the essence of identity is comparison, whereby the people compare with similar others in the course of social encounters based on social categorizations. These classifications are by its actual nature stereotypically based since they mark out the approved boundaries of group membership.[7] According to Tajfel and Turner, the main reason behind intergroup comparison is based on the need for positive social identity.[8] Identity construction is a work in progress; it is not rigid. Hence Smit maintains that identity construction of women is multiple.[9]

The study also draws on Merchant's idea of ecological theory, which considers "the relation between human beings and the non-human world as reciprocal, when humans alter their surroundings, "'nature' responds to those changes through laws."[10] This view to nature is applicable to the Sotho-Tswana environmental ideals. As put by Worster, Cronon, and Jacobs, the environment does not just represent a historical backdrop, but is an agent in its own right, providing a "material base for the power to dominate others" as well as the "power to endure domination."[11]—meaning that the environment plays an active part in life's component. Hence, in the Sotho-Tswana language environment is described as having power (*matla)* because it is *lefa* (inheritance) from ancestors.

Language plays a major role in identity construction. As suggested by Giles, language has been used by ethnic clusters to assert their positive uniqueness from other groups. It is thus important to "re-language" African concepts so as they can be understood as they are within the English language. "Re-languaging" is part of the Africanist approach, which has also provided an intellectual foundation for this study, which insists on the agency of Africans. Feminism also advocates for such agency of women in making their own history. The Sotho-Tswana define nature as *tlhago,* that "which is created." The term also includes *lefatshe* (land) and everything in it which is environment. For Africans "nature" is an inclusive term that goes beyond merely what is seen and touched. Nature is biography of the imagination of being—being that is deeply embedded in the collective unconscious of those who lost their original space through colonization. Thus, *thlago* and *lefatshe* go beyond Eurocentric understanding of nature. *Tlhago* is revelation of creation in any space called "home." This is because "traditionally, among Batswana, there is no clear distinction between the sacred and the profane, the spiritual and the material, the celestial and the purely mundane, that which is above and that which is below, for all things are summed up in *Modimo,* the Creator and Sustainer of the universe."[12] The research uses a phenomenological approach, which is qualitative. Phenomenology endeavors to apprehend people's insights, perspectives, and understandings of a specific situation (or phenomenon).[13] The genre allows the researcher to produce rich information and to understand community beliefs from within and not judge their beliefs or practices.[14] Tosh mentions a major limitation of interviews when he states that "it is naive to suppose that the testimony represents a pure distillation of past experience, for in an interview each party is affected by the other."[15] So this methodology is used in this study in conjunction with archival and other secondary sources in order to fill the gaps created by informants' forgetting and the myths created by their nostalgia. Open-ended interviews were employed in this study because, in my experience, many interviewees prefer open discussions to a prescribed format and thus much information is attained via this process. In keeping with the research ethics, all the names of the interlocutors in this chapter are pseudonyms.

Interviews were conducted in Ga-Rankuwa in 2004, 2006, and lastly in 2014, mainly among the Sotho-Tswana women community who were forcibly removed from Lady Selborne between 1960 and 1969. For the purpose of this project, women were the focus group in order to understand how forced removals affected their identity construction. The researcher had to redo interviews at different intervals with the same informants to fill the gaps that were encountered while transcribing data. Twelve women were interviewed over the age of forty-five. The fact that I had to redo interviews on different intervals helped in trustworthiness of the data collected. The number chosen was determined by the availability and the quality of the information required for the project, as Cohen, Manion, and Morrison have argued that in qualitative research there are no clear rules on the size of the sample; size is informed by "fitness for purpose."[16] The study also draws on Merchant's idea of ecological theory, which considers "the relation[ship] between human beings and the non-human world as reciprocal, when humans alter surroundings, 'nature' responds to those changes through laws.[17] A tape recorder was avoided because, though useful, it tends to intimidate informants.

SOTHO-TSWANA WOMEN AND IDENTITY CONSTRUCTION

Women classification in Sesotho and Setswana falls under *mo—ba*, (*mo-sadi—basadi*), while they are classified under other categories if deemed less than human. Ellenberger argues that the Sotho-Tswana word *motho* (human being) indicates "the power of speech, a speaking being distinct from monkeys or baboons, which have something like human shape, but cannot speak."[18] For example, a prevocal baby girl is called *ngwanyana* but is termed *mosetsana* after speech is learned, conjecturing they are human. Thus, denial of "speech" via disenfranchisement and other rights implies a loss of humanness. The Apartheid-induced devaluing of a human being is explained by Ngubane as "a sense of translation into experience the pessimistic and devaluative view of being human" because it led to widespread degradation of African women's self-esteem.[19] Ngubane also emphasizes the dynamic nature of self-perception and its reliance on social context.[20]

The Sotho-Tswana ideology toward the environment and land issues "was a positive one which embraced and connected the individual to the environment via interwoven physical spiritual and cultural links"—it helped women identity construction.[21] This stems from the fact that the Sotho-Tswana perceive *motho* as part of nature and nature as *motho*'s companion from the origin of humanity.[22] This is based on their myth of origin which at its heart lies identity construction. The Sotho-Tswana believe that the first people and animals emerged from the "the hole in the ground."[23] The Batswana locate the hole at Ga-Ditshweni (lit., "the Place of the Baboons") in Bophuthatswana in the eastern Free State.[24]

Gender roles played an important role in defining the Sotho-Tswana's relationship with the land and environment. Women often performed traditional roles as food-producing agriculturalists, and some were ecologists who performed rainmaking rituals but they were continually subjugated.[25] Women as rainmakers played the role of environmental nurturers.[26] Such high-profile women are termed as *basadisadi* (real women) because of their influential position in society. According to Guy, the history of women in South Africa is one of oppression, and the nature of that oppression is dynamic and has undergone qualitative change over time.[27] Such change is also portrayed in their identity construction.

Women in the precolonial era had to contribute to agricultural labor directly through their own labor and indirectly through fertility, and got married through the *magadi* (lit., "bride wealth") system. In such settings, they saw themselves as important because they worked the land to produce food for their families. Their food production duties ensured that they became "pillars" of their communities despite the dominant ideology of patriarchy at the time. Jacobs argues that the role of cultivator was a less propitious form of production, but that role was important because it provided subsistence.[28] In environmental history, according to Dankelman and Davidson, it is only from the 1980s that scholars recognized that poverty is linked to environmental problems and this implies an inherent sexism.[29] Patriarchy ensured that they identified themselves as the lower class—*basadi,* those who are left at home looking after land and the children. Supporting Hogg and Abrahams views that power and status relations between groups has a bearing on social identity in the sense that "the dominant groups in society have the power and the status to impose the dominant value system and ideology which serves to legitimate and perpetuate the status quo."[30]

Precolonial Sotho-Tswana women's perceptions of themselves transformed dramatically after the industrial revolution of the 1860s and forced removals of 1913 onward because landownership by Africans was curtailed. Through contact with the West, they had to adhere to scientific authority and a new set of social practices and policies. As the South African economy became more capitalist during the late nineteenth century, creditworthiness became a yardstick for land tenure and title deeds were introduced.[31] Women were hit hard because the dominant ideology favored men as landowners. They appropriated the identity of the underclass of *bomme* being mothers left at home to do household chores because their environment was taken away from them.

Capitalism transformed gender roles by preventing men from working the land, forced to engage in the migrant labor system. Male labor was controlled in mines and markets and no longer controlled female labor.[32] Even though women deepened their environmental roles in rural agriculture because of the absence of their male counterparts, social and economic crisis ensued. But despite the crisis in food production women became more important in society because "through their fertility they became not objects of exploitation but as bearers of value in the technical, wider, non-technical sense."[33] They often became more important than males in a practical sense because they provided food and related more to the soil and nature. Accordingly, from the 1930s onward many unmarried or divorced women started establishing independent households while most men established independent homes through marriage.[34] Women realized that they could survive without men because they had to fulfill the role of "food makers." In this sense capitalism entrenched positive identity for women. As suggested by Turner, for social change to occur, the low-status group normally penetrates the boundaries set by the high-status group and they then adopt positive social identity.[35] This process is not based on competition but assimilation which involves the adoption of the positive features of the high-status group by the lower-status group.

Some women saw themselves as being less of women because their husbands could not purchase land. Hence the name *mme* because of the land that was curtailed and many families could not have access to such properties and the roles of such women were that of looking after children. The infiltration of colonial ideals on land ownership rights violated the African women ideology on their identity in terms of land rights. The philosophy of land as '*lefa*' was violated by white ideology of title deeds as those who could not buy land were regarded as less human (*ga se batho*). This suggests that when people are threatened in any way, in many instances they tend to change their perceptions of reality to adapt to the new situation. This reflects a constructionist approach, which shows that identities are not static but fluctuating, influenced by and reacting to changing social environments, processes, and interactions. In this instance, women faced discrimination from African culture and westernization.

FROM LADY SELBORNE TO GA-RANKUWA: WOMEN'S IDENTITY CRISIS

Lady Selborne was more than a geographic or residential space for the Sotho-Tswana women because they could hold title to land and managed to perform their precolonial duties on the fertile land they were exposed to in the township. The township was a "home," a space for positive identity construction. Ga-Rankuwa became a place of affirmation of positive identity to former tenants, and denigration a state of negative identity for former landlords because they could not purchase land in the new township. But both types of women became dehumanized by the fact that the soil was infertile and land was small and they could not engage in food production.

Conversely, former tenants who continued to rent houses in Ga-Rankuwa were initially excited at the move but became unhappy when they realized they could not engage in food production.[36] Ross maintains that cultural meanings must be emphasized when dealing with the "home."[37] Certainly, interviewees in this study described a "home" as a cluster of traits—an inheritance, a site for agricultural production, a sacred space for religious rituals and a place for constructing identity.

Displaced informants have affirmed the community in Lady Selborne lived as a family and that this created a sense of belonging. This grounded sense of identity established positive self-esteem among local women, evinced in what they called "being human." Implying that land dispossession transformed this sense of identity caused those displaced to describe themselves as being "less human." The women's understanding of what their "homes" meant was reflected in their lived reality and in the way they engaged closely with their environment and with one another.

The social engineering of the Group Areas Act of 1956 both physically destroyed Lady Selborne and changed the ideological relationship of the Sotho-Tswana women with their environment and impacted negatively on their identity. As indicated by Mphahlele, land continued to play a historical and spiritual role in the memories of the Sotho-Tswana women even though the "spiritual and mystical bond between the soil and its users around which so much of their folklore, poetry, religion and language were constructed was miscued."[38] The ideology of land that the Sotho-Tswana held was mentally intact, but empirically they did not want to continue living their history of Lady Selborne in Ga-Rankuwa and had to flee from history by applying environmental resistance in the resettlement area. This was another turning point in identity construction for women as they had to now lose their inheritance that affirmed their identity—land. These women became squatters on the relocation area and agriculture was crippled. According to Bundy, such a history of land dispossession became a "punitive untenable allocation of land and land rights to land" because African women had to settle on unviable lands with small plots which to date are not supporting food production but are meant for housing.[39] Areas that were found suitable for white settlers were appropriated and the Sotho-Tswana system of land tenure was slowly but surely destroyed.[40] Land dispossession led to an untenable positive identity that some women enjoyed in Lady Selborne. As the interviewee Tshweni could state:

> By losing our houses in Lady Selborne during forced removals, our humanness was impacted negatively because we lost the places where we performed rituals. And we lost our homes, our inheritance from our parents.

Resettlement in Ga-Rankuwa instilled positive identity in former women tenants of Lady Selborne because they were given an equal opportunity with former landlords to buy or lease plots. It is interesting that such tenants never mentioned feeling less human about the fact that they did not own plots in Lady Selborne; their only dehumanizing factor there was having to clean up sewerage spilled by bucket collectors.[41] Interviewees claim that tenants were incorporated into the community as residents of Lady Selborne. This implies discrimination in terms of land ownership was not profound. This substantiates the concept of self as suggested by Comaroff and Comaroff as "a constant work-in-progress, indeed a highly complex fabrication, whose complexity was further shaded by gender, generation, class, race, ethnicity, and religious ideology among other things."[42] This implies that *botho* (lit., "humanness") was not a static concept but had to transform under different historical and social influences. This can perhaps be ascribed to the romantic nostalgia felt for Lady Selborne by those living in Ga-Rankuwa, and the voluntary nature of their former tenancy. As Bachelard observes, "The human imagination always builds walls of impalpable shadows, comforting itself with the illusion of protection, and so carries the 'notion of home' into any really inhabited space, whether cognitive or physical."[43]

Certainly, some former tenants and former landlords (who were able to buy plots) were able to inculcate the notion of a "home" and positive identity when they arrived in Ga-Rankuwa. But most former landlords could not because the resettlement did not afford them the same rights of property ownership. Such former landlords felt a sense of insecurity and a loss of dignity. This shift in property relations and the concomitant shift in power relations have been remembered as a degrading experience for former landlords. This suggests that ownership of land and identity went hand in hand, and gave people a sense of dignity (*seriti*). As described by Comaroff and Comaroff, "Personhood was everywhere seen to be an intrinsically social construction. . . . The identity of each and every one was forged, cumulatively, by an infinite, ongoing series of practical activities."[44] This suggests that a "home" can be made because it consists of persons and emotions and can be transformed into a habitable space. As suggested by Rapport and Overing: "One dwells in a mobile habitat and not in a singular or fixed physical structure."[45]

The changes in perception of "home" from Lady Selborne to Ga-Rankuwa in affirming humanness deteriorated as people adapted to the situation in Ga-Rankuwa. Former landlords who became tenants in the resettlement area perceived themselves as less human: "*dilo*."[46] This corroborates the argument by Comaroff and Comaroff that "contemporary Tswana personhood is not referred to a state of being but to a state of becoming."[47] Many resettled women interviewed, especially former landlords, fostered negative self-perceptions and saw those without title to land as *dilo*. This is supported by Ngubane, that "a philosophy of a definition of a human person succeeded or failed in proportion to the degree that it harmonised the personality."[48] Such negative perception led to serious environmental degradation in the resettlement space that was supposed to be *legae* (home) but was instead often referred to as *ntlu* (house).[49] In this regard forced removals were a betrayal of the concept of *botho*, "an ethical concept that expresses a vision of what is valuable and worthwhile in life."[50] This inferred death of former landlords' identity which had to be resurrected in the new space. As expressed by Shutte, the loss of *botho* had to materialize because "the morality of *botho* is intrinsically related to human happiness and fulfilment" and "can take more aggressive forms such as anger and defiance in face of injustice."[51]

CONCLUSION

This chapter has argued that Apartheid-forced removals brought with it untenable effects of identity crisis among the Sotho-Tswana women of Ga-Rankuwa. By undermining the indigenous ethics of land tenure and the significance of the ecological roles of women, land dispossession violated the spiritual importance of land in affirming women's identity. In this sphere Apartheid left women in a state of border identity construction because it curtailed land for women and more so relocated them in areas that were infertile for food production. This explains why displacement destroyed the positive identity of many of the Sotho-Tswana women of Ga-Rankuwa as they saw land as more than a shelter and property: It was sacred and had spiritual connotation; it was part of their identity, a place for making history where family and neighbors socialized. Losing it meant the loss of *lefa* and identity.

Thus Ga-Rankuwa was difficult to make a "home" as people hankered after their "lost home" and positive identify in Lady Selborne. Many women residents became apathetic toward environmental conservation which affected their identity construction and put it at a border situation–identity crisis. Despite these frustrations, the "pursuit" continued in the face of crippling environmental degradation, and this "quest" requires drastic steps by the South African government to assist in ensuring that the resettlement areas become "homes" so that the women can regain their fullness in positive identity construction. Improvement of the soil and increasing land sizes can help a great deal in this venture. As suggested by Davies, for such women their "identity are never closed they are always multiplied, determined by all the past, present and future migratory experiences and relations."[52] Meaning that such women are engaged in resistance discourses on construction of their identity, signifying their agency in constructing their history in the midst of homelessness. This is the politics of identity construction beyond the constraints of forced homelessness whereby male domination is resisted in the process and allows women to reinterpret, represent, and reconstruct their identity in a multifaceted manner. This I can say is a depiction of the Sotho-Tswana women's political mobilization strategies by using indigenous knowledge on land rights in constructing their identity.

NOTES

1. Alfred Crosby, *Ecological Imperialism: The Biological Expansion of Europe 900–1900* (Cambridge: Cambridge University Press, 1986), 94.

2. "Africa," Dictionary.com, <http://www.dictionary.com/browse/africa?s=ts/> [Accessed: June 18, 2017].

3. Jane Carruthers, "Urban Land Claims in South Africa: The Case of Lady Selborne Township, Pretoria, Gauteng," *Kleio* 32 (2000): 2.

4. M. C. Kgari-Masondo, personal collection, interviews, Ga-Rankuwa: Isabel Mvula, domestic worker, Johannesburg, June 2004, September 15, 2006, and March 21, 2014; Ruth Kgari, domestic worker, Isando, June 27, 2004; Madumo, housewife, June 30, 2004; Matilda Manamela, housewife, July 2, 2004 and June 28, 2004; Violet Maphalare, housewife, March 21, 2014 and June 28, 2004; Matlaila, housewife, June 29, 2004; Julia Motshetshane, cleaner, Ga-Rankuwa Hospital, April 13, 2006 and 27 June, 2004; Mohlahledi, housewife, June 28, 2004; Poo, housewife, March 21, 2014; Hilda Ntsoko, entrepreneur, Mabopane, March 22, 2014; Sekhu, housewife, June 28, 2004; Tshidi Tshweni, domestic worker, Isando, June 28, 2004.

5. The case study of Lady Selborne stems from my PhD at Stellenbosch University supervised by Professor Sandra Swart in 2008.

6. Henri Tajfel, "Social Categorisation, Social Identity and Social Comparison," *Differentiation between Social groups: Studies in Psychology of Intergroup Relation* (1978): 61–76.

7. Suzanne Skevington and Deborah Baker, *The Social Identity of Women* (London: Sage, 1989), 2.

8. Henri Tajfel, and John Turner, "An Integrative Theory of Intergroup Conflict," *The Social Psychology of Intergroup Relations* 33/47 (1979): 74.

9. Johannes Smit, "Black Women and Writing Identity," *Alternation* 3/2 (1996): 196–207.

10. Carolyn Merchant, "The Theoretical Structure of Ecological Revolutions," *Environmental Review* 11/4 (1987): 269.

11. Donald Worster, "Theories of Environmental History," *Environmental Review* 11/4 (1987): 251–53; William Cronon, "Modes of Prophecy and Production: Placing Nature in History," *Journal of American History* 76 (1990): 1122–31; Nancy Jacobs, *Environment, Power, and Injustice: A South African History* (Cambridge: Cambridge University Press, 2003), 219.

12. James Amanze, *African Traditional Religions and Culture in Botswana* (Gaborone, Botswana: Pula Press, 2002), 302.

13. Michelle Byrne, "Understanding Life Experiences through a Phenomenological Approach to Research," *AORN Journal* 73/4 (2001): 830–32.

14. Thomas Ryba, *The Essence of Phenomenology and its Meaning for Scientific Study of Religion* (New York: Peter Lang, 1991), 34.
15. John Tosh, *The Pursuit of History: Aims, Methods and New Directions in the Study of Modern History* (London: Longman, 1991), 213.
16. Louis Cohen, Lawrence Manion, and Keith Morrison, *Research Methodology in Education*, 7th ed., (Abingdon: Routledge, 2011).
17. Kenny Chow and Mick Healey, "Place Attachment and Place Identity: First-Year Undergraduates Making the Transition from Home to University," *Journal of Environmental Psychology* 28 (2008): 362–72.
18. Frederic Ellenberger, *History of the Basuto: Ancient and Modern* (New York: Negro University Press, 1969), xxi.
19. Harriet Ngubane, *Original Peoples: Zulus of Southern Africa* (Hove, UK: Wayland, 1986), 81.
20. Jordon K. Ngubane, *Conflict of Minds* (New York: Books in Focus, 1979), 92.
21. Es'kia Mphahlele, foreword to *Land Reform in South Africa: A Black Perspective*, ed. Essy M. Letsoalo (Johannesburg: Skotaville, 1987); Farieda Khan, "Contemporary South African Environmental Response: An Historical and Socio-Political Evaluations with Particular Reference to Blacks" (unpublished master's thesis, University of Cape Town, 1990).
22. Gabriel M. Setiloane, *African Theology: An Introduction* (Johannesburg: Skotaville, 1986), 40.
23. Setiloane, *African Theology*, 7.
24. Setiloane, *African Theology*, 7–8.
25. I. Schapera, introduction to *Apprenticeship at Kuruman: Being the Letters of Robert and Mary Moffat 1820–1828*, ed. I. Schapera (London: Chatto & Windus, 1951), xviii.
26. Isabel Apawo Phiri, cited in Terence Ranger, "Women and Environment in African Religion: The Case of Zimbabwe," in *Social History and African Environments*, ed. JoAnn McGregor and William Beinart (Oxford: James Currey, 2003), 76.
27. Jeff Guy, "Gender Oppression in Southern Africa's Pre-capitalist Societies," in *Women and Gender in Southern Africa to 1945*, ed. Cherryl Walker (Cape Town: David Philip, 1990), 33–47.
28. Nancy Jacobs, "The Colonial Ecological Revolution in South Africa: The Case of Kuruman," in *South Africa's Environmental History: Cases and Comparisons*, ed. Stephen Dovers, Ruth Edgecombe, and Bill Guest (Athens, OH, and Cape Town: Ohio University Press and David Philip, 2002), 22.
29. Irene Dankelman and Joan Davidson, *Women and Environment in the Third World: Alliance for the Future* (London: Earthscan, 1988).
30. Cited in Skevington and Baker, *The Social Identity of Women*, 2.
31. Letsoalo, *Land Reform in South Africa*, 10.
32. Guy, "Gender Oppression," 43,
33. Guy, "Gender Oppression," 45.
34. William F. Lye and Colin Murray, *Transformations on the Highveld: The Tswana and Southern Sotho* (Cape Town: David Philip, 1980), 107–8.
35. John C. Turner, "Towards a Cognitive Redefinition of the Social Group," *Social Identity and Intergroup Relations* (1982): 15–40.

36. Personal collection, interviews: Mvula, March 21, 2014, September 15, 2006, and June 24, 2004; Mohlahledi, June 28, 2004; Kgari, June 27, 2004; Madumo June 30, 2004; Matlaila, June 9, 2004; Poo, March 21, 2014; Ntsoko, March 22, 2014.

37. Fiona Ross, "Making Home in the New South Africa" (unpublished paper, University of Cape Town, 2003), 2–3.

38. Mphahlele, foreword to *Land Reform in South Africa.*

39. Colin Bundy, "Land, Law and Power: Forced Removals in Historical Context," in *No Place to Rest: Forced Removals and the Law*, ed. Christina Murray and Catherine O'Regan (Cape Town: Oxford University Press, 1990), 11.

40. Cosmas Desmond, *The Discarded People: An Account of Africa Resettlement in South Africa* (London: Penguin African Library, 1971), 13.

41. Personal collection, interviews: Kgari, Ntsoko, Mohlahledi, Madumo, and Matlaila.

42. Jean and John L. Comaroff, "On Personhood: An Anthropological Perspective from Africa," *Social Identities* 7/2 (2001): 268.

43. Gaston Bachelard, cited in Nigel Rapport and Joanna Overing, *Social and Cultural Anthropology: The Key Concepts* (London: Routledge, 2000), 159.

44. Comaroff and Comaroff, "On Personhood," 268.

45. Cited in Rapport and Overing, *Social and Cultural Anthropology*, 58.

46. Personal collection, interviews: Tshweni and Motshetshane.

47. Comaroff and Comaroff, "On Personhood," 271.

48. Jordon K. Ngubane, *Conflict of Minds*, 92.

49. Personal collection, interview: Tshweni.

50. Augustine Shutte, *Ubuntu: An Ethic for a New South Africa* (Pietermaritzburg, South Africa: Cluster, 2001), 2.

51. Shutte, *Ubuntu*, 132.

52. Cited in Smit, "Black Women and Writing Identity," 199.

NINE

Reenacting "Destiny"

Masculinity and Afrikaner Identity in "Religious" Post-Apartheid South Africa

Kennedy Owino

INTRODUCTION

The intersection between religion, race, politics, social and economic factors are key in an attempt toward explaining changing perceptions of identities among men in post-Apartheid South Africa. We cannot speak of men as gendered beings unless we engage on issues around masculinity. It is therefore important to state upfront that masculinity as an identity for men must be understood as both relational and personal. In this case, new challenges in South Africa bring to the fore the use of the phrase "masculinity in crisis," and if crisis does exist, an important question that also arises is how religion is applied to address such crises. Essentially, the history of South Africa is one that bears substantial influence of religion, and more so, religion significantly contributed in establishing, for example, "ideal" perceptions of being male among Afrikaners. At the core of this identity, studies confirm how the history of the Afrikaners focused solely on the God who chose the Boer race and created a divinely planned destiny for them, a belief that established a hegemonic representation of Afrikaner masculinities during the colonial and Apartheid eras. The supposed covenant the *Voortrekkers* made with God at Bloedrivier (Blood River) on December 16, 1838, led to the establishment of the Afrikaner masculine nation.[1] From the historic events that followed, the Afrikaner people held a popular belief that the *Voortrekkers* and their descendants were "God's chosen people" to lead and build South Africa—a stereotype, if not "historical myth," that has been romanticized by the Afrikaner elite since the mid-nineteenth century. However, this misconceived "special destiny" has been challenged by historians and biblical scholars alike.[2] In general, "Afrikaner identity is evolving"[3] and the "fall of Apartheid, and the failure of Afrikaner nationalism," represents an extreme crisis for Afrikaner identity.[4] Furthermore, in a context where "whites position themselves as victims of a changing racial order,"[5] Steyn argues that "in its fiercely reactionary nature, Afrikaner whiteness has long shown characteristics which are being identified in contemporary reactive white identities."[6] In the face of political and economic changes in post-1994 South Africa, this chapter seeks to explore how Afrikaner Christian men are reconfiguring an articulation of previously constructed historical identity.

"TYPOLOGICAL REENACTMENT": THE CONSTRUCTION OF AFRIKANER IDENTITY

The historical and construction of identities in the Republic of South Africa has a unique religious and theological history, founded as one of the major white Christian settlements in Africa.[7] Steyn argues that "the early settlers of mixed European, though primarily Dutch ancestry, unified in a common identification as *Afrikaners*, people of Africa, and retained little actual or sentimental attachment to their European homelands."[8] Hence, the Dutch Boers (farmers) in previous centuries became the ancestors of the present Afrikaners who, as Templin observer, "developed a strong nationalist spirit in the nineteenth and early twentieth centuries."[9]

A distinction between Afrikaner nationalism and Afrikaner identity is therefore not possible. There is a strong consensus among scholars for the close relation between the two notions where Afrikaner nationalism informs Afrikaner identity in the process of constructing an Afrikaner self-identity and understanding.[10] In this case, to apply the notion of ideology in interrogating Afrikaner nationalism that sought to give meaning to Afrikaner identity, I borrow Templin's observation arguing that ideology seeks "to make an autonomous politics possible by providing the authoritative concepts that render it meaningful."[11] It is in this sense that a nationalist ideology would shape the former Apartheid era through the Afrikaner nationalist government coming into power in 1948. This ideology established the contours of a superior Afrikaner racial identity thereby creating a hierarchical "political dispensation that said black people [and other races — *my addition*] were different and therefore inferior."[12] Using the words of Steyn, this ideology "institutionalised abuse of state power and implemented extreme racial oppression."[13] As an ideology, the Afrikaner nationalist "spirit," I would argue, is therefore not only linguistically, ethnically (or traditionally) driven and established but was (is) also a conscious religiously constructed ideology that sought to give Afrikaans-speaking white South Africans a sense of identity, self-esteem, self-image, and a sense of belonging to the African continent. A question therefore arises in this case: How has the demise of this ideological identity brought about, especially among Afrikaner men, a sense of disillusionment, vulnerability, and a "crisis" of an existential identity in this new area? This, I argue, necessitates a renegotiation of Afrikaner identity in post-Apartheid South Africa. In this case, religious spaces are a ferment that gives rise to possibilities of exploring ways in which alternative identities are being negotiated.

Templin shows how Afrikaner ideologies would closely associate a religious sense of nationalism with particular historical theological motifs that became adopted and transformed for various existential reasons, political, sociological, or cultural.[14] It is therefore obvious to begin by positing that in order to understand the complexities and challenges present in post-Apartheid South Africa, it would perhaps require one to explore some theological ideas that constructed and maintained the historical formulations that shaped *Afrikanerdom*. A current question should further explore whether such theological ideas continue to give meaning in present cultural, racial, economic, and political crises. For such an exploration to be useful, the value of looking at the concept of "typological reenactment" within the significance of religion in shaping discourses of identity cannot be avoided.

Typological reenactment can be described as "a method or lens of biblical hermeneutics whereby one discerns one's context, calling or life direction by identifying with personalities in the biblical narrative" with the purpose of encouraging one (or a group of people) "to emulate faithful biblical personalities."[15] Originally applied by Templin, typological reenactment can be understood as a "folk theology sustained by popular piety" where situations that seemed similar to biblical events are interpreted as direct signs from God.[16] In this case, Templin maintains that the Boers assumed that "God's plan for *Afrikanerdom* was a typological re-enactment of various Old Testament episodes on the South African frontier."[17] According to Templin, in applying typological reenactment, the *Groot Trek* became the new Exodus, where with the help of Joshua, Gideon, and others, the conquest of the land was blessed by God and divine providence was therefore "on the side of the Boers' freedom fight against both African and British."[18] Templin further observes that "in battles against the Zulu's the Boers kept the stories of Gideon and Jephthah before their eyes as examples of God's favour. Their success against the Zulu chieftain, Dingane, in 1838 was interpreted as confirmation of the covenant constructed on the basis of the Abrahamic covenant."[19] Historically, Afrikaner identity to a wider extent is seen to have been drawn majorly and founded on particular firmly interwoven discourse centering on "themes of religious, racial and cultural purity, superiority, calling and the struggle for autonomy against oppression—which included the struggle for an independent language."[20] Hence, an essentialist *Afrikanerdom* (Afrikaner nation) was to be established through a quest for a "pure" ethnic Afrikaner identity which could only be realized once other cultural groups had been exorcised.[21]

By taking these historical formulations seriously, the theological imagery at the center of typological reenactment, which requires interrogation, is the concept of an elect people, which underlies the Afrikaner cultural and ethnic identity. In his analysis, Templin indicates two sources of tradition that are often used to characterize the Afrikaners' self-understanding, namely: Calvinistic theology and the Bible.[22] In other words, the Afrikaner cultural and religious tradition became rooted in the biblicism of the Calvinistic Reformed tradition where their "interpretation of themselves as elect or chosen was always a permutation, an adaptation of the original doctrine, taken from the invisible realm of high theology, transformed radically, and returned to the ethnic context of Old Testament."[23] The assumption of divine election that took central place in the Calvinistic Reformed traditions of other groups such as the French Huguenots and the German Reformed movements[24] established the idea of Afrikaner racial superiority as God's "special people" called to a "promised land," which is South Africa. This self-understanding developed what Templin calls "a pioneer life."[25]

With such biblical interpretation, which Bosman notes to have dominated the middle of the nineteenth century,[26] the role of religion in theological formulations was used not only to established a false tradition of "pioneer life" in southern Africa, but also later became influential in the formation of the Union of South Africa in 1910, the promulgation of so-called Apartheid legislation following the election of the National Party in 1948, and the subsequent establishment of a republic in 1961.[27] Furthermore, it becomes evident that the ideology of Afrikaner as a "chosen race" also established hegemony of power around Afrikaner men with a dominant form of masculinity that was authoritarian, unforgiving, and unapologetic. The post-1948 hegemonic white-Afrikaner masculinity, for example, was based on the identity of Afrikaner self-determination which used political power to popularize new perceptions of masculinity.[28] Du Pisani points out the core values identifying Afrikaner hegemonic masculinity as expressed in the membership requirements of the Afrikaner Broederbond, which entailed that one be white, financially independent, Afrikaans speaking, Protestant by faith, and male—thereby adhering to Reformed Protestant Christianity and being a baptized member of one of the three dominant Dutch Reformed Church denominations in South Africa.[29] Important to note is the constructed Afrikaner identity around the notions of Protestant Christianity and "whiteness." White English- and Afrikaans-speaking men in Apartheid South Africa therefore generally constructed their masculine identities partly in relation to the way they saw women and men of color.[30] This context accordingly established a hegemonic white-Afrikaner and white-English masculinities which marginalized "other" forms of masculinities by silencing or stigmatizing them. In this way, Christian beliefs were used to reinforce ethnic identity and cultural models of "ideal" Afrikaner manhood within the Afrikaner Broederbond in Apartheid South Africa.

THEORETICAL AND METHODOLOGICAL CONSIDERATIONS

Critical studies on men and masculinity have gained increased interest in African scholarship especially in the past decade or so. Although new foci in this field of study are constantly emerging, concerns around HIV and AIDS, sexual abuse, and gender-based violence against women and girls by men, issues around gender, sexuality, and health have prompted, among others, a continuous response especially from theologians.[31] Among theologians and other scholars, the focus has shifted to another emerging field, namely, the study of men, masculinities, and religion within critical studies of religion and gender in Africa.[32] With this new academic foci, the emergence of the Mighty Men Conference (MMC) becomes of special interest, considering what I have argued elsewhere, that such movements constitute "sub-cultural spaces" through which conventional forms of masculinities are reproduced as men seek social, religious, and theological beliefs to inform what it means to be men in changing contexts.[33] However, most African theologians agree that religion can be a means of positive dialogues in envisioning alternative masculinities.

The process of envisioning alternative forms of being men therefore makes it useful for scholars working within Christian communities to understand masculinity as not simply a definition in opposition to femininity, but instead, masculinity as primarily concerned with how men negotiate and make sense of themselves as men in varied settings. In other words, masculinity refers to a specific gender identity belonging to individuals who have specific experiences of what it means (i.e., feel, think, and behave) to be a male person.[34] As a gendered identity for men, masculinity refers therefore "to a cluster of norms, values and behavioural patterns expressing explicit or implicit expectations of how men should act and represent themselves to others."[35] In her initial analysis in *Gender and Power*, Raewyn Connell shows that there are bound to be multiple masculinities and further argues that masculinity is not equivalent to men but masculinities are characterized by internal complexities, contradictions, and are bound to change historically, hence the concept "masculinities."[36] This description of masculinity as multiple is crucial especially when examining Christian faith communities where men are often encouraged "to act like men" with an understanding that masculinity is God-designed, divinely attained, and that masculinity equals "man." Essentially, with this multiplicity of understandings of the theoretical meaning of masculinity, men are to be seen as expressing their meaning of being men in varied ways. This theoretical understanding sets masculinity as a discursive construction and enactment of male identities. Thus "men are not born with masculinity as part of their genetic make-up; rather masculinity is a gendered identity into which men are acculturated and is composed of social codes of behaviour, which men learn to reproduce in culturally appropriate ways."[37] It is therefore in order that one understands masculinity as a set of practices socially constructed as men contest various changes within processes of seeking to understand their masculine selves. With this in mind, the intersectionality approach becomes applicable as a perspective for theorizing and discussing masculinity in contemporary identity construction.

Originally intersectionality as a research paradigm embraced the idea that one must take into consideration multiple factors (variables) during a process of analysis in order to properly examine the various ways through which gender, race, and class interact (combine/intertwine) to shape multiple dimensions that subjugate black women in the context of race/sex and class oppression.[38] According to Patricia Hill Collins, the concept of intersectionality is characterized by a "matrix of domination" identifying race and gender, or sexuality, class, and nation as intersecting scenes characterized by intersecting oppressions.[39] Central to Collins's argument, as opposed to examining gender, class, sexuality, race, religion, and nation as separate systems (or variables in identity construction), intersectionality must explore how these social forces mutually construct one another or how they "articulate" with one another to shape identity constructions.[40] It is from this understanding that I apply intersectionality toward theorizing constructions of Christian male identities and masculinities in a post-Apartheid context. Significant therefore is the emphasis that factors/variables that inform constructions of identities cannot be treated as mutually exclusive categories. Within this understanding, it is difficult to conceptualize construction of identity and masculinities in a linear manner. Accordingly, this calls one to examine the interwoven web of sociopolitical, cultural, economic, race, class, and religious factors and identity categories that operate together to influence (intersect to inform) reproduction of masculinities. It is within this web of intersection, for example, that the desire to retrieve "historical myths" that provide meaning in constructing ethical identities within the ideology of typological reenactment become meaningful in contemporary contexts of various changes.

Two primary methodologies are utilized for this chapter and are derived from an original study that was based on a qualitative research project conducted with men who attended the MMC.[41] Initially, the objective of the study was to inquire about the resolve of Angus Buchan and the MMC on calling men to "return to godly manhood." The study was thus intended to establish the experiences of men on what constituted understandings of becoming "Mighty Men" as a perception of "goodly manhood" archetyped in what Buchan envisioned as "recreating masculinity." Data was collected through semi-structured individual in-depth interviews conducted with thirty-five men between January 2011 and July 2012 in Pietermaritzburg, South Africa. The study applied purposive sampling due to its convenience in terms of cost and time. The sample was chosen, first, from male participants who adhered to three different theological strands, and an active blend of ecclesiastical confessions that embrace broad-church Evangelical Christianity[42] (either Conservative mainline,[43] Charismatic, or Pentecostal). This sample was adopted based on the basis that the MMC is not a homogenous Christian phenomenon. All the selected male participants for interview had attended a minimum of two or more MMCs consecutively. Second, Buchan's faith discourse and data from interviewed participants were supplemental to my personal observations which took place during the MMC gatherings.[44]

MASCULINE REFORM: THE MIGHTY MEN'S CONFERENCE AS A CONTESTED SPACE

The MMC arose in the early 2000's in Greytown of the KwaZulu-Natal midlands as an initiative of Angus Buchan, a South African white farmer of Scottish descent[45] who later became a Charismatic itinerant evangelist/preacher.[46] As a family man, Buchan is married to Jill Buchan and together they have five children, with nine grandchildren. Buchan describes his father as a "man's man" and his mother as a "very feminine woman."[47] Emphasizing a "traditional model" of household governance in one of his sermons, Buchan refers to this traditional model as "*the* biblical model" for all Christian families, and speaks of his wife:

> I'm so grateful to God that I don't have to compete with my wife Jill. She is a very feminine lady, an excellent cook, a wonderful housekeeper, mother and grandmother. I have been privileged that it was not necessary for her to work from the day we got married. I said on our wedding day, "you will not work unless obviously it's absolutely a case of life and death." If we have to eat maize meal and sour milk, then that's what we'll eat, but I want you to be at home bringing up our children.[48]

With this traditional model in mind, Buchan seems to believe that Christian men should follow his example and become responsible "godly men" in a changing social, political, and economic context. Grappling with the new challenges in a democratic South African context, what appears clear from Buchan is a resistance to change, especially when he points out: "I keep stressing to the ladies that this Mighty Men concept was initiated and born through a heart that we have for the family so that men can be the prophet, priest and king that they are meant to be in their own homes."[49]

This changing context, according to Buchan's understanding, has brought about a crisis in masculinity and identity among South African men. This is evident when Buchan describes the genesis of the MMC when God specifically instructed him: "I want you to mentor young men. There are very few spiritual fathers in our nation and the world . . . . Young men are desperately seeking role models and mentors."[50] This perceived crisis of identity and masculinity among Christian men is described further through intentions that focus on lack of fathers and especially spiritual fathers/mentors, lack of leadership in homes, and the effect of societal pressure, a concern that is central for Buchan. Accordingly, he states:

> I recently saw again how young men have reached a stage in their lives where they don't know what they, as men, are supposed to do. Society has broken the man down so much that he is not sure how far to go or what he needs to do to lead his household. That is the whole gist of the term "Mighty Men."[51]

In this case, Buchan alludes to an essentialist thinking that implore men to return to a specific identity that is "lost," a position that seeks to reassert male dominance and reaffirm male power over the household and a rightful place as leaders in society. Such an essentialist position portrays a detached assumption that understands masculinity as a divine given and ordained of God. Using Kimmel's words, this desire to reestablish control in the home represents "the second coming of patriarchy."[52] The notion of reforming a "lost masculinity" therefore brings to the fore a preoccupation with a traditional form of patriarchal masculine identity and is thereby used to justify what underlies understandings of masculinity among the MMC and Buchan's "godly manhood." The MMC is therefore described by Buchan as a "God phenomenon," and an "initiative of God"[53] where "God is calling His [*sic*] men back to Himself [*sic*] from every denomination, every class, race and creed, every age group, and He's [*sic*] calling them together in His presence."[54] In so doing, Buchan contends:

> When we begin to understand what God wants a man to be, Christianity becomes exciting, challenging and worthwhile. That is what God is doing at the moment, not only in our beloved South Africa but in the whole world. Men are beginning to understand what is required of them by God and they are implementing it by looking at examples of real men.[55]

The MMC understood as being of "supernatural origin" is perceived by Buchan as God restoring masculinity in an area of "crises" of masculinity among Christian men. Buchan states: "The Lord is restoring man's masculinity. When men start to hear what God can do through nobodies. . . . A completely different paradigm shift takes place and happens especially in the midst of multitudes of men. Men start to realise again what they have been created for and why they are on this earth."[56] A quest to "restore lost masculinity" as an appeal to join the MMC following South Africa's transition to a new democracy post-1994 calls for further investigation. A popular interpretation of the MMC as a "new awakening" among South African men should be questioned within a context of shifts in gender relations and roles, political and economic transitions. From fairly small beginnings, the first MMC gathering in 2004 as an informal men's get-together recorded 240 men attending. In the last decade, the movement has seen exponential growth with 600 men attending the conference in 2005; 1,060 in 2006; 7,500 in 2007; 60,000 plus in 2008; 200,000 delegates in 2009; and as Buchan claims, "acres of men" (600,000 plus) in 2010,"[57] thereby becoming one of the largest Christian men's movement of its kind in contemporary times.[58]

Several important questions need particular interrogation. Could this be a reactionary movement, through which men seek to cope with fear and vulnerability precipitated by constitutional change and gender shifts necessitated by the political change of power from one racial group to another? What do we make of the rising magnitude of the MMC gatherings? What are the reasons for the increased attraction of men to attend the MMC? Important to note as a striking feature for the MMC is its demographic attraction, where over 80 percent of men attending this movement are predominantly white Afrikaans- and English-speaking South African men.[59] Why is this "new awakening" (and revival as Buchan puts it) particularly attractive to white South African men across both language groups? This chapter wrestles with such questions while it locates the MMC as a religious space within which white Afrikaans-speaking Christian men are seeking to reenact eroded identities in contemporary Evangelical Protestantism in a post-Apartheid South Africa. The MMC especially provides white Afrikaans-speaking men a space of safety, hope, and acceptance to enable them romanticize the past religious historical myth that they can be "mighty" again despite political powerlessness. The question is whether or not faith discourses by Buchan and the MMC have equipped men to positively transcend an idealized historically constructed white Afrikaner male identity. As discussed in the next section, analysis indicates that the focus of the MMC on becoming "Mighty Men for God" offers opportunities for both an alternative and reenactment of past masculinities and ideas/narratives of destiny. Such narratives were characterized by nostalgia of a "lost identity" within transitions of sociopolitical changes in shifting realities of race and economic factors in post-Apartheid South Africa.

"REENACTING DESTINY": A QUEST FOR AN ALTERNATIVE IDENTITY AS "MIGHTY MEN"

Identities are consciously or unconsciously being constructed and negotiated in a context where white South African men seem not to adapt easily to change in a democratic South Africa. This perceived resistance to change is revealed in an interview with a fifty-year-old Afrikaans-speaking white respondent who stated:

> So, as the country has come to the point where you got Mandela saying: "Okay, you know what, it's now, it is over." And all over sudden, you had Afrikaners. . . . The English adapted very quickly to the change. But you had Afrikaners that came to the point and said, "You know what, this is a lot of rubbish, we somehow have to find forgiveness" . . . and this Mighty Men's Conference came up, they said, "You know what, men, let's go. Let's come together and see, let us ask God for forgiveness, we cannot continue this way."[60]

Although, white English-speaking men seem to have adapted much faster to the political and economic changes in South Africa post-1994 democracy, the resistance to political change by Afrikaner men was unmistakable. Accordingly, what is being considered "rubbish" by the above respondent requires further questioning. Understood within the context of this response, it is evident that the veiled status of Afrikaner "privilege identity" as God's elect and chosen people is delusional given the social, economic, and political change in South African post-1994 context.

With regard to addressing the challenges that white political hegemony is facing in South Africa's new democracy, a window for dealing with disillusionment appears with the coming of the MMC. To deal with their sense of an eroded, vulnerable identity, the solution for these Afrikaner men was to *"ask God for forgiveness"* and not continue in a state of resistance to change. With the immanent fall of white power, it is obvious why this feeling of resistance toward a South Africa in political transition continued among Afrikaner men. In this light, the MMC affirms the notion of internal inconsistency of masculinities among men where alternative forms of masculinities are being continuously constructed and reconstructed within ideals of godly manhood. Historically, the formation of Afrikaner nationalist identity heightened through a pervasive social, political, economic, and cultural force engineered through the Apartheid policies. One can argue that this established a deliberate Afrikaner essentialist "imperial identity" as *Volk* (lit., "nation," "people"), a formulation in which religion was a major resource, among others. Steyn describes this imperialism as racial domination entrenched "as emanating from a group that felt secure in their power."[61] This false sense of security, power and "might" was established with little awareness that the wheel of history would soon turn and become a threat to Afrikaner ethnic identity that idealized the "destiny" of the white race.

The turning of the wheel of history brought democracy to South Africa. This stripped off the "imperial" ethnic identity of Afrikaner men, so much so that the need for "forgiveness" seemed the only solution. Could it be that the need for forgiveness is also false, arising from a feeling of being abandoned by God?[62] Glimpses of the historical myth of a people "divinely appointed" by God which was used to establish a *Volk* theology for an "ideal" Afrikaner identity was evident within the MMC. A fifty-five-year-old white Afrikaans-speaking middle-class working man alluded to this notion when he stated:

> You see, I will tell you something, in the Mighty Men Conference, if we put, let's put it down to a hundred thousand men. Out of that hundred thousand, I will tell you eighty thousand are probably Afrikaans speaking. You know what, the white Afrikaners believed, "I am going to tell you something that is quite amazing." White Afrikaners believed we were chosen by God. If you will go and read the story of Blood River, "I don't know if you have ever read that?" You see King Shaka came with all his men to fight a sea of Afrikaner, these Boers. Now when the Boers went and made that circle with their things, before they went they asked God, and they said to God, "God, if you help us win this battle today, we will build a church. We will build a church for you." That was their promise to God. So, when the Zulus came they were outnumbered. Maybe a hundred to one. When they came, they were in the camp and they won the battle. When the Boers won the battle over King Shaka, because King Shaka had come with spears and the Boers came with guns. They did not know what these things were. They just saw their men falling. Ahahahaha! Then they see blood: "What are these white people throwing at us?" Thousands of Zulus died. So when they won that battle, so they said, "We will build a church for you." Then they built a church. So as Afrikaners we walked around with that thing. God, God had given us the victory. So we are the chosen people who can build this nation. But they had to come to a realization; from the Mighty Men, we have to come and ask for forgiveness, God have this.[63]

The "*walking around*" with a consciousness of a special destiny, as "*the chosen people who can build this nation,*" was for Afrikaners an identity that was swiftly swallowed up by the coming of a democratic state. The anguish of a lost ethnic identity is often heard in social "white-talk" around what the Afrikaner people feel they had lost since 1994. Lydia Dekker in this case argues:

> The narratives were specifically about having lost "our" flag, "our" anthem, and "our" country and how what was important to "us" as Afrikaners was ripped away from us—torn from our hearts. In these stories, South Africa was viewed as "our" country, and "we," i.e., the Afrikaner, continuously blamed "our leaders," mistakes made under National Party governmental rule.[64]

Accordingly, Buchan's faith discourses on men becoming "Mighty Men" begins to make sense in a context where a majority of Afrikaner men need to deal with the fear of emasculation that comes with post-Apartheid democracy seeking to repress Afrikaner identity in previous established educational policies, language, and symbols. In seeking to recreate and restore "godly manhood" in a mainly white Mighty Men's movement, Buchan imagines a "new" man in a "new" South Africa. He contends, "We are Mighty Men of God in a time and era where everything else is falling apart, where nothing is substantial and where there is nothing and no one a young man can look up to. Young men are desperately seeking role models and mentors."[65] Further, Buchan observes:

> I have taken quite a lot of stick for that during the last seven or eight years, especially from many pharisaical men who have asked, "How can you call yourselves Mighty Men? Where is the humility in that?" In 1 Chronicles 11:10, God speaks about David's thirty mighty men, who are listed in the Bible. These men did amazing things. One of them killed three hundred men with his spear. . . . The three other mighty men broke through the ranks of the enemy, ran down through the gate to the well of Bethlehem, filled a container with water and took it back to David. The men performed extraordinary feats for God. How we long for men like that. The good news is that they are among us.[66]

The MMC is a proof that masculinities are constantly being defended and that this is always at a cost. In this case, in citing biblical assertions of King David's thirty or so "Mighty Men" warriors in 2 Samuel 23:8–39 / 1 Chronicles 11:10–47, Buchan uses perceptions of courage, strength, and conquest to constantly remind men that they must not be "soft" or weak. As such, the MMC offers alternatives in the case of masculinities.

How then does the notion of "Mighty Men" speak to men in a context where historically established hegemonic Afrikaner masculinities are threatened in post-1994? A review of Steyn gives an insight to this phenomenon as she reviews how white identity has been affected in a changing South Africa. This is summarized in her title: "Whiteness Just Isn't What It Used to Be."[67] The application of 2 Samuel 23:8–39 / 1 Chronicles

11:10–47, in Buchan's thinking can therefore be understood as a form of contemporary typological reenactment envisioned to reenact and bring back a particular historical identity in a context where men seem no longer to measure up to certain manly expectations. Indeed, analysis suggests that the gist of becoming "Mighty Men" is equated to a quest for a patriotic identity where men are being called upon to stand together and fight back for a "common good." This call is sugarcoated in Buchan's faith discourses and thus requires critical interrogation. Such faith discourse easily feeds into palatable Afrikaner neo-ethno-nationalism in an era where men are called to devote to their heritage, their beloved *vaderland*, and their ethnic identity. In the case of the Afrikaner imagination as a chosen nation, one could argue that the MMC is a platform for reenactment. The notion of becoming "Mighty Men" for God is therefore applied in a religious socio-ideological context that seeks to reenact a lost destiny toward an alternative identity seeking to reempower white Afrikaans- and English-speaking men in contemporary South Africa. This is in a context where Buchan feels men are not "mighty" as they once were or as they should be.

CONCLUSION

This chapter has shown that typological reenactment is an important framework through which Afrikaner construction of identity can be interrogated. This chapter has demonstrated how the MMC offers opportunities for both alternative and reenacted understandings of masculinities and ideas/narratives of destiny. The premise of the chapter strongly argues that religious notion of becoming "Mighty Men" should be understood as a crutch toward a search for alternative masculinities, on the one hand; while on the other, the MMC offers a space for reenacting Afrikaner ideology of themselves as God's chosen people in post-Apartheid South Africa as it was applied in its historical context in Afrikaner formulations of ethnic identity and destiny. It is in such a context that Walker contends:

> Being a man in post-Apartheid South Africa is of necessity different yet, the present does not represent a complete break with the past. Rather, current models and practices of manhood are historically embedded. The crisis of masculinity in contemporary South Africa may therefore be different but it is certainly not new.[68]

To what extent should contemporary men seek to embrace the notion of "Mighty Men" if its goal seeks a reenactment of the lost Afrikaner destiny of a "special people"? Bosman addresses a similar concern stating that a "careful attention to the hermeneutical context during the middle of the nineteenth century is required."[69] Along with other historians who believe that the notion of "God's chosen" people is an ideology among "Afrikaner elite attempting to ensure social cohesion in transitional times,"[70] Bosman shows that a "primitive Calvinism" as a paradigm might have developed in the nineteenth-century biblical interpretation in South Africa, purposefully engineered to give "rise to a sense of divine calling and mission amongst the *Voortrekkers* and their descendants"[71] and this must be considered a "historical myth." The inclination to merge the religio-cultural history of the Afrikaner people with the history of Israel as depicted in the religious texts of the Hebrew Bible, reached its "climax with the publication of *De Voortrekkers of Het Dagboek van Izak van der Merwe* in 1893 by two Dutch Reformed ministers, John D. Kestell and Nico Hofmeyr."[72] According to Bosman, the assumption that a primitive Afrikaner Calvinism was a cornerstone of *Voortrekker* society remains a highly contested notion among modern historians and is a trend that was actually "developed by English and Afrikaans historians and popularised by novelists, locally and abroad."[73] This ideological quest for a religious identity of the Afrikaner people as a "chosen race" is therefore a much later development emerging from a "reconstructed" Afrikaner history. Hence, faith discourses focusing of "Mighty Men" can, in various ways, feed alternative forms of desired masculinities while the MMC could be a space for a nostalgic reenactment of Afrikaner imagination of themselves as God's special destined people reminiscent of a bygone time and a lost identity.

NOTES

1. According to most historians, the *Voortrekkers,* loosely translated as "those who first started traveling" or "those who traveled in front" were part of the twenty thousand inhabitants of the Cape Colony, mostly Cape Dutch–speaking farmers between the years 1835 and 1845 (see Jan C. Visagie, *Voortrekkerstamouers 1835–1845* (Pretoria: UNISA, 2000), x. Several reasons have been given for this "trek" into the interior of southern Africa, but one that remains relevant and central to the focus of this essay is that of "a growing need to establish political independence" (see Hendrik Bosman, "The '*Jerusalemgangers*' as an Illustration of Resistance against the British Empire and Nineteenth Century Biblical Interpretation in Southern Africa," in *In the Name of God: The Bible in the Colonial Discourse of Empire,* ed. Carly L. Crouch and Jonathan Stökl (Leiden, Netherlands: Brill, 2014), 151–52.

2. See Bosman, "The '*Jerusalemgangers*'"; Johan Degenaar, "The Church and Nationalism in South Africa," in *Church and Nationalism in South Africa,* ed. Theo Sundermeier (Johannesburg: Ravan Press, 1975).

3. Cornel Verwey and Michael Quayle, "Whiteness, Racism, and Afrikaner Identity in Post-Apartheid South Africa," *African Affairs* 111/445 (2012): 552.

4. Verwey and Quayle, "Whiteness, Racism, and Afrikaner Identity," 557.

5. Melissa E. Steyn, "Rehabilitating a Whiteness Disgraced: Afrikaner White Talk in Post-Apartheid South Africa," *Communication Quarterly* 52 (2004): 148.

6. Steyn, "Rehabilitating a Whiteness Disgraced," 148.

7. J. Alton Templin, *Ideology on a Frontier: The Theological Foundation of Afrikaner Nationalism, 1652–1910* (London: Greenwood Press, 1984).

8. Steyn, "Rehabilitating a Whiteness Disgraced." 148.

9. Templin, *Ideology on a Frontier*, 3. However, citing scholars such as Dubow, 1992; Fredrickson, 1981; Porter, 2000; Vail, 1989, Steyn argues that "the rise of extreme Afrikaner nationalism in the early part of the twentieth century is generally understood as a reaction to the defeat of the Boer forces in the South African (Anglo-Boer) War of 1899–1902. Steyn, "Rehabilitating a Whiteness Disgraced," 147.

10. See Verwey and Quayle, "Whiteness, Racism, and Afrikaner Identity," 553; Steyn, "Rehabilitating a Whiteness Disgraced."

11. See Templin, *Ideology on a Frontier*, 4.

12. Antjie Krog, *Begging to Be Black* (Cape Town: Random House Struik, 2009), 94.

13. Steyn, "Rehabilitating a Whiteness Disgraced," 147.

14. Templin, *Ideology on a Frontier*, 4.

15. Scott Everett Couper, "'Bond by Faith': A Biographic and Ecclesiastic Examination (1898–1997) of Chief Albert Luthuli's Stance on Violence as a Strategy to Liberate South Africa" (unpublished PhD diss., School of Anthropology, Gender and Historical Studies, University of KwaZulu-Natal, 2008).

16. Templin, *Ideology on a Frontier*, 117.

17. See Templin, *Ideology on a Frontier*, 117–18.

18. See Templin, *Ideology on a Frontier*, 117.

19. See Templin, *Ideology on a Frontier*, 117–18.

20. Verwey and Quayle, "Whiteness, Racism, and Afrikaner Identity," 553. Further, Afrikaner nationhood was artificially established within "a mythology that celebrated the courage of a people who refused to be subordinated to the British Empire on more than one occasion in their history." See Steyn, "Rehabilitating a Whiteness Disgraced," 147.

21. Steyn, "Rehabilitating a Whiteness Disgraced," 149.

22. Templin, *Ideology on a Frontier*, 6–7.

23. Templin, *Ideology on a Frontier*, 9.

24. Templin, *Ideology on a Frontier*, 6.

25. Templin, *Ideology on a Frontier*, 7

26. Bosman, "The '*Jerusalemgangers*,'" 159.

27. Templin, *Ideology on a Frontier*, 7.

28. Robert Morrell, Rachel Jewkers, and Graham Lindegger, "Hegemonic Masculinity / Masculinities in South Africa: Culture, Power, and Gender Politics," *Men & Masculinities* 15/1 (2012): 11–30.

29. Kobus Du Pisani, "Puritanism Transformed: Afrikaner Masculinities in Apartheid and Post-Apartheid Period," in *Changing Men in South Africa*, ed. Robert Morrell (Pietermaritzburg, South Africa: University of Natal Press, 2001), 157.

30. Debbie Epstein, "Marked Men: Whiteness and Masculinity," *Agenda* 34 (1998): 50.

31. See Adriaan S. van Klinken, "Transforming Masculinities towards Gender Justice in an Era of HIV and AIDS: Plotting Pathways," in *Religion and HIV and AIDS: Charting the Terrain*, ed. Beverley Haddad (Pietermaritzburg, South Africa: University of KwaZulu-Natal Press, 2011); Ezra Chitando, "'Even When There Is No Rooster, the Morning Will Start': Men, HIV, and African Theologies," *Journal of Feminist Studies in Religion* 28/2 (Autumn 2012): 141–45.

32. For a review, see Ezra Chitando and Sophie Chirongoma, eds., *Redemptive Masculinities: Men, HIV, and Religion* (Geneva: World Council of Churches, 2012); Adriaan S. van Klinken, *Transforming Masculinities in African Christianity* (Burlington, VT: Ashgate, 2013).

33. See Kennedy Owino, "The Mighty Men Conference as a 'Safe Space' for 'Born Again' Men to Express Conflicting Masculinities?" *Journal of Gender & Religion in Africa* 18/2 (2012): 65–81.

34. Raewyn W. Connell, Jeff Hearn, and Michael S. Kimmel, introduction to *Handbook of Studies on Men and Masculinities*, ed. Michael S. Kimmel, Jeff Hearn, and Robert W. Connell, (London: Sage, 2005), 1–12.

35. Stephen F. Miescher and Lisa A. Lindsay, introduction to "Men Masculinities in Modern African History," in *Men and Masculinities in Modern Africa*, ed. Lisa A. Lindsay and Stephen F. Miescher (Portsmouth, NH: Heinemann, 2003), 4.

36. Raewyn W. Connell, *Gender and Power: Society, the Person and Social Politics* (Stanford, CA: Stanford University Press, 1987).

37. John Beynon, *Masculinity and Culture* (Philadelphia, PA: Open University Press, 2002), 2.

38. Kimberlé Williams Crenshaw, "Demarginalizing the Intersection of Race and Sex: A Black Feminist Critique of Antidiscrimination Doctrine, Feminist Theory and Antiracist Politics," (University of Chicago Legal Forum, 1989), 39; Shan Simmonds, "Intersections of Gender, Religion and Culture in Adolescent Girls' Narrative: Curriculum Considerations for Religion Education (RE)," *Journal of Gender & Religion in Africa* 18/2, supplement (2012): 115.

39. Patricia Hill Collins, "It Is All in the Family: Intersections of Gender, Race and Nation," *Hypatia* 13/3 (Summer 1998): 63.

40. Collins, "It Is All in the Family," 63.

41. Pseudonymous names are used for all the respondents in this study in order to protect their anonymity.

42. Evangelicalism as broadly understood in South Africa is a brand of Christianity emerging from the pietistic stream of Reformed theological tradition and is epitomized in the nineteenth century South African Dutch Reformed Church leader Andrew Murray (1828–1917) (see Anthony Balcomb, "From Apartheid to the New Dispensation: Evangelicals and the Democratisation of South Africa," *Journal of Religion in Africa* 34/1/2 (February–May 2004): 9; Owino, "The Mighty Men Conference as a 'Safe Space,'" 71. In this case, the MMC as a movement confessionally adheres to Characteristics of Evangelical Christianity as clearly stated in its published Statement of Faith. See <http://www.shalomtrust.co.za/inside-shalom/angus-buchan-biography/77-statement-of-faith/> [Accessed: April 11, 2013].

43. "Conservatives" in this context refers to groups within the Evangelical strand which mainly comprises mainline denominational churches in South Africa which include for example the Church of England in South Africa, the Dutch Reformed Church, the Baptist Church, and the Presbyterians. The conservative wing of Evangelicals in South Africa is mainly characterized by those who supported Apartheid because of the biblical injunction to submit to the authority of the day, opposed, or supported attempts to oppose, any resistance to Apartheid. In post-Apartheid South Africa, the conservatives now oppose various changes that have taken place in the new dispensation. (See Balcomb, "From Apartheid to the New Dispensation," 9.

44. For a detailed elaboration on method, see Kennedy Owino, "'Godly Manhood': Evangelical Constructions of Masculinities in a South African Context: A Case Study of the Mighty Men's Conference (MMC)" (unpublished PhD diss., University of KwaZulu-Natal, 2014).

45. Angus Buchan was born in 1947 in Bulawayo, Zimbabwe, to Scottish parents. At the age of six, his family moved to the Copperbelt in Zambia, where he completed his schooling. In 1978 Buchan sold his farm and moved to South Africa with his family due to political, social, and economic unrest that Zambia was experiencing at that time. See Angus Buchan, Shalom Ministries, 2012, <http://www.shalomtrust.co.za/> [Accessed: June 10, 2012].

46. See Angus Buchan, *The Mighty Men Journey* (Vereeniging, South Africa: Christian Art Publishers, 2012); Owino, "The Mighty Men Conference as a 'Safe Space,'" 65–84.

47. Buchan, *The Mighty Men Journey*, 214.

48. Buchan, *The Mighty Men Journey*, 214.

49. Buchan, *The Mighty Men Journey*, 165.

50. Buchan, *The Mighty Men Journey*, 17.

51. Buchan, *The Mighty Men Journey*, 18.

52. Michael S. Kimmel, "Promise Keepers: Patriarchy's Second Coming as Masculine Renewal," *Tikkun* 12/2 (1997): 46–53.

53. Buchan, *The Mighty Men Journey*, 11.

54. Buchan, *The Mighty Men Journey*, 161–62.

55. Buchan, *The Mighty Men Journey*, 147.

56. Buchan, *The Mighty Men Journey*, 166.

57. Buchan, *The Mighty Men Journey*, 12–52.

58. Owino, "Godly Manhood."

59. See Owino, "The Mighty Men Conference as a 'Safe Space,'" 72.

60. Interview with Mighty Men's respondent no. 22, Pietermaritzburg, South Africa, field notes, June 20, 2012.

61. Steyn, "Rehabilitating a Whiteness Disgraced," 147.

62. I have dealt with the notion of forgiveness among the Mighty Men in an earlier publication. See Owino, "The Mighty Men Conference as a 'Safe Space.'"

63. Interview with Afrikaner male, November 20, 2011, Pietermaritzburg, South Africa.

64. Lydia Dekker, "Identity Construction of Afrikaner Car Guards in Durban" (unpublished master's thesis, University of KwaZulu-Natal, 2011), 8.

65. Buchan, *The Mighty Men Journey*, 18.

66. Buchan, *The Mighty Men Journey*, 10.

67. Melissa Steyn, "'Whiteness Just Isn't What It Used to Be': White Identity in a Changing South Africa," in *Interruptions: Border Testimony(ies) and Critical Discourse/s*, ed. Henry A. Giroux (New York: State University of New York Press, 2001).

68. Liz Walker, "Men Behaving Differently: South African Men since 1994," *Culture, Health & Sexuality* 7/3 (2005): 225–38.

69. Bosman, "The '*Jerusalemgangers*,'" 160.

70. See Bosman, "The '*Jerusalemgangers*,'" 160; André Du Toit, "No Chosen People: The Myth of the Calvinist Origins of Afrikaner Nationalism and Racial Ideology," *American Historical Review* 88 (1983): 920–52; André Du Toit, "Puritans in Africa? Afrikaner 'Calvinism' and Kuyperian Neo-Calvinism in Late Nineteenth-Century South Africa," *Comparative Studies in Society & History* 27 (1983): 209–40.

71. Bosman, "The '*Jerusalemgangers*,'" 159.

72. See Bosman, "The '*Jerusalemgangers*,'" 159.

73. Bosman, "The '*Jerusalemgangers*,'" 160.

TEN

"Some LGBTIQs Are More Unequal than Others"

Determinants of LGBTIQ Marginality in South Africa

Scott Everett Couper

PREFACE

In October 2016 the *Sunday Times* reported that gay rights activists Beverly Ditsie, Thami Kotlolo, and celebrity makeup artist Muzi Zuma were not attending nor supporting the Johannesburg gay pride event, saying that it is only "'celebration of whiteness and freedom' while gay people living in townships continue to be persecuted."[1] Critics claimed the event, first held in 1988 by Beverly Ditsie and the late Simon Nkoli, was "no longer inclusive," "has lost its focus and no longer celebrates the life and struggle of all gay men, transgender people and lesbians in the country."[2] Critics feel that white gay men feel no imperative to protest injustices despite "continuing attacks on homosexuals—particularly lesbians—in townships."[3] What explains this defection of a subaltern within a subaltern?

INTRODUCTION

This chapter responds to the query "How does 'whiteness' (race) inform constructs of gender and sexual identities within South Africa?"[4] Given that the subject matter relates to people's existential experiences, it is prudent to disclose that I am a white, heterosexual, North American male who has resided in South Africa for seventeen years.[5] I do not intend for my own nationality, race, sex, or sexual preference to substantively, if at all, reflect my thinking on LGBTIQ marginality. Nonetheless, my class (and thus my education and mobility) has influenced my thinking on issues related to LGBTIQ issues and therefore my writing suggests I have an advocacy agenda. As I am a historian by discipline, I primarily source

South African history, particularly that which relates to the LGBTIQ experience and activism.[6]

This chapter adopts a "constructionist" paradigm that interprets LGBTIQ sexuality to be disparate and "influenced by specific cultural, historical and social contexts" as opposed to an "essentialist" paradigm that interprets varied LGBTIQ identities to be "cohesive" and share a common "consciousness."[7] A constructionist paradigm demonstrates that because patriarchy privileged males, male LGBTIQs were historically less marginalized than female LGBTIQs.[8] Furthermore, a constructionist paradigm demonstrates that because racial legislation socially and economically privileged whites during the colonial and Apartheid eras, white LGBTIQs were less marginalized than those of color.[9] Patriarchy enabled males and white supremacy enabled whites who were LGBTIQ to enjoy to a greater degree a gay lifestyle than women and people of color. In short, patriarchy and white supremacy colluded to render socioeconomics, that is class, the primary determinant of LGBTIQ marginality.

As it regards degrees of marginality, both within and outside of the LGBTIQ community, generically, white males have been less disadvantaged than black males, white females have been less disadvantaged than black females, white females have been less disadvantaged than black males and black males have been less disadvantaged than black females.[10] Premised on class (determined in large part by race/Apartheid and sex/patriarchy), a hierarchical social "social ladder" can be conceived, in which those of a higher class are able to better avoid LGBTIQ marginality:

White male LGBTIQ
White female LGBTIQ
Black male LGBTIQ
Black female LGBTIQ

Mark Gevisser's chapter, "A Different Fight for Freedom," reflects white male privilege as the book in which it is found "reflects, to a large extent, white, male and middle-class experience."[11]A quintessential example of the above experience is: Justice Edwin Cameron as a white male was less marginalized by his LGBTIQ identity than was Eudy Simelane, a black female. *Despite* his openly gay identity, as a prominent attorney Cameron advised the National Union of Mine Workers, the Chamber of Mines, and Centre for Applied Legal Studies on issues related to HIV and AIDS, cofounded AIDS Consortium, "helped secure the expressed inclusion of sexual orientation in the South African Constitution," and currently sits on South Africa's Constitutional Court as a judge.[12] In contrast, *because* of her openly lesbian identity, Simelane was a victim of "corrective gang rape" and murdered in KwaThemba. In fact, the term "corrective" rape may be inaccurate as no "correction" is realistically intended (especially when death follows the rape). Though not the central message of a lecture given on April 7, 2016, Cameron states that lesbians and, I would add, black lesbians "are particularly vulnerable."[13] To more starkly frame the argument, has one ever heard reported that several heterosexual black women engaged in a corrective gang rape and murder of a gay white man? No.[14]

A "hierarchy of marginalization" thesis is predicated on the assumption that in a racist society, whites are less marginalized than Blacks and in a patriarchal society, men are less marginalized than women. Therefore, it stands to reason that white male LGBTIQs (personified by Edwin Cameron) are less marginalized than black male LGBTIQs. If males are less marginalized than females, then it stands to reason that white female LGBTIQs are more marginalized than white male LGBTIQs. The hierarchy is completed, whereby black female LGBTIQs (personified by Eudy Simelane) are more marginalized than black male LGBTIQs.

But do statistics verify the above assumed hierarchy? Statistics demonstrating LGBTIQ marginality and differentiating that marginality by race and sex are scarce.[15] The Other Foundation states that, generally, South Africans "are deeply homophobic and unaccepting of gender diversities."[16] Yet it is really not known what South Africans really think, and thus it is not known how and to what extent the LGBTIQ communities are marginalized "because hardly any work has been done to gather and analyse the views of the public in a structured way."[17] First, "marginality" is not particularly quantifiable—it includes myriad forms of discrimination that are not and cannot be substantively documented and collated. Empirical evidence of LGBTIQ marginality can perhaps be gleaned from "sexual offenses" and "hate crime" statistics. But hate crime statistics will only be available after the Prevention and Combatting of Hate Crimes Bill is tabled before Parliament in September 2016 and made law thereafter.[18] Yet it is uncertain if those statistics will differentiate victims' race and sex—let alone class.

Though scarce, statistics that demonstrate degrees LGBTIQ marginality do exist. Recently, and for the first time, the Other Foundation released a scientifically valid, nationally representative data on homosexuality in South Africa. The Other Foundation reported that 530,000 South Africans indicated that they identified themselves as LGBTIQ, the same ratio of LGBTIQ people in other countries. Yet, the only statistics in the study that documented LGBTIQ marginality (solely through physical violence) and differentiated it somehow by race and sex were: "Ninety percent of both black and white adults say they have not physically hurt gender non-conforming women and 'would never do it'" (with five percent of blacks and five percent of whites indicating they would) and "one percent of both black and white adults reported physically harming gender non-conforming women in the past year" (with one-half percent of Blacks and one-half percentage of whites indicating they had).[19] These statistics do not tell us much about marginality as a whole. Nonetheless, questions that *only* ask how many people assault non-gender-conforming women (and not men) imply that LGBTIQ women are more marginalized than men.

Benjamin Roberts and Vasu Reddy conducted the South African Social Attitudes Survey. The survey provides statistics regarding LGBTIQ marginality. First, contrary to the Other Foundation's findings examining race as a determinant, the survey concluded that "there exists a *small* racial gradient of difference in tolerance of homosexual behaviour" (Couper's emphasis) with Blacks reporting higher levels of disapproval of homosexuality than whites; second, there exists a geographic gradient of difference in tolerance of homosexual behavior, with rural areas, informal urban, and formal urban demonstrating decreasing degrees of prejudice, respectively; lastly, the survey concluded that "prejudiced views on same-sex relations appear closely related to education, with more highly educated people being more tolerant."[20] The survey suggests that there exist divides between blacks and whites, rural and urban (informal, formal), and undereducated and educated populations whereby the former are least tolerant and the latter more tolerate of LGBTIQs. The intersectionality of these three divides, containing strong socioeconomic parallels, suggests that class is the primary determinant of LGBTIQ marginality.

Though race and sex seem to be the predominant demographic determinants for marginalization of the heterogeneous LGBTIQ community, today it is class that supersedes them both. For societal acceptance, or conversely the denial of humanity, is commodified. A human's worth (in society's view) is determined by commodity fixation. Illegally, this assumption is painfully evident in the case of slavery or human trafficking. Legally, a person's class determines whether he or she can financially afford to supersede or depart from his or her environmental context to move to a context that is more accepting of LBGTIQ status. So class directly influences mobility from less accepting environments to more accepting environments. A human's worth, and thus agency, is determined by his or her access to power, and thus money. Hence, class is the primary determinate of LGBTIQ marginality though it is manifested most observably through race and sex due to the historical legacy of white supremacy and patriarchy, respectively. For example, there are assumptions regarding the degree of marginality drawn from context (class and space). "Hate crimes," many or most of which involve homophobia (again, currently statistics that differentiate *types* of hate crimes are not tabulated), occur in townships/rural spaces because they are far less inclusive compared to suburban and urban spaces. Vasu Reddy, Nonhlanhla Mkhize, Jane Bennett, and Relebohile Moletsane confirm the hierarchy by documenting hate crimes experienced by black lesbian women.[21] Also, Deevia Bhana's extensive research on sexual violence experienced by (black) girls in township environments lends much credence to the existence of a "hierarchy of marginalization," with black women most affected.[22] Commenting on Bhana's work, Paula Key wrote, "During a fifteen-year time frame, thirty lesbians have been brutally murdered in what often is a 'corrective rape' gang session. Torture is also added—these lesbians have had their throats slit, eyes removed, a water hose pumped into their stomach and vaginal mutilation."[23] Bhana's research emphasizes class or environment (space) is a primary determinate for marginality: "Large-scale social and economic inequalities structure African girls' risk to and experience of sexual violence. . . . Under conditions of chronic poverty and unstable living conditions, girls' vulnerability to sexual violence is increased."[24]

Roger Southhall's text "The New Black Middle Class in South Africa" reveals that *some* Black's socioeconomic conditions are improving since 1994, although one can rightly argue not sufficiently enough. Southhall reveals that whites have been "overtaken by Blacks as the largest population group within the middle class."[25] Southhall also reveals that "the middle class as a whole has become significantly more multiracial, recording a growing presence of black Africans (4.947 million in 2008, compared with 2.217 million in 1993) compared to a declining presence of whites (down 3.093 million in 2008 from 4.175 million in 1993).[26] Crudely speaking, if a direct corollary exists between socioeconomics and agency, as this chapter claims it does, then members of the LGBTIQ community who belong to a higher class should correspondingly be able to increasingly live out a LGBTIQ lifestyle without negatively affecting their worth (net or otherwise) or safety. Ceteris paribus, as time passes with the improving socioeconomic status of Blacks, class (rather than race or sex) should continue to become the primary factor affecting LGBTIQ marginality. In other words, as legislated racism and Black economic empowerment continue and as patriarchy diminishes, class, rather than race or sex, should continue to be the primary demographic influencing LGBTIQ marginality. Improved class, rather than race (Apartheid) or sex (patriarchy), is becoming the predominant means by which one is able to travel, access information, escape unsafe environments and domiciles, and network within a chosen community.

Yet, Africanist leaders who harbor and advocate an imagined indigenous past free of homosexuality threaten to increase the false conceptualization of race as the primary determinant for homosexual marginality.

WHITE MALE LGBTIQ MARGINALIZATION

White male homosexuals have, unsurprisingly, been the least marginalized of those whose sexualities have been ostracized and persecuted by heterosexuality's social hegemony. This reality is most easily viewed when surveying the history of the LGBTIQ advocacy movement. Intuitively, it is those who are least marginalized within the LGBTIQ community that would be the first to speak out and defend their rights.

A cursory read of Mark Gevisser's history of South African lesbian and gay organizations from the 1950's to the 1990's reveals that gay white men were at the forefront of social justice advocacy efforts. In almost all the cases of LGBTIQ rights organizations chronicled, Gevisser identifies that the initiates were middle-class professionals, and thus white men. Middle-class gay white men were primarily professionals with incomes that allowed them to transcend the otherwise restrictive barriers of a closeted lifestyle.

In 1968 "a small group of gay professionals, led by a prominent gay advocate," organized the Homosexual Law Reform Fund.[27] The action group's goal was to raise funds to thwart proposed legislation before the Parliamentary Select Committee. Notably, Gevisser states that the action group was composed of "middle-class white gay men." Gevisser further states that the action group had little solidarity with, and therefore did not include, black homosexuals as "they barely existed themselves as an organised or even informal entity."[28] Following the relatively successful 1968 legal effort, a somewhat "formalised gay culture" evolved, "creating . . . gay venues . . . and meeting places for those gay white men and women who were allowed in."[29] Yet "those who were black or could not afford . . . the entry-fee . . . were left, quite literally, out in the cold."[30]

The only South African attempt of establishing a gay rights movement in the early 1970's took place at the University of Natal in Durban when Mark West announced the formation of the South African Gay Liberation Movement. Notably, West made the announcement at a predominately male and exclusively white institution of higher learning (and thus middle class) where freedom of thought and expression had the best opportunity to be exercised. West declared, "I believe, as do my followers, that homosexuals should come forward and demand their rights. We should not be forced to meet in dark bars."[31] This was the first time a gay person had openly placed gay rights within a framework of human rights.

In 1976, a gay man, Bobby Erasmus, founded South Africa's first gay organization since the Law Reform days of 1968: Gay Aid Identification Development and Enrichment (GAIDE). GAIDE could be considered diverse. Yes, 40 percent of the supporters were women. But it would be hyperbolic to state that "GAIDE cut right across class" simply because "there were people ranging from high powered professionals to post-office workers."[32] And it was not multiracial as many within the white gay community were, from a racial perspective, politically and socially conservative.

From 1979 to 1981 the South African LGBTIQ community formed "supper clubs." One group formed in Johannesburg, Unité, composed of men and women. Also in 1981 a social group founded the 6010 Supper Club in Cape Town. John Pegge recalled, "We would hire a restaurant once a month and take it over. The motivation was to make a space. We were mainly middle-class white men who had contact with Western Europe and America, and we saw the value of social organisations outside the bar and the club."[33] Pegge's comment demonstrates that financial capital is required to create safe spaces that allow for LGBTIQs to live open and free lifestyles. During the 1960's and 1970's, when Apartheid and patriarchy were strong, only white men and some white women were able to participate in an organized LGBTIQ subculture.

In 1982 the Gay Association of South Africa (GASA) was founded as an amalgamation of three political groups, one of them Unité. Yet, again, the organization primarily represented approximately a thousand white middle-class gay male members. Soon after its founding, GASA sponsored a Gay Jamboree and in 1985 held a convention. Attendees at the convention were "almost exclusively white and male."[34] Even within GASA, the negative ramifications of patriarchy were felt by lesbians, so few women joined.

The consistent common denominator for the above legal and social organizational examples is that historically race and sex bestows socioeconomic privilege thus rendering white males the least marginalized of the LGBTIQ community. Socioeconomics enables one to escape the confines of a repressive environment and affords one the ability to migrate to and/or create a new environment for self-expression and fulfillment, be it physical (sexual), vocational, spiritual, and/or personal.

WHITE FEMALE LGBTIQ MARGINALIZATION

In his lecture dedicated to the life of Eudy Simelane, Edwin Cameron emphasized the heterogeneity of the LGBTIQ community and thus affirmed this chapter's emphasis on a constructionist paradigm: "Lesbians, as a sub-group, experience distinct and additional human rights violations compared to gay men."[35] Patriarchy, both existentially and financially, limits women, be they white or black. Yet, black female LGBTIQs suffer all the forms of marginalization that white female LGBTIQs do and more. Therefore, the section below intentionally focuses on marginality on women in general, while specifically sampling the voices of white women's experiences. The voices of black female LGBTIQs will be sampled later in the chapter, while noting that they experience the same marginalization as their white counterparts but with the increased threat of lethal violence.

Lesbians suffer the societal patriarchal psychosis that is threatened by female same-sex relations. Historically, women had to engage in more subterfuge than their male counterparts to meet other homosexuals. In his chapter "A Different Fight for Freedom," Mark Gevisser sought to highlight "the marginality and invisibility of lesbian voices in the white and black subcultures" by capturing their stories.[36] Yet, most of the stories heard where those of white female LGBTIQs.

Human Dignity Trust understands that "homosexuality is often seen as an assault on both the gendered structuring of society and the institution of the traditional family."[37] In the 1950's, "There was room in society for the 'gay bachelor' and for independent or transient men, but the pressure on women to marry and have children was—and remains—greater."[38] Amnesty International asserts that lesbians are "a threat to men's position in society; choosing to have sex with other women can be seen as a rejection of male ownership of their bodies, as well as disconnecting sex from reproduction."[39] Lesbians who opt into heterosexual marriages and have children are compelled to "stay in the closet," not so much to avoid matrimonial infidelity and divorce, but to avoid the possibility of losing access or custody of their children.

During Apartheid, South Africa's Dutch Reformed civil religion maintained a relatively conservative society whereby patriarchy, white supremacy, and heterosexuality mutually reinforced one another. There was not a strong bohemian culture and there certainly was not a substantive feminist movement. Space to engage in an open lesbian identity remained smothered. During the 1950's and 1960's, white lesbians primarily met at small parties in flats or within sporting clubs. For example, one white woman from Durban recalled:

> The only way you could meet someone was through cricket—there was no other place. . . . We knew that "those girls" played cricket, so we joined too. . . . The girls used to play at Albert Park, and every week we'd have a "Plaza Night": we'd meet at someone's home for supper, a few drinks and a game of darts.[40]

Lesbians suffer the societal oppression of patriarchy which creates for them a class disadvantage. Women's vocational options and earning potential are limited by patriarchy. Historically, women have been relegated to the health and educational sectors—the service industry—and hence did not have the means to overcome societal strictures against homosexuality with financial strength. For example, the hiring of restaurants and the purchasing and founding of clubs was rarely, if ever, an option for lesbians. Thus, public gathering spaces for lesbians remained isolated. One white woman recalled that though lesbian communities existed during the 1950's and 1960's, they had to be far stealthier than their male counterparts:

> We were all poor and hard-working. You had to remember that in those days women as a matter of course earned much less than men. And also, we were by definition independent. We didn't have men to look after us. So, we had to earn a living. And for middle-class women in the 1950's, that was unusual. There were very few professions open to us, and we could not afford to lose our jobs—there was no hubby to go running back to. This dictated how we ran our lives.[41]

If a woman had employment, their sexual identity could not be disclosed. If women enjoyed a middle- or high-class lifestyle, it was usually dependent upon a heterosexual marriage contract. Heterosexual institutions, like marriage, were more restrictive for women then they were for men.

BLACK MALE LGBTIQ MARGINALIZATION

The trend for the white male LGBTIQ community from the 1960's to the 1980's was to move from the bars and clubs to more open and public spaces—out of the "social" closet, so to speak. For the black male LGBTIQ community this was not a possibility until the 1980's. Due to restrictive Apartheid laws such as the Separate Amenities Act, Blacks as a whole were prohibited from entering "whites-only" locations or properties.

In addition to the societal marginalization that black LGBTIQs experienced, internal discrimination within the open, predominately white, LGBTIQ community also existed. For example, Simon Nkoli joined the Gay Association of South Africa (GASA) in 1983 and he complained:

> The best thing about membership was that, apparently, your little pink card got you into clubs at discounted prices. I got my Link/Skakel in the mail, and it was a feast of possibility: The Dungeon, the Butterfly, Mandys. I tried Mandys and they said "no Blacks." The Dungeon. "No Blacks." I showed them their ad in Link/Skakel: "All GASA members, welcome at a discount." "I'm a member of GASA," I'd say. "Yes," they'd reply, "but you're black. What if the police come?" The only place I managed to get in was somewhere in Jeppe Street: I was the only black person there and I felt so intimidated that I never went back.[42]

In the above testimony, two factors related to class are submerged within the issue of race. First, the public open spaces available to gay white middle-class men were often unaffordable to gay black men. Hence, Nkoli's strong interest in GASA membership for discounts. Second, black men still resided with nuclear and extended families in cramped, overcrowded domiciles and thus did not have private spaces to explore their sexuality. Because black gay men's freedom within GASA was limited, they actually had no other options. Even into the late 1980's, white males primarily composed GASA's membership.

Arguably South Africa's most prominent gay activist is the founder of the Gay and Lesbian Organisation of the Witwatersrand, the above quoted Simon Nkoli. In an interview with Mark Gevisser, Nkoli stated, "If you are black in South Africa, the inhuman laws of Apartheid closet you. If you are gay in South Africa, the homophobic customs and laws of this society closet you. If you are black and gay in South Africa, well, then it is really all the same closet."[43]

Hein Kleinbooi, technically a Colored who considers himself a Black, commented clearly on the marginality of black LGBTIQ men as compared with white LGBTIQ men. Kleinbooi attended the University of Cape Town in the early 1990's where he found "the culture, predominately white and racist, was alienating." At university, he encountered an analogy that compared heterosexism (or its dominance) to white supremacy. Kleinbooi, in opposing the analogy, reflected on the intersectionality and hierarchy of sexuality, race, and most importantly, class.

> To say that heterosexism is the same as racism is actually trivialising racial oppression. A lesbian or gay person born into a white middle class family somewhere in sunny South Africa inherits so many social privileges, and is in no way exposed to the brutalities of forced removals or police attacks in his or her own dwelling just for being gay.[44]

South Africa is very much a multiracial country whose racist past still permeates the socioeconomic context. Other sub-Saharan countries contain vastly different demographics, whereby whites feature far less prominently and therefore a thesis concerning "degrees of marginality" as it concerns race become less relevant. Also public or state violence against black male LGBTIQs is less common in South Africa due to its progressive 1993 interim and 1996 final constitution (Bill of Rights) which expressly prohibits discrimination based on sexual orientation and its Constitutional Court rulings (e.g., the 2006 Civil Union Act approving same-sex marriages) that do not subtly or overtly sanction public or state discrimination or violence against the LGBTIQ community.[45] Comment therefore must be made on Africa, as opposed to South Africa, where black male LGBTIQ marginalization is that which is most evidenced and reported.

In Nigeria, Uganda, Malawi, and Kenya public violence against black male LGBTIQs is frequently reported. In many African (and Middle Eastern) countries, legislation, and thus state policy, legalizes imprisonment and violence against homosexuals, arguably numerically affecting black males far more than white LGBTIQs or female LGBTIQs of any race in those nations.[46]

BLACK FEMALE MARGINALIZATION IN THE LGBTIQ COMMUNITY

Black female lesbians suffer all the same *and more* patriarchal biases as do white lesbians, thus rendering black lesbians with a higher degree of social marginality within and outside the LGBTIQ community. For example, one black woman who confided to her father that she was a lesbian stated, "My father said I am insulting men—why was I so bad—and said he could not believe my mother had given him this kind of child."[47]

While Edwin Cameron acknowledged in his Eudy Simelane Memorial Lecture that the LGBTIQ community is not homogenous, he ironically did not recognize the subgroup within the subgroup of the lesbian community: black lesbians. Cameron's statement, "For lesbians, the 'intersectionality' between discrimination against women and against gays and lesbians 'creates a particularly *lethal* combination,'" is actually more accurate and thus appropriate if it referred to "black lesbians" and not "lesbians" generically (Couper's emphasis).[48] Likewise, Cameron's assertion that "homophobic and transphobic violence are forms of patriarchal social control—and are directed with particular *anger and force* at same-sex oriented [women] who dare challenge patriarchy" is a statement that more accurately reflects the marginality of black lesbians as opposed to white lesbians in South Africa (my emphasis).[49] This chapter asserts that black LGBTIQ women in South Africa, as opposed to white LGBTIQ men and women, suffer a much greater degree of marginality because they are the predominate victims of violence characterized by "hate crimes." Specifically, black lesbians are arguably the primary sufferers of "corrective rape." Hence, the question posed at the beginning of the chapter: Has one ever heard a report of a gay white male that was correctively raped by a mob of black heterosexual women? No.

In the context of the lecture remembering Eudy Simelane, a black lesbian who was correctively raped and murdered, Edwin Cameron's failure to identify and highlight the subgroup within the subgroup is arguably a further marginalization of black lesbians by one of the LGBTIQ community's greatest and most well-known advocates. In Mark Gevisser's history of lesbian and gay organizations from the 1950's to the 1990's, only one reference is made specifically to "black lesbians." Cheryl-Ann Potgieter states that there exists a "paucity of [black lesbian] voices being heard" and recognizes that black lesbian voices "have been rendered invisible or non-existent."[50] Furthermore, Potgieter's study found that "society renders lesbian experiences of violence, both by their partners and when they are victims of hate crimes, invisible."[51]

Perhaps Edwin Cameron's failure to identify the degree to which black lesbians are marginalized as compared to white lesbians is due to "political correctness" because in most cases the violence committed against them is by black males. And perhaps this political correctness is more than appropriate. The differing findings of the Other Foundation and the South African Social Attitudes Survey cited earlier justify Cheryl-Ann Potgieter's warning against assuming, as is often done, "that black communities are more homophobic" than white communities.[52] Potgieter cites a 2004 study that suggests that black communities are no or little more homophobic (81 percent) than all communities at large (78 percent).[53] By assuming Blacks are more homophobic than whites, one might be "entrenching a racist stereotype."[54] Despite the manner in which Eudy Simelane was murdered, Cameron in his discretion may be "tipping his cap" to Potgieter's warning. Nonetheless, even if black communities are marginally more homophobic than communities of all races, the viciousness in which that homophobia is meted out to black lesbians within the black community (perhaps due to class, unsafe domiciles, and lack of security and law enforcement) is not reflected in the percentages cited.

AFRICAN LEADERS "ENTRENCHING A RACIST STEREOTYPE"

One would project that as South Africa's new democratic dispensation increasingly bestows greater socioeconomic opportunities to people of color and women, socioeconomics (class) alone, disassociated from race and sex, will increasingly become the primary (if not sole) determinant of LGBTIQ marginality. However, this trend toward class being the primary determinate of LGBTIQ marginality is being thwarted by populist African leaders (such as Yoweri Museveni, Robert Mugabe, Jacob Zuma, and King Goodwill Zwelithini) who appeal to an imagined, idealized and romanticized African culture to claim LGBTIQ identities are a white and Western phenomenon and not universal. For example, in November 2009, Yoweri Museveni told young Ugandans, "I hear European homosexuals are recruiting in Africa. . . . We used to have very few homosexuals traditionally."[55] In the legal case against Winnie Mandela, it was claimed that "white rapists made Coloureds (and homosexuals)."[56] Mandela's defense strategy, which was by George Bizos, "characterised homosexual practice as a white, colonising depredation of heterosexual black culture. 'Homosex is not in black culture,' read a placard held by one of Mandela's supporters outside the court."[57] An example of this viewpoint was expressed by one black lesbian: "My father got angry and said I just needed men to show me how good sleeping with them were. He also said this was a white thing, totally not part of his culture. He then chased me away."[58]

Populist African leaders' primary constituency is to the "masses" who are, for the most part, socioeconomically deprived, and their words may ironically cause LGBTIQ marginality to again be racialized despite the fact that the amelioration of Blacks' socioeconomic conditions should move the primary determinant of marginality to class. A two-fold racialization can occur: First, white westerners can again perceive Blacks as sociologically stunted and thus inferior and, second, black LGBTIQs will again be marginalized by those of color while accepting and thus privileging white LGBTIQs in comparison. In this sense, Africanist leaders revive a racial "essentialism among whites," be it "traditional" (Blacks are racially inferior) or "liberal" (Blacks, while not racially inferior, are uncivilized and require Western tutelage).[59] This entrenchment of a racial stereotype that Blacks are culturally and scientifically regressive as it regards the acceptance of homosexuality is most ironic given that it was white westerners, by means of colonialism, who formalized and legalized homophobia though the imposition of Judeo-Christian values, legislation, and even violence. The supposed arbiters and protectors of African culture are actually, out of ignorance of their own African culture, rehegemonizing an archaic white and Western culture when much of postmodern white Western culture perceives that same homophobic culture as passé and the victimizing of gays and lesbians as uncivilized. The ironies are piled high.

When the question "Who is an African?" is asked, it is accurate to affirm that LGBTIQs are. Edwin Cameron rightly stated in his Eudy Simelane Memorial Lecture that:

> In reality, same-sex orientation is a simple variant—between five percent and ten percent of every race, every continent, every culture, every language, every religion has some measure of same-sex orientation. All classes and sectors; every school, community, congregation, neighbourhood; every family has LGBTI[Q] members.[60]

Marc Epprecht is perhaps the most prominent academic who has documented the existence of homosexuality in precolonial Africa. In his book

Hungochani, Epprecht "illuminated the rich history of same-sex practices and ideas in southern Africa, stretching back well before contact with Europeans."[61] Furthermore, in his book *Heterosexual Africa?* "Epprecht argues that European colonial authorities, settlers, and scholars, *did not* introduce homosexual practices to Africa, but *did* introduce their own homophobia and racism, projecting those ideas onto studies of sexuality in Africa."[62] Wazha Lopang also acknowledges the presence of homosexuality in precolonial Africa and demonstrates that in their denial of African homosexuality, colonial African writers described it as evil or "ignored it altogether" and thus contributed to the trope that homosexuality is alien to Africa.[63]

Thabo Msibi is another scholar that has written extensively on the existence and practice of homosexuality in precolonial Africa. In his article "The Lies We Have Been Told," Msibi concurs with Epprecht that "same-sex sexual attraction and expression were known to occur in usually hidden but sometimes even culturally accepted ways."[64] Furthermore, Msibi presents "evidence that homophobia is not only publicly approved by African leaders, but relies on unsubstantiated claims of an imposed homosexual identity, contradictory ideas on morality and the use of outdated laws."[65] Given that "there is no doubt that homosexuality existed in pre-colonial Africa" and given "the iconographic representation that homosexuality is un-African," Robert Kuloba has recently "situated homosexuality in the context of African hybridity."[66] An African in the postcolonial era is a hybrid offspring, incorporating Western-sourced homophobia and incorporating it and identifying it as "African." Hence, Kuloba's hybrid Africa is a fusion or grafting of that which is African (the existence of homosexuals) with homophobia (that which is a Western colonial import).

There is nothing un-African about accepting what was always there. There is nothing un-African about cultural change. There is nothing un-African about changing social mores influenced by scientific knowledge. There is nothing un-African about the acceptance of LGBTIQs.

CONCLUSION

Race (given South Africa's Apartheid past) and sex (given South Africa's patriarchal societies, both white and black) are key determinants for LGBTIQ marginality. However, class supersedes race and sex as a determinant despite the reality that race and sex can be impediments to class mobility in a (still) racist and patriarchal country. Therefore, the reduction of homophobic attitudes and acts of violence is dependent upon improving law enforcement (and rights often do not translate to justice) and the collection of statistics for hate crimes with the passage of the Prevention and Combatting of Hate Crimes Bill, the provision of quality education (particularly life orientation) to South Africa's most marginalized populations, and the cessation of homophobic utterances by populist African leaders. Above all, as the intersectionality of race, geographic location, and education (South African Social Attitudes Survey) demonstrates, the number of homophobic acts of violence will be reduced if LGBTIQ's socioeconomics afford them the mobility to escape hostile environs and move to more inclusive ones.

NOTES

1. Khanyi Ndabeni, "'White' Joburg Gay Pride Bashed as Frivolous," *Sunday Times*, October 23, 2016, 6.
2. Ndabeni, "'White' Joburg Gay Pride Bashed as Frivolous."
3. Ndabeni, "'White' Joburg Gay Pride Bashed as Frivolous."
4. The various gender and sexual identities can be summarized with the acronym LBGTIQ or Lesbian, Bisexual, Gay, Transgender, Intersex, and Queer.
5. In this essay, I do not capitalize racial characters such as "white" when it is used grammatically as an adjective ("a single white male"). I do capitalize racial groups such as "Blacks" when referring to specific race group as a proper noun ("Blacks are the majority").
6. For the history, I primarily source chapters from: Mark Gevisser and Edwin Cameron, eds., *Defiant Desire: Gay and Lesbian Lives in South Africa* (Johannesburg: Ravan Press, 1994). Gevisser and Cameron's text contains a minefield of narratives from which I can draw personal narratives reflecting the experiences of white, black, male, and female LGBTIQs. Neither the history nor the narratives are by any means comprehensive; I offer only "samples."
7. Mark Gevisser, "A Different Fight for Freedom: A History of South African Lesbian and Gay Organisations from the 1950s to the 1990s," in *Defiant Desire: Gay and Lesbian Lives in South Africa,* ed. Mark Gevisser and Edwin Cameron (Johannesburg: Ravan Press, 1994), 16–17.
8. I use the acronym LGBTIQ (Lesbian, Gay, Bisexual, Transgender, Intersex, Queer) as a noun inclusive of various sexual identities that are associated with homosexuality. Although, a white "male," "LGBTIQ" may be somewhat redundant (male and G) and contradictory (male and L), I intentionally choose not to omit the "L" for lesbian for the sake of consistency.
9. When I refer to "people of color," I speak of Blacks, Coloreds and Indians—all socially constructed racial categorizations imposed on South Africans during the colonial and Apartheid eras.
10. Of course, there exist anomalies. It might be that a gay white working-class male's experience might be more negative than a rich black lesbian's.
11. Gevisser, "A Different Fight for Freedom," 17.

12. Brochure, "Inaugural Eudy Simelane Lecture," Ujamaa Centre, School of Religion, Philosophy and Classics, University of KwaZulu-Natal, program, April 7, 2016, 2.

13. Edwin Cameron, "Eudy Simelane Memorial Lecture," inaugural lecture on behalf of the Other Foundation and the Ujamaa Centre, University of KwaZulu-Natal, Pietermaritzburg, South Africa, April 7, 2016, 4. This lecture was given at the conference, entitled "Homophobia and the Churches in Africa: A Dialogue," at the Seth Mokitimi Methodist Seminary, Pietermaritzburg, South Africa, April 7–8, 2016.

14. A gay black man was gang raped and set alight by other men in Lerato Park, Kimberly. So this chapter does not deny that violent homophobic acts are committed against white males and females and black males. See Ludovica Luccino, "South Africa: Gay Man Gang-Raped and Set Alight in Homophobic Attack," *International Business Times*, March 31, 2014, <http://www.ibtimes.co.uk/south-africa-gay-man-gang-raped-set-alight-homosexual-attack-1442690/> [Accessed: May 19, 2016].

15. Quantitative studies on marginalization based on sex do exist. For example, the Commission for Gender Equity has a text (unpublished) entitled "Gender Equity in South Africa: Progress and Challenges," compiled by its commissioner, Janine Hicks.

16. The Other Foundation, "Progressive Prudes," <http://theotherfoundation.org/progressive-prudes/> [Accessed: October 17, 2016]. See also the Human Sciences Research Council's survey: <http://www.hsrc.ac.za/uploads/pageContent/1607/Pride%20and%20Prejudice.pdf/> [Accessed: October 23, 2016].

17. The Other Foundation, "Progressive Prudes," <http://theotherfoundation.org/progressive-prudes/> [Accessed: October 17, 2016].

18. Republic of South Africa, South African Criminal Law Sexual Offenses and Related Matters Amendment Act No. 32 (Pretoria: Government Printers, 2007); Gideon Muchiri, "The Upcoming Hate Crimes Bill: A Welcome Development in the Fight against Xenophobia and Hate Crimes in South Africa," *AfricLaw* 5 (August 2016), <https://africlaw.com/2016/08/05/the-upcoming-hate-crimes-bill-a-welcome-development-in-the-fight-against-xenophobia-and-hate-crimes-in-south-africa/> [Accessed: October 1, 2016].

19. The Other Foundation, "Progressive Prudes," <http://theotherfoundation.org/progressive-prudes/> [Accessed: October 17, 2016].

20. Benjamin Roberts and Vasu Reddy, "Pride and Prejudice: Public Attitudes toward Homosexuality," South African Social Attitudes Survey, Human Sciences Research Council, *HSRC Review* 6/4 (2008): 9–11. <http://www.hsrc.ac.za/uploads/pageContent/1607/Pride%20and%20Prejudice.pdf/> [Accessed: October 24, 2016].

21. Vasu Reddy, Nonhlanhla Mkhize, Jane Bennett, and Relebohile Moletsane, *The Country We Want to Live In: Hate Crimes and Homophobia in the Lives of Black Lesbian South Africans*, (Pretoria: HSRC Press, 2010).

22. Deevia Bhana, *The Regulation of Sexualities in South African Secondary Schools* (Cape Town: Modjaji Books, 2015).

23. Paula Key, "The Regulation of Sexualities in South African Secondary Schools," Stories 4 Hotblooded Lesbians, January 14, 2015, <http://stories4hotbloodedlesbians.com/regulation-sexualities-south-african-secondary-schools/> [Accessed: October 17, 2016].

24. Deevia Bhana, "When Caring Is Not Enough: The Limits of Teachers' Support for South African Primary School-Girls in the Context of Sexual Violence," *International Journal of Educational Development* 41 (2015): 262.

25. Roger Southhall, *The New Black Middle Class in South Africa* (Dunkeld, South Africa: Konrad Adenauer Foundation, 2016), 53.

26. Southhall, *The New Black Middle Class in South Africa,* 50. Southhall cites Justin Visagie, "The Development of the Middle Class in Post-Apartheid South Africa," a paper presented at the Micro-Econometric Analysis of South Africa Data Conference, Salt Rock Hotel, October 2011, table 2, 8.

27. Gevisser, "A Different Fight for Freedom," 32–33.

28. Gevisser, "A Different Fight for Freedom," 34.

29. Gevisser, "A Different Fight for Freedom," 34.

30. Gevisser, "A Different Fight for Freedom," 37.

31. Gevisser, "A Different Fight for Freedom," 43; Gevisser cites *Natal Daily News,* April 20, 1972.

32. Gevisser, "A Different Fight for Freedom," 45.

33. Gevisser, "A Different Fight for Freedom," 46.

34. Gevisser, "A Different Fight for Freedom," 49.

35. Cameron, "Eudy Simelane Memorial Lecture," 4. Cameron cites Human Dignity Trust, *Briefing Note: Breaking the Silence: Impacts of Criminalisation of Homosexuality on Lesbians,* London, March 2015,17.

36. Gevisser, "A Different Fight for Freedom," 17.

37. Cameron, "Eudy Simelane Memorial Lecture, 5. Cameron cites Human Dignity Trust, *Breaking the Silence,* 18.

38. Gevisser, "A Different Fight for Freedom," 22.

39. Cameron, "Eudy Simelane Memorial Lecture, 5. Cameron cites Amnesty International, *Making Love a Crime: Criminalisation of Same-Sex Conduct in Sub-Saharan Africa,* 25 June 2013, AFR 01/012/2013, 47.

40. Gevisser, "A Different Fight for Freedom," 21. Gevisser cites *Sunday's Women,* September 1990.

41. Gevisser, "A Different Fight for Freedom," 22.

42. Gevisser, "A Different Fight for Freedom," 52. As a qualification, it may not have been "club racism" but rather "legal restrictions" that marginalized Blacks. In 1983 the Separate Amenities Act was still enforced. Licensed establishments had to comply, but unlicensed establishments (who presumably could not sell alcohol) did not have to comply with segregation laws.

43. Simon Nkoli, "Wardrobes: Coming Out as a Black Gay Activist in South Africa," in *Defiant Desire: Gay and Lesbian Lives in South Africa,* ed. Mark Gevisser and Edwin Cameron (Johannesburg: Ravan Press: 1994), 249–50.

44. Hein Kleinbooi, "Identity Crossfire: On Being a Gay Black Student Activist," in *Defiant Desire: Gay and Lesbian Lives in South Africa,* ed. Mark Gevisser and Edwin Cameron (Johannesburg: Ravan Press, 1994), 266–67.

45. Cameron, "Eudy Simelane Memorial Lecture," 4. Cameron cites "National Coalition for Gay and Lesbian Equality vs Minister of Justice," 1999 (1) SA 6 (CC) paras. 107 and 127, per Sachs J.

46. Cameron, "Eudy Simelane Memorial Lecture," 2. Cameron mentions the cases of Steven Monjeza and Tiwonge Chimbalanga of Malawi.

47. Cheryl-Ann Potgieter, "Sexualities? Hey, This Is What Black South African Lesbians Have to Say about Relationships with Men, the Family, Heterosexual Women and Culture," in *Performing Queer: Shaping Sexualities 1994–2004*, vol. 1, Social Identities South Africa Series, ed. Mikki van Zyl and Melissa Steyn (Roggebaai, South Africa: Kwela Books, 2005), 186.

48. Cameron, "Eudy Simelane Memorial Lecture," 4. Cameron cites Human Dignity Trust, *Breaking the Silence*, 17.

49. Cameron, "Eudy Simelane Memorial Lecture," 4. Cameron cites Triangle Project (Lee, Lynch, and Clayton), "Your Hate Won't Change Us: Resisting Homophobic and Transphobic Violence as Forms of Patriarchal Social Control" (2013), 28. Triangle Project cites H. Moffett, "'These Women, They Force Us to Rape Them': Rape as Narrative of Social Control in Post-Apartheid South Africa," *Journal of Southern African Studies* 32/1 (2006): 129–44.

50. Potgieter, "Sexualities?,"176.

51. Potgieter, "Sexualities?," 181.

52. Potgieter, "Sexualities?," 187.

53. Potgieter, "Sexualities?," 187. Potgieter cites S. Rule, "Rights or Wrongs? Public Attitudes towards Moral Values," *Human Sciences Research Council Review* 2/3 (2004): 4–5.

54. Potgieter, "Sexualities?," 187.

55. Matt Swagler, "The Myth of 'Heterosexual Africa,'" *International Socialist Review* 71, (May 2010), <http://isreview.org/issue/71/myth-heterosexual-africa/> [Accessed: October 17, 2016].

56. Rachel Homes, "'White Rapists Made Coloureds (and Homosexuals)': The Winnie Mandela Trial and the Politics of Race and Sexuality," in *Defiant Desire: Gay and Lesbian Lives in South Africa*, ed. Mark Gevisser and Edwin Cameron (Johannesburg: Ravan Press, 1994), 284.

57. Homes, "'White Rapists Made Coloureds (and Homosexuals),'" 284–85.

58. Potgieter, "Sexualities?," 186.

59. Mohamed Adhikari, "From Narratives of Miscegenation to Post-modern Re-imagining: Towards a Historiography of Coloured Identity in South Africa" in *Burdened by Race: Coloured Identities in Southern Africa*, ed. Mohamed Adhikari (Cape Town: University of Cape Town Press, 2009), 7–9.

60. Cameron, "Eudy Simelane Memorial Lecture," 3. Cameron cites Academy of Sciences of South Africa, *Diversity in Human Sexuality—Implications for Policy in Africa*, May 2015.

61. Swagler, "The Myth of 'Heterosexual Africa.'"

Swagler references Marc Epprecht, *Hungochani: The History of a Dissident Sexuality in Southern Africa* (Montreal: McGill-Queen's University Press, 2004).

62. Swagler, "The Myth of 'Heterosexual Africa.'" Swagler reviews Marc Epprecht, *Heterosexual Africa? The History of an Idea from the Age of Exploration to the Age of AIDS* (Athens: Ohio University Press, 2008). See also Saheed Aderinto, "*Marc Epprecht: Heterosexual Africa?*" *Gender Forum* 23 (2008), <http://www.genderforum.org/issues/face-to-race/marc-epprecht-heterosexual-africa-the-history-of-an-idea-from-the-age-of-exploration-to-the-age-of-aids-athens-ohio-ohio-university-press-2008/> [Accessed: October 17, 2016].

63. Wazha Lopang, "No Place for Gays: Colonialism and the African Homosexual in African Literature," *International Journal of Humanities & Social Science* 4, 9/1 (July 2014): 77.

64. Thabo Msibi, "The Lies We Have Been Told: On (Homo) Sexuality in Africa," *Africa Today* 58/1 (Autumn 2011): 55.

65. Msibi, "The Lies We Have Been Told," 55.

66. Robert Kuloba, "'Homosexuality Is Unafrican and Unbiblical': Examining the Ideological Motivations to Homophobia in Sub-Saharan Africa: The Case Study of Uganda," *Journal of Theology for Southern Africa* 154 (March 2016): 15.

ELEVEN

Rituals of Female Solidarity

The Role of Imbusa in Promoting Social Cohesion among Married Women in Pietermaritzburg, South Africa

Mutale M. Kaunda and Chammah J. Kaunda

INTRODUCTION

The 2015 Johannesburg Carnival's 10th edition, which came but a few months after xenophobic attacks in KwaZulu-Natal, was about celebrating South Africa's cultural diversity. Foreign nationals across the continent were invited to showcase their different cultures. It was seen as an opportunity to learn about different cultural traditions of various foreign nationals living in the country. The deputy director of communications of the city of Johannesburg, Nthatisi Modingoane, emphasized, "One of the key objectives of [South Africa] is really to build what we call social cohesion."[1] The carnival's emphasis on the distinctiveness and multiplicity of identities is commendable, but all is based on promoting cultural distinctiveness without deliberately cultural value exchange. Contemporary life is based on interaction of foreign bodies and public security depends on cultural exchange in order to experience harmonious symbiosis among different groups. They have specificities and different cultures; yet, they live in the same space. Hence, are there some innovative ways that different groups engage in some forms of cultural exchange in order to create social cohesion?

The aim of this chapter is to examine how women are creatively promoting social cohesion through intercultural exchange in Pietermaritzburg in South Africa. Taking the institution of *imbusa*—the Bemba premarital initiation rite through which a young woman is prepared for becoming an ideal married woman—this chapter will demonstrate how *imbusa* ritual in diaspora functions as a space for promoting social cohesion and female solidarity among foreign nationals and local nationals. The rite seems to be going through an acculturation process as women report adopting and adapting *imbusa* to various cultures.

This chapter argues that promotion of adaptive cultural traditions such as *imbusa* has potential to contribute to prevention of xenophobia alongside anti-xenophobia policies being developed in South Africa which too often exhibit legalism without accompanying attitudinal transformation toward foreign nationals. The implications of this study for policy matters is important, especially for public understanding that immigrant cultural traditions have much to contribute in promoting social cohesion. Most African cultural traditions have been situated within the broader context of cultural pluralism in South Africa. However, there are scarce studies that have been done regarding how some foreign traditional cultures such as *imbusa* function to promote social cohesion in the diaspora. Perhaps because such rites are too often done in semipublic spaces with only women in attendance, they remain virtually invisible to mainstream society.

In Pietermaritzburg, *imbusa* acculturation as an approach to issues of diversity, married woman identity construction and peaceful coexistence seem to be viable tools. The data for this study was gathered through participant observation and in-depth interviews conducted with eight Zambian women and two South African women living in Pietermaritzburg in 2012.[2] Initially, there were fifteen women who had agreed to the interview, but five later pulled out for one reason or another. The most common reason they gave was that they were too busy. The women interviewed came from an economic and age cross section of society, but this study is focused on married women who in 2012 were in the age range between twenty-three and forty-five years, and had been married for two to twenty-five years. Most of these women had gone through *imbusa* prior to their coming to South Africa or within South Africa. *Imbusa* teachings are specifically for women about to be married, and it is only married women who have the information that is contained in the rite.

This qualitative study begins by unpacking how *imbusa* is understood within Bemba cultural context before moving on to analyze how Zambian women are renovating and transforming *imbusa* for adequacy in diaspora contexts.

IMBUSA IN THE BEMBA CULTURAL CONTEXT

Imbusa as a rite occupies a central place among the Bemba people of Northern, Muchinga, Luapula, and Central Provinces of Zambia and represent the largest ethnic group in the country.[3] The Bemba precolonial social structure was matrilineal,[4] matrilocal[5] and monogamous based with a well-entrenched matriclan system of organization. Unlike patriarchal cultures, in Bemba cosmology, ancestry is traced through the woman.[6]

From the onset, it is important to distinguish two rituals for young women within the Bemba culture. The first rite is for girls at their first menstruation, called *icisungu*, a word derived from the noun *icisungusho* (a miraculous or shocking event). The girl's experience of her first menstruation was cerebrated as *ukuwa icisungu* or *ukuwilwa ne cisungusho* (lit., "the miracle has fallen on her or experiencing a miracle), through which the girl received the divine gift of feminine sexuality from *Lesa* ("God").[7] But it was also a miracle/*icisungusho* due to the girl's astonishment at her first menstrual blood—for nothing prepares her for the first menstrual blood.

The second ritual of *imbusa* on which this chapter focuses is a rite of passage given to young women a month or three weeks prior to their wedding. Practiced by almost all ethnic groups in Zambia, the ritual involves older married women giving indigenous wisdom, explicit sexual lessons, and other homemaking skills before entering into marriage.[8] As a semiprivate space exclusively for married women, *imbusa* creates safe spaces where women empower each other about female solidarity, sexuality, and marriage longevity.

Due to the sacredness associated with femininity, these lessons are communicated in symbolic terms. *Banacimbusa* (lit., "the ones who chisels or moulds, or are guardians of divine femininity") utilize indigenous methodologies including songs, dance, riddles, folklores, kitchen utensils, methods of preparing certain types of food, and so on.[9] The concept of *imbusa* is etymologically derived from the word *imbaso*—a chiseling tool for making wood artifacts. From this perspective, *imbusa* is a process designed or tailored to chisel and curve out the woman in the girl, to bring out her divine feminine status as given by *Lesa*.[10] Thera Rasing rightly argues *imbusa* is a transition ritual that is perceived as a means to cross boundaries, changes in time, and social status.[11] Mutale Kaunda highlights the twofold aim of *imbusa* within Bemba cosmology.[12]

First, *imbusa* is an instrument that women utilize to subvert the status quo in their marriages and society. It is a form or method used by Bemba women for premarital counseling of women for viable marriages and social transformation. It is not only the initiator who benefits from this institution, but it works as a marriage improvement and female sociocultural education program where every woman who has undergone the ritual has an opportunity to reengage in discussions about what it means to be a married Bemba woman.

Second, *imbusa* is a tool for creating female "cohesion and solidarity."[13] *Imbusa* brought women together in solidarity concerning marriage and society so that transformation can take place. Mushibwe affirms that women need each other's loyalty in order to stand in solidarity in the community.[14] Although Rasing contends that since *imbusa* is a woman-centered rite, it aids the "construction of female identity, pride, autonomy and meaning."[15]

In this critical rite, Bemba women are also skillfully taught sexual and social agency. Although *banacimbusa* are the key instructors, the rite is open to all initiated women as long as they are ready to pass on their marriage and social experiences and sexual skills to new brides.

In this space, every initiated married woman is both a spectator and critical participant. Thus, as the teaching goes on during *imbusa*, everyone participates to help shape the young bride as well as remind other women of the value of femininity. It is an exciting moment for women who narrate memories of their own daily experiences in their marriage and society. *Imbusa* takes women on the journey of learning and relearning, evaluating and reevaluating their experiences in marriage and society before passing them to the young. It is also a safe space of learning from the other *banacimbusa* and married women. In this way, a bond and solidarity among these women is formed as they begin to understand their common experiences as women.

THEORIZING *IMBUSA* AS DIASPORA RITUAL

How do we conceptualize and imagine *imbusa* as a diaspora ritual? What model best fits the profile and identity it advocates?

Most of the studies done on *imbusa* have focused on the Zambian context.[16] It was Mutale M. Kaunda in her master's dissertation, in which she aimed to demonstrate the continuity of *imbusa* in the diaspora context. In this pioneering empirical research, she discovered that "the institution of *imbusa* has in many ways exhibited resilience and tenacious adaptability in the context of modernisation and globalisation but has also shown continuity in the different contexts of the Zambian Diaspora."[17] She argued that among the women in the diaspora, the Zambian women do not consciously associate *imbusa* with the cultural past of the Bemba people. This aspect is not perceived as obligatory like those who perform the rite within the Zambian Bemba context do.

Utilizing current system theory in cultural studies reveals that migrants often uncritically reproduce their cultural traditions, rituals, and religion in diaspora contexts. Scholars have further argued that settlement patterns of most migrant communities tend to further the maintenance of socio-cultural ideals of their nationality ties in addition to minimizing the effects of social, religious, political, economic, and cultural disequilibrium in the host nation.[18] In addition, cultural researchers argue that the migrant communities too often seek to reproduce their cultural identity in diaspora contexts for retaining their identity but also as a means of connection with their nationalities.[19]

Our central finding is that *imbusa* is transnationalized to transcend the Zambian-Bemba perspective as a means of attaining and constructing social fields, as well as integrating host cultural values together with values from the transcultural traditions of other immigrant African communities. This means that *imbusa* as reenacted within diaspora contexts demonstrates that the rite is going through a process of transformation and expresses specific diasporic contextual functions, actions, and symbols that have little or less resemblance to Zambian *imbusa*. The diaspora *imbusa* is reconstructed to embrace the circumstances and experiences of being in a hostile diaspora context. For example, women who have never gone through *imbusa* and those cohabiting are allowed into *imbusa* space without discrimination. In fact, one of the *banacimbusa* acknowledged she never went through *imbusa* before she got married. In the Zambian context of *imbusa*, such women are never allowed to enter the sacred space of *imbusa*, being regarded as *bachitongo* (lit., "unformed girls, who are untaught and uncultured"). Without undergoing *imbusa* teaching, these women would be regarded as girls, unfit to handle marriage and can never be a part of married women's teaching space, least of all become *nacimbusa* (lit., "ritual guardians").

In diaspora contexts, the Bemba initiation rite of *imbusa* is linked to orthopraxy and its cultural benefits are often inconsequential. The *imbusa* teaching in diaspora contexts has to contend with the fact that the specialist *banacimbusa* are not only absent but have to function in a context of a "cultural salad" in which cross-national women seek to participate in the ritual context. Hence, the search for integration within the new contexts that Zambian women find themselves has to do with negotiating new cultural terrains, which in turn necessitates transformation in *imbusa* performance. For *imbusa* in diaspora contexts, therefore, transformation is not a luxury, but indicates the struggle for survival of transnational women and the search for relevancy in the context of the (often) harsh socioeconomic realities of their host countries.

The forgoing does not mean that *imbusa* has abandoned all ritual aspects, but instead has sought to reproduce itself, albeit, in a reconstructed manner. Accordingly, the ritual continues to serve as sacred space for preparing young brides for marriage, the promotion of female sexual agency, and functions as a space for female solidarity both for immigrant and local women. This means that collective female identities among these women that transcend ethnic or national structures of belonging are most probably constructed. Some of these Zambian women appear to deliberately and consciously subvert their ethnicity to counter objectifying ethnocentric discourse prevalent in South Africa.

RITUALIZATION OF FEMALE SOCIAL COHESION

The ritual of *imbusa* in the Zambian diaspora in South Africa has shown its ability to adapt to changing contexts. Accordingly, it has loosened its ritual boundaries to accommodate multicultural female initiation rites of passage from other African nations. Despite the fact that *imbusa* is more pronounced as the framework for teaching young brides, it is the majority of Zambian women teaching in the diaspora. It has nevertheless embraced various elements from other African cultures including that of Zulu women. For example, Lynn,[20] a Zambian *nacimbusa* and Zambian diaspora living in Pietermaritzburg, could report:

> I can say that I have not been teaching ladies from many other African nations only it's like people just have some confidence in Zambian teaching on marriage having witnessed the thoroughness of our teaching. Women of other nations have just had confidence in us to be able to teach their daughters or nieces etc. . . . I have mostly taught Zimbabweans, Malawians, and South Africans. Usually those who approached me are those who have heard me teaching or because they have seen me teaching. We have to find out from the guardians on their marriage practices before we teach the brides from other nations. We mix these practices with those from Zambia.

For this, it is clear that the emphasis of *imbusa* in diaspora contexts is not about its distinctiveness, but instead about the value it contributes to other cultural identities, all of which claim their position in South African society. *Imbusa* in diaspora contexts is not about promoting Zambian cultural distinctiveness and ethnic identity but the promotion of a collective identity. Natasha,[21] who is also a *nacimbusa*, came to South Africa in 1998 and has taught *imbusa* for over nine years in Pietermaritzburg. She narrates that "we have taught on several occasions more than four brides from other African countries." Mpika[22] further explains:

> When I mention that they do have teachings, their guardians indicated that they do have teachings but when they have come in South Africa they are not giving to their children those teachings. They are depending on a community of women, regardless of where those women come from to teach. . . . When we sit down to agree on what to teach as different women, then you find that those guardians would speak. For example we were teaching a particular girl, the topic was on sex and intimacy in the bedroom, two Malawians, two Zambians, and two South Africans teaching this girl, as we were teaching we just touched on the aspect of the bedroom privacy how to respect the bedroom; and three nationalities represented there we found that they respected the bedroom differently. One of the nationalities said, "For us it's nothing, kids can walk in friends can walk in, etc." whereas for us a bedroom is a sacred place because that's your place so kids and your sisters

> have to knock. The way things are kept in the bedroom is critical for a married woman. Then one of the nationalities went to the extent of saying that for them not only are you supposed to knock, but the maid can't even go in and clean or wash your beddings, so the very same topic was discussed but the depth or the extent or degree that the teachings apply was totally different and as we sat there then we are learning from each other as well. With the teachings I believe that we come from different cultures and embrace our cultures and you can't force one particular culture on the girl especially if the girl doesn't belong to your culture. When teaching a Zambian she had to understand the Zambian culture, and the others would come in just as variations so that she understands that this thing is not only peculiar to Zambia because sometimes when people think this is a Zambian thing and we are living in the diaspora, they might think it doesn't matter with others. But when they hear that it also occurs where they come from, they learn to respect the culture. But if we are teaching a girl that's not a Zambian we lay all of this and if there's nothing from her side, then we say to her, among all of this what are you feeling comfortable to take with?, because we don't want her to say, am not taking any because we have seen it working in our own cultures/marriages that this is how you keep bedroom issues.

We have quoted Natasha at length because in her comment, she demonstrates how *imbusa* in diaspora contexts is not simply a means for preparing a bride for marriage. Instead, its goal is a process in which women can engage in rethinking about their cultures and retune them for their specific goal within diaspora contexts. Hence, these women perceive *imbusa* as an educational space where they discuss their cultural traditions and enrich one another. Natasha[23] recollects that having "recently taught Zambian girl, we invited a South African lady in her sixties, and two South African ladies in their early thirties [Zulu and Xhosa], there were Malawians, then there were Zambians." In this case, *imbusa* is seen as inclusive tradition helping to build customary and national traditions that unify both African foreign nationals and local nationals. As such, it helps to promote a strong national integration at least for women. In her research on *imbusa* in the Zambian diaspora in South Africa, Kaunda discovered that the ritual in its diasporic reenactment still returns its Bemba teaching methodology which is mostly done through song, dance, and the collective participation of any married woman.[24] As Natasha[25] affirms:

> We do teach through songs and dance and when we are putting together a committee, for example, the one lady from Kenya has approached us to teach her daughter, then I'd sit and say who in the committee would assist because I know that they are coming with that rich experience. So, they would come with a song and we dance but all of it carrying a message. For example, you sing, "when child cries feed the child" [*mwana akalila munyonshe*], but from the face value you would think we are just talking about breastfeeding a

> child, but what we are saying is that even if you are breastfeeding, sex in the bedroom you must still carry on.

Imbusa is also seen as a ritual enabling the transformation of relationships among women in diaspora contexts, especially that "some South African women believe that foreign women have powerful love potions that make their husbands to remain faithful in marriage despite several beautiful women around. They think that only *muthi*[26] can make a man remain faithful to the wife."[27] Consequently, Natasha[28] believes that *imbusa* functions as a platform through which foreign women communicate, share ideas or the so-called secrets of marriage longevity. In this way, *imbusa* helps to reduce mutual suspicion and promotes female solidarity and social cohesion. This means the space *imbusa* creates for women depends much on the intercultural identities of women from various cultural groups who come together to form an integrated *imbusa* among them, each incorporating different elements, while retaining the cultural distinctiveness of each ethnic.[29] We thus argue that *imbusa* space in diaspora contexts is based on the mutual exchange of cultural ideas, beliefs, and activities, rather than comparison and competition among the values held by women from different cultural groups.[30]

In her interview, Natasha[31] reported some laxity in the promotion of social cohesion. She remembers that *imbusa* had been

> a very strong driver in the cohesion of women to an extent that we would meet to pray and discuss HIV and AIDS and all these things. But . . . we relaxed and had to start the groups afresh but it's a place where women draw identity, because then we realised that we are all women here whether you are from Rwanda or wherever. We draw that and you find that the women that come for these meetings, you find that the cohesion begins to build. You have just reminded me of what I forgot, that we prayed together as women and so on.

According to this statement, *imbusa* represents a traditional Bemba worldview that affirms women's agency, subjectivity, and solidarity. In diaspora contexts, these values have been shown to be inclusive for all women from various nationalities.[32] This is similar to the observation made by Rasing, that while undergoing *imbusa*, women do not just gather to pass "norms and values concerning gender, production and reproduction, and cosmological ideas rite," but they also express "and confirm solidarity and unity among women."[33] In her interview, Lynn[34] was found in agreement with Natasha[35] when she stated:

> These teachings are quite social and brings solidarity personally, my perception and desire is that if we can have these meetings more often we can uphold the richness of our cultures, those values that we come with from our countries, they can help strengthen not only marriages but during that time

> also as we come together as women we are also going to unite, we are also going to help one another.

Natasha[36] further stressed:

> We literally remind each other of what we should have been doing in our homes, marriage, and bedroom. We receive many such comments. You find that even ladies that are not scheduled to teach they will ask you if they can just come and listen in. You have four ladies teaching but it's a group of twelve women in the meeting and others are just sitting. Currently they bring notebooks. It just brings us women together from different nationalities and we won't see the difference. And I call it a blessing . . . a very strong space where we can learn as such. When you talk about a space where you are teaching a bride, all the ladies who were in the teaching space have been thoroughly reminded for example there are about nine sessions that she attends before her wedding. It's not just sex to learn, there is communication, business, etc., all of those things. I see a gap for before and for after. We don't do a postmortem. The taught girl lives as though she's an expert, she's not an expert; therefore, I don't see a problem with women who are married doing a postmortem on themselves and thereby strengthening themselves, in fact we would only help ourselves to teach ourselves better. And that for me is solidarity and if we stood and if we stood and did postmortems of our marriages, few would be breaking or be on the rocks. In fact, women would stand together and pray together, that for me should be the result of that solidarity such that when someone comes with a problem we first of all pray together and as women we begin to investigate. There is a solidarity but not to the extent that I think we can.

Similarly, Lynn[37] reported that:

> My desire is actually to see more marriages being strengthened in the long run even those that are already married when we have these teachings, we invite them just to be there to just listen and you find that it is also another way of trying to refresh the women, probably you've lagged behind in upholding some of those teachings. My vision is having more of such teachings, we indeed learn as we teach the young girl. When we come to teach it's just to celebrate together as women from different nations and when we finish teaching and we have a kitchen party it's another way of advertising that there is this teaching that we have as women. And because I believe that every woman out there has something to contribute when we come together and invite more women you find that we are promoting more and more of such gatherings and female solidarity.

These two Zambian women in the Zambian diaspora context of South Africa are aware that strengthening local marriages is as imperative as strengthening their own. They see themselves as having a duty to empower local women to take control of their marriages in order to realize peaceful coexistence. Consequently, *imbusa* helps women in diaspora contexts "to stand in solidarity concerning marriage and help each other to have better marriages."[38] Women in diaspora contexts have learned that they do not only need one another's loyalty as foreigners, but also the loyalty of local South African women in order to stand in solidarity and build life-giving marriages and community. In our field interviews, Thandi,[39] a young South African woman who had gone through the ritual of *imbusa*, narrated that it was

> a worthwhile experience because it makes you feel that you are part of the womanhood community in context because you can't be a woman without undergoing that kind of teachings. It also makes you become aware that there are good things you can learn from other cultures.

CONCLUSION: IMPLICATIONS FOR POLICY MAKERS

In response to the outbreak of xenophobia in 2015, Lindiwe Zulu, national minister of Small Business Development, argued that "it's important for the foreigners to share with the South Africans about what it is that makes it possible for them to be successful."[40] This statement was used in the context of business, but as seen in terms of the argument above, it is also applicable in the marriage context. It is in this context that *imbusa* as a space of sharing marriage secrets with local South African and other African women becomes significant. The space creates connecting bonds among married women and may place emphasis on supranational marriage rite traditions. The realization of the significance of *imbusa* in diaspora contexts as transcultural marriage rites may be combined with government-sponsored social cohesion strategies in order to reveal such rites to local married women and make couples realize the benefits they may gain from such traditions. Hence, the role of local authorities is to promote such cultural traditions as a locus for promotion of social cohesion based on the mutual sharing of cultural values, especially when some local national women seem to have already embraced *imbusa* rites in its diasporic manifestation. Local authorities and policy makers alike need to take into consideration that the common denominator for integrating foreign nationals and local nationals is found in such all-embracing cultural traditions that are already unifying people in different communities.

NOTES

1. ENCA, "In Pictures: City of Joburg Carnival's 10th edition," <https://www.enca.com/south-africa/pictures-city-johannesburg-carnivals-10th-edition-1/> [Accessed: June 6, 2016].

2. In terms of research ethics, throughout this chapter pseudonymous names have been used throughout and all the participants had given their consent for the research to take place. Mutale Kaunda, having gone through *imbusa* herself and living in diaspora like the interviewees, was unthreatening to them.

3. We are aware that these ethnic cultures are different although they share most values and beliefs, but for this chapter, the notion of Bemba people includes the Bemba, Chishinga, Tabwa, Ushi, Mukulo, Lala, and the Lunda of Mwata Kazembe.

4. The term matrilineal means family line is through the mother and not the father.

5. Matrilocal means a marriage custom where the husband moves to the wife's community at marriage.

6. In Bemba cosmology, blood is passed on from generation to generation through the woman. The man's semen merely activates the foetus—hence children belong to the mother. In this culture, the father has no right over his children.

7. Alfred C. Mupeta, "Communication as a Factor in the Perpetration and Prevention of Domestic Violence against Women among the Bemba People of Mwamba's Village in Kasama District" (unpublished master's thesis, Communication for Development, University of Zambia, 2014).

8. Naomi Haynes, "Change and *Chisungu* in Zambia's Time of AIDS," *Ethnos* 80/3 (2015): 364–84; Mupeta, "Communication as a Factor."

9. Mutale M. Kaunda, "A Search for a Life-Giving Marriage: The *Imbusa* Initiation Rite as a Space for Constructing Wellbeing among Married Bemba Women of Zambia" (unpublished MTh diss., University of KwaZulu-Natal, Pietermaritzburg, 2013), 2.

10. Mutale M. Kaunda and Chammah J. Kaunda, "*Infunkutu:* The Bemba Sexual Dance as Women's Sexual Agency," *Journal of Theology for South Africa*, special edition 155 (2016): 159–75.

11. Thera Rasing, *Passing on the Rites of Passage: Girls Initiation Rites in the Context of an Urban Roman Catholic Community* (London: African Studies, 1995), 34. See also: Hugo Hinfelaar, *Bemba-Speaking Women of Zambia in a Century of Religious Change (1892–1992),* (Leiden, Netherlands: Brill, 1994).

12. Kaunda, "A Search for a Life-Giving Marriage," 15–16. See also Mutale M. Kaunda and Sarasvathie Reddy, "Pedagogies of Subservience? A Feminist Exploration of the Institution of *Imbusa* among the Bemba," *Journal of Gender & Religion in Africa*, special edition 19/2 (2013): 124–27.

13. Kaunda, "A Search for a Life-Giving Marriage," 16; Kaunda and Reddy, "Pedagogies of Subservience?," 126.

14. Christine P. Mushibwe, "What Are the Effects of Cultural Traditions on the Education of Women? The Study of the Tumbuka People of Zambia" (unpublished PhD diss., University of Huddersfield, 2009), 119.

15. Thera Rasing, *The Bush Burnt, The Stones Remain: Female Initiation Rites in Urban Zambia* (London: African Studies Centre, 2001), 23.

16. Audrey Richards, *Chisungu: A Girl's Initiation Ceremony among the Bemba of Zambia* (London: Tavistock, 1956); Jacob Corbeil, *Mbusa: Sacred Emblems of the Bemba* (Mbala, Zambia: Moto-Moto Museum, 1982); Thera Rasing, "The Persistence of the Female Initiation Rites: Reflexivity and Resilience of Women in Zambia," in *Situating Globality: African Agency in the Appropriation of Global Culture,* ed. Wim

Van Bisbergen and Van Dijk Rijk (Leiden, Netherlands: Brill, 2004), 277–314; Lillian Siwila, "Culture, Gender, and HIV and AIDS: United Church of Zambia's Response to Traditional Marriage Practices" (unpublished PhD diss., University of KwaZulu-Natal, Pietermaritzburg, South Africa,2011).

17. Kaunda, "A Search for a Life-Giving Marriage," 13.

18. Babatunde Adedibu, "Migration, Identity, and Marginalisation: The Case of Britain's Black Majority Churches," *Journal of Africana Religions* 2/1 (2014): 110–17.

19. Francisa Cho and Richard K. Squier, "Religion as a Dynamic and Complex System," *Journal of the American Academy of Religion* 81/2 (2013): 357–98.

20. Interviewed by Mutale M. Kaunda, Pietermaritzburg, South Africa, May 12, 2012.

21. Interviewed by Mutale M. Kaunda, Pietermaritzburg, South Africa, May 26, 2012. In terms of research ethics, the respondent's real name has been withheld and a pseudonym given in order to protect the anonymity of the individual concerned.

22. Interviewed by Mutale M. Kaunda, Pietermaritzburg, South Africa, May 26, 2012.

23. Interviewed by Mutale M. Kaunda, Pietermaritzburg, South Africa, May 26, 2012.

24. Kaunda, "A Search for a Life-Giving Marriage," 16; See also Kaunda and Reddy, "Pedagogies of Subservience?," 126.

25. Interviewed by Mutale M. Kaunda, Pietermaritzburg, South Africa, May 26, 2012.

26. *Muthi* is simply "medicine" or a concoction of herbs that heals a person from wrongdoing.

27. Mugara was interviewed by Mutale Kaunda in Pietermaritzburg, South Africa, June 16, 2012.

28. Interviewed by Mutale M. Kaunda in Pietermaritzburg, South Africa, May 26, 2012.

29. Mark C. Hopson, Tabitha Hart, and Gina Castle Bell, "Meeting in the Middle: Fred L. Casmir's Contributions to the Field of Intercultural Communication," *International Journal of Intercultural Relations* 36/6 (2012): 789–97.

30. Eugenia Bitsani, "Promoting Traditions of Multicultural Communities as a Tool for Social Cohesion in Trieste, Italy," *Procedia-Social & Behavioural Sciences* 148 (2014): 412–19.

31. Interviewed by Mutale M. Kaunda, Pietermaritzburg, South Africa, May 26, 2012.

32. Kaunda, "A Search for a Life-Giving Marriage."

33. Rasing, "The Persistence of the Female Initiation Rites," 280; See also Mushibwe, "What Are the Effects of Cultural Traditions on the Education of Women?," 118.

34. Interviewed by Mutale M. Kaunda, Pietermaritzburg, South Africa, May 12, 2012.

35. Interviewed by Mutale M. Kaunda, Pietermaritzburg, South Africa, May 26, 2012.

36. Interviewed by Mutale M. Kaunda, Pietermaritzburg, South Africa, May 26, 2012.

37. Interviewed by Mutale M. Kaunda, Pietermaritzburg, South Africa, May 12, 2012.

38. Kaunda, "A Search for a Life-Giving Marriage," 16.

39. Interviewed by Mutale M. Kaunda, Pietermaritzburg, South Africa, June 2, 2012. In terms of research ethics, the respondent's real name has been withheld and a pseudonym given in order to protect the anonymity of the individual concerned.

40. Amogelang Mbatha, "S. African Minister Says Foreigners Must Share Trade Secrets," Bloomberg, January 28, 2015, <http://www.bloomberg.com/news/articles/2015-01-28/s-africa-minister-says-foreigners-must-share-to-avoid-looting/> [Accessed: June 22, 2016].

III

RELIGION, PROTEST, AND AFRICANNESS

TWELVE

"Sing unto the LORD a New Song" (Psalm 98:1)

Aspects of the Afrikaans Punk-Rock Group Fokofpolisiekar's Musical Spirituality as Rearticulated Aspects of the 1978 Afrikaans Psalm–en Gesangboek[1]

Christo Lombaard

PLAY IT CONTINUOUSLY, SAM

Analyzing the religious identity of Afrikaans speakers is fraught with the usual difficulties associated with understanding any group that transverses the boundaries of race, class, gender, geography, and more. Diversity prevents the fuller phenomenological representivity that homogeneity would enable. The range of identity theories[2] on which to draw does nothing to simplify the matter, nor the interpretative dynamic related to being an insider or an outsider[3] to the group being analyzed, nor the never-static nature of identity.[4] Surprisingly, writings on Afrikaner[5] identity tend to eschew going into substantial depth on its foundational religious aspects.[6] When spiritual[7] identity is the focus, other general identity markers are generally not made much of.[8] The reason for this may well be that, in order to escape the vast complexities that only a book-length analysis could deal with adequately, a very specific focus is in each instance offered, as is also the case here, all the while acknowledging that what is left unsaid by a large measure outweighs what is being said. The focus here is on the spirituality implicitly present in one of the most successful and influential Afrikaans rock music groups over recent years.

The nature of artistic creativity is such that, apart from a whole range of personal-psychological and social, and perhaps even mystic ("the muse") aspects,[9] it also bears historical and contemporary dimensions: The old is drawn on in order to create something original; the contemporary thus gives voice to the historical.[10] Such "citations" or references, in all genres of art such as literature and dance and painting and music, can occur either with approval or in rejection, concerning important or (previously regarded as) insignificant aspects of the past that are then drawn on deliberately. Yet, even hardly "audible" properties from the past can in this way be given barely noticeable, subtle or non-cognizant / subconsciously implied continuance. The latter may be termed implicit allusions.

In distinction to deliberate allusions, which are actively created re-expressions or "quotations" by artists, implicit allusions (or perhaps silent, latent, or passive allusions) would be constituted by the reactivation of aspects of the past in a way that the artist/s concerned did not intend. It may have escaped the artists' notice that they incorporate the past in such ways, but the past inadvertently insinuates itself in the new work of art. (In a way, a client's unintentional self-disclosure to a psychologist may serve as a parallel here: The counselor hears more, in greater analytic depth and with fuller historical validity, than the person had thought to convey. The client's words "say" more than just the information intentionally communicated, at least to an informed ear.) In this quite natural way, cultural perpetuation occurs.

Such cultural perpetuation is something that humanity cannot escape from, and which in many ways had formed all of us into whom we are (or who we think we are—identity formation being as complex as it is). For instance, negatively in politics, such unintended continuance is demonstrated by the phenomenon that successful revolutionaries have often tended to become like their former oppressors, or in less politically correct but more classical philosophical language: Slaves become like their past masters,[11] in some respects, at least. Artistic expression, relies in many ways on "deep learning": fluid, positivistically indeterminable cultural and existential awarenesses that are difficult to give verbal expression to, which come to the fore in ways that cannot but draw in assorted ways on the past to speak to the present, even when revolutionizing (aspects of) the present.

It is two such implicit/silent/latent allusions in the music of the influential Afrikaans punk-rock band Fokofpolisiekar that are indicated at the conclusion of this contribution—this not as a denial of a multitude of other influences on their music, nor to evaluate aesthetically the originality or the quality of their art.[12] Rather, what is offered here is a sympathetic, hermeneutical analysis of cultural continuance, which can be found in at times surprising ways.[13] First, though, a brief orientation to the music of this band is required.[14]

HEAVENLY LYRICS

Religion has never been far removed from the music of the band Fokofpolisiekar, nor faith from the lives of its members. Though in the interpretation of literary texts (particularly in so-called New Criticism) biographical/authorial information tends to be strongly eschewed, in the kind of historical textual analyses I engage with in all my work on ancient and modern signification, all possible sources of information are drawn on in order more fully to gain insight into the text concerned, thus enabling a richer description of the texts. In the case of Fokofpolisiekar, the cogency of such an approach is demonstrable: In the lives of all of the members of the band Fokofpolisiekar, religion had been a strongly formative factor. Religion can variously be seen in their biographies[15] as formative early-life influence. Faith served as source for (then still religious) rebellion by finding alternate expressions of Christianity in a way that had been emblematic for many in their generation: charismatic groups (more socially-experientially than dogmatically oriented, in a more modern style). Churches had also served as their initial social and music-related networking environment. Lastly—the aspect that had received the most public attention in the news media[16] serving the strongly religious Afrikaans community—in their rejection of Christianity, religion had been a formative creative force for Fokofpolisiekar.

The latter is testified to in one of their earlier scandals, namely, when one band member at a music event wrote the words "Fok God" on a fan's wallet in the early morning hours.[17] This writerly[18] act became national news. The group had already been known for their explicit lyrics; however, in this respect they were not unique in Afrikaans, as another parallel innovation in Afrikaans music, the adoption of the rap genre, made clear, with, mildly, Jack Parow, more extremely, Die Antwoord, and lately Dookoom liberally employing the f-, p- en c-words. (Had the ice been broken by Koos Kombuis with his song "AWB-tiete"?) Profanity was not entirely new in Afrikaans rock either. (Already Johannes Kerkorrel ventured "My God, Gert, dis 'n splinternuwe ossewa" in his song "Ossewa.") However, to swear in such a dismissive (and quite poetic) way at God or about God[19] seemed to be some kind of trigger. Fobbing the idea of God off made for a new kind of Afrikaans newsworthiness; reactions by members of Fokofpolisiekar to this (e.g., on LitNet) in a way simply cemented the idea that matters religious matter.

Aspects of religiosity (e.g., God, church, death, the meaning of life) remain a recurring theme in many Fokofpolisiekar songs. In 2012, on their ten-year anniversary compilation CD, there is no song among the twenty-two that is without religion. (More accurately, twenty-three, but "Hemel op die Platteland" is found twice, as opening and closing tracks, the latter being an acoustic version.) This ranges from deeply self-reflective religio-philosophical overtones (e.g., "Ek skyn, ek skyn heilig" in the song "Ek Skyn (heilig)") to explicit (e.g., "Kan iemand dalk 'n god bel en vir hom sê ons het hom nie meer nodig nie" in the song "Hemel op die Platteland") to—unexpected in the generally raucous[20] tenor of Fokofpolisiekar's oeuvre—a fully reverent tone in the song "Tiny Town" that stays with one as a kind of ambient mood long after the song has ended, approaching perhaps the most beautiful religious song in Afrikaans popular music, Koos du Plessis's "Gebed."

The conclusion presents itself: There has, outside of Gospel music circles, never been a more religiously inclined popular music band in Afrikaans, and probably in South African popular music *in toto*, than Fokofpolisiekar. Precisely the rejection of traditional Afrikaans religiosity and of aspects of faith in general in their music make this sustained theme palatable. With Fokofpolisiekar, God rocks. (Even if He rocks off.)

Let us take a closer look at their breakthrough song, which remains one of their most popular ones:

Table 12.1. Translation of "Hemel op die Platteland"[1]

"Hemel op die Platteland"	*"Heaven in the Countryside"*
1. Kan jy my skroewe vir my vasdraai?	1. Can you tighten my screws for me?
2. Kan jy my albasters *vír* my vind?	2. Can you find my marbles for me?
3. Kan jy jou idee van *nórmaal* by jou gat opdruk?	3. Can you stick your idea of normality up your arse?
4. Kan jy?	4. Can you?
5. Kan jy apatie spel?	5. Can you spell apathy?
6. Kan iemand dalk 'n god bel	6. Can someone perhaps phone a god?
7. En vir hom sê ons het hom nie meer nodig nie	7. And tell him we don't need him any more
8. Kan jy?	8. Can you?
9. Kan jy apatie spel?	9. Can you spell apathy?
10. Reguleer my	10. Regulate me
11. Roetineer my	11. Routinate[2] me
12. Plaas my in 'n boks en merk dit veilig	12. Put me in a box and mark it "safe"
13. Stuur my dan waarheen al die dose gaan	13. Then send me to where all boxes (idiots/cunts) go
14. Stuur my hemel toe	14. Send me to heaven
15. Ek dink dis in die platteland	15. I think it is in the countryside
16. Dis hemel op die platteland (x3)	16. It's heaven in the countryside (x3)

Notes

1. The translation here was first undertaken by me, after which it was slightly edited in comparison with various, mostly poor, Web-published translations.
2. This word, although it occurs in English, is clearly an uncomfortable translation here, employed simply for the sake that the more idiomatic "put me into a routine" would fit poorly with the poetic conventions followed in this lyric.

Following the numbering of the lines above, a brief running commentary on this lyric is provided: Line 1 can easily seem a little mystifying, especially initially, since the context is not immediately clear. Line 2 clearly refers to a child seeking help for locating scattered toys, and this contextualizes Line 1 somewhat, raising the possibility of reference in Line 1 to a child requiring assistance with something like a toy Meccano set. Still, unsettlingly, the reference in Line 1 could be to something more general, perhaps even sinister, such as being caged. Then the question that is Line 1 could well be meant ironically, as already rebelliously tinged. In such a case, it might be possible to reread Line 2 as referring to "losing one's marbles," with an apt explanatory pun here, "going off one's rocker." Or are these lines perhaps expressing a longing for child-time securities?

Line 3 breaks harshly from any possible earlier childlike innocence and dependence, though. All such standard matters are outrightly rejected. This rejection may be posed as a question, but it is meant as a forceful statement.

Line 4 can be taken as either an iteration of the previous question, or a preparation-in-brief for the question that follows in Line 5. This question, which lies at the heart of the song (hence the repetition in Line 9), carries a range of cultural references that may well at the time of writing have congealed into this expression. (Whether this was at that time a deliberately construed act of reinterpretation, though, or one of those quirky flashes of linguistic happenstance that at times occurs when one writes lyrics, only the author of this song could really know.) An older Afrikaans putdown expression is drawn on here: "hy/sy kan nie pateties spél nie," with the tonal nuance that becomes evident only when said loudly, namely, that "s/he can't even *spell* pathetic," implying that the objects of reproach are so wretched that they do not have the ability even to put to language correctly what they are: "pathetic." "Kan jy apatie spel?" is therefore no slightly probing question, but an accusation in the superlative: The addressees are in fact stated outright to be so apathetic that they could not be bothered even to make plain what they are. This linguistically playful turn of phrase is therefore both compact in its expression and imaginative in its cultural relay.

The meaning of Line 4, thus: It responds to the questions in Lines 1 and 2, answering them by means of accusation—*nobody* helped. The plaintiff, perhaps even supplicant, feels left alone. Given the broader referential context of the Fokofpolisiekar members and their music: Those who had been trusted and of whom securities were expected have let the speaker down, by implication: have left the youth feeling let down.[21] Given that such disillusionment is a recurring realization that (at least some members of) each generation has to deal with in their coming of age, the attractiveness of such a universalizing questioning—which is a feature of good poetry—becomes clear. Given that this generationally cyclical "rude awakening" has now been put into both the linguistic and musical registers with which to ask the question as if anew on behalf of a cohort of Afrikaans teens to thirty somethings open to both those registers, the cultural phenomenon of Fokofpolisiekar's success can be better understood. Fokofpolisiekar is not *just* a band; they are, like earlier generations of Afrikaans word artists,[22] poets who speak directly to an aspect of their time. As illustrated by for instance the classic 1993 movie *Dazed and Confused,* and given voice to by Fokofpolisiekar biographer Klopper,[23] "ons is almal deurmekaar" (at least some members of): This youthful group experiences bewilderment. These psychological and social insecurities are the generationally recurring, stirring realization that little remains of what had seemed firmly set in an imagined safe childhood.

Clearly, part of the center of this disillusionment is—Line 6 and 7—God. God is experienced as existentially distant: At least part of the metaphoric intent of phoning God is to express that the divine is no longer accessible by usual means, such as prayer and the experience of existential warmth. For precisely that reason, Line 7: The "services" of God[24] are no longer required. Whether God is dead or not (the eternal post-Nietzschean question) is not touched on, but God *is* out of reach. The experienced distance has rendered God, in this interpretation, superfluous.

Why "a god," and not "God," as it had been in an earlier version of the lyrics?[25] Precisely because of the same distancing effect created by the telephone metaphor in the previous line. Though the extent of deliberate intentionality here is unclear, this kind of reference to the divine echoes similar wording in the broader Afrikaans religious debate in popular-scientific books and on the broadly influential literary website LitNet.[26] Such wording includes for instance renderings such as "gotte" (gods, in a novel plural form), meant to be irreverent, humorous, and novel, yet interestingly still does not break off completely the visible terminological continuance, as had been done with divine referentiality in, for instance, some forms of feminist theology.

The fact that Lines 4 and 5 are mirrored precisely in Lines 8 and 9, thus forming a lyrical *inclusio* that circles Lines 6 and 7, stresses the centrality of the religious issue that forms part of the heart of this song (as it does of the Fokofpolisiekar oeuvre, psyche and appeal).

Lines 10 to 13 express the sense of experienced constriction, probably here more social than religious, putting in new language the same matter objected to in the 1979 and still popular, highly influential Pink Floyd song, "Another Brick in the Wall" (from *The Wall*).[27]

Lines 14 to 16 recoup the religious thematics, unexpectedly expressing a yearning for an existential *heimat,* albeit in a slightly humorous, slightly irreverent way. Still, it seems, the yearning for a spiritual home is itself not dead. What is evident, though, is that it is someplace else; not here, where the author finds himself. This "other" place is romanticized as a heaven, with the interesting recouping here of the older Afrikaans literary trope of sketching the countryside as an idyllic other, set over against a bad urban life in the here and now. Here too, though, the intentionality of the author on this matter cannot be determined from the text alone, but at the very least this is an Afrikaans cultural-literary meme available within the referential frame of the author, on which he could have drawn, either explicitly or implicitly.

If this geographical reference had indeed been a deliberate play on that older literary trope, the countryside thematic here would constitute a return to the childlike innocence of Lines 1 and 2, thus rendering this lyric with a classic *inclusio* opening and closing motif. The artistic technique of this lyric as poetry would be well spoken to by such thematic craftsmanship.

However, the idea that a spiritual home could be sought in a place known for conservatism and traditional values would then be a poor fit with the prominent idea in the rest of the lyric, most explicitly in Lines 5 to 7, namely, of rejection of these things. If this were a biblical text, the latter consideration would prompt the theory that a different hand had been responsible for these closing lines, 14–16 (as is the case with, for instance, the Book of Ecclesiastes in the Old Testament section of the Bible), or perhaps the same hand, but at a different time and in a different, more optimistic mood (as, equally, is the case with the closing pericope of Ecclesiastes).

"Hemel op die Platteland" (was the song title chosen to summarize the theme of religious distancing, or because it is the most repeated phrase of the song, or—in keeping with the paragraph immediately above—as a later addition to the whole?) is thus a chorus of rebellion against social and religious restriction. Freedom is sought, in the face of experienced earlier false securities; or if not freedom, then integrity. This yearning is expressed in what is clearly a high-quality artistic creation, with ample cultural referentialities and intertextualities, of the deliberate, implied and, perhaps, uncertain kind. Moreover, this is done in a surprisingly structured manner (even more so than seems to have been band members' own estimation, later, of their music in general,[28] and certainly more than is the general perception of Fokofpolisiekar's music): One would have expected the turmoil of such heartfelt agitation to be reflected more clearly in the compositional structure of the lyrics.

THE INFLUENCE OF THE *PSALM–EN GESANGBOEK* (1978)

Given the strongly religious elements in the personal biographies and in the music of Fokofpolisiekar, it should not be surprising that aspects of their religious heritage found also implicit reflection in the formal composition of their music. Some "implicit/silent/latent/allusions" indicated above can be indicated in the way Fokofpolisiekar's songs are composed.

The two highlighted here are the elements of word-tone congruence and of caesurae. Amongst the prominent characteristics of the music of Fokofpolisiekar, namely, that they often exhibit extraordinary occurrences of these traits, which would generally be regarded as a faux pas in modern music.

Two examples of each will illustrate this; first, the imprecise word-tone congruence:

> From Line 3 in "Hemel op die Platteland" above:
> "Kan jy jou idee van *nór*maal by jou gat opdruk?"
>
> Then, from the song "Brand Suid-Afrika":
> "in die bosse buite *jóú* huis in die nag," but especially:
> "ons hou ons *gé*wetens skoon."

Here can be seen that the natural syllabic emphasis within the Afrikaans language idiom is relocated in order to fit with the melodic accent. Although this had occurred in Afrikaans music before, as in rock genres in general, this phenomenon had never been as pronounced as with the music of Fokofpolisiekar. Moreover, since their rise to popularity, this phenomenon can be detected more readily in the music of their spin-off bands and the South African bands that have risen to prominence in their direct wake.

Examples of poor caesurae in the music of Fokofpolisiekar include:

> From the song "Ek Skyn (Heilig)":
> "Genade on-
> beskryflik groot"
>
> From the song "Vernietig Jouself":
> "jou verleppende per-
> soonlikheid"

Not completely unrelated to the matter of word-tone congruence indicated above, here the natural ending of the musical phrase and the natural ending of the word do not coincide. This leaves an atypical word-break pause at the end of the musical phrase, with the usual expectation being that the word could not be hyphenated here. Although the uneasiness this creates on the part of the listener could be used to good poetic-psychological effect in cases where it is done deliberately, in the music of Fokofpolisiekar in general that intent does not seem evident. The origin of this recurring phenomenon lies elsewhere.

For most modern music tastes, these occurrences fall strangely on the ear; instances such as these described above create the sense that more compositional effort should have been put into rounding off the songs, in order to have them accord more fully (rare exceptions will always occur) with accepted musical convention.

Probably, in the case of the music of Fokofpolisiekar, occurrences such as these spring from the way in which their songs had often come into being, at least in the early days of the band: lyrics/poems are written and then set to music. However, achieving a successful setting to music of a preexisting text is a most difficult compositioning exercise, precisely in overcoming complications such as those highlighted here; perhaps the more so for musicians who, like me, are not musicologically trained.

However, the fans of Fokofpolisiekar forgave them these "sins" in their early songs,[29] allowing these features to become more prominent in later songs.

Playfulness with the conventions of music is certainly one of the characteristics of the punk rock genre; especially in the early British days of punk, melodies and lyrics could be shockingly unrefined and vulgar—in the sense of being unsophisticated, naive, and even bland. Deliberately so. However, the punk influences on the music of Fokofpolisiekar are much more modern; this is shown clearly by their melodies, which do not reflect the early British punk styles in this respect. Though the two elements of word-tone congruence and of caesurae referred to above could in Fokofpolisiekar's case still be said to mirror unintentionally and in a nondirect way some of that earlier purposive punk unsophistication, a more direct source, I propose, could be found closer to home: in the old Afrikaans *Psalm–en Gesangboek*.[30]

This hymnal contains the kind of church music most of the Fokofpolisiekar band members would have grown up with, hearing it regularly and singing it actively. Given the strongly religious background of the band members, especially with the lead singer and initially primary songwriter being raised in a Dutch Reformed Church parish, such an idea is, although also initially amusing, historically and phenomenologically speaking not entirely preposterous. The reasons for the revision of the older *Psalm–en Gesangboek* precisely included problems with word-tone congruence and caesurae[31] (on the move from older to newer Afrikaans hymnals, see the literature below).[32]

One of the prime examples of the identified caesurae problem can be seen with Psalm 48 in this hymnal—a Psalm that was widely sung in Afrikaans church services since the late 1970s, even becoming beloved. Nobody could attend Afrikaans church services regularly and not become familiar with the melody and most of the verses. Noteworthy is that in this religious song, and others in the same collection, awkward caesurae occur more frequently than in any other earlier Afrikaans music. In a sense, poor caesurae had become an identifiable trait of Afrikaans church singing, to the extent even that it would hardly be expected elsewhere. Much the same could be said of poor word-tone congruence.

In the Psalm 48 text copied below (*Psalm–en Gesangboek* 1978), as just one illustration to serve the purposes here, the problem of poor caesurae is indicated at the end of each line in which it occurs in extreme measure (thus not indicating cases where it may be argued that the pause is lyrically or musically functional) by means of a tilde sign (~). The matter of poor word-tone congruence occurs only once in this song (though more frequently in other instances, most particularly in the Psalms), namely, in the fourth line of the fourth verse, indicated below in the same manner as above, by means of italics and acute signs over the vowels. The "sins" referred to above are identifiable without much effort:

1. Die HEER is groot waar Sions top ~
hom wentel uit die dieptes op.
Hy is lofwaardig, waar verhewe
die berg en stad in songlans bewe,
en Sion teen die noorde ~
blink, bó die lof van woorde.
Daar waar in vlekkelose wit
die Koning van die wêreld sit,
het Hy, wat teen die vyand waak,
as rotsburg Hom bekend gemaak.

2. Die konings van die heidendom
het met hul leërs aangekom,
die aanvalsmag wat hul gekeur het.
Maar nou? Hul weet nie wat gebeur het –
plots kom oor hul verbasing, ~
verskrikking en verdwasing.
Die helde deins verward terug,
'n oomblik—en hul 't weggevlug!
En Sion, rotsburg van die HEER,
blink in sy oue glorie weer.

3. Soos een wat beef in moedersmart,
so raak hul daar verskrik, verward.
Die God van mag, van kragbewyse,
verbreek die skepe, pragpaleise ~
van Tarsis: oseane ~
spring op voor sy orkane!
Soos ons gehoor het, sien ons oog:
Die HERE Sebaot rys hoog!

Hy sal sy stad, die mens ten spyt,
bevestig tot in ewigheid.

4. Ons wil, o HEER, wat redding skenk,
aan al u goedheid bly gedenk ~
as ons tesaam is in u woning.
Net sóós u Naam is, grote Koning,
so is u glansverskyning:
die vyand se verdwyning ~
word aan die volkere bekend ~
tot by die aard' se verste end.
U hand wat nooit die kwaad gedoog,
rys vol geregtigheid omhoog.

5. Laat Sions berg weerklink van vreug!
Laat Juda's dogters hul verheug,
omdat Gods oordeel hul verbly het –
dié oordeel wat sy volk bevry het.
Aanskou die stad met skanse, ~
paleise, toringtranse -
hoedat hul pryk met nuwe prag. ~
En meld dit aan die jong geslag:
Die God is onse God, en Hy ~
sal tot die dood toe ons gelei.

That such influences from Psalm 48, as one instance among many other popular hymns, would constitute *deliberate* creative reception on the part of the Fokofpolisiekar songwriters is scarcely possible: Their kind of rejection of religion would hardly allow for this. However, could it be that these musical influences insinuated themselves into the songwriting of Fokofpolisiekar? Could the notion of implicit/silent/latent allusions touched upon in the opening paragraphs of this essay explain these two characteristics of the music of Fokofpolisiekar? Or is this altogether too playful a suggestion?

NOTES

1. Paper read at the Third International Conference on Spirituality and Music Education, "Music Education and Spirituality: Theory and Application," School of Music and Conservatory, North-West University (Potchefstroom campus), March 25–27, 2015. See <http://www.spirituality4 mused.org/> . I herewith thank Mrs Elsabé Nell, librarian at the University of South Africa, for her efforts in sourcing many of the materials required for researching this paper. Not only has she a longstanding interest in "alternative" Afrikaans music; she has always been an excellent librarian, whose most professional services I could not do without.

2. Summarized in Robert Andrew Dunn, "Identity Theories and Technology," in *Handbook of Research on Technoself: Identity in a Technological Society*, ed. R. Luppicini (Hershey, PA: Information Science Reference, 2013), 26–44, esp. 27–29.

3. Cf. M. E. Rabe, "Are You Out When You Are Not In? Revisiting 'Insiders' and 'Outsiders' as Social Researchers," *African Sociological Review* 7/2 (2003): 149–61.

4. Cf. Julie Aaboe, "The Other and the Construction of Cultural and Christian Identity: The Case of the Dutch Reformed Church in Transition" (unpublished PhD diss., University of Cape Town, 2007).

5. It remains surprising how often the term "Afrikaner" is misspelt in English academic works as "Afrikaaner," somehow breaking the spelling sense of both the Afrikaans and English languages.

6. Even when the term "civil religion" is employed in the academic tradition influentially established by T. Dunbar Moodier, *The Rise of Afrikanerdom: Power, Apartheid, and the Afrikaner Civil Religion* (Berkeley, CA: University of California Press, 1975).

7. Spirituality is here meant as the experienced or sensed aspect of religion; the lived yet intellectually hardly ever reflected upon faith, which is internalized and processed as part of normal acculturation processes in a society and particularly certain spheres of it.

8. Cf. Christo Lombaard, "Om die Skrif tot stilte te bring . . . Gewaarwordinge oor Afrikaanse Bybelse spiritualiteit," *Litnet Akademies (Godsdienswetenskappe)* 9/3 (2012): 929–95; J. W. Hofmeyr, "Spiritualiteit in die NG Kerk van die 21ste eeu teen die agtergrond van Calvyn en die Nadere Reformasie," *Ned. Geref. Teologiese Tydskrif* 50/3-4 (2009): 595–606; Erna Olivier, "Afrikaner Spirituality: A Complex Mixture," *HTS Teologiese Studies / Theological Studies* 62/4 (2006): 1469–87; G. J. Steyn, "Die NG Kerk se identiteitskrisis, Deel 2: Huidige bewegings, tendense of mutasies," *Ned. Geref. Teologiese Tydskrif* 47/3-4 (2006): 661–76; L. Christo Lombaard, "'Afrikaans, Reformed and Internetted': Some Outlines of Current Afrikaans e-Spiritualities," in *White Matters / Il bianco in questione*, ed. S. Petrilli (Athanor, anno XVII, nuova serie, 10, 2006-2007), (Rome: Meltemi editore, 2006), 202–15; Christo Lombaard, "Gewaarwordinge. 'n Gesprek oor Afrikaans-Christelike geloofsprikkels in ons tyd," *Pomp* 1 (2006): 291–93.

9. Cf. in nonacademic format, Chrisman Baard, "Dis die klein verdraai-inkies wat tel," *Rapport Perspektief*, January 23, 2005, 3; <http://152.111.1.87/argief/berigte/rapport/2005/01/23/ R1/27/01.html/> [Accessed: August 22, 2016]; Chrisman Baard, "My onsigbare vriende por my aan om te skryf," *Rapport Perspektief*, February 2, 2005, 3; <http://m.news24.com/rapport/XArchive/ Perspektief/My-onsigbare-vriende-por-my-aan-om-te-skryf-20050205/> [Accessed: August 22, 2016]; Chrisman Baard, "Koop 'n kitaar vir kreatiwiteit," *Rapport Perspektief*, February 20, 2005, 3; <http://152.111.1.87/argief/berigte/rapport/2005/02/20/R1/23/02.html/> [Accessed: August 22, 2016].

10. The implications of this include that the original is never from nowhere, *ex nihilo*, while the past is never predictably only in the past. On more fully fledged philosophy of history, drawn on here implicitly, see, e.g., Philip Sheldrake, *Spirituality and History* (New York: Crossroad, 1992); Jurie le Roux, "The Nature of Historical Understanding (or: Hermeneutics and History)," *Studia Historiae Ecclesiasticae* 19/1 (1993): 35–63.

11. Cf., e.g., Friedrich Wilhelm Nietzsche, *Zur Genealogie der Moral*, Eine Streitschrift (Berlin: Holzinger, [1887] 2013).

12. During one of the controversies in which Fokofpolisiekar became embroiled (cf. Annie Klopper, *Biografie van 'n bende. Die storie van Fokofpolisiekar* [Pretoria: Protea Boekhuis, 2011], 172–83), mine was one of the early appreciative analytical voices in the press on the matter: Christo Lombaard, "Fokofpolisiekar laat ons weer oor God dink," *Rapport*, February 2, 2006, *Perspektief*, bl. 7, <http://152.111.1.87/argief/berigte/rapport/2006/02/26/RP/7/01.html/> [Accessed: August 22, 2016]. That article was later in, for instance, the negative reaction to my "Buchan brou" article on the literary website LitNet: cf. Christo Lombaard, "Buchan brou," *LitNet* (2010), <http://www.litnet.co.za/Article/buchan-brou/>, and elsewhere, from conservative theological circles held against me. The newspaper heading of that article, "Fokofpolisiekar laat ons weer oor God dink," was taken up in the artwork in the approved biography of the band: cf. Klopper, *Biografie van 'n bende*, 182–83. However, as has been pointed out to me, the layout of the graphics on the latter pages may well create the impression, at first glance, that my voice counted amongst the detractors of the Fokofpolisiekar phenomenon. As should be clear in the addendum to this contribution, which contains the text of that journalistic piece, that is not the case. More recent appreciative analyses are: Christo Lombaard, "Persoonlike Jesus," (October 29, 2014) <http://teo.co.za/persoonlike-jesus-christo-lombaard-3/>, of the Marilyn Manson rendition of "Personal Jesus," and Christo Lombaard, "Is daar iets soos Nuwe Afrikaanse Spiritualiteit? (Oor Dookoom se "Larney jou Poes")," De Ark Boektiek-kunstefees, Lydenburg, (November 5, 2014), of the local rap act Dookoom's song "Larney jou poes."

13. As a parallel instance on the Bible in popular culture, aspects of such continuance have been discussed in, e.g., Wim Beuken and Sean Freyne, eds., *The Bible as Cultural Heritage* (London: SCM Press, 1995).

14. Cf. Annie Kloppers, "Die opkoms van Afrikaanse rock en die literêre status van lirieke, met spesifieke verwysing na Fokofpolisiekar," MA-verhandeling: Afrikaans en Nederlands, (Stellenbosch, South Africa Universiteit van Stellenbosch, 2009); Kloppers, *Biografie van 'n bende*.

15. Cf. Kloppers, *Biografie van 'n bende*, 148–57.

16. Cf. R. Kahn, "Oop vir Interpretasie: An Examination of the South African Media's Take-up and Representation of the Music of Fokofpolisiekar" (unpublished research report, master's thesis, Journalism and Media Studies, University of the Witwatersrand, Johannesburg, 2009).

17. Cf. Kloppers, *Biografie van 'n bende*, 172–83; Lombaard, "Fokofpolisiekar laat ons weer oor God dink."

18. I employ this term in the productive sense given it by, e.g., Anthony Thiselton, *New Horizons in Hermeneutics* (Grand Rapids, MI: Zondervan, 1992), 98: writerly texts elicit responses, and multiply so.

19. For mostly international precursors, cf. Christo Lombaard, "Fokofpolisiekar laat ons weer oor God dink."

20. The title of Ross's description of classical music is *The Rest Is Noise*. Alex Ross, *The Rest Is Noise: Listening to the Twentieth Century* (New York: Farrar, Straus & Giroux, 2003). With Fokofpolisiekar and many similar bands, locally and internationally, the noise is precisely part of the point.

21. Cf. Burgert A. Senekal and Cilliers van den Berg, "'n Voorlopige verkenning van postapartheid Afrikaanse protesmusiek," *LitNet Akademies* 7/2 (2010), 98–128.

22. Antjie Krog, Die beautiful woorde van Van Wyk Louw (NP van Wyk Louw Gedenklesing), (Johannesburg: University of Johannesburg, 2004).

23. Klopper, *Biografie van 'n bende*, 219.

24. Relatively few Afrikaans people are open to the problem of gendered language when referring to God. This is in itself interesting: The God problem is experienced as foundational, not referential. Once the foundational problem has been resolved, in the cases where faith is retained, the resulting religion tends to be traditional in at least sentiment, and conservative. The oppositioning within this kind of choice world is telling.

25. Klopper, *Biografie van 'n bende*, 85–88.

26. Cf., e.g., Erns Grundling, Etienne Van Heerden, and Thomas Mollett, *Die omstrede God. Bestaan God of nie?* (Stellenbosch, South Africa: Rapid Access, 2004).

27. Locally, M. Odendaal, "Qohelet and the Dark Side of the Moon," paper presented at the Conference on Music and Philosophy: Perspectives from Europe and Africa, University of Pretoria, September 20–23, 2004); cf. E. A. Akrofi, "Conference on Music and Philosophy: Perspectives from Europe and Africa," *SAMUS* 23 (2003): 97 has proposed an interesting biblical intertextuality to the earlier Pink Floyd record album *The Dark Side of the Moon* (1973).

28. Klopper, *Biografie van 'n bende*, 148.

29. If the reason for this had been that "the cause" was felt to be so important that much else is left aside, then it is in this respect too that the music of Fokofpolisiekar approaches closely much of what happens in the popular Gospel genre.

30. *Psalm–en Gesangboek* (Kaapstad: NG Kerk Uitgewers, 1978).

31. Cf., e.g., Annie Kloppers, "'n Nuwe psalmomdigting in Afrikaans: uitgangspunte, beleid, probleem," *Hervormde Teologiese Studies* 56/1 (2000): 192–204; C.J.A. Vos en T. Gouws, "Op hom die groot hosannas: perspektiewe op die bewaring en vernuwing van die kerklied," *Skrif en Kerk* 11/2 (1990): 209–21.

32. Francois Paul Fourie, "'n Geskiedenis van die kerklied in die Nederduitse Gereformeerde Kerk," DTh-proefskrif, Pretoria: UNISA, 2000; W. M. Louwrens Strydom, *Sing nuwe sange, nuutgebore. Liturgie en lied* (Bloemfontein, South Africa: UOVS, 1994); Redakteur J.H.H. du Toit (red.)*'n Geskiedenis van die Afrikaanse Protestantse Kerklied* (Pretoria: NG Kerkboekhandel, 1983); Gawie G. Cillié, *Waar kom ons Afrikaanse Gesange vandaan?* (Kaapstad: Tafelberg, 1982); J. A. Loader, (red.), *'n Nuwe lied vir die Here* (Pretoria: HAUM, 1979); Frederik Malherbe Gaum, "Die Afrikaanse evangeliese gesang: 'n literêre ondersoek," DLitt-proefskrif, Bloemfontein: UOVS (1969); Kongres oor die Kerkmusiek, *Die Gereformeerde Kerklied deur die eeue. Referate gelewer by die Kongres oor die Kerkmusiek gehou in Kaapstad op 9 en 10 Oktober 1962* (Kaapstad, South Africa: Tafelberg, 1964); W. J. B. Serfontein. *Die Psalm as kerklied: Teologiese agtergronde van die Afrikaanse Psalmberyming,* (Nijkerk, Netherlands: Callenbach, 1956); E. C. Pienaar, *Die ontstaan van ons Afrikaanse Psalms–en Gesangboek* (Kaapstad, South Africa: Tafelberg, 1944).

THIRTEEN

Rastafari Perspectives on African Identities

Lucky Dube's "Different Colours / One People" in Conversation with Peter Tosh's "I Am an African"

Roderick R. Hewitt

INTRODUCTION

Contemporary global political discourses have found currency around the subjects of race, ethnicity, and color in the construction of national identities. The growing strength of extreme right-wing nationalist groups have given rise to politics of hate especially against immigrants and other groups that are considered threats to their national identity. Xenophobia, bigotry, and suppression of the human rights and dignity of minority groups have now become fashionable in societies that previously abhorred such antidemocratic values. Within the African continent, conflicts linked to the political rights and privileges of ethnic identities have resulted in some countries becoming failed states.[1] Factors relating to the access of land and mineral resources and the inability of government to create the right conditions that can lead to increased job creation and investment in the economy have led to disillusionment in the status quo of governance.

South Africa, since the start of European colonialism, has evolved with different competing narratives about its peoples' identities. There is no one history of the country, but competing interpretations. Those that control political and economic power tend to write history that supports their political agenda and interest. The heroes and villains of the nation depend on who is telling the story. Although the Apartheid system of governance was constitutionally defeated in 1994 when a new era of democratic governance was ushered in, the negative effects of colonial policies and its nondevelopmental policies against black South Africans continues to impact their development through the legacies of poor housing, inadequate education, and lack of employment opportunities.[2] Disillusionment with the progress made by the democratic project since 1994 is expressed in the many contemporary public demonstrations against the lack of adequate service deliveries in housing, electricity, jobs, and water.[3] Michelle Adato, Michael R. Carter, and Julian May describe the South African context as one shaped by poverty traps and social exclusion of its majority black population.[4] The inequality and inadequate social cohesion that are affecting the economic development of the nation are intricately linked to how race and identity politics have been practiced within the development of the nation over many centuries. This has bequeathed an unjust socioeconomic system that seems to prescribe privileges according to the ethnic identity of persons, "If you are white . . . then you are right, if you are Colored . . . stick around, but if you are black . . . stay back."

THE NEED TO INTERROGATE IDENTITY POLITICS

Being an African Jamaican living in South Africa, shaped by the philosophies and opinions of Marcus Mosiah Garvey (1887–1940),[5] the Jamaican Pan-Africanist who interrogated the politics of the race and identity, the unfolding debate within race and identity politics in South Africa has piqued my academic interest. Indeed, the historical construct of race and identities within the Jamaican context mirrors, to some extent, the South African experience and therefore constitutes a relevant sociopolitical mirror through which to reflect on the dynamics of race and identity.[6] According to James D. Fearon, identity is a social reality shaped by membership rules that is a blurred but important term used in political discourse to classify issues concerning race, ethnic, national, and gender roles.[7] It is also "a socially distinguishing feature that a person takes a special pride in or views as unchangeable but socially consequential (or [a] and [b] at once). In the latter sense, 'identity' is modern formulation of dignity, pride, or honour that implicitly links these to social categories."[8]

To some extent, it could be argued that South Africa is experiencing what Donald Horowitz describes as "Ethnic groups in Conflict."[9] Ethnic identities are defined by Kanchan Chandra as "a subset of identity categories in which eligibility for membership is determined by attributes associated with, or believed to be associated with, descent."[10] However, he argues that based upon this definition, ethnicity is not important in explaining the outcomes of violence, democratic stability, and patronage. According to Bekker, if the old Apartheid racial and ethnic identity constructs continue to dominate the new democratic South African society, then a new life-giving common national identity will fail to emerge and develop.[11]

This chapter argues, to the contrary, that the experiences of African victims of sustained political and economic oppression over many centuries cannot be dismissed as unimportant, and race and ethnic identities politics according to a Rastafari[12] hermeneutics of suspicion have been used by imperial and colonial forces to subjugate all peoples of African descent.

The neoliberal economic order that dominates the new democratic era of South Africa continues to promote unjust and unequal models of national development that masks the unresolved legacies of black pain and underdevelopment within the nation. Lubabalo Ntsholo, a spokesperson for the Economic Freedom Front (EFF) party in South Africa, has argued that the issue of the African identity in South Africa must be linked to the subject of land injustice and "the reorganisation of the economy in the countryside, and is less to do with race as both a historical and present determinant to access social and economic power, and the centrality of race-based land ownership as a facilitator of inequality."[13]

This thorny issue of land has remained unresolved since 1994 out of fear by the government of triggering a negative economic response from the white minority citizens that own 90 percent of the best productive land in the country, which in turn may contribute to a major economic downturn within the economy.[14] Since land is so important to the construct of people's identity, conflicts can easily erupt,[15] and if just solutions are not found, then individuals or groups may engage in the seizure of land to reclaim their historic rights to ownership.

The objective of this chapter is not to give a detailed discourse on Rastafari influence within South Africa, but to offer a limited reflection on how their ideology offers a decolonial countercultural perspective on the dynamics of race and identity politics. The issues of identity and race are inescapable. These are phenomena that permeate every aspect of life. At the core of this debate on ethnic identity is the meaning of being African. Who can be called African? This chapter employs the contrasting narratives of two Rastafari, South African Lucky Dube (August 3, 1964—October 18, 2007) "Different Colours / One People" and Jamaican Peter Tosh OM (October 19, 1944—September 11, 1987) "I Am an African," to interrogate race and identity issues. Both narratives offer contrasting perspectives on how to build a racially just nation with diverse ethnicities, but Africans are in the majority. Dube offers a hybrid model of building a common national identity in which the quest for unity is achieved not by emphasizing ethnic differences but by affirming the human dignity of all within the one nation. However, Tosh offers a radical alternative decolonial discourse[16] in which the centrality of being African must be affirmed because of the historical forces of imperial and colonial oppression that have been unleashed upon peoples of African descent to deny them of their access to their political, cultural, and economic resources linked to the land.

RASTAFARI AS AN AFRO-CENTRIC IDENTITY MOVEMENT

Rastafari constitutes a decolonial movement of the Black Consciousness Movement linked to the Coronation of H.I.M. Haile Selassie as Emperor of Ethiopia in 1930[17] and the pride and hope that it gave to the peoples of African descent who were living in a socially, politically, and economically depressed state under colonialism within Jamaica, the wider Americas, and Africa. It was the philosophy and opinion of Marcus Mosiah Garvey at the beginning of the twentieth century advocating for a global black/African civilization renaissance that laid the foundations for the birth of the revolutionary decolonial religio-political movement of Rastafari. His Afrocentric philosophy constitutes a strategic lens to interrogate oppression from the perspective of race and identity because its ideology unmasks the false foundation of life that is used as a strategy of colonization.[18] The early Rastafari interpreted Selassie's coronation as emperor as a fulfillment of Garvey's prophesy that they should "look to Africa where a Black King shall arise."[19] Africa became the organising and operating principle for which peoples of African descent should ensure "consistency and coherence to their way of life" and affirmation of their identity.[20] Garvey also affirmed the blackness of God as the operating theological principle for the affirmation of the African identity.[21] As a decolonial liberation movement, Rastafari advocate for the full reclamation and restoration of land justice[22] for all peoples of African heritage and others who have suffered through the Babylon system[23] of modern imperial, political, economic, and religious forces that benefited from the wealth generated through colonialism, capitalism, and slavery. Garvey's African theology of liberation therefore offered a philosophy of race consciousness and land justice that Rastafari embraced within an Afrocentric worldview.[24]

SOUTH AFRICAN RASTAFARI MOVEMENT

Within the city of Pietermaritzburg reside groups of Rastafari that give serious attention to interrogating issues linked to the subject of African identities within the South African context that they refer to as Azania[25] (lit., "land of black people"). The use of the term Azania reclaims the nonimperial civilization identity and movement of African people who migrated from East Africa down into Zimbabwe and Gauteng during the fourteenth century. The Rastafari of Pietermaritzburg embody the politics of belonging because of the inherent threats to their existence by imperial forces of oppression. They reject the name of South Africa as an imperial and colonial construct of African identities and instead embrace Azania.[26] These Rastafari constitute a concrete South African contextual expression of a global decolonial Rastafari movement of African resistance against imperial forces of oppression against the African peoples.[27]

Like the early Jamaican Rastafari movement that drew its early membership largely from the alienated men (primarily) in the urban and suburban areas that lived on the margins, so too the Rastafari movement that evolved in South Africa soon after April 1994 and the inauguration of the new democratic era drew its membership from disenchanted young black men in the townships.[28] They embraced the twin black heritage of Ethiopianism,[29] (the symbol of black hope, dignity, and ownership of Africa) and the philosophy of Marcus Garvey.[30] The Rastafari symbols and colors of Marcus Garvey, Haile Selassie, clothing adorned in colors of red, green, and gold, the lion as symbol of royal strength, the use of marijuana (ganga), and the growing of dreadlocks were embraced by the local movements and later adopted by sections of the public as a countercultural statement to the status quo of white values.[31]

An interesting perspective on race and identity within the South African context was articulated by Rastafari leaders at a religion and governance conference, "Nation Building in Democratic South Africa," at the School of Religion, Philosophy and Classics, University of KwaZulu-Natal, that was held on October 26, 2012. The core questions that the conference sought to explore were: What does it mean to be an African and to build an African nation together? And, what does it mean to be a free African that refuses to imitate any other people and reconnects with the African's true identity?[32] Prof. R. Simangaliso Kumalo, the University of KwaZulu-Natal (UKZN) staff organizer of the conference, questioned why it was so easy for white people from other countries, but especially from Europe, to settle in South Africa since 1994, and for black people from African countries to encounter so much antiforeigner sentiment.[33] Kumalo argued that the Rastafari of South Africa constitute a special community that knows and defines what it means to be African and openly accepts Africans from the wider African continent and insists that those from the African diaspora should be welcomed into the community.[34] He expressed concerns how the issue of African identity continues to be constructed and defined by perceptions around access to economic and financial resources. The Apartheid era of governance used racism as a political policy to legalize the racial inferior identity construct of local Africans and those within the African continent and beyond. This nationalistic ideology constructed on the superiority of the European race over other races left an indelible legacy of negative perceptions of the African race that are still unaddressed in the educational programs of the post-Apartheid era.

The Pietermaritzburg Rastafari group began their presentation at the UKZN conference with their anthem in which they sang and celebrated unapologetically an Afrocentric identity that embodied Africanness at the core: *"I am proud to be black, I am an Ethiopian."*[35] Their song echoed the identity formulation of Rastafari prophet Bob Marley's poignant narrative, *"We refuse to be what you wanted us to be, we are what we are and that's the way it's going to be."*[36] Their love of reggae music[37] included the songs of South African Rastafari Lucky Dube, Jamaican Rastafari Bob Marley and Jamar Rolando McNaughton Jr., known by his stage name Chronixx, and the revolutionary Afrocentric lyrics of Peter Tosh.

The local Rastafari in Pietermaritzburg rejected the modern world order that they claimed is defined and dominated by imperial power systems. Instead, they offered a counter narrative that makes Ethiopia (blackness) synonymous with their African identity. They argued for a radical political reconscientization of their South African racial identity that is constructed around the themes of black pride and land justice. In addition, they used a radical hermeneutical model of reading and interpreting the Bible as an authentic African text that is central to their black identity. Therefore, it could be argued that for these Rastafari their movement should be defined less as a religion and more as a way of life, dedicated to the respect and advancement of humanity, especially those that experience oppression.

The local Rastafari used the concept of Africa and blackness to cover multiple identities of people, not only those within South Africa and the wider African continent but also from the African diaspora who have migrated by free will or been forced from the continent by imperial and colonial systems of oppression. Their interrogation of issues on race and identities within South Africa employed an African philosophical worldview, humanism, spirituality, proverbial wisdom, and Rastafari teachings, especially those that are bequeathed through the teachings of Marcus Mosiah Garvey[38] and other Rastafari leaders that are communicated through their worship, reasoning sessions, chanting with reggae music. Their chanting articulated powerful resources and retrieval of memories of African resistance against oppression that they will never forget in their contemporary struggle against oppression by the South African Babylonian system.

REGGAE MUSIC AS A DECOLONIAL LENS TO CRITIQUE RACE AND IDENTITY POLITICS

The global influence of reggae music, the medium through which Rastafari spreads its liberative message of resistance against the evils of the Apartheid system, empowered township resistance movements. The early Jamaican Rastafari used language and music that was intrinsically linked to the hybrid Jamaican language that combined the retention of West African languages with European languages of colonization such as Spanish, English, and French. More importantly, Rastafari developed its own anticolonial lexicon to disrupt and deconstruct the dominant meaning systems of Babylon and reconstruct with life-affirming meaning systems.[39] Language and music for Rastafari are music of the soul and mind.[40] Reggae and ska evolved out of the struggles of poor and working-class Jamaicans living in the city ghettoes and became vehicles to communicate their messages of love and political resistance in a society that was not life giving. Among the many local musicians like Jimmy Cliff that took reggae music to the world, it was the phenomenal impact of Bob Marley's music and his Rastafari-embedded ideology and theology of resistance against global imperial forces of oppression that were universalized.[41] Bob Marley and the Wailers' reggae music with their explicit political message exploded on the scene during the 1970's and 1980's when the anti-Apartheid struggle was making South Africa ungovernable. Reggae music became a liberative force that empowered the township youth with a positive black identity to resist and subvert the oppressive system.[42]

DUBE'S RAINBOW CONSTRUCT OF RACE AND IDENTITY

Rastafari communicates its way of life through words, sounds, and music,[43] and they serve as tools to educate their community and the wider public. Lucky Dube, as the most famous South African Rastafarian, used music to construct a rainbow vision of nation building in which all races have their identity respected in a common pursuit of national unity. He wrote the song "Different Colours / One People" that contributes to the title of this chapter. It was first released on the 1993 album *Victims* and later became global in his 1996 nineteenth anniversary album, Serious

Reggae Business.[44] Dube described the relevance of his songs for the South African context as responding to "people's fears, people's joys, people's dreams and everything. *Feel Irie* talks more about people's fears and my fears as well, because it says there that no man can hide from his fears. Since they're part of him, they'll always know where to find him."[45] He gave attention to those issues that exposed the fears of people and haunt them with negative political consequences. Arthur Goldstruck, who interviewed Dube in 1996,[46] described his song "Together as One" (released in 1990 in the album *Captured Live*) in which he critiqued the Apartheid system stating that:

In my whole life My whole life, I've got a dream, I've got a dream
Too many people hate Apartheid, why do you like it? Why do you like it?
Hey you, Rasta man, Hey European, Indian man. We've got to come together as one[47]

Within the contemporary post-Apartheid era these words may appear to be tame, but in the dying days of Apartheid when the system was most vicious in silencing its critics who were deemed to be threats to the social order, it meant that Dube could have been imprisoned. His Rastafari principles of cultivating a peaceful lifestyle of nonviolence, envisioned the coming together of the different ethnic groups of South Africans and overcoming their differences through forgiveness and reconciliation. The South African Broadcasting Corporation (SABC) classified the song's lyrics to be political and threatened to ban it.[48] Dube's stinging assessment of the Apartheid system concluded it was a failure: "*All those years fighting each other, but no solution, but no solution.*" He used the medium of music to communicate a message of peaceful resistance to the oppressive system and also coexistence and unity among the different peoples. He argued that peaceful change was the only viable future for the nation. Dube's humble upbringing in rural South Africa had exposed him to the deep sociopolitical and economic threats to life, and his songs generally reflected on the challenges that he experienced. He envisioned a South African nation in which all races are equal and equally empowered. His song embodied a commitment to the pursuit of equal rights and justice for all people and a message of love that overcomes hate and revenge to settle wrongs.

Dube's discourse called into question whether it is possible for the South African rainbow identity nation to evolve into an inclusive "melting pot" of ethnic identities that affirm and celebrate their differences without being exclusive. His songs also exposed some inherent contradictions present within the society that hinder people, especially those that live on the margins, from realizing their full human potential. Among his many songs, this chapter critiques the song "Different Colours / One People," which was influenced by his experience of the Euro-Australian struggle to deal with racial challenges with the aboriginal people. He used their theme, "Different Colours" to reflect on his South African context and therefore penned the following selective words to the song "Different Colours / One People."

Breaking those barriers all over the world was not an easy thing
Yesterday your mouth was shut yeah couldn't make a sound eh boy
But it's such a good feeling today when I can hear them from across the ocean[49]

In this narrative, Dube argues for the need to break the entrenched systemic barriers that separate peoples from each other. He blamed the dehumanizing politics practiced by different governments for the disunity in race relations within the South African society. Using the Hebrew biblical narrative about creation, Dube states that God created "man" (human beings) in God's image (*"And who are you to separate them"*) and no reference or distinction was made about the significance of race or ethnicity. Therefore, people should rise up and (kick away) such false identities that separate people from one another. Therefore, acceptance of the other constitutes the discourse through which South Africa, with its many ethnic differences, can become one people. Dube's songs offered an inclusive vision of a common South African nation that encompasses people of all races and backgrounds. His Rastafari ideology on race and identity adopted a liberative hermeneutic that embraced the diversity of the national community, where everyone, regardless of ethnicity, must be included. Dube's quest for a common South African identity embraces multiculturalism ("Out of Many—One People") rather than nativism. His perspectives echoed Tutu's theo-political discourse that human beings are shaped in the image of God and that human worth and human freedom does not depend on the incidentals of race, religion, and social status.[50] His views are contrary to those of the then South African president, Jacob Zuma, who stated that, "You have more rights because you're a majority; you have less rights because you're a minority. That's how democracy works."[51] Zuma's interpretation of democracy is built on how "more rights for the majority" can be delivered by the system of governance. However, if these rights are not influenced by principles of justice, then this model of governance will become dictatorship of the majority.

One could therefore ask whether Dube's vision of a new South Africa is a naive and impractical solution for restorative justice to the black majority that suffered so much injustice. His model for nation building built on the promotion of peace and unity could be summarily dismissed as utopian in praxis. Some pertinent questions should therefore be asked: Was it the oppressed black majority that requested for South Africa to be known as "a rainbow nation" or was it a theme created by the privileged minority class as a way to still exercise power and influence during the democratic era? Could it be that the quest for a peaceful and united South African nation is being fashioned through the suppression of deep-seated, unresolved pains of the majority black population? The identities based on race, ethnicity, and color bequeathed by the Apartheid era should never be accepted as fixed and unchangeable realities but must be interrogated in the light of the post-1994 democratic experience. Indeed, Dube's Rastafari perspectives on race and ethnic identities seem to compromise the strong Afrocentric hermeneutic that is inherent in his Rastafari faith and worldview for the sake of promoting unity among all South Africans. His focus is on the need for all South Africans to flourish and that such flourishing must include other Africans and peoples from other nations living within the nation.

PETER TOSH'S ALTERNATIVE MODEL OF BUILDING AFRICAN IDENTITY

Dube's choice of embracing a Rastafari faith and reggae music as his medium of communication would have exposed him to the strong Afrocentric narratives of the rebellious and fiery Jamaican Rastafari Peter Tosh who was a founding member of the well-known Bob Marley and the Wailers reggae band. Tosh became famous for his global anthem "Legalise It," which demanded the decriminalization[52] of marijuana.[53] Rastafari do not smoke the herb merely as an act for personal pleasure but as their natural divinely sanctioned medium through which their identity is realized.[54] In other words, it "has religious significance to Rastafarians who usually call it 'wisdom weed' or the 'holy herb.' They believe that it increases the feeling of community and that it produces visions of religious and calming nature."[55] Tosh's "Legalise it" anthem mobilized the Rastafari community against what it considered to be an onslaught of the Babylon system that wanted to control the resources that would economically empower the African.[56] Tosh was an ardent follower of Garvey's ideology to "Let Africa be our guiding star: Our star of destiny"[57] and therefore affirmed his identity as an African, as advocated by Marcus Garvey and the Rastafari movement.[58] His narratives employed a decolonial hermeneutics of suspicion to analyze and reappropriate black dignity and pride to overcome the dominant Eurocentric cultural and political alienation.[59]Garvey taught that the oppression of black people around the world was the result of an unjust colonial economic order perpetrated through capitalism and slavery.[60]

Tosh was the most vocal anti-Apartheid Rastafari activist who was not afraid in the 1970's to call for the overthrow of the Apartheid regime. This revolutionary Rastafari rhetoric did not rule out violence as a legitimate tool to overcome systemic oppression. However, his political lyrics also seem to embrace a more universal, peace building, one-humanity affirmation of unity that is very similar to Dube's narrative. He argued that all people connected to Africa are part of the black experience of colonial and imperial oppression and should embrace the identity of being African. Accordingly, "I Am an African" became a potent statement of resistance against the forces of imperialism that were prescribing identities to peoples they wished to oppress. His message was simple and potent: To be African is not determined by nationality, color, and religion. As long as the person recognizes herself/himself to be part of the black experience they should recognize themselves as Africans. Selective extract from the lyrics of his song focus on explaining the African identity:

Don't care where you come from, As long as you're a black man, you're an African
No mind your nationality, You have got the identity of an African . . . No mind your complexion . . . No mind denomination that is only segregation You're an African[61]

Tosh seems to define African identity as one that includes all of the rainbow mixtures of peoples of the world who are classified as "black." In doing so, he refuses to use nationality as the principal criterion to determine the African identity. However, he has left unclear what the African identity really represents.

Tosh uses the term both as a social and personal category to describe African identities. His recurring narrative states:

Don't care where you come from, As long as you're a black man, you're an African
No mind your nationality, You have got the identity of an African

His song emerged within the social context of Jamaica shaped by colonial forces that utilized a system of social death[62] through slavery to unleash physical brutality and cultural genocide. Conflict and alienation shaped all forms of human relation. The enslaved population was under pressure to lose their personal and corporate identity and their social environment.[63] According to Ashley Smith, the years of socialization bequeathed a psyche of self-hate, self-contempt, lack of confidence, an inordinate respect for things from the European culture and a sense about things African.[64] The Jamaican people being addressed by Tosh were reminded that they should not surrender their human dignity to forces of division bequeathed by colonialism and slavery. What is important is to recover and retain their unity as African people regardless of their ethnic locations. Oppression and suffering had molded them into one people.

Tosh identified local and regional political boundaries that separate people from each other and give them competing identities to fight each other. Indeed, within the Caribbean, Anglophone-speaking populations who were classified as belonging to the British West Indies were called West Indians; this became a travesty to their authentic identities that evolved primarily out of West Africa and Asia. Tosh's Rastafari perspective is built on the notion that the peoples' experience of colonialism has sought to deprive them of the positive heritage of their African identity. Therefore, the color stratification bequeathed by the colonial system, based upon pigmentation of skin color of white, brown, black, colored, and mulatto, and the religious segregation based upon denominational differences, are false divisions among the people that must be rejected. Finally, Tosh pushed the definition of African identity into the international sphere to include those peoples of African identities living in North America, Europe, and Asia. Of significance is Tosh's failure to list South America, where Brazil constitutes the nation with the most people of African identity outside of the African continent with over ninety-seven million.[65]

The significance of Tosh's narrative for the rainbow nation of South Africa is that he argues that the common identity of being Africans should be the inclusive identity affirmation of all ethnic groups before they embrace any other identities that separate them from others. To be African is constitutive of a deep level of identity conscientization that is constructed to resist colonizing imperial forces of oppression.

CONCLUSION

This chapter argues that the contemporary discourse on race and identities within South Africa constitutes part of a wider global debate on identity politics. The intensity of pressures from global migration, economic decline, and the rise in far-right political movements has impacted negatively on the rise in identity politics. The context of South Africa with its negative legacy of Apartheid has exacerbated the problem and made race and identity issues central to every facet of life. Among the different methods that are being employed to interrogate these issues, Rastafari hermeneutics as embraced in the musical narrative of local Rastafari groups in Pietermaritzburg seems to offer a positive corrective response to the societal challenges. The perspectives of Lucky Dube in "Different Colours / One People" and Peter Tosh, "I Am an African," offer contrasting and at times complementary responses to the identity challenges faced by the African race living in a multiethnic society in which they are numerically the majority, but economically they live as the minority because of historic forces of inequality.

What then is the significance of the narratives offered by Dube and Tosh in their contrasting perspectives on African identities? The narrative of both Rastafari reggae artists placed the unity of the people who have been oppressed by global and local imperial forces as a key counterforce of resistance in reshaping their quest for liberation. Their different Rastafari lenses of constructing African identities appear on the surface to be somewhat contradictory. However, an in-depth analysis of their competing perspectives suggests that they have much in common. They placed the common good of all citizens living in harmony and flourishing in their context the overriding and urgent mission for nation building.

Dube's "Different Colours / One People" sought to unite all residents of South Africa into a common identity as South Africans, not one in which their different ethnic identities become barriers to national unity. Tosh's emphasis is on appropriating ones' African identity by owning, affirming, and celebrating ones' "blackness" as a central strategy to resist the minority privileged class who falsely claim that "color does not matter" but uses the slogan as a strategy to maintain their economic and political power. The concept of "blackness" is also more than a specific ethnic identity and neither is it restricted to national identities. Rather, its identity is broadened to include people who have been shaped by experiences of oppression and suffering that is deemed to be a kind of "black experience." Whereas Tosh called on all black people to affirm their African identity, Dube's emphasis is on calling for all who live in South Africa to embrace a common South African identity regardless of ethnic background. The factors of race and the African identity will therefore continue to challenge all South Africans because social cohesion and issues that pertain to inequality are all linked to the construct and working-out of policies linked to race and identity.

NOTES

1. Within the African continent for 2010, the following countries were classified as failed states: Somalia, Chad, Sudan, Zimbabwe, and Democratic Republic of Congo. AllAfrica.com, "Africa: Seven Nations Named in Top Ten 'Failed States.'" <http://allafrica.com/stories/201006240615.html/> [Accessed: August 22, 2016].

2. Rich Elfers, "Apartheid Impacts Are Still Felt in South Africa," http://www.courierherald.com/opinion/174619881.html [Accessed: August 22, 2016].

3. Phillip de Wet, "New Stats Show That Nine out of 11 Protests a Day are Peaceful," <http://mg.co.za/article/2016-06-07-new-stats-show-that-nine-out-of-11-protests-a-day-are-peaceful/> [Accessed: August 22, 2016].

4. Michelle Adato, Michael R. Carter, and Julian May, "Exploring Poverty Traps and Social Exclusion in South Africa Using Qualitative and Quantitative Data," *Journal of Development Studies* 42/2 (2006): 226–47.

5. Erskine, *From Garvey to Marley-Rastafari Theology*, 59.

6. Roxanne E. Burton, "Globalisation and Cultural Identity in Caribbean Society: The Jamaican Case," <http://ojs.mona.uwi.edu/index.php/cjp/article/viewFile/285/185/> [Accessed: August 16, 2016].

7. James D. Fearon, "What Is Identity (As We Now Use the Word)?" <https://www.researchgate.net/profile/James_Fearon2/publication/229052754_What_is_identity_(as_we_now_use_the_word)/links/0f31752e689dc3f2a7000000.pdf/> [Accessed: August 16, 2016].

8. Fearon, "What Is Identity," 1.

9. Horowitz L. Donald, *Ethnic Groups in Conflict* (Berkeley: University of California Press, 1985), xii, 697.

10. Chandra Kanchan, "What Is Ethnic Identity and Does It Matter?" <https://www.nyu.edu/gsas/dept/politics/faculty/chandra/ars2005.pdf/> [Accessed: September 23, 2016].

11. Simon Bekker, Martine *Dodds*, and *Meshack M. Khosa*, eds., *Shifting African Identities, Identity? Theory, Politics, History* (Pretoria: Human Sciences Research Council, 2001).

12. The Rastafari movement derives its name from Selassie's pre-coronation title, Ras Tafari Makonnen. Ladi Opaluwa, "Haile Selassie and the Rastafari Movement in Britain," <http://thisisafrica.me/lifestyle/haile-selassie-rastafari-movement-britain/> [Accessed: June 30. 2016].

13. Lubabalo Ntsholo, "South Africa Can't Speak about Land without Speaking about Race," <http://www.dailymaverick.co.za/opinionista/2016-06-20-south-africa-cant-speak-about-land-without-speaking-about-race/#.V3PN31V97IW/> [Accessed: June 20, 2016].

14. Leighton Luke, "Challenges Confronting South Africa: Land Reform," <http://www.futuredirections.org.au/publication/challenges-confronting-south-africa-land-reform/> [Accessed: August 22, 2016]. According to Luke, "Less than ten percent of the target set in 1994 of returning thirty percent of the land taken under colonialism and Apartheid has been transferred to its previous owners."

15. The phenomenon of landlessness describes a historical and structural organization of a nation's economy in which land is excessively owned or possessed by a handful of people. See Mahmood Hasan Khan, M. Ghaffar Chaudhry, and Sarfraz Khan Qureshi, "Landlessness and Rural Poverty in Underdeveloped Countries," *Pakistan Development Review* 25/3, part I [Autumn 1986]: 371–402 (papers and proceedings of the Third Annual General Meeting of the Pakistan Society of Development Economists, August 10–12, 1986.

16. The term decolonial refers to: "The term means to suggest both resistance to the "colonial" and that the "colonial" and its discourses continue to shape cultures whose revolutions have overthrown formal ties to their former colonial rulers." See Cultural Theory, "XI. Postcolonial/Decolonial Theories," <http://culturalpolitics.net/cultural_theory/postcolonial/> [Accessed: September 23, 2016]. In Rastafari understanding and practice, its teachings offer critical reflection on race and ethnicity that deconstruct modernity and its deceptive systems of enslavement.

17. Nathaniel S. Murrell, William D. Spencer, Adrian A. McFarlane, *Chanting Down Babylon: The Rastafari Reader* [Philadelphia, PA: Temple University Press, 1998), 159–65.

18. Roderick R. Hewitt, *Church and Culture* (Pietermaritzburg, South Africa: Cluster Publications, 2012), 98.

19. Erskine, *From Garvey to Marley-Rastafari Theology*, 59.

20. Erskine, *From Garvey to Marley-Rastafari Theology*, 44.

21. Swami Anand Prahlad, *Reggae Wisdom-Proverbs in Jamaican Music* (Jackson, MS: University Press, 2001), 8.

22. Roderick R. Hewitt, "Stealing Land in the Name of Religion: A Rastafari Religio-political Critique of Land Theft by Global Imperial Forces," *HTS Teologiese Studies / Theological Studies* 72/1 (2016): a3347, DOI: 10.4102/hts.v72i1.3347.

23. Babylon symbolizes the oppressive state, the formal social and political institution of Anglo/American imperialism. Carolyn Cooper, *Noises in the Blood: Orality, Gender and "Vulgar" Body of Jamaican Popular Culture* (Durham, NC: Duke University, 1995), 121.

24. Tony Martin, *Marcus Garvey: Message to the People: The Course of African Philosophy* (Dover, MA: Majority Press, 1986), 1–18.

25. George Wauchope, "Azania: Land of the Black People," <https://azanian-revolution.wordpress.com/historical-azania/> [Accessed: June 30, 2016].

26. Wauchope, "Azania: Land of the Black People."

27. See Murrell, Spencer, and McFarlane, *Chanting Down Babylon*, 159–65; Erskine, *From Garvey to Marley-Rastafari Theology*, 59.

28. Midas Chawane, "The Appearance and Significance of Rastafari Cultural Aspects in South Africa," <https://dspace.nwu.ac.za/bitstream/handle/10394/13374/No_71(2014)_6_Chawane_M.pdf?sequence=1/> [Accessed: September 18, 2016].

29. P. Napti, "Jamaicans of Ethiopian Origin and the Rastafarian Faith" <http://www.zhurnal.ru/music/rasta/napti.htm/> [Accessed: September 23, 2016].

30. Alemseghed Kebede and J. David Knottnerus, "Beyond the Pales of Babylon: The Ideational Components and Social Psychological Foundations of Rastafari," *Sociological Perspectives* 41/3 (1998): 499–517.

31. Kebede and Knottnerus, "Beyond the Pales of Babylon."

32. "Rastafari for Nation Building in Democratic South Africa," symposium video clip (4′ 55″), Askhulume Media Production, October 26, 2012.

33. "Rastafari for Nation Building," (4′ 00″).

34. "Rastafari for Nation Building," (3′ 00″ to 9′ 00″).

35. "Rastafari for Nation Building," (10′ 15″).

36. J. Richard Middleton, "Identity and Subversion in Babylon: Strategies for 'Resisting against the Babylon System,'" in *Religion, Culture and Tradition in the Caribbean*, ed. Hemchand Gossai and Nathaniel Samuel Murrell (New York: St Martin's Press, 2000), 181–205.

37. The word "reggae" has evolved in meaning from its Yoruba rege-rege meaning "rough" to symbolize in Jamaica how the "rough" poor people in the ghettoes of Kingston, Jamaica, use their musical resources to renew and reinvent themselves. Olive Senior, *Encyclopaedia of Jamaican Heritage* (Red Hills, Jamaica: Twin Guinep, 2003), 412.

38. Murrell, Spencer, and McFarlane, *Chanting Down Babylon*, 152.
39. Afari Yasus, *Overstanding Rastafari: Jamaica's Gift to the World* (Kingston, Jamaica: Senya Cum, 2007), 113–26.
40. Yasus, *Overstanding Rastafari*, 128
41. Erskine, *From Garvey to Marley-Rastafari Theology*, 169–70.
42. Erskine, *From Garvey to Marley-Rastafari Theology*, 178.
43. Erskine, *From Garvey to Marley-Rastafari Theology*, 169–70.
44. Lucky Dube was named the world's best-selling African recording artist at the World Music Awards for his "Serious Business 10th Anniversary Album." See "Lucky Dube: A Complete Human Being," Thought Leader, *Mail & Guardian*, October, 19, 2007, <http://thoughtleader.co.za/amablogoblogo/2007/10/19/lucky-dube-a-complete-human-being/> , [Accessed: June 30, 2016].
45. Thought Leader, "Lucky Dube: A Complete Human Being."
46. Thought Leader, "Lucky Dube: A Complete Human Being."
47. Metro Lyrics, "Together as One Lyrics," <http://www.metrolyrics.com/together-as-one-lyrics-lucky-dube.html/> [Accessed: June 4, 2016].
48. Metro Lyrics, "Together as One Lyrics."
49. Song Lyrics, "Lucky Dube: Different Colours Lyrics," <http://www.song-lyrics.com/lucky-dube/different-colours-lyrics/#eTwcToI5uXRDuHOA.99/> [Accessed: June 26, 2016].
50. Tinyiko S. Maluleke, "Desmond Tutu's Earliest Notions and Visions of Church, Humanity, and Society," *Ecumenical Review* 67/4 (2015): 572–90.
51. The Economist, "African Democracy: The March of Democracy Slows," <http://www.economist.com/news/middle-east-and-africa/21705355-threats-democratic-rule-africa-are-growing-time-and-demography-are?fsrc=scn/tw/te/pe/ed/themarchofdemocracyslows/> [Accessed: June 26, 2016].
52. "Decriminalization" is the term used to describe laws that are intended to reduce the legal sanctions for possession of small amounts of marijuana to penalties other than imprisonment. See Eric Single, "The Impact of Marijuana Decriminalisation: An Update" <http://www.michelepolak.com/200spring11 / Weekly_Schedule_files/Single.pdf/> [Accessed: June 26, 2016].
53. Peter Tosh, "Legalise It," <http://genius.com/Peter-tosh-legalize-it-lyrics/> [Accessed: June 26, 2016].
54. Joseph Owens, *Dread: The Rastafarians of Jamaica* (Kingston, Jamaica: Sangster, 1976).
55. Joseph Owens, "Rastafari: Liberation of Misplaced Black Community," <https://colleenday .wordpress.com/tag/joseph-owens/> [Accessed: April 1, 2017].
56. This Babylon system is expressed through the social, religious, and economic systems of Euro-American imperialism. According to Cooper, Babylon symbolizes the oppressive state, the formal social and political institution of Anglo/American imperialism. Cooper, *Noises in the Blood*, 121.
57. Jacques-Garvey, "Philosophy and Opinions of Marcus Garvey."
58. Erskine, *From Garvey to Marley-Rastafari Theology*, 59.
59. Erskine, *From Garvey to Marley-Rastafari Theology*, 146–64.
60. Roderick R. Hewitt, "Bob Marley's Redemption Song in Conversation with de Gruchy's Olive Agenda," *Alternation*, special edition 14 (2015) 169–89.

61. See Peter Tosh, "African Lyrics," <http://www.songlyrics.com/peter-tosh/african-lyrics/#2djXm4y73fiDE5iu.99/> [Accessed June 26, 2016].

62. Orlando Patterson, *Sociology of Slavery* (London: Oxford University Press, 1967), 72.

63. Maulana Karenga, *Introduction to Black Studies* (Los Angeles: University of Sankore Press, 1993), 128.

64. Ashley Smith, *Emergence from Innocence* (Mandeville, Jamaica: Eureka Press, 1991), 10.

65. The 2010 census of Brazil shows that ninety-seven million Brazilians, or 50.7 percent of the population, claim African identity, <https://www.theguardian.com/world/2011/nov/17/brazil-census-african-brazilians-majority/> [Accessed: August 22, 2016].

FOURTEEN

On Locating Islam and African Muslim Identity within Africana/ Islamica Existential Thought

A Preview

Tahir Fuzile Sitoto

INTRODUCTION

Of African identities, black African Muslim identity, more especially in the context of South Africa, if not a contested identity, remains an anomaly. Unlike in some other African countries such as Senegal, Mali, Nigeria, or even Tanzania in East Africa—to mention but a few—where large sections of the African population have been Muslims for centuries, in South Africa, this is not the case. Due to the presence of the Asian diaspora with large numbers of Muslims, to be black, African, and Muslim in the country is understood as a serious contradiction. Black Africans who have turned to Islam as the religion of choice, as well as an aspect of their identity, irrespective of their social, professional, or even political standing, are often accused of being guilty of cultural treason. The outcry against Chief Mandla Mandela (grandson of the late Nelson Mandela), when news broke that he had converted to Islam, is a case in point. Journalists had a scoop reporting that the Congress of Traditional Leaders of South Africa (Contralesa), as represented by its provincial chair and Bhala Traditional Council head, Chief Mwelo Nonkonyana, was "angered" by "Mandla Mandela's conversion to Islam."[1] Contralesa's statement went so far as to demand that the young Mandela be stripped of his chieftaincy. Although Chief Mandela had quietly converted to Islam in late November 2015, what news journalists had exposed was the controversy surrounding his highly publicized marriage to Rabia Clarke, a Muslim from Cape Town.

This chapter, however, is not about the cultural politics of Mandela's conversion to Islam. Nor is it about dramatizing his turn to Islam. Instead, by opening with Chief Mandela's story and the reactions to his adopted faith, my caveat is to highlight a subtler point, viz., the rejection of Islam as being incompatible with African identity. Such rejection is also discernible in surprisingly enlightened circles through what is referred to in this chapter as discursive blindness or prejudice toward Islam. By this I mean the almost absent treatment of Islam as a category worth serious examination in most African philosophical discourse.

Besides the introduction and conclusion, this chapter consists of three main sections. The first section provides a rationale as to why the conceptual and philosophical is privileged over the social and political aspects of African identity—not that there is a distinct separation between these categories; but that is a discussion for elsewhere. In addition, the section concedes that there is a context to the polemic against Islam and its subsequent negation as an aspect of black and African identity. Rather than offer a spirited defense of Islam, the section identifies some of the possible reasons for such an attitude. Extending the discussion, the second section offers a critique and appraisal of the work of two African Muslim intellectuals considered "insiders" to Islam, who have paid critical attention to Islam and its place within African thought and philosophy. This is followed by a third section where through a preview of work in progress, this researcher argues that a more meaningful way of appreciating Islam as an aspect of black and African identity can be found by locating Islam as a critical discursive concern within Africana and Islamica existential philosophy. What is implied by black and Africana existential philosophy in the context of this chapter will complete the discussion.

WHY PRIVILEGE THE PHILOSOPHICAL OVER THE POLITICAL?

If the notion of identity in its expansive sense is understood as consisting of "a compendium of different elements that are nevertheless interconnected," as argued elsewhere by Olajubu, then surely African identity, and by inference philosophical discourse, cannot be an exception to such a view.[2] But then again, the doyen of the Pan-Africanist movement, Prah reminds everyone in the first opening epigraph: "If everybody is an African, then nobody is an African." Prah's insistence is that there has to be something that binds and gives content to African identity, and, by inference, a philosophy that claims to be African. In the absence of this unique something, then any claim to African identity is questionable. Put differently, what is it that gives substance and content to what is conceived as an African identity? And in exactly what specific sense is Prah referring, when he refers to African identity? Is it in the "chauvinistic" and "xenophobic" sense, or is Prah demanding a far deeper probing of what is conceived as an African identity?[3]

Without attempting to even critique Prah's otherwise nuanced position, the view expressed in his quote nevertheless highlights the almost impossible task of defining identity and, not least, African identity.[4] Indeed, there are times as Olajubu asserts, when, "time and settings" often "dictate which aspects of an individual's identity are prioritised" while others are downplayed.[5] Take the example of North African identity. In North African social and political history, there are times when North Africans have punted a pan-Arab identity over an African one. But there are also times when the opposite is true. During the later years of Muammar Gadhafi's rule in Libya, there was a discernible shift from pan-Arabism to a Pan-African orientation in Libyan identity.[6] Of course, to speak of African identity in the latter sense would entail speaking of African identity in its strictly social and political contexts. This in turn would suggest among other things delving into a discourse around the quest for continental unity or what Muchie has termed, the "making of the Africa-Nation."[7] However, to indulge in such a discussion would defeat the purpose of the present study.

As noted, the purpose of this chapter is to explore—if it is possible at all—to imagine and reconfigure Africana existential thought beyond its privileged categories, foundational logic, and essentialist framings. Indeed, if closed notions of African identity are to be challenged, then in addition to dealing with the crude political aspects of African identity, the seemingly abstract, conceptual, and philosophical questions pertaining to such an identity, regardless of how it is understood, remain crucial. After all, part of the problem with notions of who is African and who is not, is based on internalized self-understandings that were, as argued by Zeleza, "manufactured" within the academy. Also, such an assertion finds support in Mamdani's critique of the history and formation of African studies at the University of Cape Town, when he observed, "If the thrust of Apartheid was to produce a racial identity among its victims, to what extent were these racial identities grounded in the knowledge produced by the academy?"[8]

Mamdani's question is not trivial. In fact, in a dense chapter, "Philosophy in South Africa under and after Apartheid," More provides a survey and critique of how the discipline of philosophy was manipulated to legitimize Apartheid. Among other issues, he highlights how, for example, some "Afrikaans university professors explicitly defended Apartheid" by mobilizing an array of philosophical traditions. And as he notes further, "The defence was so vigorous and extensive" to the extent that even "Rawls theory of justice was construed to be compatible with the basic tenets of Apartheid."[9]

The project to broaden the discursive and conceptual categories in black and African intellectual traditions such as philosophy should not be confused with the old polemic among those claiming to be professional African philosophers over the problem of its definition and method. As Oladipo, who calls "for relevance," and Matolino, who among others has argued that while "debates on style and method of African philosophy were important," the imperative "today," is to begin "work in those areas where there is a need for philosophical investigation."[10] Without claiming to offer any philosophical investigation of any sort, this present study concedes that one of the glaring omissions in the African philosophical literature, in both its African and African diasporal contexts, is the almost neglect, if not absence, of Islam as a category worth critical examination. This is not to say there is hardly any mention of Islam in African philosophical literature. It is common to find prominent professional African philosophers making some references to Islam in one way or another. However, such references as noted by Diagne are either to augment arguments on the multiple nature of African identity, or to prove that both Islam and Christianity are no longer external but an internal aspect of African identity. Accordingly, the concern is not so much with the view that offers an extensive investigation of African Muslim identity.[11] Instead, could the ambivalence toward Islam be based on a sub-conscious cultural or cognitive prejudice toward this tradition as being non-African?

The Senegalese philosopher Blaise Diagne thinks that the absence of Islam in African philosophical reflection is not only based on cultural prejudice but reflects a gross neglect of African intellectual history. Souleymane Bachir Diagne is convinced that it is virtually "impossible to give a proper account of the history of philosophy in the African continent while ignoring totally the significance of the penetration of Islamic knowledge in Africa."[12]

In particular, he is referring to the Islamic intellectual legacy that remains largely buried in the rich Timbuktu manuscripts written in Arabic and other similar archives, such as those in Zanzibar, East Africa.[13] However, without analyzing such materials here, Diagne's "pre-colonial African Philosophy in Arabic" provides a useful index on the content and significance of Arabic African archives. Besides debunking notions that prior to the encounter with Europe and Western modernity Africa lacked any written culture, Diagne's contribution illustrates how as far back as "pre-colonial times," African Muslim scholars in African locales such as Timbuktu were already engaged in forms of "philosophical writing and thinking," albeit conducted through Arabic.[14]

Inasmuch as Diagne raises critical questions regarding the content of the African intellectual legacy in Arabic materials, as a professional philosopher trained at the Sorbonne in France, with a specialization in mathematical philosophy and Boolean logic, as his studies on Bergson reveal, initially his interests were invested more on continental European philosophy. Curiously, even in his work on Islam, Diagne was inclined to devote more attention to the Indo-Pak Muslim philosopher-poet Allama Iqbal Iqbal.[15] Alternatively, Iqbal is studied with a view to compare his thought with that of Senghor. That is, where the two thinkers are read through Bergsonian lenses. This is certainly the case with his essay "Bergson Postcolonial: *le élan vital dans la pensée de* Léopold Sedar Senghor *et de* Mohamed Iqbal."[16] This characterization of Diagne although partly correct, since his relocation to the United States, where he is currently professor of philosophy and French literature at Columbia University, as Hogarth has observed, there has been a remarkable shift in his work toward "cultural philosophy."[17] I shall return to some discussion of Diagne later in this chapter.

With regard to other works on the place of Islam in African philosophy, scholarly analysis tends to be either hopelessly shallow, or alternatively, Islam is treated through a triumphalist language that insinuates its implicit superiority over, say, African traditional thought. Nasseem's essay "African Heritage and Contemporary Life" represents the latter example.[18] On the surface, the essay is premised on an earnest quest to treat Islam as a critical heritage among Africans. Unfortunately, what is deemed African heritage and Islamic are often analyzed through a binary logic that treats them in essentialist ways as oppositional categories. Hence, Nasseem is at pains to prove the futility of reconciling two "conflicting systems of epistemology" that represent different understandings of cosmogony. As he writes: "The Islamic heritage" advances "one single and absolute cosmogony"; whereas African cosmogony "postulates" as reflected in the "traditional African mind . . . a divine who can participate with the finite in the same locus."[19] Without getting into the problematic of Nasseem's simplistic representation of African cosmogony, and not to mention its essentialist undertones that conscript the African to a static ontology of the "traditional mind," his stance toward what is African cosmogony is highly problematic.[20] Hence, notwithstanding black Muslim defenses against what is sometimes perceived as an unfair criticism of Islam as a cultural imposition on Africanity, Nasseem unwittingly feeds into such criticism.[21]

Similarly, Lajul in his recent *African Philosophy: Critical Dimensions* is also dismissive of the relevancy of Islam in Africa. In his essay he pairs Islam with Christianity and treats it under the heading, "Modern African philosophy of religion." While initially appearing to affirm Islam when, as with Christianity, he argues, both religious traditions "are capable of providing new myths . . . and inspirations for thinking afresh," Islam is suddenly dismissed, "because [Islam] has not itself awoken to the demands of the day due to its legalism and inflexibility."[22] A fair point, it could be argued. However, while it is not my intention to reduce this chapter to a discussion of Christian/Muslim polemics, Lajul's simplistic treatment of Islam betrays the complexity shown in the treatment of other themes and concerns that his text has treated. Without any account of internal diversity within Islam, it is relegated to a cultural monolith. Nor is there any reference to the Sufi orders or mystical fraternities, which enjoy more prominence in African Islam than legalistic Islam. To borrow language used elsewhere that foreground notions of African agency, the reverse is indeed true. Accordingly, other scholars have argued that when "possessed by Africans," religious traditions such as Islam have been given new meanings that are in concert with African realities.[23] The resultant question that must be asked with regard to Lajul's reference to Islam is: Why should Islam in a philosophical text be reduced in a simplistic fashion, to a cultural monolith? Could this be another instance of cultural and cognitive prejudice toward Islam in the African intellectual tradition and associated philosophical texts?

SEEKING ALTERNATIVE READINGS: ENGAGING MAZRUINA'S "TRIPLE HERITAGE" AND DIAGNE'S "AFRICANITY AS DIFFERENCE"?

Given Mazrui's huge intellectual corpus in what has become known as "Mazruina," any writing that reflects on the place of Islam in African intellectual traditions and identity cannot afford to ignore his work.[24] Never dull and always brilliant, as observed by Umari: "Whatever one may say about Ali Mazrui's writing, it is hardly boring."[25] Through what has become his trademark, "the triple heritage," hence, in addition to Christianity, the presence of Islam in African traditional culture and religion constitutes for Mazrui one of the central pillars of African identity.[26] Accordingly, Morewedge and others such as Nyang regard Mazrui as someone who has made the most "original contributions" in situating Islam as a critical dimension of African heritage.[27]

Notwithstanding Mazrui's impressive contribution on Islam as an integral component of African identity, what admirers of Mazrui often miss is that besides affirming Islam as integral to African heritage, there is often a lack of a sustained meta-theoretical reflection on the very meaning of the affirmed Islamic component within Africa's identities. This is not to say his writings on Islam lack any brilliant insights. On the latter, I agree with Umari's characterization that Mazrui's strength rests rather in his brilliance as "the generator of the intellectual framework" and "hypotheses."[28] However, there is a need to move beyond "the hypothesis" that affirms Islam as a critical signature of the triple heritage. The question that begs for attention is: "What is, beyond the descriptive level, the deeper meaning of the interface between Islam and Africanity?" With regard to the latter question, Diagne's entry as another "insider of the Islam / Africa phenomenon," to use Morewedge's description of Mazrui, represents a promising reading of the place of Islam within African identity.

Diagne's "Islam in Africa: Examining the Notion of an African Identity within the Islamic World" provides an opportunity to take a closer look at his reflections on Islam and African identity. In particular, Diagne's approach on Islam within African identity revolves around a careful analysis of two identical but, as he argues, different concepts, namely, *L'Islam Noir* (lit., "Black Islam") and the "Africanisation of Islam."[29] The first concept is examined mainly through the history of its construction and how it has come to enjoy usage through what Diagne terms "colonial ethnology." Accordingly, through the construction of the concept *L'Islam Noir*, colonial strategy, argues Diagne, was to cut off and thus separate African Muslims from the rest of the Muslim world.[30] Constructed as "difference" through *L'Islam Noir*, African Muslims were not quite like other Muslims. "Black specificity," therefore, maintains Diagne, was used in a "derogatory" way to delegitimize African Islam. Furthermore, the colonial strategy through the designation *L'Islam Noir* served another political purpose, viz., to "shield the sub-Saharan areas from [the] so-called pan-Arabic and pan-Islamic threat to Western colonial domination."[31]

However, the Muslim world is also not spared from Diagne's critique. But how different was the attitude of the latter toward the Africans? Ethnological thinking within the Muslim world and its attitude toward "Muslim Africa," Diagne asserts, was in the form of Arab "tribal thinking," which ironically contradicts Islam. Such thinking, he asserts, is expressed through implicit and at times explicit considerations of "the Arab peoples to be at the centre of the *Ummah*" (i.e., the universal community of Muslims), and by such definition, the only legitimate custodians of Islam. The logic of such "a chauvinistic viewpoint," Diagne maintains, was to disregard "Muslim Africa" and place it on the margins of the supposed "'truly' Islamic world."[32]

Significant as reflections on colonial and Arab Muslim "ethnologism" are, what interests this researcher is how Diagne deals with the second concept: viz., the "Africanisation of Islam." Interestingly, with regard to this second concept, Diagne's emphasis is on the need for "internal understanding" of Islam as lived and practiced by African Muslims and not as dictated by external players. While I agree with such a shift in emphasis, unfortunately, by his own admission, Diagne's work represents a kind of "bibliographic sample." Unfortunately, he has yet to illustrate fully how the project of "internal understanding" should unfold. This does not mean Diagne has not raised deep and important questions; nevertheless, they remain questions that require further probing.[33]

Having briefly surveyed Mazrui's and Diagne's treatment of Islam and its place within African identity, what remains to be asked is: In what way does this author's research pertaining to the place of Islam on African identity either endorse or depart from the views advanced by these two prominent African Muslim scholars and others sharing similar views?[34]

A POINT OF DEPARTURE: WHY PRIVILEGE AFRICANA EXISTENTIAL PHILOSOPHY—A SUBJECTIVE BIAS OR A METHODOLOGICAL AND THEORETICAL DEMAND?

Without weighing down this contribution with substantive content from this researcher's work, what is shared in this section are really morsels from a work still in progress. And work in progress as invoked here implies both the metaphorical and literal sense. Literal, in the sense that the ideas explored here, even though this chapter is independent, more especially the latter sense, emerging from data from a forthcoming research work and hence this chapter does not claim to be solely based on an exclusive "empirical data" of its own. And by work in progress in the metaphorical sense, the reference is to an extent this researcher's personal narrative on why Africana existential philosophy is proposed in this chapter as the method to locate a critical enquiry on black African Muslim identity.

Not persuaded with how black African Muslim identity has been written about thus far, this researcher has been searching for a concept and method that would best articulate, among other concerns, the meaning of what it means to be black, African, and Muslim in the world? That is, not so much in the historical, political, social, or even anthropological sense. Instead, my point of departure is found in this existential question: What does it mean really to be a subject that is forever cast as *Otherness*? More especially, in a context such as South Africa where the African Muslim subject is cast through what can best be described as the "dialectic of Otherness."[35] First, it is *Otherness* in the sense of a subject construed as the misguided African *Other* through her/his association with Islam. In the second, it is cast as the Muslim *cultural Other* and hence the *proverbial* convert. That means, although a Muslim, the individual can never become "a complete Muslim," no matter how committed and dedicated they are to Islamic adherence, rituals, and practice.

With the above unashamedly self-subjective note, the question of Islam and African identity is approached in the work of this researcher from a slightly different angle, where Islam is not pursued from the premise of a tradition, culture, or religion detached from its adherents. Rather, what is privileged is the ontological location of Islam as lived and embodied by black African Muslims as an existential reality and presence—and thus is already a part of their identity. Subsequently, this quest to find a concept or method adequate enough to fully capture such a complex mode of being has turned out to be more than mere academic inquiry, but a lifetime commitment. In particular, it was exposure at the State University of New York, Binghamton's now defunct philosophy, interpretation, and culture program, during a three-year course of study, that exposed this researcher to the work of Gordon and others working within black and Africana existential philosophy, in particular. When returning to South Africa and deciding to resume an aborted research project, the subject matter and its data demanded that Africana existential philosophy should anchor such a research project. In particular, what intrigued the present researcher was that the preferred method was not to be externally imposed but rather informed by the content (and data) of his research.[36]

Building on the previous work of Lucius Outlaw Jr., Lewis Gordon has defined Africana existential philosophy as "a branch of Africana philosophy and black philosophies of existence."[37] The emphasis on "philosophies of existence" is a deliberate strategy on the part of Gordon, and those working in this area such as the South Africans More and Maart, for example, to distinguish its privileged discursive parameters and concerns.[38] While the influence of Sartre is acknowledged as the "unusual catalyst in the history of black existential philosophy," Gordon cautions that it would "be an error to construct Africana existential academic philosophy as a fundamentally Sartrean or 'European based phenomenon.'"[39] Accordingly, without erasing Sartre's influence as "European thought," and by inference, existential philosophy, "Africana existential philosophy," as the argument taken up by More illustrates, can be understood as an "intertextually embedded discursive practice,"[40] with great importance being placed on the "situation of being Black in the world." [41]

Without a critique of the latter position—at least not in this contribution—the conceptualization of Africana existential philosophy as an "intertextually embedded practice" has proved particularly attractive. Rather than frustrate the dialogue, it opens up possibilities to explore new and alternative ways of creating knowledge not yet fully explored. As I argue elsewhere, black African Muslim identity, more especially in the context of South Africa, remains poorly interpreted. Accordingly, the questions explored in my research with regard to the latter identity, are premised on a different order of questions. Instead of asking the banal question of *why* Africans become Muslims, significance is rather attached to the micro and individual level, with a view to making proper sense of African Muslim identity, the sense of self, and subjectivity.[42] However, in seeking to do this, there is a double theoretical challenge.

If, as it is claimed, African Muslim identity is as much a question about African identity as it is a question of Islam (Mazrui and Diagne), inarguably such a claim presents a double bind. It is therefore not so much the strength of the claim that concerns this researcher as *how* the claim can be theorized and interpreted. Theoretically, the double bind is this: While Islamic thought is generally silent on black African Muslim identity—except through the narratives of conversion—the same is true with African philosophy in general and Africana existential philosophy in particular.[43] Accordingly, inasmuch as Africana existential philosophy is privileged to situate my research, I am not unmindful of its own theoretical omissions and blindness. It is with the latter view in mind that the work in progress is conceptualized as: "A Thesis on the Idea of Africana/Islamica Existential Thought with a Focus on Don Mattera and the Question of Transcendence." However, to guard the integrity of the project, and in respect of academic protocols, the least that this study can do for now is to merely comment thinly on what the conceptual formulation "Africana/Islamica existential thought" entails.

Although Lewis Gordon's signature is written all over the title, as noted, except for thin commentaries, Islam as a critical category is conspicuously absent, not just in African philosophy but also in Africana existential philosophy. The conceptual formulation in the title "Africana/Islamica existential thought," is thus intended to operate as a double concept, thereby serving as a conceptual bridge that can facilitate the self-negotiation of black African Muslim identities, subjectivities, and sense of self as both an African and Islamic identity without any serious schisms occurring in the process.

CONCLUSION

As intimated in the foregoing section, although captured more fully in a forthcoming research work, the conceptual formulation "Africana/Islamica existential thought," as postulated in the context of my research, is intended to act as a critical bridge to foreground the theoretical interface that takes place when categories that are generally understood as "Islamic" and "African," are treated together as a mutual discursive concern and not as if they are irreconcilable entities. Accordingly, if the possibility of finding new and open ways to read black and African identities is to be explored, there is not only the need to guard against the tyranny of existing discursive orthodoxies and their foundational logics but also to critically explore ways of thinking that go beyond existing conventions and categories. Admittedly, this chapter is limited to an exercise that points forward to how conceptual maps and horizons need to be broadened in the explication of black African Muslim identity.

NOTES

1. See "Mandla Mandela's Conversion to Islam Angers Contralesa," *The Citizen*, <http://www.citizen.co.za/ 985357/mandla-mandelas-conversion-to-islam-angers-contralesa/88/2/2016/> [Accessed: July 25, 2016].

2. Although Olajubu's reference to "identity" is in the context of discussing women in Yoruba culture and religion, her insights on identity formation in general are useful. For a detailed view, see Oyeronke Olajubu, *Women in the Yoruba Religious Sphere* (Albany, NY: SUNY Press 2003), 65.

3. For example, in making his claim, Prah is quick to assure his readers that he is "not suggesting anything chauvinistic" nor does he represent "an inward-looking essentially xenophobic mind." For a detailed discussion of his position, see Kwesi Kwaa Prah, *Beyond the Colour Line: Pan-Africanist Disputations: Selected Sketches, Letters, Papers, and Reviews* (Trenton, NJ: Africa World Press, 1998), 34. See also Kwesi Kwaa Prah, *Tracings: Pan-Africanism and the Challenges of Global African Unity* (Cape Town: CASAS Book Series, 2013).

4. For example, without referring to Prah specifically, Mbembe has characterized the position held by Prah on the "uniqueness" of African identity as representing a form of nativist thinking. Space and the nature of my own focus in this chapter do not allow for either a proper account of Mbembe's position or counterpoints to it. For further details, see Achille Mbembe, "African Modes of Self-Writing," *Public Culture* 14/1 (2002): 239–73.

5. Olajubu, *Women in Yoruba Religious Sphere*, 65.

6. See Akram Hawas, "Pan-Africanism and Pan-Arabism: Back to the Future?" in *The Making of the Africa-Nation: Pan-Africanism and the African Renaissance*, ed. Mammo Muchie (London: Adonis & Abbey, 2003): 296–97.

7. See Mammo Muchie, *The Making of the Africa-Nation: Pan-Africanism and the African Renaissance* (London: Adonis & Abbey, 2003).

8. For an extensive discussion on the formation of African Studies as an academic discipline within the academies of the global north, in particular, see Tiyambe Zeleza, *Manufacturing African Studies and Crises* (Dakar, Senegal: Codesria Book Series, 1997); Mahmood Mamdani, "Centre for African Studies: Some Preliminary Thoughts," *Social Dynamics* 22/2 (1996): 1–14.

9. Mabogo P. More, "Philosophy in South Africa under Apartheid," in *A Companion to African Philosophy*, ed. Kwasi Wiredu (Cambridge: Blackwell), 152–53.

10. See Olusegun Oladipo, *The Idea of African Philosophy: A Critical Study of the Major Orientations in Contemporary African Philosophy* (Ibadan, Nigeria: Hope Publications, 1998), 13; Bernard Matolino, *Personhood in African Philosophy* (Pietermaritzburg, South Africa: Cluster Publications, 2014), xiii–xvi.

11. Diagne cites as a specific example the case of Appiah, when he argues that Islam and Christianity are no longer external but have become internal to African identity. See Souleymane Bachir Diagne, "Precolonial African Philosophy in Arabic," in *A Companion to African Philosophy*, ed. Kwasi Wiredu (Cambridge: Cambridge University Press, 2004), 67; Kwame Anthony Appiah, *In My Father's House: Africa in the Philosophy of Culture* (Oxford: Oxford University Press, 1992), 107.

12. Souleymane Bachir Diagne, "Toward an Intellectual History of West Africa: The Meaning of Timbuktu," in *The Meanings of Timbuktu*, ed. Shamil Jeppie and Souleymane Bachir Diagne (Cape Town: HSRC Press, 2008), 19–21.

13. See R. Sean O'Fahey, "Arabic Literature in the Eastern Half of Africa," in *The Meanings of Timbuktu*, ed. Shamil Jeppie and Souleymane Bachir Diagne (Cape Town: HSRC Press, 2008), 333–47; Anne K. Bang, "Textual Sources on an Islamic African Past: Arabic Material in Zanzibar's National Archive," in *The Meanings of Timbuktu*, ed. Shamil Jeppie and Souleymane Bachir Diagne (Cape Town: HSRC Press, 2008), 349–59.

14. Souleymane Bachir Diagne, "Precolonial African Philosophy in Arabic," in *A Companion to African Philosophy*, ed. Kwasi Wiredu (Cambridge: Blackwell, 2004), 74. See also Diagne, "Toward an Intellectual History of West Africa," 19.

15. See Souleymane Bachir Diagne, *Islam and Open Society: Fidelity and Movement in the Philosophy of Muhammad Iqbal* (Dakar, Senegal: CODESRIA, 2010).

16. Soulaymane Bachir Diagne, "Bergson Postcolonial: *le elan vital dans la pensee de* Léopold Sédar Senghor's *et de* Mohamed Iqbal," *American Catholic Philosophical Quarterly* 83/1 (2011): 79–94.

17. See Christopher Hogarth's "Entre Deux Générations D'Intellectuels Africains': Souleymane Bachir Diagne," in *The Contemporary Francophone African Intellectual*, ed. Christopher Hogarth and Natalie Edwoods (Cambridge: Cambridge Scholar Publishing, 2013).

18. Subair Nasseem, "African Heritage and Contemporary Life," in *Philosophy for Africa: A Text with Readings*, ed. P. H. Coetzee and A.P.J. Roux (Johannesburg: Thompson, 2002).

19. Nasseem, "African Heritage and Contemporary Life."

20. Robin Horton's notion of a "two-tiered" cosmology offers a far more complex take on African cosmology. See Robin Horton, "African Traditional Thought and Western Science," in *African Philosophy: An Anthology*, ed. Emmanuel Chukwudi Eze (Oxford: Blackwell, 1998), 181–92.

21. For example, Sherman Jackson has labeled dismissal of Islam as an aspect of black and African identity a form of "Black Orientalism," a term first coined by Ali Mazrui. See Sherman Jackson, "Black Orientalism," in *Islam and the Blackamerican: Looking toward the Third Resurrection* (Oxford: Oxford University Press, 2005), 99–129; Ali Mazrui, "Black Orientalism? Further Reflections on 'Wonders of the African World,'" *West Africa Review* 1/2, <http://www.icaap.org/iuicode?101,1,2/> [Accessed: August 13, 2016].

22. Wilfred Lajul, *African Philosophy: Critical Dimensions* (Nairobi: Fountain Publishers, 2013), 204.

23. See Gerald O. West and Tahir Fuzile Sitoto, "Other ways of Reading the Qur'an and the Bible in Africa: Isaiah Shembe and Shaykh Ahmadu Bamba," *Postscripts: Journal of Sacred Texts & Contemporary Worlds* 1/1 (2005): 47–76.

24. See Abdul Bemath, *The Mazruina Collection Revisited: Ali A. Mazrui Debating the African Condition: An Annotated and Select Bibliography 1962–2003* (New Delhi: New Dawn Press, 2005).

25. Umari Kokole, introduction to *Mazrui: Portrait of a Global African*, ed. Kole Umari (Trenton, NJ: AWP Press, 1998), 5.

26. See Ali Mazrui, *The Africans: A Triple Heritage* (London: BBC Publications, 1986).

27. See Parvez Morewedge, "The Onyx Crescent: Ali A. Mazrui on the Islamic/Africa Axis," in *Ali Mazrui: Portrait of a Global African*, ed. Kole Umari (Trenton, NJ: AWP Press, 1998), 123–24. Due to limited space, Nyang's work is not discussed here. For details, see Sulayman Nyang, *Islam, Christianity and African Identity* (Chicago: Kazi Publications, 1999).

28. Kokole, introduction to *Mazrui*, 5. In fact, a study of the neologisms that Mazrui has coined over the years on different topics could be an interesting study on its own.

29. Soulaymane Bachir Diagne, "Islam in Africa: Examining the Notion of an African Identity within the Islamic World," in *A Companion to African Philosophy*, ed. Kwasi Wiredu, (Malden, MA: Blackwell, 2004), 375.

30. A similar practice can also be identified in how Islam in the context of North America was often framed as a different practice through the label "Black Muslims." See, for example, C. Eric Lincoln, *The Black Muslims in America* (Trenton, NJ: AWP Press, 1961; repr., 1994).

31. Diagne, "Islam in Africa," 376.

32. Diagne, "Islam in Africa," 376.

33. His brief discussion, for example, on Ahmad Baba, the eminent scholar and philosopher of Timbuktu, deserves a critical independent study of its own. See Diagne, "Precolonial African Philosophy in Arabic," 67.

34. For this chapter, and for considerations of space, I have deliberately limited my focus to Mazrui and Diagne as my immediate interlocutors insofar as the place of Islam and its relationship with Africanity is concerned.

35. For the term "dialectic of otherness," which I use to describe the peculiarity of black Muslim identity in South Africa, I am indebted to Mazrui's usage where he refers to African American identity and its relationship with Africa as a "dialectic of diversity." See Ali Mazrui, "Global Africa in Flux: The Dialectic of Diversity in the Black World," in *African Presence in the Americas*, ed. Carlos Moore, Tanya R. Saunders, and Shawna Moore (Trenton, NJ: Africa World Press, 1995), 457–76.

36. Here I am referring to my research work on the South African poet, writer, journalist, and Black Consciousness activist turned Muslim in the 1970's, Don Mattera. See forthcoming PhD thesis by Fuzile Tahir Sitoto, "A Thesis on the Idea of Africana/Islamica Existential Thought with a Focus on Don Mattera (1935–) and the Question of Transcendence" (University of Cape Town).

37. Lewis R. Gordon, *Existentia Africana: Understanding Africana Existential Thought* (New York: Routledge, 2000), 5. See also Lucius Outlaw, "African, African American, Africana Philosophy," in *African Philosophy: An Anthology*, ed. Emmanuel Chukwudi Eze (Oxford: Blackwell, 1998), 23–42.

38. Gordon has singled out Mabogo More and Rozeena Maart's work on Black Consciousness and Steve Bantu Biko as part of work that could be assembled under the "gathering notion" of Africana existential philosophy. See Lewis Gordon, "A Phenomenology of Biko's Black Consciousness," in *Biko Lives! Contesting the Legacies of Steve Biko*, ed. Andile Mngxitama, Amanda Alexander, and Nigel C. Gibson (New York: Palgrave, 2008), 83.

39. Gordon, *Existentia Africana*, 8–9.

40. Percy Mabogo More, "Biko: Africana Existential Philosopher," in *Biko Lives! Contesting the Legacies of Steve Biko*, ed. Andile Mngxitama, Amanda Alexander, and Nigel C. Gibson (New York: Palgrave, 2008), 46.

41. More, "Biko: Africana Existential Philosopher,"47.

42. See, for example, the essay on Mattera by Tahir Fuzile Sitoto, "'Complex Subjectivities': Don Omaruddin Mattera's Conversion to Islam. Beyond a Political Reading and a Biographical Essay," *Journal for Islamic Studies* 34 (2014): 153–76.

43. For example, out of its twenty-one chapters Gordon's first anthology on black existential philosophy does not have a single chapter that addressed either Islam or black Muslim identity, notwithstanding the Nation of Islam as part of the black religious and cultural experience. See Lewis Gordon, *Existence in Black: An Anthology of Black Existential Philosophy* (New York: Routledge, 1997). In this regard, the work of Anthony Pinn stands out for its inclusive take on what is black religion and African American religion and cultural experience. See Anthony Pinn, *Terror and Triumph: The Nature of Black Religion* (Minneapolis, MN: Fortress Press, 2003).

FIFTEEN

Urban Immigrant Pentecostal Missiology

The Case of an Immigrant Zambian Pentecostal Pastor in South Africa[1]

Chammah J. Kaunda

INTRODUCTION

Migration to urban centers marks the contemporary post-Apartheid South African landscape. Scholars have documented the momentous reformation that has been taking place in cities—political, financial, religious, spatial, industrial, racial, and internal and external migrations have all contributed to reconfiguring and restructuring the way life is experienced in South African cities.[2] This alteration has come with enormous challenges for the young democracy. Whereas the cities are understood as engines of economic well-being, most post-Apartheid South African cities are spaces that are deeply entrenched with socio-cultural and economic contradictions. The majority of black South Africans live in squatter camps located in proximity to some of the richest neighborhoods in South Africa. Yet they experience radical exclusion from all the affluences associated within the cities.[3] Scholars have argued that "South Africa is a violent country."[4] Accordingly, South African cities are spaces fraught with death, crime, xenophobia, poverty, identity crisis, cultural pluralism and fragmentations, strangeness, and so on. This situation can be described as a titanic collision "of bodies in need."[5]

In his *To Change the World*, James Hunter poses some meaningful questions: How do believers live out their faith under the conditions of the [city]? "How does a community that longs for shalom" relate to the city?[6] In other words, how does an immigrant pastor articulate her/his engagement in the mission of God in the hosting city in order to contribute to the needed change in today's urban context? These contextual and practical questions are more than academic debates, insofar as they require reflection on how the church can articulate its urban *missio Dei*.[7] Stanley Hauerwas maintains that while Christianity has an important message for engaging with urban life, the Christian ethic is largely alien to, and inadequate to redress, contemporary urban life.[8] He stresses that the Christian ethic is offensive and subversive to most of urban life because its language is based on what Walter Brueggemann calls "singular holiness of God."[9] For Hauerwas therefore, "The issue is how the church can provide the interpretative categories to help Christians better understand the positive and negative aspects of their societies and guide their subsequent selective participation."[10] Christians make a difference by being a colony of the kingdom of God in a world that cannot fathom God's mission.

Hauerwas's view raises a question on how the church can function as a source of social cohesion in the city. To be fair, Hauerwas believes that an adequately formulated Christian ethic has the potential to respond to challenges of urban life. His argument is that the Christian community must live faithfully within their strange culture and as aliens amidst urban life that do not appreciate their divinely given social cohesion. It appears that this is the reasoning within which Apostle Ernest Mulenga Chitabo (aka Pastor Mulenga) conceives of social cohesion in the migrant Christian communities, in particular, immigrant Zambian Pentecostal Christianity in Pietermaritzburg, South Africa.

In this study of urban immigrant Pentecostal missiology, I will utilize the phenomenological theological method. This method is a qualitative method that does not assume that there are hidden meanings in the responses of the interviewees; rather, they are based on intentions. Allan Savage argues that this approach is not "particular to the agent and is not bound to the objective and external social constructs of any given culture."[11] This does not entail that the Christian perspectives of immigrants are free from value judgments or the influences of their culture of origin and specific religious imaginations.[12] In fact, the very interpretations Pastor Mulenga ascribes to social cohesion in the context of xenophobia could be informed by consciously or unconsciously internalizing the immigrant communities' socially constructed meanings. The strength of this method is that it seeks to liberate human interpretations from historical and social constructions that replicate uncritically held interpretations of the declaration.[13] In utilizing this method, the study investigates how Pastor Mulenga, as an immigrant Zambian pastor in urban ministry, articulates his urban immigrant Pentecostal missiology utilizing the notion of the culture of the kingdom of God as a basis for social cohesion among his transnational, multiethnic, multiracial church members. The central objective is to demonstrate how immigrant pastors contribute to developing an urban immigrant Pentecostal missiology that promotes social cohesion in their hosting countries. The second objective is to suggest some contours for constructing urban immigrant missiology.

ABOUT THE STUDY

The Bethel City Church International (Restoration Cathedral) was established in 2008 by Pastor Mulenga, an ordained minister in the Apostolic Church in Zambia (ACZ). The ACZ was established in Zambia by Danish missionaries from the Apostolic Church in Denmark in 1957. The ACZ must be distinguished from the Apostolic Faith Mission (AFM) in Zambia which spread to Zambia from South Africa through Afrikaner expatriate mining workers on the Copperbelt.[14] While Bethel City Church is affiliated with the ACZ, the church functions from an independent neo-Pentecostal model. It is also financially and structurally autonomous. Pastor Mulenga is the sole founder and senior pastor of the church. Mulenga defines his church as Pentecostal-Charismatic. It has about two hundred full members from various nationalities in approximately the following proportions: seventy-seven South Africans (thirty-two Zulus, fifteen Xhosas, seventeen Coloreds, nine Indians, and four Sotho), forty-three Malawians, thirty-seven Zimbabweans, ten Congolese, six Kenyans, ten Rwandese, five Tanzanians, four Zambians, three Lesotho, and two white North Americans. As these figures show, the church has more foreigners (about 126), but the number of locals as a whole is more than foreign nationals, at least in their segments. The church appears to be committed to diversity.

The collection of data presented in this study began some time ago, through informal conversations with Mulenga. Accordingly, I became fascinated by the ethnic diversity of the church. This does not mean that other churches in Pietermaritzburg are not as ethnically diverse. However, most Zambian pastors who have churches in Pietermaritzburg have attracted mostly Zambians and foreign nationals from other parts of Africa. I wanted to dig deeper and understand his theological approach to issues of diversity, identity construction, and peaceful coexistence especially in the context of xenophobia. Finally, I decided to engage him in an interview which consisted of an unstructured, face-to-face, in-depth interview schedule, comprising open-ended questions. The interview language traversed between English and Bemba. Bemba is the mother tongue of Mulenga. This conversational approach—traversing between English and Bemba—is normative within the Zambian urban context. The interview was conducted at the Bethel City Church International building in the town center of Pietermaritzburg. It was recorded on a digital voice recorder with the consent of Mulenga. The length of the interview was about sixty minutes. The participant observation was done in advance through church-service attendances, informal discussions with Mulenga and some of the church members.

AN URBAN MIGRANT MISSIOLOGICAL TURN: "SEEK THE PEACE OF THE CITY"

Urbanization is a "process of sociocultural shifting"[15] embedded in "distinctive forms of human relationships, interconnection, and complex patterns of cultural, economic, and political life that transcend the close-knit patterns of smaller communities."[16] Nathan Bills in his editorial preface, "Urbanised Mission," notes, "Urbanisation generates not one but multiple urbanisms—kaleidoscopic ways of living fostered by the urban matrix."[17] He therefore advises, "Christians located in the cities must learn to think and live in critical dialogue with this variegated, urban world."[18]

The principles of the *missio Dei* that orient the life of the church are embodied and enacted through the liturgy and life of the church in its critical dialogue with a multicolored world. In missiological perspective, the church could be understood as a divine reenactment of the redemptive work of Christ in the world. The church seeks to bring transformation to human life, nations, and cities by exhorting believers to faithfully reenact the values of the kingdom of God discerned through Scripture, church traditions, experience, and human cultural traditions.[19] In his essay "Being Urban Matters," Andrew Davey directs that urban migrant missiological practice lies "in wise counsel of Jeremiah to "seek the peace of the city, an embrace, an acceptance of the city, with all its diversity and contradiction, as the context of a new performance based on redemption and grace seeking God's order glimpsed of earth as it is in heaven."[20] This missiological approach is noticeably explained by Brueggemann in his *Living toward a Vision*. There he argues that in a migrant context, the "hated" social ethics of Babylon metropolis[21] should be regarded as "the location, context and foundation of a new urban ethic."[22]Some Pentecostals clergy such as Bishop Bernard Nwaka have called upon other Pentecostal leadership to begin *invading the Babylonian system* as a strategy to bring about sociopolitical transformation. They have argued that "you cannot change the system by being outside the system. You change the system by being inside the system."[23] The Prophet Daniel in the Hebrew Bible is constantly perceived as a typical example of immigrant religio-political mission in Babylon. In his *The Mission of God's People*, Christopher J. H. Wright demonstrates how Daniel embraced key aspects of Babylonian culture and at the same time rejected certain aspects that intended to alienate him from Jewish identity (Daniel 1). He accepted a Babylonian name, education, language, and employment but refused to worship Babylonian idols.[24] The Babylonians used religion to promote xenophobia against immigrants such as Daniel, who refused to worship the golden idol and was accused of destroying their religio-cultural heritage. The golden idol was used as a tool to instill fear of immigrants among the Babylon people. In response, Daniel also used religion to witness to the peace and justice of God within the Babylonian context.

As with the migrant Daniel or immigrant Savior, Jesus Christ who migrates from the celestial City of God into earthly spaces, embracing an urban migrant *missio Dei,* is parallel to that of an immigrant pastor entering into a significant dialectic of a city that can be voracious and ferocious but also an arena of incarnation and redemption.[25] In giving the directive to "seek the peace of the city," God is not necessarily calling migrant Christians to be in alliance with political forces, or those who negatively shape the city. Instead, God is calling them into partnership with any movement or organization directed at promoting the peace of the city. James Connolly and Justin Steil, in their "Introduction: Finding Justice in the City," can observe:

> Awareness of exploitation, and attempts to challenge it, bring us closer to realising the too often unfulfilled promise that cities have long represented the promise of liberation and opportunity. But to search for a Just City is to seek something more than individualised responses to specific injustices. It requires the creation of coherent frames for action and deliberation that bring the multiple and disparate efforts of those fighting against unjust urban conditions into relief and relate their struggles to each other as part of a global orchestration improvised around the single tenor of justice.[26]

Embracing those already struggling for peace is an act of prophetic subversion of the imperial metropolis. The migrant pastor should never be indifferent to the city's quest for peace for its only within a just and peaceful city that the urban migrant church thrives. This remains a divine vision for all migrant Christians who are exposed to the harsh realities of living in foreign cities. Urban migrant missiology affirms "that God's *Shalom* is known only by those in inclusive, caring community."[27] The city will always be a space for a large intersection of both locals and migrants and can only thrive if there is mutual commitment to their mutual wholeness and well-being. Consequently, the need to recognize that wherever there is a wellspring of life, they should always team up with lots of migrants and the poor. The urban migrant missiology has to do with finding new ethics to redefine mutual coexistence. It is about acts of resistance, the active pursuit of *shalom in ecclesia,* as well as strategies to develop a community of faith that seeks to recover the divine vision of urban life based on the ethic of fullness of life for every city dweller.[28] Immigrant spirituality only thrives if there is commitment to peaceful coexistence—commitment to the city and its well-being, where welfare is recognized as the common good for all. It is within this missiological framework that I explore Mulenga's emerging immigrant missiological thinking in the context of migration in South Africa.

MULENGA'S URBAN IMMIGRANT PENTECOSTAL MISSIOLOGY

Mulenga's urban migrant missiology is embedded in the biblical notion of the kingdom of God. He perceives the Christian community as alien in the world. Christians are in the world to demonstrate alternative values and principles that can transform human social organization. This perspective is similar to the interpretation of Hauerwas of "the church as an alternative political community."[29] To fully appreciate Mulenga's missiological thinking, it is important to understand how he connects the kingdom of God to social cohesion.

Healing and Deliverance

Mulenga explained that he came to South Africa because he discovered that post-Apartheid South Africans needed "healing and deliverance" in order to build themselves up as a nation. He remembers that after praying, the ACZ discovered that the kind of deliverance that was being performed in South Africa by most Pentecostal churches was inadequate for the context, which "has gone through a lot of pain looking at the many years of segregation." He highlights that God sent him to South Africa because "a number of people, emotionally have been hurting, a number of people, spiritually have been hurting." He stressed, "I remember President Zuma confirming, 'we are a hurting nation.'" He notes, "When you look at the people demonstrating, most of the demonstrations turn into violence and property destruction. Now, how do you look at that situation?" Mulenga believes that "it is because of some emotional damages." This means that "when your life is not together, you find a way to vent your frustration—burn that building, shoot someone; you do all sorts of things because you're not okay." Mulenga believes, "No one can fix that problem but the Word of God." He argues that "when we say we want to see a nation that is healed, it is from the platform of the Word of God—the solution is the Word of God." Mulenga is aware of the fact that the Apartheid regime used Scripture as a tool for promoting segregation and racial hatred. He argues, "When a snake has beaten you, you must use the exact snake's venom as anti-venom to heal that poison." Mulenga is citing Mensa Otabil, a Ghanaian Pentecostal theologian and founder of International Central Gospel Church, headquartered in Accra. Otabil argues that the Bible is "anti-oppression serum"[30] to bring healing, emancipation, and restoration to African people. These Pentecostals are in agreement that the Bible was misused as a tool of oppression against African people. However, they contend that it was not the fault of the people but the carnality of the oppressors. The Bible is a spiritual book and unspiritual or carnal mind cannot comprehend or understand the things of the Spirit. This is based on Paul's scriptural injunction in 1 Corinthian 2:14—"The person without the Spirit does not accept the things that come from the Spirit of God but considers them foolishness, and cannot understand them because they are discerned only through the Spirit." Mulenga stresses that only the interpretation empowered by the Holy Spirit has power to bring authentic healing and restoration to the damaged African humanity. He insists the problem is not the Bible, but the carnality of the interpreters. The interpreter empowered by the Holy Spirit is motivated by love. The Holy Spirit is the power of love and "when you are motivated by love—genuine love is not destructive, it is not self-seeking." The person who preaches hatred is not motivated by the Spirit of love, but is possessed by a destructive spirit. The Word of God when preached in love empowers believers in such a way that instead of viewing their differences with fear and hatred, they come to view them with love and compassion.

It is from this perspective that Mulenga also understands deliverance. He stresses that "deliverance is more than just demons screaming and going out of somebody. Deliverance is the mind—your mind—because once your mind is not transformed, is not changed, you're not delivered. Then you will preach hatred as good news." Accordingly, Mulenga focuses on the "transformation of the mind. What makes a person live differently is when you change what is in the mind." He argues that "the devil and demons were assigned a place called darkness." He links darkness to ignorance. According to his view, the demonic forces thrive in ignorance. For him, "The solution to darkness is light" which he equates with "knowledge." This "knowledge is from the Word of God which is a manual" for human functioning in the world. Deliverance begins by letting the light shine into the mind. Once that takes place, the person is set free. In other words, "Deliverance is getting darkness out and let the light enter." Yet Mulenga does not think deliverance is a one-off event. Instead, he believes that deliverance is a lifetime process. For as long as darkness exists in the world and human hearts, deliverance has to continue to take place in order for believers to overcome their inner darkness so as to live as a "*shalom* community" in a context "permeated by forces of darkness that manifests in hatred, superiority complex, inferiority complex, oppressions, racism, violence."

In terms of xenophobic attacks that took place across South Africa, Mulenga was of the opinion that there were demonic forces at play: "as a preacher as I don't look at xenophobia only as natural thing. It has also demonic aspects." He thus questions, "Tell me, how can you justify a situation where a person is burnt alive? You put a tire on the person and then you put petrol to burn them?" Mulenga thinks this "is not normal . . . There is a force that is making a person behave that way." In classifying xenophobia as a demonic rather than a social issue, the best response for Mulenga is nonviolent resistance. This he views not only as a coping mechanism but as a tool for advancing the deliverance discourse. Since it is a demonic issue, it is not really the fault of the perpetrators; instead, they are seen as victims of the spiritual forces of evil. In this way, Mulenga's immigrant missiology seems to function as a means of soothing the consciences of the South African members in his church who are exonerated of any responsibility with respect to the xenophobic attacks. It also helps the foreigners in his church to embrace South Africans as victims of spiritual attack. While this strategy might not be the best solution to xenophobia, it nevertheless helps foreign nationals express love toward South Africans as a means of winning them to Christ.

According to Mulenga, this means, "When I begin to speak to people, I don't need to speak to them on the platform where there are. I speak to them on the platform where they can be—that is my paradigm." Deliverance has therefore to do with "bringing the light of the Word of God to shine in the darkness of their minds to set them free from bitterness and anger which was put there through years of segregation in the darkness of Apartheid." He further explains, "We deliberately name our church 'Restoration Cathedral' because people are broken, lives are shattered. We want to bring back what has been lost in society—we are a paradise of restoration."

Culture of the Kingdom and Mind Kingdomization

Mulenga sees the church as an extension of the kingdom of God and a symbol of God's enduring "yes" response to the world.[31] This is described by David Bosch as the *missio Dei*. It is a framework through which God is actively seeking to restore humanity to its humanness, justice, and the alleviation of oppression and human need in the world. But Mulenga's perspective also resonates with the perspective of Stanley Hauerwas and William Willimon in their (1989) book *Resident Aliens: Life in the Christian Colony*, in which they argue that "the church is a colony, an island of one culture in the middle of another."[32] Holding a similar perspective, Mulenga argues that while "believers are a society which belongs to the kingdom," they are "not here to promote a nationalistic mind-set." He clarifies, "We love our nations. We're responsible citizens of our nations but we are promoting another kingdom—the kingdom of God is what makes us effective citizens in this world." Mulenga further narrates:

> We don't want to basically promote any cultural values because if we do that, then we will be separated. What we want is to promote the culture of the kingdom. We want to have people's minds kingdomized. Where they are

not thinking in terms of where I am coming from and the values from my culture because if I begin to do that I think "this one is better than the other."

A statement such as that above can easily be misinterpreted as promoting what contemporary Western anthropologists have classified as an African Pentecostal's discourse of a "complete break with the past."[33] In terms of Ghanaian diasporic Pentecostalism as practiced in Gaborone, Botswana, Rijk van Dijk argues that it tries "to decentre a Ghanaian-versus-local type of discourse within their congregations by stressing their multinational composition and transnational way of operation."[34]In contradistinction, while Mulenga's respect for local and foreign national cultural traditions is deemed necessary, it does not replace the culture of the kingdom. In this way, unlike the Ghanaian diasporic model, which appears to abandon its African cultural heritage,[35] Mulenga's church cannot be perceived as abandoning any African cultural heritage. Instead, in terms of Restoration Cathedral within the Zambian diaspora in South Africa, it is reinterpreted through the notion of the culture of the kingdom of God.

Mulenga's culture of the kingdom of God functions as an alternative culture that promotes values that are distinguishable from African traditional culture. His kingdom culture integrates in significant ways certain values of African cultural tradition without giving in to assimilation as it promotes reconceptualized sets of beliefs, interests, and means of interaction for the community (both migrants and nationals alike) that sees itself as living in an earthly diaspora or sojourn. In one of the Sunday services I attended, Pastor Mulenga led the congregants in the prayer of declaration in which the entire congregation was asked to repeat after him. Part of the declaration was, "We belong to God! We have the culture of the kingdom! I'm not only South African, I am not just Zambian, I'm not just Zimbabwean, I'm not only Congolese . . . I belong to God! The phrase "I'm not only" suggests a kind of balance that Mulenga seeks to strike between national identity and kingdom identity, ideas that are not perceived as being in conflict with each other. For example, Mulenga began his sermon by explaining that he was requested to represent one of his Zimbabwean congregants to act as a go-between for *lobola*[36] negotiations. He narrated how he was fascinated by how this particular Zimbabwean culture possessed values that could help his congregants to live effectively for the kingdom of God in the world. Mulenga's interpretation of the church as a kingdom's colony does not immunize the church from cultural values in the world; rather, the church actively integrates some cultural values without losing its distinctiveness. This is at variance with Hauerwas and Willimon, in their description of the church as a "beachhead, an outpost, an island of one culture in the middle of another, a place where the values of [the kingdom] are reiterated and passed on to the [the faith community], a place where the distinctive language and life-style of the resident aliens are lovingly nurtured and reinforced."[37] Their argument portrays the church in colonial terms as a reality that cannot incarnate and engage with human experiences. Mulenga's argument brings the balance in the way the reality of the church should be understood in the world. He thus argues:

> We want everyone who comes here to have a kingdom mind that is transformed by the Word of God. The culture of the kingdom is one in which we have Jesus as Lord. Where we begin to think that we are not from here. Though we are in South Africa, we are from above. But we have to live effectively in South Africa. Learn the culture and the language.

Mulenga believes that the culture of the kingdom is superior to any human culture. Hence, priority must be given to modeling the Christian lifestyle. He gives an example of the Samaritan woman at the well in John, chapter 4. He sees this woman as a metaphor for collective human approach to life before Kingdomization. He reminds his listeners:

> You remember the woman at the well. She said to Jesus, when he said, "I need a drink." She said, "You're a Jew, I am a Samaritan. Jews and Samaritans do not mix." She was thinking from that level of a person who is not kingdomized but Jesus was from above." So, he speaks to her, he says, "If you knew who you are talking to, you would ask him for the drink." He changes the question. "Because the drink I will give you, you will not be coming here again for it." Then she says, "If you have that kind of the drink, give it to me so that I don't need to come here."

For Mulenga, as with everyone who does not possess a kingdom mindset, this woman's thinking was constrained by the natural limits of human consciousness and Samaritan culture. However, "Jesus was thinking from above"—outside the box of natural human consciousness and culture. Jesus helped the woman at the well realize that kingdom values have no geopolitical restrictions, "nor devotion to any particular ethnic group or nationality."[38] Such kingdom thinking transcends them all by simultaneously assimilating its life-giving values. According to Mulenga, Jesus's "interpretation of reality was kingdom-value-shaped." Mulenga consistently argues:

> We are in the world to be effective as human beings. But we are representing the kingdom from above. We honor the governments, we honor the leaders from the platform of the Word of God which tell us to honor our leaders. But we have a culture of the kingdom which tells us this is how we live, this is how we talk, this is how we honor secular leaders, this is how we do things. We are not doing them according to the world's way of doing things. We are doing them according to the kingdom way of doing it.

Unlike Gregory Boyd who understands that the kingdom of God is "completely different from the world's way,"[39] Mulenga believes that there are values that are already enshrined in human cultures that resonate with the values of the kingdom of God. Accordingly, he tries to demonstrate that Christian believers must find the intricate balance between being "in the world" and not "of the world." As Mulenga explains:

> If I say, "I am a Zambian," . . . it will make other people to feel awkward. I know I am a Zambian and I know I need to respect my uniqueness and cultural identity but I don't want to make it take the center stage of my relationship with other brothers. Because then we are going to be segregated, we will have these xenophobic things [*sic*] because you see me as a Zambian and not a person loved by God. So, from the platform of the kingdom culture, we are able to get this one who is Indian to think that "I am not just Indian, I am a child of God." The other one from Zimbabwe, from Sotho, Zulu background, they begin to think, "I am not just a Zulu person, I am a kingdom person," because of the Word of God.

Mulenga thinks with the clarity of his conviction firmly rooted in an inclusive kingdom thought. He does not perceive the kingdom mind-set or culture as something exclusively for Christians. He believes that the values of the kingdom of God are inherent in every human being from all walks of life, color, creed, race, ideology, and religion. He quotes Matthew 5:45 to demonstrate that God's grace is deeply rooted in all creation. "He makes the sun to shine on everyone, good and evil, and sends rain to them all." He compares that just as light is everywhere, so these values are embedded in every human being. For Mulenga, "You don't need to be a Christian to have the kingdom mind-set." He gives an example of the Good Samaritan, who, he argues, "didn't need to be a Jew in order to offer help to the victim of robbery. He had a kingdom mind-set that finds meaning in the humanity of others." Here we see that Mulenga's understanding of the kingdom of culture has been influenced by the Bemba notion of *Ubwananyina* (lit., "of the same mother") explained below.

As with Desmond Mpilo Tutu, Mulenga holds that "God is not a Christian. His kingdom values cannot be restricted to any religion." [40] This means that the values of the kingdom manifest in other contexts apart from Christianity. Mulenga observes that "the Good Samaritan did not question the character, culture, or religion of the victim. Are you a Jew? Are you religious? Are you homosexual? Or anything else?" He believes that "it was not religion but "self-sacrificial, unconditional love and kingdom-like love that defined the character of the Good Samaritan as 'Good' because there were bad Samaritans as well." Mulenga recollects, "The Samaritans were seen as lesser humans by the Jews, but he refused to give in to anger and bitterness and vent it on others because he functioned with a kingdom mind-set." This is similar to David Leong's view that the Good Samaritan embodied what could be considered "a Christlike ethic of love and service to neighbor." According to Leong, the Good Samaritan's actions "should call into question the ways in which racialisation and class consciousness have accentuated the segregation of neighbours in the urban context."[41]

Mulenga continues by saying that the Good Samaritan took the strange, helpless victim and integrated him back into the context of life (in the inn) at his own expense. He also promised to do more upon his return. For Mulenga, the just actions of the Good Samaritan demonstrate that promoting kingdom culture has nothing do with converting people to Christianity or any religion for that matter. Instead, he stresses, "You don't accept the homosexuals in the church in order to convert them. You accept them because they are human. The rest is up to God and themselves." This is the Good Samaritan paradigm. The metaphor of the Good Samaritan is a collective representation of the church and anyone with a kingdom mind-set. The church as an agent of God's mission in the world is meant to be "the Good Samaritan" in the world. Those outside must see the manifestation of the kingdom values. Mulenga thus emphasizes:

> What makes a difference is how we are living, not in the church building, but how we are living outside in the world. Our mission work is not in the church but in the world—in our work places, in our businesses, whatever we are doing to promote the well-being of the nation. How are we living? Can we be trusted as Christians? Can your word be your bond? What will make me to live to honor my obligations in the city as a child of God is because I esteem the kingdom values. The church is there to instill these values. People move from here [church], the way they live after is what is important. When you come here is like you come to receive some injection—given some motivation to out and live kingdom values. They come for some empowerment to go and win outside. The battle is between Monday to Friday to Saturday that is where they have to prove that they are kingdomized.

Hauerwas and Willimon make a similar argument that suggests that "the message that sustains the colony is not for itself but for the whole world—the colony having significance only as God's means for saving the whole world."[42]

AN URBAN IMMIGRANT PENTECOSTAL MISSIOLOGICAL MODEL

The forging highlights the missiological challenge to study urban immigrant African pastors without presupposing ethnic cultural reenactment or a quest to break with an African cultural past. But to understand how they creatively and innovatively critique and search for balance between African cultural traditions and a culture of life using Christian metaphors such as the culture of the kingdom of God as the case of Mulenga. Urban immigrant pastors in South Africa find themselves in complex political, social, economic, transcultural, multi/trans-identities and multilayer spiritualities that demand they use language that promotes collectiveness. Accordingly, Mulenga's notion of kingdom culture can be read as a form of cultural critique proclaiming to the general public that immigrant pastors have the potential to promote a new culture of compassion, self-sacrificial, Christ-like love and unconditional acceptance. This in turn can help develop a collective worldview for both locals and foreign nationals alike in their socio-relational interactions. Mulenga's kingdom culture as a Christian collective identity thus possesses the potential to prevent xenophobic attacks, more so than some South African government policies.[43] Immigrant pastors such as Mulenga are seeking to diffuse such inhospitable host cultures by articulating an alternative culture independent of both the local xenophobic culture and the immigrants' culture which is often perceived with suspicion by the local hosts. The new culture is informed by values that both the immigrant and local nationals desire. So what contours can we glean from all of this for constructing an urban immigrant *missio Dei*?

First, urban immigrant missiology seeks to deconstruct and reconstruct or reconceptualize African cultural values through the notion of the kingdom of God in order to promote the common good. The alternative culture forged does not major on minor issues, but seeks instead to be radically inclusive by centering on social challenges or existential needs as a basis for good neighborliness. As a consequence, the focus of urban immigrant missiology is on empowering the community of faith through the Good Samaritan missiological framework, where the neighbor becomes the essence of being human.

In the Bemba worldview, the Good Samaritan is encapsulated in the notion of *Ubwananyina* (lit., "of the same mother"). This notion goes beyond that of *ubuntu*, which states: "I am because we are." Instead, *Ubwananyina* refers to the radical equal standing of all human beings before one another because they share the same substance or essence, being children of the same mother. In other words, the mother can never mistake her children for someone else's.[44] This accords with the Bemba tradition, which is matrilineal, where everyone descends from the same female ancestor, *Lesa* (God)—where maternal aspects of God are far more pronounced in traditional Bemba society than paternal. The Bemba tradition therefore references the intrinsic cosmic, social, and moral oneness of all human beings. This means that those who belong to the same mother take care of one another. The recognition that *tulibananyina* (lit., "we are of the same mother") is based on an affirming just-love without conditions and a radical, unconditional acceptance and constructive engagement with one another.

Ubwananyina is encapsulated in Bemba thinking with the notion of *munda ni mucabu* (lit., "the womb is a ferry"). The womb is thus likened to *Lesa* (God),[45] which means that *Lesa* is a ferry within which every individual is nurtured and brought out to the safe haven of earthly life in the way *Lesa* destined them to be. Individuals have no right to dictate the way any person is to be born (e.g., sick, color, looks, disabilities, height, etc.)—that is the decision of *Lesa* (God). Accordingly, difference can never be the basis for rejecting, denouncing, discriminating, or denying anyone else their rights to the fullness of life—with all of its contradictions. For we are all of the same mother (*bonse tulibananyina*). In short, radical neighborliness within *Ubwananyina* thinking is based not so much on a neighbor as another human being in need (as in Lukan narrative). In these terms, the just-love of the other is expressed because humans are different pieces of the same puzzle. In other words, human beings need each other to complete the complex divine puzzle of life. *Ubwananyina* respects difference, because therein concealed is the strength of the oneness of the puzzle. The adage is therefore true: "Respect every human being; you never know which one fits into your shape as a piece of the divine puzzle."

Second, it is decolonial *missio Dei*,[46] as it focuses on mind decolonization using a language that is religiously accepted in specific church traditions such as Mulenga's notions of deliverance and mind kingdomization. An urban immigrant missiology is representative of decolonial missiology because it is concerned with overcoming Apartheid and colonial mentalities deeply rooted in the mind-sets of most African Christians, which Mulenga defines as darkness, (i.e., demonic). This is "a process of identification, articulation and representation—a critical positioning which provides a sense of place, a context from which to develop . . . insights, ideas and responses, a strategic site that allows sufficient rounding for specific forms of thought, speech and representation to emerge and gain meaning"[47] that can engender new African experiences. Decolonial missiology is about deliverance from life-denying thought forms and the systems of living informed by inferiority complexes, superiority complexes, racism, ethnicity, xenophobia, ethnocentrism, and the like. From such modes of darkness and demonic engagement, the faith community must resist, both in their individual lives and collectively within society.

Third, it focuses on the promotion of a culture of self-reliance among the members. In turn, this encourages hard work such as entrepreneurial spirituality or education, reinterpreted as forms of prophetic resistance to the ineffective service delivery by the government. In this regard, Mulenga organizes a special yearly service to recognize and honor those church members who have graduated from school or university, been promoted at work, found jobs, or started new businesses. The value of this is that both national and immigrant believers are called by God to "constructive engagement in the world—because it is God's world, created, loved, valued and redeemed by him."[48] This is important because their constructive engagement in South Africa justifies their earnings through hard work and care of the less fortunate. Immigrants should never be apologetic in their engagement with the world, for "the earth is the Lord's and fullness thereof" (Psalms 24:1). Immigrant believers must always be aware that God has a purpose for them in South Africa. Through constructive engagement with South Africa and its people, "They become salt and light" and "are both missional (they are used for a purpose) and *confrontational* (they challenge decay and darkness, corruption)"[49] by exposing the treasures of the land hidden from the eyes of the masses. This can bring about social transformation. For example, in response to the outbreak of xenophobic attacks in 2015, the minister of Small Business Development, Lindiwe Zulu, argued that "it's important for the foreigners to share with the South Africans about what it is that makes it possible for them to be successful."[50] This shows that immigrants have business strategies that can promote mutual development between the immigrants who have needed skills and the nationals in need of skills. As Mulenga himself argues, "Daniel worked hard and was beneficial and not a liability to Babylon." In the biblical account, Daniel did his work so well that his political enemies could not find any fault in his work: "At this, the administrators and the satraps tried to find grounds for charges against Daniel in his conduct of government affairs, but they were unable to do so. They could find no corruption in him, because he was trustworthy and neither corrupt nor negligent" (Daniel 6:4, New International Version). As Wright suggests, "One can imagine that life for ordinary Babylonians was better when Daniel was in charge of civic affairs."[51] As demonstrated above, Mulenga understands that he came to South Africa to make it a better place after the demise of Apartheid. Hence, for him, self-reliance is critical for immigrant *missio Dei* for it proves that foreigners are here to make the country better.

Fourth, the goal of urban immigrant missiology is not to struggle to take over political power, but to become the manifestation of God's love for the city. The immigrant pastors' function is that of being a prophetic enabler to help the community of faith discern the demonic forces at work in the city and seek strategic ways to exorcise them from the minds of the people—this is prophetic opposition to evil in the city. The implications are that the church is not there to seek to replace the secular government with the kingdom of God, but to live out faithfully the values of the kingdom as a prophetic witness. This requires practicing nonviolent resistance for this reaffirms Jesus's alternative community which reenacts the kingdom of God's principles of justice, peace, and righteousness. As Amos Yong can argue, immigrant missiology "does not rely on Christians having or exercising political authority but on their capacity to promote the healing reconciliation essential to a peaceful, just, and beautiful world order."[52] The question that arises from this is important: How does an urban immigrant missiology function in the face of political violence, oppression, dehumanization, etc? Furthermore, in the 2016 municipal elections, South Africa witnessed a change in voting patterns and allegiances, especially in the metropolitan areas. The question that arises from this is of equal importance to the first: In what way can an urban immigrant missiology be relevant in this context if South Africans are also members of these churches?

Fifth, an urban immigrant missiology is informed and operated in partnership with social movements within the context of the struggle for *Shalom* in society, such as in the context of worker's rights, women's rights, gender justice, children's rights, human rights and dignity, homosexual rights, animal rights, and climate justice. These also function as sources of theological insight for urban immigrant pastors.

CONCLUSION

This chapter examined the missiological perspective of an immigrant pastor from Zambia living and ministering in Pietermaritzburg, KwaZulu-Natal, to demonstrate that South Africa is a creative space for new missiological imagination, embedded as it is in notions of social cohesion and mutual coexistence.

Part of the intention of this chapter was to demonstrate that focusing exclusively on the xenophobic attacks sometimes causes scholars to undervalue the stories of hope, mutual love, new creativities, and innovative identities that are being fashioned among various foreign nationals living in South Africa. In other words, South Africa is not one monolithic story. This does not dispute the fact that we need to see the bigger picture of the struggles and stresses that shape immigrant life in South Africa, such as the narrative of the xenophobic attacks of 2008 and 2015. Nevertheless, we must not forget the stories of hope, compassion, love, and joy that are mutually shared between local nationals and immigrants. These two stories must be bridged for the world to know that not all hope is lost.

NOTES

1. Throughout this chapter, all the quotations from Pastor Mulenga are taken from Ernest Mulenga Chitabo, interview with the author, Bethel City Church International Pietermaritzburg, April 2, 2016.

2. Pieter Kok, Michael O'Donovan, Oumar Bouare, and Johan van Zyl, *Post-Apartheid Patterns of Internal Migration in South Africa* (Cape Town: HSRC Press, 2003); Pieter Kok, Marie Wentzel, Johan van Zyl, and Catherine Cross, "Contemporary South African Urbanisation Dynamics," *Urban Forum* 21/3 (2010): 331–48.

3. Duncan Ranslem, "'Temporary' Relocation: Spaces of Contradiction in South African Law," *International Journal of Law in the Built Environment* 7/1 (2015): 55–71.

4. Henri Boshoff, Anneli Botha, and Martin Schönteich, *Fear in the City: Urban Terrorism in South Africa*, no. 63 (Pretoria: Institute for Security Studies, 2001), 4.

5. Abdou Maliq Simone, *For the City Yet to Come: Changing African Life in Four Cities* (Durham, NC: Duke University Press, 2004), 3.

6. James D. Hunter, *To Change the World: The Irony, Tragedy, and Possibility of Christianity in the Late Modern World* (New York: Oxford University Press, 2010), ix, 230.

7. Andrew Davey, "Being Urban Matters: What Is Urban about Urban Mission?" in *Crossover City: Resources for Urban Mission and Transformation*, ed. Andrew Davey (London: Continuum, 2010), 24–36.

8. Stanley Hauerwas, "Why the 'Sectarian Temptation' Is a Misrepresentation: A Response to James Gustafson," in *The Hauerwas Reader*, ed. John Berkman and Michael Cartwright (Durham, NC: Duke University Press, 2001), 90–110. In this chapter, Hauerwas responds and rejects James Gustafson's argument that Christian language must translate its language into a familiar one that can be understood in contemporary society. See James Gustafson, "The Sectarian Temptation: Reflections on Theology, the Church, and the University," *Proceedings of the Catholic Theological Society* 40 (1985): 83–94.

9. Walter Brueggemann argues that once the church has lost this language its "religious power has become self-serving ideology." See Walter Brueggemann, *Interpretation and Obedience: From Faithful Reading to Faithful Livin,* (Minneapolis, MN: Fortress Press, 1991).

10. Hauerwas, "Why the 'Sectarian Temptation,'" 102.

11. Allan M. Savage, *Ecology: A "New to You" View: An Orthodox Theological Ecology* (CreateSpace Independent Publishing Platform, 2008), 78.

12. Henry A. Giroux, *Border Crossings: Cultural Workers and the Politics of Education* (New York: Routledge, 1992); Klaus Nürnberger, *Faith in Christ Today: Invitation to Systematic Theology*, vol. 2, *Involved in God's Project*, (Pietermaritzburg, South Africa: Cluster Publications, 2016).

13. Allan M. Savage, *Phenomenological Understanding of Certain Liturgical Texts* (Lanham, MD: University Press of America, 2001); Allan M. Savage, "Phenomenological Philosophy and Orthodox Christian Scientific Ecological Theology," *Indo-Pacific Journal of Phenomenology* 8/2 (2008): 1–9.

14. Naar M'fundisi, "Pentecostal and Charismatic Spiritualities and Civic Engagement in Zambia (1964–2012)" (unpublished PhD diss., University of Birmingham, 2014).

15. Harvie M. Conn and Manuel Ortiz, *Urban Ministry: The Kingdom, the City, and the People of God* (Downers Grove, IL: InterVarsity Press, 2001), 167.
16. Bryan P. Stone and Claire E. Wolfteich, *Sabbath in the City: Sustaining Urban Pastoral Excellence* (Louisville, KY: Westminster John Knox, 2008), 2.
17. Nathan Bills, "Urbanised Mission," preface to *Missio Dei: A Journal of Missional Theology & Praxis* 3/2 (August 2012), <http: / / missiodeijournal.com / article.php?issue=md-3-2&author=md-3-2-preface / > [Accessed: May 4, 2016].
18. Bills, "Urbanised Mission."
19. Davey, "Being Urban Matters," 24–36.
20. Davey, "Being Urban Matters," 35.
21. Walter Brueggemann, *Living toward a Vision: Biblical Reflections on Shalom* (Philadelphia, PA: United Church Press, 1982), 23.
22. Davey, "Being Urban Matters," 35.
23. Bernard Nwaka, *Invading the Babylonian System* (Lusaka, Zambia: Campus Voice Publishers, 2007), 115.
24. Christopher J. H. Wright, *The Mission of God's People: A Biblical Theology of the Church's Mission* (Grand Rapids, MI: Zondervan, 2010).
25. Davey, "Being Urban Matters," 25.
26. James Connolly and Justin Steil, "Finding Justice in the City," introduction to *Searching for the Just City Debates in Urban Theory and Practice,* ed. Peter Marcuse, James Connolly, Johannes Novy, Ingrid Olivo, Cuz Potter, and Justin Steil (London: Routledge, 2009), 1.
27. Brueggemann, *Living toward a Vision,* 23.
28. Davey, "Being Urban Matters," 35.
29. Hauerwas, "Why the 'Sectarian Temptation,'" 102.
30. Mensa Otabil, *Beyond the Rivers of Ethiopia: A Biblical Revelation of God's Purpose for the Black Race* (Lanham, MD: Pnuema Life Publishing, 1993), 21.
31. David Bosch, *Transforming Mission: Paradigm Shifts in Theology of Mission* (Maryknoll, NY: Orbis, 1991), 10.
32. Stanley Hauerwas and William H. Willimon, *Resident Aliens: Life in the Christian Colony* (Nashville, TN: Abingdon Press, 1989), 12.
33. Birgit Meyer, "'Make a Complete Break with the Past': Memory and Postcolonial Modernity in Ghanaian Pentecostalist Discourse," *Journal of Religion in Africa* 28/3 (1998): 316–49.
34. Rijk van Dijk, "Localisation, Ghanaian Pentecostalism and the Stranger's Beauty in Botswana," *Africa: Journal of the International African Institute* 73/4 (2003): 560–83.
35. Rijk van Dijk, "The Soul is the Stranger: Ghanaian Pentecostalism and the Diasporic Contestation of 'Flow' and 'Individuality,'" *Culture and Religion* 3/1 (2002): 59.
36. *Lobola* is vaguely referred to as bride price, but most African traditional cultures understood it as a gift of appreciation and acknowledgment that the parents of the bride have well-groomed and nurtured her. It was not a price but a gesture of appreciation and acknowledge.
37. Hauerwas and Willimon, *Resident Aliens,* 12.
38. George West, "Book Review: 'The Myth of a Christian Nation,'" *Faith and Values* (2007), <http: / / www.independentmail.com / features / faith / book-review-

--the-myth-of-a-christian-nation-ep-416878774-341668631.html/> [Accessed: May 6, 2016].

39. Gregory A. Boyd, *The Myth of a Christian Nation: How the Quest for Political Power is Destroying the Church* (Grand Rapids, MI: Zondervan, 2007), 14–15.

40. Desmond Mpilo Tutu, *God Is Not a Christian and Other Provocations,* ed. John Allen (New York: Harper One, 2011). Tutu's argument that "God is clearly not a Christian is popular in many Christian circles. It is possible that Mulenga may have been influenced by Tutu's view of unChristianness of God.

41. David P. Leong, "Reading the City: Cultural Texts and Urban Community," *Missio Dei: A Journal of Missional Theology & Praxis* 3/2 (August 2012), <http://missiodeijournal.com/article.php?issue=md-3-2&author=md-3-2-leong#sthash.bR1gslq1.dpuf/> [Accessed: May 4, 2016].

42. Hauerwas and Willimon, *Resident Aliens*, 29.

43. van Dijk, "Localisation," 558.

44. In the world without DNA paternity testing, only the mother truly knew the true father/s of her children.

45. Hugo Hinfelaar, *Bemba-Speaking Women of Zambia in a Century of Religious Change (1892–1992)* (Leiden, Netherlands: Brill, 1994).

46. For detailed discussion on decolonial missiology, see Chammah J. Kaunda and Roderick R. Hewitt, "Toward Epistemic Decolonial Turn in Missio-Formation in African Christianity," *International Review of Mission* 104/2 (2015): 378–92.

47. Joan Borsa, "Frida Kahlo: Marginalisation and the Critical Female Subject," *Third Text* 4/12 (1990): 36.

48. Wright, *The Mission of God's People.*

49. Wright, *The Mission of God's People.*

50. Amogelang Mbatha, "S. African Minister Says Foreigners Must Share Trade Secrets," Bloomberg, January 28, 2015, <http://www.bloomberg.com/news/articles/2015-01-28/s-africa-minister-says-foreigners-must-share-to-avoid-looting/> [Accessed: June 22, 2016).

51. Wright, *The Mission of God's People.*

52. Amos Yong, *The Missiological Spirit: Christian Mission Theology in the Third Millennium Global Context* (Eugene, OR: Cascade Books, 2014), 230.

SIXTEEN

Why Read the West?

Messianicity and Canonicity within a Postcolonial South African Context

Justin Sands

INTRODUCTION

Currently there is an intense discussion in South Africa as to why their universities still teach from a curriculum developed primarily from the so-called "Western canon," a process and historical legacy often called westernization. Postcolonialism (or postcolonial studies) forms this discussion's philosophical foundation, asking how African thought can reconcile its colonial past and retrieve its deleted history without falling into a cycle of violence that forsakes reconciliation for recovery. As one can see with the #feesmustfall[1] student protests throughout South African universities, westernization's influence has become crucial to South Africa's future. This campaign has expanded its protest beyond student fees to also include pushing for a decolonized university, even protesting monuments depicting the supporters of a colonial or Apartheid past (cf. the #rhodesmustfall protests).[2] In October 2016, for example, University of Cape Town students held a forum about decolonizing science in which one student asked why scientific research does not take into account African beliefs and practices such as what she called "African magic." In a YouTube video of the forum, the student states that science must be "scratched out," rethought from the bottom up, or done away with altogether.[3] This forum garnered great attention with commentators mostly mocking this student and, in turn, the whole project of decolonization. For some who are suspicious of decolonization, this student represents all that is wrong with these efforts.

This video is only an example of the clash between the decolonization movement against westernization's dominance and its set of "proven" and "acceptable" epistemologies. Of course, the question of decolonization has been pervasive throughout these protests with varying emphases depending on the campus and which set of students are protesting. I raise this particular example to show how decolonization embodies a cluster of issues rather than just a singular question of curricula. I think it also reveals the tacit differences between decolonization and the concept of "Africanization," as well as the question of what is the importance of a South African university within a global context. In what follows, I will explore how a postcolonial reassessment of South Africa's intellectual and religious heritage might lead to a critical rereading of the Western canon, reshaping the canon itself. I will do so through examining the dichotomy between decolonization and Africanization, and will argue that reading Western texts from a South African perspective would provide great insights and critique for a global community that often deems Western thought and religiosity as normative. From this perspective, I anticipate that South African intellectual and religious thought might develop a degree of self-understanding and self-determination where their own voices, within their own contexts, represent their communities' specific concerns, prayers, and desires. I will do so through exploring Achille Mbembe's work regarding decolonization versus Africanization, in order to establish the context from which I see the issue, and then will suggest a possible framework for this reflection through the work of Colby Dickinson, focusing especially upon his reconsiderations of the concepts of canonicity and messianism.

AFRICANIZATION AND DECOLONIZATION: ACHILLE MBEMBE

To begin, it is important to address South Africa's global standing and the current state of higher education at large. Mbembe, amongst others, critiques the commodification of higher education where students are treated as clients at best, customers at worst, and where the general goal of receiving a diploma is obtaining a credential for a future job.[4] In short, there is no higher education, just a ladder to higher employment in a global marketplace that sees the self only as human capital to be ushered along for greater profits.[5] This facilitates a resistance to decolonizing the curricula for fear that South African students will become "further behind the times" in comparison to students around the globe, where they become less and less capable of capitalizing upon their education in the world's marketplace. Yet who is keeping time here? Why should South Africans comport their worldviews, cultures, and intellects to the global market just to be competitive? South Africans already live within the fallout of modernity and its colonialism, so it seems preposterous that their success should be dictated by markets fashioned through regimes that profited from their exploitation.[6] The problem of decolonization thus begins with the question of the university itself, or as Jeremiah Arowosegbe puts it: "What differences exist between *a university in Africa* and *an African university?*"[7]

According to Mbembe's essay "Decolonising the University: New Directions," this issue is the crux between decolonization and Africanization. Decolonization, for him, entails questioning the "large systems of authoritative control" and standardization for the sake of commercial accountability and viability. I find that the increasing popularity of using global university rankings for a calculative assessment of a university's worth is a stark example of this. Thus, decolonization's first movement entails replacing this system built upon "scientific capacity and addiction to study and inquiry by salesman-like proficiency."[8] Part and parcel of this salesman-like proficiency, with its scientific-calculative evaluation of the classroom and its marketeering to customers (not students), is an acceptance of a standardized education that can be evaluated on a global scale. Outside of its historical and colonial legacy, which cannot be overlooked, this is one of the primary reasons why the Western canon still thrives globally: It represents an authoritative education.[9] Mastering this Eurocentric canon proves one to be an intellectual with a employable CV, as seen with how STEM classes are marketed as corridors to global and prosperous futures.[10] It also exists in the humanities where philosophers, for example, adopt Western philosophy as normative and anything else—mainly coming from Asia, South America, or Africa—as hyper-specialized fields. If one wants to join the global marketplace of ideas, one needs to master this canon and, perhaps, adopt its epistemologies and ontologies.

Yet decolonization is not a new trend and Africana and postcolonial academic programs have proliferated throughout the world.[11] However, there is a concern that the revolution against colonial epistemologies will become a new canon that is just as hegemonic and destructive. Drawing upon Fanon's *The Wretched of the Earth,* Mbembe highlights that the counter-trend to westernization, a so-called "Africanization," tends to be just as destructive given its nationalist tendencies that typically assimilate "colonialist thought in its most corrupt form."[12] Lacking any spiritual depth, and adopting the framework that established colonial epistemologies, Africanization becomes itself an ideology that subverts self-determination into a nationalized "consciousness," dictating what is and is not acceptable along what is perceived as "African" or "Western." Mbembe also addressed this issue in his earlier work, *On the Postcolony,* when describing the concept of "commandment" and the legitimization of postcolonial regimes and governments.[13] In short, a heavily politicized nationalism, based upon an ideological construct of a pure "Africa," follows a similar path of legitimization that colonial empires employed; they just replace "European" concepts with "African" ones, without addressing the structures of power. In both texts, Mbembe follows a particular reading of Fanon by arguing that some decolonization efforts are merely superficial and do not get to the heart of what it means to be colonized.[14] Africanization's intellectual attempt is thus one that seeks to do away with the Western canon but keep its sovereignty. In this vein, "scratching out" the Western scientific method does nothing to help diversify the classroom, or to give South Africans intellectual freedom, since it proves to be just as hegemonic. Furthermore, I find that Africanization's attempt to remove Western canons does so at the expense of African contributions to these canons, such as how Western medicine appropriated indigenous herbs and practices for pharmaceuticals and therapies. Or how African literature and histories are integral for understanding why the West became a dominant cultural force. Africa's intellectual, religious, and cultural history is inextricably tied to the West, for very abhorrent reasons I might add, but removing the Western canon from African classrooms would obscure these legacies for the sake of a purer concept of "Africa."

Countering this trend, Mbembe highlights Ngugi wa-Thiong'o's *Decolonising the Mind*, which explores the politics of language as a measure of liberation from colonialization without falling into a colonial mentality.[15] Situated between poststructuralism and existential phenomenology, Mbembe's vision for decolonization seeks a new textual paradigm that reinscribes African voices back into Africa's diverse cultures, in turn requiring "a geographical imagination that extends well beyond the confines of the nation state" in the colonial sense and the one latent within Africanization.[16] Hence, the reinscription of African voices needs to break beyond the geopolitical barriers erected by Western nationalization that first corralled and suppressed them. But doing so, to "Write Africa" as Mbembe often calls it,[17] does not mean writing Africa out of colonialization, but rather to write Africa as a rupture that criticizes and questions this colonial narrative. Instead of destroying the modern project, decolonization breaks it open. As Mbembe sees it, its outcome is not a "decolonized university" as such, but a "plurivisity" that is not merely an extension of the Eurocentric model of universal education; it is an institution that encourages "a process of knowledge production that is open to epistemic diversity. It is a process that does not necessarily abandon the notion of universal knowledge for humanity, but which embraces it via a horizontal strategy of openness to dialogue among different epistemic traditions."[18]

I find that, on the one hand, Fanon's critique that superficially removing colonialism from Africa merely replaces one regime for another informs Mbembe's thinking, particularly in *On the Postcolony*. On the other hand, poststructuralists like Ngugi who focus on the possibility of language as means of liberation to open a space for Africans to speak amongst other voices informs Mbembe's quest to "Write Africa." Returning to decolonizing science, the student proposed "scratching out" Western science in order to give South Africans a new voice, but her articulation kept the same colonial mentality of forcefully replacing one canon with another, maybe even an anticanon of forbidden ideas. However, perhaps the best path to decolonizing science involves a messianic breaking open of Western science instead of eliminating it. This messianic desire is not a force that removes the canon, it is a prophetic voice that scrutinizes the authority given to the canon and it questions whose voices and texts are authoritative. Furthermore, it strikes at the heart of the contemporary state of the university as a commercial institution. If decolonization's goal of a pluriversity is realized, then the whole financial structure that has grown around the university becomes questioned as well. In this new paradigm, African voices not only find their self-determination, they also push the global discussion forward by revealing the oversights and superficial justifications for what stands as knowledge.

However, a question arises as to what gets included in "writing Africa" and what counts as Africanization. This is an especially pertinent question given that several students and adjacent protestors have resorted to violent means to get their message across: Do petrol bombing university buildings or burning a university's paintings—its Apartheid and post-Apartheid cultural heritage—count the same as demanding that monuments to John Cecil Rhodes must fall?[19] Who gets to decide? One can see that the #feesmustfall protests are happening in a flux where decolonial or postcolonial thought meets Apartheid-era forms of protest. South Africa's past, present, and its indeterminate future are colliding at a rapid rate to where one cannot truly separate these violent measures—which at one time were justified in the face of an oppressive regime built upon white supremacy—from the intellectual thought that seeks an Africa inscribed to Africans of all races and cultures. Mbembe's work has been critiqued in a similar fashion regarding what gets to count as an acceptable epistemology in this plurivocal discourse. Jeremy Weate, for example, questions whether Mbembe's emphasis on post-structural analysis actually succeeds in giving more people voices in the discussion or if it proves to be just as silencing.[20] Indeed, there is a problem within Mbembe's pluriversity since there would still be an apparatus that decides which emerging epistemologies are deemed worthy to join the discourse, and even the rejection of a universal discourse (within the concept of the university) is a dismissal of a particular epistemology.

This is where Colby Dickinson's *Between the Canon and the Messiah* informs our discussion, where the debate between Derrida's messianic gesture from within the canon and Agamben's archaeological search for a pretextual origin can unveil the inherent violence within both decolonialization and Africanization. Dickinson's assessment of this debate might push forward the South African discourse on the nature and worth of its universities by embracing the messianic force latent within canonical structures, thereby suspending (or at least mitigating) the violent nature of these canonical forms by rupturing them from within, where Africanization's revolutionary character, its "scratching out" of Western hegemony, finds a more effective and just expression of itself from within the canons it seeks to dismantle.

CANONICITY AND MESSIANICITY: COLBY DICKINSON

Interestingly, Dickinson's lines of thought run alongside Mbembe's and, to a degree, Fanon's in that all three seek to understand, deconstruct, or otherwise demythologize the canonical structure in order to find a space for unheard and silenced voices to speak. Drawing upon Walter Benjamin's "weak messianism," or desire to change societal structures without complete upheaval, the canon, for Dickinson, "signifies a cultural, symbolic reality" whereas the messianic represents a quasi-heretical impulse to break open orthodoxy.[21] The canon's political force stems from its dialectical sifting of what is deemed legitimate for a culture and what is not. Dickinson seeks a possible reconciliation between the canon and the messianic through putting the canon's dialectical structure into direct tension with its messianic opposition, thereby exposing it to new and plurivocal ideas. The revolution gets teleologically suspended into the dialectic it wishes to topple, if you will.

The text in part examines the debate between Derrida and Giorgio Agamben regarding the political nature of the canon within belief systems, where Dickinson argues that the "religious desire to transcend all representations (its "messianic" force) is to be understood in relation to our formulations of shared sovereign power (its "canonical" manifestation)."[22] Our privately held beliefs have a public dimension and representation since they are shared and / or mediated throughout culture, and thus play a part in the sovereignty given to society, or the political. The establishment of political sovereignty for any society is its approval of certain beliefs that are legitimized as authoritative through the establishment of canons. Hence, "a canon is only a force which determines how certain norms will become legible to the subjects who are in turn subjected to them."[23] This is where canonicity's inherent violence arises: It necessarily rejects some ideas—and often those who hold them—when legitimating others. Therefore, any permanent interruption of these dynamics follows the same trajectory as the canon: The elimination of all canons excludes those who adhere to the canon, thus merely replacing one dialectical set for another. The dialectic of "approval" versus "disapproval" still remains, resembling Mbembe's reading of Fanon and proving that "scratching out" science is equally violent as solely following science.[24] Furthermore, it also proves that Mbembe's rejection of Africanization is a silencing, a rhetorically violent act, regardless of its good intentions.

Space and scope preclude us from deeply going into the debate Dickinson presents between Derrida and Agamben, but in short, it pertains to whether or not we need canons at all. For Derrida, the canon is a social inevitability—just as there is nothing that is not textual or subjective—and canons function as a binding of a community's sense of justice.[25] Not only do these canons authorize what we see as culturally important but, going back to their political force, they also symbolize what we see as "right" or just, further increasing their violent and silencing nature.[26] The canon, in the course of meting out justice, tends to absolutize its findings, enhancing its sovereignty and authority. Yet, this absolutization can only hold for so long and, as it tightens its grip upon sovereignty, it eventually breaks itself apart. This is where the messianic arises but, interestingly, Derrida's deconstruction of the canon comes from within the canon itself while recognizing that it can never actually destroy the canon: "The (spectral) messianic forces that run throughout any canonical form will always disturb, though the canonical form will yet always persist."[27] One task of deconstruction is to break down canons and texts in order to reveal and explore these messianic forces, thereby opening canonical justice to heretofore uncovered, and perhaps "indecent," justices that have been silenced.[28] Mbembe's "writing Africa" carries with it a similar task of justice, and breaking open the universal within the university reveals the uncovered pluralities that were silenced. Importantly, though many African epistemologies were otherwise muzzled by the Western canon, their spectral voices still remained within it, either obliquely or in tune with other silenced voices such as feminist voices, queer voices, and/or voices from other religions.[29] This is one reason why I think post-structuralism and phenomenologies of alterity play such a pertinent role within postcolonial thought: They seek to uncover these voices, often through a hermeneutics of recovery or an archaeology.

The role of philosophical archaeology in breaking down these sovereign structures is where Agamben critiques Derrida. Whereas Derrida approaches the origins of the canon with "almost a holy distance," Agamben attempts to seek what is behind canons and all texts in order to find the pre-linguistic origin before all inscriptions.[30] Focusing on the signification within our textual nature as our "Original Sin," Agamben seeks a path to undo the political force that undergirds our entire system: canons, texts, and contextualities.[31] In a way, similar to Fanon's desire to undo the structures of colonialism and not just its effects, Agamben wants to revolutionize how we do politics altogether and how we inscribe our own personal narratives. Deconstruction works within the system it wishes to reconstruct and Agamben thus finds Derrida complicit in continuing its violence.[32] In its place, Agamben seeks an archaeological uncovering of the significations before the canon and, once those are revealed, a "coming community" would no longer need their texts codified or authorized for any teleological aim toward justice. Furthermore, this community, not having an aim toward justice represented in canons, would not need political representation to support their narrative inscriptions; "writing Africa" does not necessitate transcending geopolitical boundaries, since these boundaries no longer exist. Justice is found in uncovering the forces behind canons, removing the transcendental barriers that stitch them together. Derrida critiques this as superficial and, one could say, lacking spiritual depth: Removing canons and seeking the archaeological origins behind them makes one fall into a sort of "archive fever" where the archaeologist who chooses which and what texts to uncover becomes the sovereign.[33] Similar to sifting through what is purely African and/or Western, and touching upon our question of who gets to decide what is either decolonization or Africanization, Derrida finds that Agamben's approach merely replaces one sovereign for another but in a much more violent way since the archaeologist is in control of what gets uncovered. Moreover, in my view, privileging a silenced text over another text, even if it were dominant at some point, replaces one sort of epistemology over another; the revolution becomes what it sought to eliminate.

Dickinson finds that the tension between Derrida and Agamben is irresolvable, but this tension becomes a source of hermeneutical creativity for the canon and for the messianic.[34] Since the messianic emerges from within the canon, it becomes a prophetic voice of creativity for a given community: If canons are inevitable, pace Derrida, then the creation of a less violent canon only comes from a deconstructive critique from within the canon. If uncovering the origins of what makes us form canons reveals a path beyond the sovereign, pace Agamben, then further archaeology aids in the creative measure of breaking open existing canons—even if we accept their inevitable formation. A hermeneutical suspicion of canons emerges, where we are constantly overturning the canon in a creative tension of accepting and questioning its authority. Regarding decolonization and the possible coming pluriversity, the former takes a deconstructive approach to westernization's canons while the latter seeks a path beyond the sovereignty given to them through the university and a "universal education." In tandem, the path to accepting new epistemologies and giving them value is through their evaluation and critique of established epistemologies—westernized or otherwise—and then finding a platform for these epistemologies to engage others. Note that these new epistemologies emerge as the messianic impulse from within the Western canon, and South Africans can find their self-determination through their critique and exposure to Western modernity and the consequences levied upon them by this intellectual and political force. Appropriating Agamben's archaeological approach, the establishment of these new epistemologies also questions what makes them sovereign in the first place: Do they aid South Africa in being with the times or do they question who gets to mark time for South Africa? Are they established on behalf of *a university in South Africa or a South African University*? In answering these questions, South African academics and students critique the normativity of the Western canon and its latent presuppositions. This opens avenues for a decolonial hermeneutics of suspicion that emerges from within these westernized traditions to rival those old masters, Freud, Marx, and Nietzsche.

CONCLUSION

Returning to our example, the student raised the concept of "African magic" and why it is not considered an acceptable topic for scientific study. For some, this is misguided since science is considered de facto an objective inquiry using re-testable and verifiable methodologies that function independently of human bias. Hence, there is a sense of purity to the hard sciences that other fields do not have; what science deems valid is true whether you accept it or not. Yet science is not so philosophically innocent; as we have seen, every question we raise is a political act—the mere fact that we find a subject worthy of questioning gives it a provisional legitimacy that is reflected by our canonically affirmed beliefs. Consider the numerous times when Western observers of indigenous communities notice that a superstition (such as slathering one's arms with a concoction of herbs and mud) may actually have value. The superstitious act may prove useful to the Westerner, and thus it becomes scientifically testable. Once it is scientifically affirmed as effective in some kind of way, it then transitions from merely being a superstition to being a medicine. A decolonial hermeneutics of suspicion would be to question where our medicines come from, and to whom go the profits and credit. Academics such as Linda Tuhiwai Smith[35] are already undertaking this necessary critique and their approach similarly follows the ones that decolonial thinkers take in the humanities: One does not need to scratch out these canons to decolonize them, one can work from within these canons—questioning their norms, accepted epistemologies, their ethical treatment of subjects and persons—in order to find a rupture, a voice for those who were heretofore silenced.

The task of decolonization entails accepting its messianic nature while also recognizing that the breaking open of the Western canon will inevitably sustain the canon's sovereign nature. However, in this recognition, one may also teleologically suspend within a decolonial framework Africanization's revolutionary impulse to "scratch out" or do away with westernization. By accepting the inevitability of political force and, according to Fanon and Mbembe, recognizing that exchanging sovereigns never replaces the issue of sovereignty, we can seek a better form of justice that constantly overturns and questions what it deems authoritative so that new epistemologies can emerge and new voices can be heard. Through critiquing the Western canon in which they find their lives and histories already inscribed, South Africans' self-determination and self-definition thus becomes not just a writing of Africa, but also a rewriting of the universal definition of what it means to have an authoritative education. If this is true, then what comes after colonization and modernity, or even decolonization and postmodernity, thus comes from the messianic impulse from within these structures and, I find, from within South Africa.

NOTES

1. Or "fallism" as it has become known since the movement has expanded its scope.

2. See Shanade Barnabas, "Engagement with Colonial Apartheid Narratives in Contemporary South Africa: A Monumental Debate," *Journal of Literary Studies* 32/3 (September 2016): 109–128.

3. "Science Must Fall?" YouTube video, 4:14, posted by UCT Scientist, October 13, 2016,<https://www.youtube.com/watch?v=C9SiRNibD14/>[Accessed: December 2, 2016]. Many public responses can be found online, but for a sample of some of the responses, see Roxanne Henderson, "UCT Student Upsets Newton's Apple Cart with the Demand That #ScienceMustFall," Times Live, October 14, 2016,<http://www.timeslive.co.za/local/2016/10/14/UCT-student-upsets-Newton%E2%80%99s-apple-cart-with-her-demand-that-ScienceMustFall1/>[Accessed: December 2, 2016].

4. For a general overview of the perspective that South African education too heavily emphasizes a capitalist framework that renders higher education into a commodity, see Anne Becker and Petro du Preez, "Ideological Illusions, Human Rights and the Right to Education: The In(ex)clusion of the Poor in Post-Apartheid Education," *Journal of Education* 64 (2016): 55–78.

5. Achille Mbembe, "Decolonising the University: New Directions," *Arts & Humanities in Higher Education* 15/1 (2016): 40.

6. See Jeremiah O. Arowosegbe's introduction to *Social Dynamics*'s special section on this topic: "Special Section: African Studies and Knowledge Production in the Universities in Postcolonial Africa," *Social Dynamics* 40/2 (2014): 243–54.

7. Arowosegbe, introduction to "Special Section," 245, emphasis his.

8. Mbembe, "Decolonising the University," 30. See also Achille Mbembe, "At the Centre of the Knot," *Social Dynamics* 38/1 (March 2012): 13.

9. Mbembe, "Decolonising the University," 33.

10. One only needs to go to a given university's "Open Day" for incoming students to see how majors from all fields are marketed, often focusing on jobs and careers rather than the student's interest in a given subject. Of course, finding employment after one's schooling is an important and necessary task; my aim here is not outright to stop this process but to question how the emphasis on the commercial viability of a given subject has underlying assumptions and consequences that need to be thoroughly evaluated.

11. Also the emergence of new journals focused solely on this issue have been established; see the following journal and its premier article: Petro du Preez, Shan Simmonds, and Anné Verhoef, "Rethinking and Research Transformation in Higher Education: A Meta-study of South African Trends," *Transformation in Higher Education* 1/1, a2. DOI: http://dx.doi.org/10.4102/the.v1i1.2.

12. Mbembe, "Decolonising the University," 33. He is citing Frantz Fanon, *The Wretched of the Earth*, chapter 3.

13. Achille Mbembe, *On the Postcolony* (Berkeley, CA: University of California Press, 2001).

14. Some may disagree with Mbembe's reading of Fanon, yet we do not have space to give a proper critique or discussion of this reading. Here, our purposes are more concerned with *how* Mbembe develops his own concept of Africanization and decolonization through Fanon's work. For a broader reading of *Wretched of the Earth*, see Robert Bernasconi, "Fanon's *The Wretched of the Earth* as the Fulfillment of Sartre's Critique of Dialectical Reason," *Sartre Studies International* 16/2 (December 2010): 36–47; Nigel Gibson, "Relative Opacity: A New Translation of Fanon's *Wretched of the Earth*—Mission Betrayed or Fulfilled?" *Social Identities* 13/1 (January 2007): 69–95; Margaret A. Mujamdar, "*The Wretched of the Earth*—Then and Now," *International Journal of Francophone Studies* 1/19 (2016): 95–103; Matthew Whittle, "'These Dogs Will Do As We Say': African Nationalism in the Era of Decolonisation in David Caute, *At Fever Pitch* and Frantz Fanon's *The Wretched of the Earth*," *Journal of Postcolonial Writing* 51/3 (2015): 269–82.

15. Ngugi, like Fanon, is a major influence on Mbembe's work as one can see from his early text "Écrire l'Afrique à partir d'une faille," *Politique Africaine* 51 (1993): 87. For an overview of Ngugi's influence, as well as how language and textuality is central to Mbembe's work, see Michael Syrotinski, "'Genealogical Misfortunes': Achille Mbembe's (Re-)Writing of Postcolonial Africa," *Paragraphs* 35/3 (2012): 407–20.

16. Mbembe, "Decolonising the University," 36.

17. See Achille Mbembe, *Sortir de la grande nuit*, Essai sur l'Afrique décolonisée (Paris: La Decouverte, 2013); Gayatri Chackravorty Spivak, "Religion, Politics, Theology: A Conversation with Achille Mbembe," *Boundaries* 2, 34/2 (2007): 151–70;

"What Is Postcolonial Thinking?" Interview with Olivier Mongin, Nathalie Lempereur, and Jean-Louis Schlegel, trans. John Fletcher, *Esprit* (2008),<http://www.eurozine.com/journals/esprit/issue/2006-12-15.html/>[Accessed: November 11, 2016].

18. Mbembe, "Decolonising the University," 36–37, emphasis his. He appropriates the term "pluriversity" from Boaventura de Sousa and Enrique Dussel.

19. For the burning of university paintings, see André Jurgens, "UCT's 'Colonial Art' Faces Threat after Burning Outrage," *Sunday Times,* February 21, 2016,<http://www.timeslive.co.za/sundaytimes/stnews /2016/02/21/UCTs-colonial-art-faces-threat-after-burning-outrage/>[Accessed: December 12, 2016]. For an international perspective, see "Whiteness Burning," *The Economist,* February 20, 2016,<http://www.economist.com/news/middle-east-and-africa/21693278-students-are-throwing-colonial-art-pyre-whiteness-burning/>[Accessed: December 12, 2016]. For an example of petrol bombings that led to the near-death of two security guards, see Tammy Peterson, "Two Guards Locked in Burning Building at CPUT," *News24,* October 12, 2016,<http://www.news24.com/SouthAfrica/News/two-guards-locked-in-burning-building-at-cput-20161012/>[Accessed: December 8, 2016)].

20. Weate specifically critiques Mbembe's approach as confused and muddled. Jeremy Weate, "Achille Mbembe and the Postcolony: Going beyond the Text," *Research in African Literatures* 34/4 (Winter 2003): 27–41. For more critiques, particularly against *On the Postcolony,* see Adeleke Adeeko, "Bound to Violence? Achille Mbembe on the Postcolony," *West Africa Review* 3/2 (2002),<http://www.westafricareview.com/vol.3.2/adeeko.html/>[Accessed: December 12, 2016]. Ato Quayson, "Breaches in the Commonplace," *African Studies Review* 44/2 (2001): 151–66; Bruce Janz, "Review of Achille Mbembe, On the Postcolony," *H-Africa, H-Net Reviews* (March 2002),<http://www2.h-net.msu.edu/africa/>[Accessed: December 12, 2016]. I highlight these critiques since Mbembe responds to them, among others, directly: Achille Mbembe, "On the Postcolony: A Brief Response to Critics," *African Identities* 4/2 (October 2006), 143–78.

21. Colby Dickinson, *Between the Canon and the Messiah* (London: Bloomberg, 2013), 47, see also 4–6 for a summary.

22. Dickinson, *Between the Canon and the Messiah,* 45.

23. Dickinson, *Between the Canon and the Messiah,* 47.

24. Furthermore, Dickinson states on page 48: "Just as messianicity must forever deconstruct any given canonical representation, so too must those 'other' representations (installed as products of revealability, the historical theologemes of a particular religious tradition or the canonical forms before us) be constantly active in our world."

25. Dickinson, *Between the Canon and the Messiah,* 53: "There are only *canons,* for Derrida, just as there are only *texts* (or *histories* or *subjectivities*), and nothing lies outside of their corresponding grids."

26. Dickinson, *Between the Canon and the Messiah,* 48–49.

27. Dickinson, *Between the Canon and the Messiah,* 53. My own example: Postmodern critique comes from within modernity but it never rids itself of modernity; it is still latched onto the latter's epistemologies, histories, and so forth.

28. I include "indecent" here because Dickinson's reading of messianic force can also be aligned with Marcella Althaus-Reid's concept of "indecent theology;" see Marcella Althaus-Reid, *Indecent Theology: Theological Perversions in Sex, Gender, and Politics* (New York: Routledge, 2000), 1–10, 19–23, 57–60.

29. One can think of Hegel's comments on African and Asian peoples in *Lectures on the Philosophy of Right* and how many thinkers, Mbembe especially, employ his negative comments as an access point to critique Western thought and to reprise these silenced voices. Hegel's own dismissal of these cultures in emphasizing the supremacy of Eurocentric thought actually becomes a way to engage Hegel and his legacy. Thus, the messianic rupture and recovery of these voices comes from critique of Hegel within his own systematic thinking.

30. Dickinson, *Between the Canon and the Messiah*, 109.

31. Dickinson, *Between the Canon and the Messiah*, 66.

32. Dickinson, *Between the Canon and the Messiah*, 70, 77.

33. Dickinson, *Between the Canon and the Messiah*, 69, 73, 80–86. For more on Agamben's response, see 92–96.

34. Dickinson, *Between the Canon and the Messiah*, 84–91. See also one of his concluding subsections for more on this creative tension, entitled "The Guises of Violence, or on the Difficulties of Constructing an Ontotheological Bridge between Metaphor and Politics," 172–89.

35. See Linda Tuhiawai Smith, *Decolonising Methodologies: Research and Indigenous Peoples* (Dunedin, New Zealand: Otago University Press, 2012).

Selected Bibliography

Aaboe, Julie. "The Other and the Construction of Cultural and Christian Identity: The Case of the Dutch Reformed Church in Transition." Unpublished PhD diss., University of Cape Town, 2007.

Adato, Michelle, Michael R. Carter, and Julian May. "Exploring Poverty Traps and Social Exclusion in South Africa Using Qualitative and Quantitative Data." *Journal of Development Studies* 42/2 (2006): 226–47.

Adedibu, Babatunde. "Migration, Identity, and Marginalisation: The Case of Britain's Black Majority Churches." *Journal of Africana Religions* 2/1 (2014): 110–17.

Adhikari, Mohamed, ed. *Burdened by Race: Coloured Identities in Southern Africa*. Cape Town: University of Cape Town Press, 2009.

Adihikari, Mohamed. *Not White Enough, Not Black Enough: Racial Identity in the South African Coloured Community*. Athens, OH: Ohio University Press, 2005.

Althaus-Reid, Marcella. *Indecent Theology: Theological Perversions*. In *Sex, Gender, and Politics*. New York: Routledge, 2000.

Altman, Miriam. "Wage Determination in South Africa: What Do We Know?" *Transformation* 60 (2005): 58–89.

Amanze, James. *African Traditional Religions and Culture in Botswana*. Gaborone, Botswana: Pula Press, 2002.

Appiah, Kwame Anthony. *In My Father's House: Africa in the Philosophy of Culture*. Oxford: Oxford University Press, 1992.

Arnowitz, Stanley, and Heather Gauntney. *Implicating Empire: Globalisation and Resistance in the 21st Century World Order*. New York: Basic Books, 2013.

Arowosegbe, Jeremiah O. "African Studies and Knowledge Production in the Universities in Postcolonial Africa." Special section, *Social Dynamics* 40/2 (2014): 243–54.

Ashforth, Adam. *Witchcraft, Violence and Democracy in South Africa*. Chicago, IL: University of Chicago Press, 2005.

Bachelard, Gaston. In Nigel Rapport and Joanna Overing, *Social and Cultural Anthropology: The Key Concepts*. London: Routledge, 2000.

Baker, Deborah, and Suzanne Skevington. *The Social Identity of Women*. London: Sage, 1989.

Barnabas, Shanade. "Engagement with Colonial Apartheid Narratives in Contemporary South Africa: A Monumental Debate." *Journal of Literary Studies* 32/3 (September 2016): 109–28.

Barnett, Ronald. "Learning for an Unknown Future." *Higher Education Research & Development* 23/3 (2004): 247–60.

Battle, Michael, J. "A Theology of Community. The Ubuntu Theology of Desmond Tutu Interpretation." *Journal of Bible & Theology* 54/2 (1995): 172–82.

Becker, Anne, and Petro du Preez. "Ideological Illusions, Human Rights and the Right to Education: The In(ex)clusion of the Poor in Post-Apartheid Education." *Journal of Education* 64 (2016): 55–78.

Bekker, Simon, Martine Dodds, and Meshack M. Khosa. *Shifting African Identities, Identity? Theory, Politics, History*. Pretoria: HSRC Press, 2001.

Bemath, Abdul. *The Mazruina Collection Revisited: Ali A. Mazrui Debating the African Condition: An Annotated and Select Bibliography 1962–2003*. New Delhi: New Dawn Press, 2005.

Beuken, Wim, and Sean Freyne. *The Bible as Cultural Heritage*. London: SCM Press, 1995.

Beynon, John. *Masculinity and Culture*. Philadelphia, PA: Open University Press, 2002.

Bezuidenhout, Andries. "Post-colonial Workplace Regimes in the Engineering Industry in South Africa." In *Beyond the Apartheid Workplace: Studies in Transition*, edited by Edward Webster and Karl von Holdt. Pietermaritzburg, South Africa: University of KwaZulu-Natal Press, 2005.

Bhana, Deevia. *The Regulation of Sexualities in South African Secondary Schools*. Cape Town: Modjaji Books, 2015.

———. "When Caring Is Not Enough: The Limits of Teachers' Support for South African Primary School-girls in the Context of Sexual Violence." *International Journal of Educational Development* 41 (2015): 262.

Biko, Steve Bantu. *I Write What I Like: A Selection of His Writings*. Edited with a personal memoir by Aelred Stubbs, C. R. Johannesburg: Picador Africa, 2002.

Bitsani, Eugenia. "Promoting Traditions of Multicultural Communities as a Tool for Social Cohesion in Trieste, Italy." *Procedia-Social & Behavioural Sciences* 148 (2014): 412–19.

Boesak, Allan, A. *Farewell to Innocence: A Social-Ethical Study of Black Theology and Black Power*. Johannesburg: Raven Press, 1977.

Borsa, Joan. "Frida Kahlo: Marginalisation and the Critical Female Subject." *Third Text* 4/12 (1990): 36.

Bosch, David. *Transforming Mission: Paradigm Shifts in Theology of Mission*. Maryknoll, NY: Orbis, 1991.

Boshoff, Henri, Anneli Botha, and Martin Schönteich. *Fear in the City: Urban Terrorism in South Africa*, no. 63. Pretoria: Institute for Security Studies, 2001.

Bourdieu, Pierre, and Loïc Wacquant. "On the Cunning of Imperialist Reason." *Theory Culture & Society* 16/1 (February 1999): 41–58.

Boyd, Gregory A. *The Myth of a Christian Nation: How the Quest for Political Power Is Destroying the Church*. Grand Rapids, MI: Zondervan, 2007.

Brain, Joy. *Christian Indians in Natal 1860–1911*. Cape Town: Oxford University Press, 1983.

Bray, Rachel, Imke Gooskens, Lauren Kahn, Sue Moses, and Jeremy Seekings. *Growing Up in the New South Africa: Childhood and Adolescence in the New South Africa*. Cape Town: HSRC Press, 2010.

Broadbridge, Helen. "Negotiating Post-Apartheid Boundaries and Identities: An Anthropological Study of the Creation of a Cape Town Suburb." Unpublished PhD diss., Stellenbosch University, 2001.

Brown, Judith M. *Global South Asians: Introducing the Modern Diaspora*. Cambridge: Cambridge University Press, 2006.

Brueggemann, Walter. *Interpretation and Obedience: From Faithful Reading to Faithful Living*. Minneapolis, MN: Fortress Press, 1991.

———. *Living toward a Vision: Biblical Reflections on Shalom*. (Philadelphia, PA: United Church Press, 1982.

Bujo, Bénézet. *The Ethical Dimension of Community: The African Model and the Dialogue Between North and South*. Nairobi: Paulines Publications Africa, 1998.

———. *Foundations of an African Ethic: Beyond the Universal Claims of Western Morality*. Nairobi: Paulines Publications Africa, 2003.

Bundy, Colin. "Land, Law and Power: Forced Removals in Historical Context." In *No Place to Rest: Forced Removals and the Law*, edited by Christina Murray and Catherine O'Regan. Cape Town: Oxford University Press, 1990.

Burns, Justine. "Inequality Aversion and Group Identity in a Segmented Society." Unpublished paper, University of Cape Town, 2004.

———. "Racial Stereotypes, Stigma and Trust in Post-Apartheid South Africa." *Economic Modelling* 23 (2006): 805–21.

Byrne, Michelle. "Understanding Life Experiences through a Phenomenological Approach to Research." *AORN Journal* 73/4 (2001): 830–32.

Cecyl, Esau. "Memories of a Political Prisoner on Robben Island, 1987–1991." *Kronos* 34/1 (2008): 41–65.

Césaire, Aimé. *A Return to My Native Land*. Harmondsworth, UK: Penguin Books, 1969.

Chipkin, Ivor. "Middle Classing in Roodepoort: Capitalism and Social Change in South Africa." PARI Long Essays No. 2. Johannesburg: Public Affairs Research Institute, University of Johannesburg, 2012.

Cho, Francisa, and Richard K. Squier. "Religion as a Dynamic and Complex System," *Journal of the American Academy of Religion* 81/2 (2013): 357–98.

Chow, Kenny, and Mick Healey. "Place Attachment and Place Identity: First-Year Undergraduates Making the Transition from Home to University." *Journal of Environmental Psychology* 28 (2008): 362–72.

Christopher, Anthony J. "Further Progress in the Desegregation of South African Towns and Cities, 1996–2001." *Development Southern Africa* 22/2 (2005): 267–76.

———. "'To Define the Indefinable': Population Classification and the Census in South Africa." *Area* 34/4 (2002): 401–8.

———. "Urban Segregation in Post-Apartheid South Africa." *Urban Studies* 38/3 (2001): 449–66.

Cillié, Gawie G. *Waar kom ons Afrikaanse Gesange vandaan?* Kaapstad, South Africa: Tafelberg, 1982.

Cohen, Louis, Lawrence Manion, and Keith Morrison. *Research Methodology in Education*. 7th ed. Abingdon, UK: Routledge, 2011.

Colin, John, Tredoux Dixon, Kevin Durrheim, Gillian Finchilescu, and Beverley Clack. "'The Inner Citadels of the Colour Line': Mapping the Micro-ecology of Segregation in Everyday Life Spaces." *Personality & Social Psychology Compass* 2 (2008): 1–23.

Comaroff, John L. and Jean, "On Personhood: Anthropological Perspectives from Africa." *Social Identities* 7/2 (2001): 267–83.

Cone, James, H. *The Cross and the Lynching Tree*. Maryknoll, NY: Orbis, 2011.

Conn, Harvie M., and Manuel Ortiz. *Urban Ministry: The Kingdom, the City, and the People of God*. Downers Grove, IL: InterVarsity Press, 2001.

Connell, Raewyn W. *Gender and Power: Society, the Person and Social Politics*. Stanford, CA: Stanford University Press, 1987.

Cooper, Carolyn. *Noises in the Blood: Orality, Gender and "Vulgar" Body of Jamaican Popular Culture*. Durham, NC: Duke University, 1995.

Corbeil, Jacob. *Mbusa: Sacred Emblems of the Bemba*. Mbala, Zambia: Moto-Moto Museum, 1982.

Crankshaw, Owen. *Race, Class and the Changing Division of Labour under Apartheid*. London: Routledge, 1997.

Crenshaw, Kimberlé Williams. "Demarginalizing the Intersection of Race and Sex: A Black Feminist Critique of Antidiscrimination Doctrine, Feminist Theory and Antiracist Politics." University of Chicago Legal Forum, 1989.

Cronon, William. "Modes of Prophecy and Production: Placing Nature in History." *Journal of American History* 76 (1990): 1122–31.

Crosby, Alfred. *Ecological Imperialism: The Biological Expansion of Europe 900–1900*. Cambridge: Cambridge University Press, 1986.

Dankelman, Irene, and Joan Davidson. *Women and Environment in the Third World: Alliance for the Future*. London: Earthscan , 1988.

Davey, Andrew. "Being Urban Matters: What Is Urban about Urban Mission?" In *Crossover City: Resources for Urban Mission and Transformation*, edited by Andrew Davey. London: Continuum, 2010.

Davis, Rebecca. "Remembering Jakes Gerwel." *Daily Maverick*, November 29, 2012.

Desai, Ashwin, and Goolam Vahed, eds. *Chatsworth: The Making of a South African Township*. Pietermaritzburg, South Africa: University of KwaZulu-Natal Press, 2013.

———. *The South African Gandhi: Stretcher-Bearer of Empire*. Stanford, CA: Stanford University Press / New Delhi: Navayana, 2016.

Desai, Ashwin. "An Exploratory Critique of the Notion of Social Cohesion in Contemporary South Africa." *Psychology in Society* 49 (2015): 99–113.

———. *Inside Indian Indenture: A South Africa Story, 1860–1914*. Cape Town: HSRC Press, 2010.

———. "The 1946–1948 Passive Resistance Campaign in Natal, South Africa: Origins and Results." In *1913, Satyagraha: Passive Resistance and Its Legacy*, edited by Devarakshanam Betty Govinden and Kalpana Hiralal. New Delhi: Manohar, 2015.

Desmond, Cosmas. *The Discarded People: An Account of Africa Resettlement in South Africa*. London: Penguin African Library, 1971.

Dhupelia-Mesthrie, Uma. *From Cane Fields to Freedom: A Chronicle of Indian South African Life*. Cape Town: Kwela Books, 2000.

Diagne, Soulaymane Bachir. "Islam in Africa: Examining the Notion of an African Identity within the Islamic World." In *A Companion to African Philosophy*, edited by Kwasi Wiredu. Malden, MA: Blackwell, 2004.

Diagne, Soulaymane Bachir. "Bergson Postcolonial: le elan vital dans la pensee de Léopold Sédar Senghor's et de Mohamed Iqbal." *American Catholic Philosophical Quarterly* 83/1 (2011): 79–94.

———. *Islam and Open Society: Fidelity and Movement in the Philosophy of Muhammad Iqbal*. Dakar: CODESRIA, 2010.

———. "Precolonial African Philosophy in Arabic." In *A Companion to African Philosophy*, edited by Kwasi Wiredu. Cambridge: Blackwell, 2004.

———. "Toward an Intellectual History of West Africa: The Meaning of Timbuktu." In *The Meanings of Timbuktu*, edited by Shamil Jeppie and Souleymane Bachir Diagne. Cape Town: HSRC Press, 2008.

Dickinson, Colby. *Between the Canon and the Messiah*. London: Bloomberg, 2013.

Diesel, Alleyn. *Shakti: Stories of Indian Women in South Africa*. Johannesburg: University of the Witwatersrand, 2007.

Disraeli, Benjamin. *England and France; Or a Cure for the Ministerial Gallomania*. London: John Murray, 1832.

———. *An Inquiry into the Plans, Progress, and Policy of the American Mining Companies*. London: John Murray, 1825.

Dixon, John, and Kevin Durrheim. "Contact and the Ecology of Racial Division: Some Varieties of Informal Segregation." *British Journal of Social Psychology* 42 (2003): 1–23.

Dixon, John, and Colin Tredoux. "Beyond the Optimal Contact Strategy: A Reality Check for the Contact Hypothesis." *American Psychologist* 60/7 (2005): 697–711.

Dolby, Nadine. *Constructing Race: Youth, Identity and Popular Culture in South Africa*. Albany, NY: SUNY Press, 2001.

Donald, Horowitz L. *Ethnic Groups in Conflict*. Berkeley, CA: University of California Press, 1985.

Dunn, Robert Andrew. "Identity Theories and Technology." In *Handbook of Research on Technoself: Identity in a Technological Society*, edited by R. Luppicini. Hershey, PA: Information Science Reference, 2013.

Dussel, Enrique. *Beyond Philosophy: Ethics, History, Marxism and Liberation Theology*. New York: Rowman & Littlefield, 2003).

Ellenberger, Frederic. *History of the Basuto: Ancient and Modern*. New York: Negro University Press, 1969.

Elphick, Richard, ed. *Christianity in South Africa: A Political, Social, and Cultural History*. Los Angeles: University of California Press, 1997.

Eze, Emmanuel Chukwudi, ed. *Postcolonial African Philosophy: A Critical Reader*. Oxford: Blackwell, 1997.

Fanon, Frantz. *Black Skin, White Masks*. Translated by Richard Philcox. Kobo ed. New York: Grove Press, 1967.

Ferree, Karen E. *Framing the Race in South Africa: The Political Origins of Racial Census Elections*. Cambridge: Cambridge University Press, 2010.

Fourie, Francois Paul. "n Geskiedenis van die kerklied in die Nederduitse Gereformeerde Kerk." DTh–proefskrif, Pretoria: UNISA, 2000; W. M. Louwrens Strydom, Sing nuwe sange, nuutgebore. Liturgie en lied. Bloemfontein, South Africa: UOVS, 1994.

Gandhi, Ela. "The 1913 Women's Marches: Learning from the Past." In *1913. Satyagraha, Passive Resistance and Its Legacy*, edited by Devarakshanam Betty Govinden and Kalpana Hiralal. New Delhi: Manohar, 2015.

Gandhi, Mohandas K. *Satyagraha in South Africa*. Translated from Gujarati by V. G. Desai. Ahmedabad, India: Navajivan, 1928.

Gevisser, Mark. "A Different Fight for Freedom: A History of South African Lesbian and Gay Organisations from the 1950s to the 1990s." In *Defiant Desire: Gay and Lesbian Lives in South Africa*, edited by Mark Gevisser and Edwin Cameron. Johannesburg: Raven Press, 1994.

Gibson, James. *Overcoming Apartheid: Can Truth Reconcile a Divided Nation?* Pretoria: Human Sciences Research Council Press, 2004.

Giroux, Henry A. *Border Crossings: Cultural Workers and the Politics of Education*. New York: Routledge, 1992.

Gooskens, Imke. "Boundaries and Crossing Points: Children, Geography and Identity in the Fish Hoek Valley." *Social Dynamics* 32/1 (2006): 135–68.

Gordon, Lewis. *Existence in Black: An Anthology of Black Existential Philosophy*. New York: Routledge 1997.

Gordon, Lewis R. *Existentia Africana: Understanding Africana Existential Thought*. New York: Routledge, 2000.

Grossberg, Arlene, Jaré Struwig, and Udesh Pillay. "Multicultural National Identity and Pride." In *South African Social Attitudes: Changing Times, Diverse Voices*, edited by Udesh Pillay, Ben Roberts, and Stephen Rule. Pretoria: Human Sciences Research Council, 2006, 54–76.

Grundling, Erns, Etienne Van Heerden, and Thomas Mollett. *Die omstrede God. Bestaan God of nie?* Stellenbosch, South Africa: Rapid Access Publishers, 2004.

Guha, Ramachandra. *India after Gandhi*. London: Pan Books, 2007.

Gustafson, James. "The Sectarian Temptation: Reflections on Theology, the Church, and the University." *Proceedings of the Catholic Theological Society* 40 (1985): 83–94.

Gyekye, Kwame. *Tradition and Modernity: Philosophical Reflections on the African Experience*. (New York: Oxford University Press, 1997.

Hansen, Thomas Blom. *Melancholia of Freedom: Social Life in an Indian Township in South Africa*. Princeton, NJ: Princeton University Press, 2012.

Hassim, Shireen. *Women's Organisations and Democracy in South Africa: Contesting Authority*. Madison: University of Wisconsin Press, 2006.

Hauerwas, Stanley, and William H. Willimon. *Resident Aliens: Life in the Christian Colony*. Nashville, TN: Abingdon Press, 1989.

Hawas, Akram. "Pan-Africanism and Pan-Arabism: Back to the Future?" In *The Making of the Africa-Nation: Pan-Africanism and the African Renaissance*, edited by Mammo Muchie. London: Adonis & Abbey, 2003.

Haynes, Naomi. "Change and Chisungu in Zambia's Time of AIDS." *Ethnos* 80/3 (2015): 364–84.

Hewitt, Roderick R. "Bob Marley's Redemption Song in Conversation with de Gruchy's Olive Agenda." Special edition, *Alternation* 14 (2015): 169–89.

———. *Church and Culture*. Pietermaritzburg, South Africa: Cluster Publications, 2012.

———. "Stealing Land in the Name of Religion: A Rastafari Religio-political Critique of Land Theft by Global Imperial Forces." *HTS Teologiese Studies / Theological Studies* 72/1 (2016): a3347. DOI: 10.4102/hts.v72i1.3347.

Hinfelaar, Hugo. *Bemba-Speaking Women of Zambia in a Century of Religious Change (1892–1992)*. Leiden, Netherlands: Brill, 1994.

Hiralal, Kalpana. "Docile Indian Women Protest—We Shall Resist: Passive Resistance in South Africa 1946–1948." *Journal of Social Science* 22/3 (2010): 153–62.

Hofmeyr, J. W. "Spiritualiteit in die NG Kerk van die 21ste eeu teen die agtergrond van Calvyn en die Nadere Reformasie." *Ned. Geref. Teologiese Tydskrif* 50/3-4 (2009): 595–606.

Hogarth, Christopher. "Entre Deux Générations D'Intellectuels Africains': Souleymane Bachir Diagne." In *The Contemporary Francophone African Intellectual*, edited by Christopher Hogarth and Natalie Edwoods. Cambridge, UK: Cambridge Scholar Publishing, 2013.

Homes, Rachel. "'White Rapists Made Coloureds (and Homosexuals): The Winnie Mandela Trial and the Politics of Race and Sexuality." In *Defiant Desire: Gay and Lesbian Lives in South Africa*, edited by Mark Gevisser and Edwin Cameron. Johannesburg: Raven Press, 1994.

Hopson, Mark C, Tabitha Hart, and Gina Castle Bell. "Meeting in the Middle: Fred L. Casmir's Contributions to the Field of Intercultural Communication." *International Journal of Intercultural Relations* 36/6 (2012): 789–97.

Hughes, Heather. "Violence in Inanda, August 1985," *Journal of Southern African Studies* 13/3 (1987): 331–54.

Hunter, James D. *To Change the World: The Irony, Tragedy, and Possibility of Christianity in the Late Modern World*. New York: Oxford University Press, 2010.

Jackson, Sherman. "Black Orientalism." Chap. 3 in *Islam and the Blackamerican: Looking toward the Third Resurrection*. Oxford: Oxford University Press, 2005.

Jacobs, Nancy. *Environment, Power, and Injustice: A South African History*. Cambridge: Cambridge University Press, 2003.

Jaffrelot, Christoph. "Communal Riots in Gujarat: The State at Risk?" *Heidelberg Papers in South Asian and Comparative Politics* no. 17. South Asia Institute, University of Heidelberg, 2003.

Kahn, R. "Oop vir Interpretasie: An Examination of the South African Media's Take-up and Representation of the Music of Fokofpolisiekar." Unpublished master's thesis, Journalism and Media Studies, Graduate School of Humanities, University of the Witwatersrand, Johannesburg, 2009.

Kalu, Ogbu. *African Pentecostalism: An Introduction*. Oxford: Oxford University Press, 2008.

Karenga, Maulana. *Introduction to Black Studies*. Los Angeles: University of Sankore Press, 1993.

Kaunda, Chammah J., and Roderick R. Hewitt. "Toward Epistemic Decolonial Turn in Missio-Formation in African Christianity." *International Review of Mission* 104/2 (2015): 378–92.

Kaunda, Mutale M. A., "Search for a Life-Giving Marriage: The Imbusa Initiation Rite as a Space for Constructing Wellbeing among Married Bemba Women of Zambia." Unpublished ThM diss., University of KwaZulu-Natal, Pietermaritzburg, South Africa, 2013.

Kaunda, Mutale M., and Chammah J. Kaunda. "Infunkutu: The Bemba Sexual Dance as Women's Sexual Agency." Special edition, *Journal of Theology for South Africa* 155 (2016): 159–75.

Kaunda, Mutale M., and Sarasvathie Reddy. "Pedagogies of Subservience? A Feminist Exploration of the Institution of imbusa among the Bemba." Special edition, *Journal of Gender and Religion in Africa* 19/2 (2013): 124–27.

Kaus, Wolfhard. "Conspicuous Consumption and 'Race': Evidence from South Africa." *Journal of Development Economics* 199 (2013): 63–73.

Kebede, Alemseghed, and J. David Knottnerus. "Beyond the Pales of Babylon: The Ideational Components and Social Psychological Foundations of Rastafari." *Sociological Perspectives* 41/3 (1998), 499–517.

Khan, Farieda. *Contemporary South African Environmental Response: An Historical and Socio-Political Evaluations with Particular Reference to Blacks*. Unpublished master's thesis, University of Cape Town, 1990.

Kimmel, Michael S. "Promise Keepers: Patriarchy's Second Coming as Masculine Renewal." *Tikkun* 12/2 (1997): 46–53.

Kleinbooi, Hein. "Identity Crossfire: On Being a Gay Black Student Activist." In *Defiant Desire: Gay and Lesbian Lives in South Africa*, edited by Mark Gevisser and Edwin Cameron. Johannesburg: Raven Press, 1994.

Kleinschmidt, Horst. *White Liberation: A Collection of Essays*. Johannesburg: Ravan Press, 1972.

Kloppers, Annie. *Biografie van 'n bende. Die storie van Fokofpolisiekar*. Pretoria: Protea Boekhuis, 2011.

Kok, Pieter. *Michael O'Donovan, Oumar Bouare and Johan van Zyl, Post-Apartheid Patterns of Internal Migration in South Africa*. Cape Town: HSRC Press, 2003.

Kritzinger, J.N.J. "South African Black Theology." Study guide 2 for MSB301–F, *Mission as Liberation: Third World Theologies*. Pretoria: University of South Africa, 1989.

Krog, Antjie. *Die beautiful woorde van Van Wyk Louw* (NP van Wyk Louw Gedenklesing). Johannesburg: University of Johannesburg, 2004.

Lajul, Wilfred. *African Philosophy: Critical Dimensions*. Nairobi: Fountain Publishers, 2013.

Lemanski, Charlotte. "Desegregation and Integration as Linked or Distinct? Evidence from a Previously 'White' Suburb in post-Apartheid Cape Town." *International Journal of Urban & Regional Research* 30/3 (2006): 564–86.

———. "Spaces of Exclusivity or Connection: Linkages between a Gated Community and Its Poorer Neighbour in a Cape Town Master Plan Development." *Urban Studies* 43/2 (2006): 397–402.

Lincoln, C. Eric. *The Black Muslims in America*. Trenton, NJ: AWP Press, 1961. Reprint, 1994.

Lombaard, Christo. "Gewaarwordinge. 'n Gesprek oor Afrikaans-Christelike geloofsprikkels in ons tyd." *Pomp* 1 (2006): 291–93.

———. "Om die Skrif tot stilte te bring . . . Gewaarwordinge oor Afrikaanse Bybelse spiritualiteit." *Litnet Akademies (Godsdienswetenskappe)* 9/3 (2012): 929–95.

Lye, William F., and Colin Murray. *Transformations on the Highveld: The Tswana and Southern Sotho*. Cape Town: David Philip, 1980.

Makwembere, Sandra. "Hallmarks of Irresponsible and Unresponsive Governance: Internal Xenophobic Attacks in South Africa's Municipalities." Special edition, *TD: Journal for Transdisciplinary Research in Southern Africa* 11/4 (2015): 118–26.

Maluleke, Tinyiko S. "Desmond Tutu's Earliest Notions and Visions of Church, Humanity, and Society." *Ecumenical Review* 67/4 (2015), 572–90.

Mamdani, Mahmood. "Centre for African Studies: Some Preliminary Thoughts." *Social Dynamics* 22/2 (1996): 1–14.

———. *Citizen and Subject: Contemporary Africa and the Legacy of Late Colonialism.* Princeton Studies in Culture/Power/History. Kampala: Fountain Publishers, 1996.

Maré, Gerhard. *De-classified: Moving beyond the Dead End of Race in South Africa.* Johannesburg: Jacana, 2014.

———. "Race Counts in Contemporary South Africa: 'An Illusion of Ordinariness.'" *Transformation* 47 (2001): 75–93.

Marie, Rowanne. "Across the Kala Pani: Untold Stories of Indian Christian Women in South Africa." *Oral History Journal of South Africa* 2/1 (2014): 89–101.

Martin, Tony, and Marcus Garvey. *Message to the People: The Course of African Philosophy.* Dover, MA: Majority Press, 1986.

Matlwa, Kopano. *Coconut.* Johannesburg: Jacana, 2007.

Matolino, Bernard. *Personhood in African Philosophy.* Pietermaritzburg, South Africa: Cluster Publications, 2014.

Mazrui, Ali. *The Africans: A Triple Heritage.* London: BBC Publications, 1986.

———. "Global Africa in Flux: The Dialectic of Diversity in the Black World." In *African Presence in the Americas,* edited by Carlos Moore, Tanya R. Saunders, and Shawna Moore. Trenton, NJ: Africa Word Press, 1995.

Mbecke, Paulin. "Anti-Afrophobia Policy Shortfall and Dilemma in the New Partnership for Africa's Development and South Africa." *TD: Journal for Transdisciplinary Research in Southern Africa* 11/4 (2015): 71–82.

Mbeki, Govan. *The Struggle for Liberation in South Africa: A Short History.* Cape Town: David Philip, 1992.

Mbembe, Achille. "African Modes of Self–Writing." *Public Culture* 14/1 (2002): 239–73.

———. "Decolonising the University: New Directions." *Arts & Humanities in Higher Education* 15/1 (2016): 40.

———. *On the Postcolony.* Berkeley: University of California Press, 2001.

———. *Sortir de la grande nuit, Essai sur lAfrique décolonisée.* Paris: La Decouverte, 2013.

McClendon, Gwyneth H. "Race and Responsiveness: An Experiment with South African Politicians." *Journal of Experimental Political Science* 3/1 (2016): 60–74.

McDonald, Michael. *Why Race Matters in South Africa.* Cambridge, MA: Harvard University Press, 2005.

Meer, Y. S. *Documents of Indentured Labour: Natal 1851–1917.* Durban: Institute of Black Research, 1980.

Metz, Thaddeus. "Just the Beginning for Ubuntu: Reply to Matolino and Kwindingwi." *South African Journal of Philosophy* 33/1 (2014): 65–72.

———. "An Ubuntu-based Evaluation of the South African State's Response to Marikana: Where's the Reconciliation?" *Politikon* 44/2 (2017): 287–303.

Meyer, Birgit. "'Make a Complete Break with the Past': Memory and Post-Colonial Modernity in Ghanaian Pentecostalist Discourse." *Journal of Religion in Africa* 28/3 (1998): 316–49.

Míguez, Néstor, Joerg Rieger, and Jung Mo Sung. *Beyond the Spirit of Empire*. London: SCM Press, 2009.

Mishra, Vijay. *The Literature of the Indian Diaspora: Theorising the Diasporic Imaginary*. London: Routledge, 2007.

Moll, Peter. "Discrimination Is Declining in South Africa but Inequality Is Not." *Journal for Studies in Economics and Econometrics* 24/3 (2000): 91–108.

Molyneux, Maxine. "Mobilisation without Emancipation? Women's Interests, State and Revolution in Nicaragua." *Feminist Studies* 11 (1985): 227–54.

Moodier, T. Dunbar. *The Rise of Afrikanerdom: Power, Apartheid, and the Afrikaner Civil Religion*. Berkeley: University of California Press, 1975.

More, Mabogo P. "Philosophy in South Africa Under Apartheid." In *A Companion to African Philosophy*, edited by Kwasi Wiredu. Cambridge: Blackwell, 2004, 152–53.

More, Percy Mabogo. "Biko: Africana Existential Philosopher." In *Biko Lives! Contesting the Legacies of Steve Biko*, edited by Andile Mngxitama, Amanda Alexander, and Nigel C. Gibson. New York: Palgrave, 2008.

Morrell, Robert, Rachel Jewkers, and Graham Lindegger. "Hegemonic Masculinity/Masculinities in South Africa: Culture, Power, and Gender Politics." *Men and Masculinities* 15/1 (2012): 11–30.

Morris, Alan. *Bleakness and Light: Inner-city Transition in Hillbrow, Johannesburg*. Johannesburg: Witwatersrand University Press, 1999.

Mosala, Itumeleng, J. *Biblical Hermeneutics and Black Theology in South Africa*. Grand Rapids, MI: Eerdmans, 1989.

Moser, Caroline. *Gender Planning and Development: Theory, Practice and Training*. London: Routledge, 1993.

Muchie, Mammo. *The Making of the Africa-Nation: Pan-Africanism and the African Renaissance*. London: Adonis & Abbey, 2003.

Mugambi, Jesse N. K. *Christian Theology and Social Reconstruction*. Nairobi: Acton Publishers, 2003.

Murrell, Nathaniel S., William D. Spencer, and Adrian A. McFarlane. *Chanting Down Babylon: The Rastafari Reader*. Philadelphia, PA: Temple University Press, 1998.

Muyeba, Singumbe, and Jeremy Seekings. "Race, Attitudes and Behaviour in Racially-mixed, Low-Income Neighbourhoods in Cape Town, South Africa." *Current Sociology* 59/5 (2011): 655–71.

Naidoo, Kesaveloo Goonaruthnum. *Coolie Doctor: An Autobiography*. Durban: Madiba Publishers, 1991.

Naipaul, V. S. *The Mimic Men*. London: Penguin Random House, 2001.

Ngubane, Harriet. *Original Peoples: Zulus of Southern Africa*. Hove, UK: Wayland, 1986.

Ngubane, Jordon K. *Conflict of Minds*. New York: Books in Focus, 1979.

Ngugi wa-Thiong'o. "Writing against Neo-Colonialism." In *Criticism and Ideology*, edited by Kristen Holst Petersen. Stockholm: Nordic Africa Institute, 1988, 92–103.

Nkrumah, Kwame. *Consciencism: Philosophy and Ideology for Decolonisation and Development with Particular Reference to the African Revolution*. London: Heinemann, 1964.

Nürnberger, Klaus. *Faith in Christ Today: Invitation to Systematic Theology*. Vol. 2, *Involved in God's Project*. Pietermaritzburg, South Africa: Cluster Publications, 2016.

Nwaka, Bernard. *Invading the Babylonian System*. Lusaka: Campus Voice Publishers, 2007.

Nyang, Sulayman. *Islam, Christianity and African Identity*. Chicago, IL: Kazi Publications, 1999.

O'Fahey, R. Sean. "Arabic Literature in the Eastern Half of Africa." In *The Meanings of Timbuktu*, edited by Shamil Jeppie and Souleymane Bachir Diagne. Cape Town: HSRC Press, 2008.

Okem, Andrew, Lucky Asuelime, and Raquel Adekoye. "Re-visiting Xenophobia in South Africa and Its Impact on Africa's Integration." *Africa Insight* 45/2 (2015): 75–85.

Oladipo, Olusegun. *The Idea of African Philosophy: A Critical Study of the Major Orientations in Contemporary African Philosophy*. Ibadan, Nigeria: Hope Publications, 1998.

Olajubu, Oyeronke. *Women in the Yoruba Religious Sphere*. Albany, NY: SUNY Press 2003.

Olivier, Erna. "Afrikaner Spirituality: A Complex Mixture." *HTS Teologiese Studies / Theological Studies* 62/4 (2006): 1469–87.

Outlaw, Lucius. "African, African American, Africana Philosophy." In *African Philosophy: An Anthology*, edited by Emmanuel Chukwudi Eze. Oxford: Blackwell, 1998.

Owino, Kennedy. "'Godly Manhood': Evangelical Constructions of Masculinities in a South African Context: A Case Study of the Mighty Men's Conference (MMC)." Unpublished PhD diss., University of KwaZulu-Natal, 2014.

Pa Anna May Say. "Reading Ruth 3:1–5 from an Asian Women's Perspective." In *Engaging the Bible in a Gendered World: An Introduction to Feminist Biblical Interpretation in Honour of Katharine Doob Sakenfeld*, edited by Linda Day and Carolyn Pressler. Louisville, KY: Westminster John Knox Press, 2006.

Pani, Kala, and Rehana Ebr-Vally. *Caste and Colour in South Africa*. Cape Town: Kwela Books, 2001.

Parry, Kevin, and Amanda Van Eeden. "Measuring Racial Residential Segregation at Different Geographic Scales in Cape Town and Johannesburg," *South African Geographical Journal* 97/1 (2015): 31–49.

Patterson, Orlando. *Sociology of Slavery*. London, Oxford University Press, 1967.

Personal collection. Interviews: Mvula, March 21, 2014, September 15, 2006, and June 24, 2004; Mohlahledi, June 28, 2004; Kgari, June 27, 2004; Madumo, June 30, 2004; Matlaila, June 9, 2004; Poo, March 21, 2014; Ntsoko, March 22, 2014.

Pienaar, E. C. *Die ontstaan van ons Afrikaanse Psalms–en Gesangeboek*. Kaapstad, South Africa: Tafelberg, 1944.

Pillay, Nesen Pillay. *The Indian South Africans*. Pinetown, South Africa: Owen Burgess, 1989).

Pinn, Anthony. *Terror and Triumph: The Nature of Black Religion*. Minneapolis, MN: Fortress Press, 2003.

Prah, Kwesi Kwaa. *Beyond the Colour Line: Pan-Africanist Disputations: Selected Sketches, Letters, Papers, and Reviews*. Trenton, NJ: Africa World Press, 1998.

———. *Tracings: Pan-Africanism and the Challenges of Global African Unity*. Cape Town: CASAS Book Series, 2013.

Prahlad, Swami Anand. *Reggae Wisdom: Proverbs in Jamaican Music*. Jackson, MS: University Press, 2001.

Ramose, Mogobe B. *African Philosophy through Ubuntu*. Harare: Mond Books, 2002.

Ranslem, Duncan. "'Temporary' Relocation: Spaces of Contradiction in South African Law." *International Journal of Law in the Built Environment* 7/1 (2015): 55–71.

Rasing, Thera. *The Bush Burnt, The Stones Remain: Female Initiation Rites in Urban Zambia*. London: African Studies Centre, 2001.

———. *Passing on the Rites of Passage: Girls Initiation Rites in the Context of an Urban Roman Catholic Community*. London: African Studies Centre, 1995.

Reddy, Vasu, Nonhlanhla Mkhize, Jane Bennett, and Relebohile Moletsane. *The Country We Want to Live In: Hate Crimes and Homophobia in the Lives of Black Lesbian South Africans*. Pretoria: HSRC Press, 2010.

Richards, Audrey. *Chisungu: A Girl's Initiation Ceremony among the Bemba of Zambia*. London: Tavistock, 1956.

Roefs, Marlene. "Identity and Race Relations." In *South African Social Attitudes: Changing Times, Diverse Voices*, edited by Udesh Pillay, Ben Roberts, and Stephen Rule. Pretoria: Human Sciences Research Council, 2006.

Roger, Southall. *The New Black Middle Class in South Africa*. Johannesburg: Jacana, 2016.

Rooberts, Benjamin, and Vasu Reddy. "Pride and Prejudice: Public Attitudes toward Homosexuality." South African Social Attitudes Survey, Human Sciences Research Council, *HSRC Review* 6/4 (2008): 9–11.

Ross, Fiona. "Making Home in the New South Africa," Unpublished paper, University of Cape Town, 2003.

Roux, Jurie le. "The Nature of Historical Understanding (or: Hermeneutics and History)." *Studia Historiae Ecclesiasticae* 19/1 (1993): 35–63.

Russell, Margo. "Are Urban Black Families Nuclear? A Comparative Study of Black and White South African Family Norms." *Social Dynamics* 29/2 (2003): 153–76.

Ryba, Thomas. *The Essence of Phenomenology and Its Meaning for Scientific Study of Religion*. New York: Peter Lang, 1991.

Saul, John, S., and Patrick Bond. *The Present as History: From Mrs. Ples to Mandela and Marikana*. Johannesburg: Jacana, 2014.

Savage, Allan M. *Ecology: A "New to You" View: An Orthodox Theological Ecology*. CreateSpace Independent Publishing Platform, 2008.

———. "Phenomenological Philosophy and Orthodox Christian Scientific Ecological Theology." *Indo-Pacific Journal of Phenomenology* 8/2 (2008): 1–9.

———. *Phenomenological Understanding of Certain Liturgical Texts*. Lanham, MD: University Press of America, 2001.

Schaefer, Richard T. *Encyclopedia of Race, Ethnicity, and Society*. London: Sage, 2008.

Scherieff, Leigh, Gillian Finchilescu, and John Dixon. "Understanding the Seating Patterns in a Residence-Dining Hall: A Longitudinal Study of Intergroup Contact." *South African Journal of Psychology* 40/1 (April 2005): 5–17.

Schrieff, Leigh, Colin Tredoux, John Dixon, and Gillian Finchilescu. "Patterns of Racial Segregation in University Residence Dining-Halls." *South African Journal of Psychology* 35 (2005): 433–43.

Seekings, Jeremy. "The Continuing Salience of Race: Discrimination and Diversity in South Africa." *Journal of Contemporary African Studies* 26/1 (2008): 1–26.

———. '"Just Deserts': Race, Class and Distributive Justice in Post-Apartheid South Africa." *Journal of Southern African Studies* 34/1 (2008): 39–60.

———. *Poverty, Policy and Politics in South Africa*. Cape Town: Jacana, 2016.

Seekings, Jeremy, and Nicoli Nattrass. *Class, Race and Inequality in South Africa*. New Haven, CT: Yale University Press, 2005.

———. *Policy, Politics and Poverty in South Africa*. London: Palgrave Macmillan, 2015.

Senghor, Léopold Sédar. *On African Socialism*. London: Paul Mall Press, 1964.

Senior, Olive. *Encyclopaedia of Jamaican Heritage*. Red Hills, Jamaica: Twin Guinep, 2003).

Serfontein, Willem Jacob Benjamin. *Die Psalm as kerklied: Teologiese agtergronde van die Afrikaanse Psalmberyming*. Nijkerk, Netherlands: Callenbach, 1956.

Setiloane, Gabriel, M. *African Theology: An Introduction*. Johannesburg: Skotaville, 1986.

Sheldrake, Philip. *Spirituality and History*. New York: Crossroad, 1992.

Shutte, Augustine. *Ubuntu: An Ethic for a New South Africa*. Pietermaritzburg, South Africa: Cluster Publications, 2001.

Simone, Abdou Maliq. *For the City Yet to Come: Changing African Life in Four Cities*. Durham, NC: Duke University Press, 2004.

Sitoto, Tahir Fuzile. "'Complex Subjectivities': Don Omaruddin Mattera's Conversion to Islam: Beyond a Political Reading and a Biographical Essay." *Journal for Islamic Studies* 34 (2014): 153–76.

Smith, Ashley. *Emergence from Innocence*. Mandeville, Jamaica: Eureka Press, 1991.

Smith, Linda Tuhiawai. *Decolonising Methodologies: Research and Indigenous Peoples*. Dunedin, New Zealand: Otago University Press, 2012.

Sniderman, Paul, and Thomas Piazza. *The Scar of Race*. Cambridge, MA: Belknap Press, 1993.

Soudien, Crain. "Constituting the Class: An Analysis of the Process of Integration in South African Schools." In *Changing Class: Education and Social Change in Post-Apartheid South Africa*, edited by Linda Chisholm. Pretoria: HSRC Press, 2004.

———. "The Reconstitution of Privilege: Integration in Former White Schools in South Africa." *Journal of Social Issues* 66/2 (2010): 352–66.

———. '"We Know Why We're Here': The Experiences of African Children in a 'Coloured' School in Cape Town." *Race, Ethnicity & Education* 1/1 (1998): 7–29.

Southhall, Roger. *The New Black Middle Class in South Africa*. Johannesburg: Konrad Adenauer Foundation, 2016.

Sparks, Alistair. *Tomorrow Is Another Country: The Inside Story of South Africa's Negotiated Settlement*. Johannesburg: Struik, 1994.

Spivak, Gayatri Chackravorty. "Religion, Politics, Theology: A Conversation with Achille Mbembe." *Boundaries* 2, 34/2 (2007): 151–70.

Steyn, Melissa. *Whiteness Just Isn't What It Used to Be: White Identity in a Changing South Africa*. Albany, NY: SUNY Press, 2001.

Stone, Bryan P., and Claire E. Wolfteich. *Sabbath in the City: Sustaining Urban Pastoral Excellence*. Louisville, KY: Westminster John Knox, 2008.
Tanner, Kathryn. *Theories of Culture: A New Agenda for Theology*. Minneapolis, MN: Fortress Press, 1997.
Telles, Edward. *Race in Another America: The Significance of Skin Colour in Brazil*. Princeton, NJ: Princeton University Press, 2005.
Teppo, Annika. "The Making of a Good White: A Historical Ethnography of the Rehabilitation of Poor Whites in a Suburb of Cape Town." Unpublished PhD diss., University of Helsinki, 2004.
Thiselton, Anthony. *New Horizons in Hermeneutics*. Grand Rapids, MI: Zondervan, 1992.
Tirmizi, S.A.I. *Indian Sources for African History*. New Delhi: Manohar, 1989.
Toit, Redakteur J.H H. du (red.) *n Geskiedenis van die Afrikaanse Protestantse Kerklied*. Pretoria: NG Kerkboekhandel, 1983.
Toress, Maldonado. "AAR Centennial Roundtable: Religion, Conquest, and Race in the Foundations of the Modern/Colonial World." *Journal of the American Academy of Religion* 82 (September 2014): 636–65.
Tosh, John. *The Pursuit of History: Aims, Methods and New Directions in the Study of Modern History*. London: Longman, 1991.
Tredoux, Colin, and John Dixon. "Mapping the Multiple Contexts of Racial Isolation: The Case of Long Street, Cape Town." *Urban Studies* 46/4 (2009): 761–77.
Turner, John C. "Towards a Cognitive Redefinition of the Social Group." *Social Identity & Intergroup Relations* (1982): 15–40.
Tutu, Desmond Mpilo. *God Is Not a Christian and Other Provocations*. Edited by John Allen. New York: Harper One, 2011.
———. *No Future without Forgiveness*. New York: Image Doubleday, 2000.
Vahed, Goolam. "Indian Muslims in South Africa: Continuity, Change and Disjuncture, 1860–2000." *Alternation* 7/2 (2000): 67–98.
———. "The Making of Indianness: Indian Politics in South Africa during the 1930s and 1940s." *Journal of Natal and Zulu History* 17 (1997).
Vahed, Goolam, and Thembisa Waetjen. *Schooling Muslims in Natal: Identity, State and the Orient Islamic Educational Institute*. Pietermaritzburg, South Africa: University of KwaZulu-Natal Press, 2015.
Walker, Cherryl. *Women and Resistance in South Africa*. Cape Town: David Philip, 1991.
Walker, Liz. "Men Behaving Differently: South African Men since 1994." *Culture, Health & Sexuality* 7/3 (2005): 225–38.
Wallis, Jim. *America's Original Sin: Racism, White Privilege, and the Bridge to a New America*. (Grand Rapids, MI: Brazos Press, 2016.
Western, John. *Outcast Cape Town*. Minneapolis, MN: University of Minnesota Press, 1981.
Wheellahan, Elizabeth Leesa. "How Markets Distort Decisions to Undertake Education, Vocational Knowledge, Provision and Qualifications." Proceedings of the 4th International Conference of Researching: Work and Learning, University of Technology, Sydney, Australia, 2005.
Wiredu, Kwasi, ed. *A Companion to African Philosophy*. Malden, MA: Blackwell, 2004.

Wiredu, Kwasi, and Kwame Gyekye, eds. *Person and Community: Ghanaian Philosophical Studies*. Washington, DC: Council for Research in Values and Philosophy, 1992.

Wright, Christopher J. H. *The Mission of God's People: A Biblical Theology of the Church's Mission*. Grand Rapids, MI: Zondervan, 2010.

Yasus, Afari. *Overstanding Rastafari: Jamaica's Gift to the World*. Kingston: Senya Cum, 2007.

Yong, Amos. *The Missiological Spirit: Christian Mission Theology in the Third Millennium Global Context*. Eugene, OR: Cascade Books, 2014.

Zeleza, Tiyambe. *Manufacturing African Studies and Crises*. Dakar: CODESRIA, 1997.

INDEX

About the Editors and Contributors

Ashwin Desai is professor in the Department of Sociology at the University of Johannesburg. He previously lectured at the University of Durban-Westville (now University of KwaZulu-Natal), Workers College in Durban, and Rhodes University. His recent book is *Reverse Sweep: The Story of Cricket in Post-Apartheid South Africa* (Johannesburg: Jacana Media, 2017).

Bernard Matolino is a senior lecturer in philosophy at University of KwaZulu-Natal. He also teaches an MPhil module in African philosophy at St. Augustine College of South Africa, Johannesburg. He has authored numerous articles on African philosophy, race, and racism in both local and international journals. He is the author of *Personhood in African Philosophy* (Pietermaritzburg, South Africa: Cluster Publications, 2014).

Chammah J. Kaunda is African research fellow, senior research specialist in Human and Social Development (HDS) of the Human Sciences Research Council of South Africa (HSRC). He is also an honorary lecturer at the University of KwaZulu-Natal, Pietermaritzburg, South Africa and Trans-Africa Christian University, Kitwe, Zambia. He is a prolific young African scholar and has written more than fifty peer-reviewed articles and book chapters. He was a co-guest editor of *Alternation*, special issue 14 (2015) under the theme Empire Religions, Theologies, and Indigenous Knowledge Systems. He is also co-editor of *Anthology of African Christianity* (Oxford: Regnum Publishers, 2016).

Christo Lombaard is professor of Christian spirituality at the University of South Africa, Pretoria. His research specializations include biblical spirituality, postsecularism, spirituality theory, sexuality and spirituality (including Song of Songs), communication media and spirituality, the patriarchs of ancient Israel, and Pentateuchal theory. He holds two doctorates: a PhD in communications (North-West University, Potchefstroom, specializing in religious communications) and a DD in theology (University of

Pretoria, specializing in Old Testament studies). He is a South African National Research Foundation–rated researcher and a regular contributor to conferences around the globe. His most accessible publication is *The Old Testament and Christian Spirituality* (Atlanta, GA: Society of Biblical Literature, 2012), which was awarded the 2013 Krister Stendahl medal for Bible scholarship by the Graduate Theological Foundation in the United States.

Goolam Vahed is an associate professor in the Department of History. He did his undergraduate studies at the University of Durban-Westville (now University of KwaZulu-Natal) and received his PhD from Indiana University-Bloomington. His research focuses on race and ethnic identity, and the role of sport and culture in South African society. He coedited *Chatsworth: The Making of a South African Township* (Pietermaritzburg, South Africa: University of KwaZulu-Natal Press, 2013).

Jeremy Seekings is professor of political studies and sociology, former director of the Centre for Social Science Research, and interim director of the Institute for Democracy, Citizenship and Public Policy in Africa, all at the University of Cape Town. He is also a visiting professor at Yale University, New Haven, Connecticut. His books include *Class, Race and Inequality in South Africa* (2005/6), *Growing up in the New South Africa: Childhood and Adolescence in Post-Apartheid Cape Town* (2010), and *Poverty, Policy and Politics in South Africa* (2016). He runs a research program on the politics of welfare reforms in contemporary Africa and is also researching the history of welfare-state building in Africa and the Caribbean since the 1930's and the dynamics of race and class in contemporary South Africa.

Justin Sands is a postdoctoral fellow at North-West University, Potchefstroom, in South Africa. He received his PhD at KU Leuven, Belgium, in 2015, researching fundamental theology and philosophy of religion, specifically focusing on the ontotheological critique of metaphysics and the work of Merold Westphal. His current research focuses upon the concepts of faith and time.

Kennedy Owino is an educator at the Seth Mokitimi Methodist Seminary (SMMS) and honorary lecturer at the School of Religion, Philosophy and Classics at the University of KwaZulu-Natal. Dr. Owino serves as the unit head for Research and Special Programmes Unit at SMMS. He is also one of the editors of the *Journal of Gender & Religion in Africa*. His academic interest is in systematic theology and its interface with various issues relating to religion, gender, and African Christianities. Dr Owino's current research focuses primarily on critical studies on men and masculinity in contemporary African societies and Christianities.

Marshall W. Murphree was born in Mutare, Zimbabwe, in 1931. He holds degrees from three American universities and a PhD from the London School of Economics and Political Science. He was a professor at the University of Zimbabwe from 1970 to 2006 and remains a professor emeritus at the university. He has been associated with the Maurice Webb Trust since 1970.

Maserole Christina Kgari-Masondo (PhD) is an ordained pastor and bishop at The People of God Christian Ministries. She is a lecturer at the University of KwaZulu-Natal, School of Education at Edgewood Campus. Her research interests are in socio-environmental concerns, indigenous knowledge, teaching and learning matters, and gender issues.

Mutale Mulenga Kaunda (PhD) is a Zambian woman living in South Africa. She is a postdoctoral research fellow at the School of Religion, Philosophy and Classics, University of KwaZulu-Natal in Pietermaritzburg. She was writing mentor to graduate students in the Gender, Religion and Health program at UKZN. She has published articles focusing on the intersection of gender, sexuality, religion, culture, and work in Africa. The most recent, copublished with Chammah J. Kaunda, is "*Infunkutu* (Sexual Dance) and Bemba Women's Sexual Agency," *Journal of Theology for Southern Africa* 155, special issue, *Sexuality in Africa* (July 2016): 159–75.

Nico A. Botha is professor in Missiology at the University of South Africa and serves as a tent-making minister in the United Reformed Church of South Africa, Middelburg-Nazareth. As an academic citizen, he serves as the general secretary of Southern African Missiological Society and as an executive member of the International Association for Mission Studies.

Nobuhle Hlongwa is a dean of teaching and learning in the College of Humanities at the University of KwaZulu-Natal. She is the former acting deputy dean of undergraduate studies in the Faculty of Humanities, Development and Social Sciences. She is the former head of the School of isiZulu Studies (2005–2007). She is the author of a scholarly book entitled *Ukuhlelwa Kolimi*, translated as language planning. She is one of the guest editors of two special issues of *Alternation*, special edition 13 (2014), with the theme "African Languages in Africa's Dispensation of Freedom and Democracy," and *Alternation* 17/1 (2010), with the theme "Multilingualism for Access, Language Development and Language Intellectualisation." She is a member of the board of directors of the International Congress of Onomastic Sciences. She is the editorial secretary of *Nomina Africana* journal. She is an executive member of International Council on Indigenous Place Names.

Roderick R. Hewitt taught at the United Theological College of the West Indies, University of the West Indies, Kingston, Jamaica, before joining the staff at the School of Religion, Philosophy and Classics, University of KwaZulu-Natal, where he is associate professor in systematic theology, lecturing also in ecumenical theology and missiology. He serves the school as academic leader for research and higher degrees. In addition to his many journal articles, his book publications include *Church and Culture: An Anglo-Caribbean Experience of Hybridity and Contradiction*. He coedited *Postcolonial Mission, Power and Partnership in World Christianity* with Desmond van der Water, Isabel Phiri, Namsoon Kang, and Sarojini Nadar, and in 2016 he coedited *Ecumenical Missiology: Changing Landscapes and New Conception of Mission* with Kenneth R. Ross, Jooseop Keum, and Kyriaki Avtzi. He was educated at the United Theological College of the West Indies, University of the West Indies, BA (Hons), and at Kings College, University of London (MPhil and PhD).

Rowanne Sarojini Marie is presently the academic dean at the Seth Mokitimi Methodist Seminary in Pietermaritzburg. She is a PhD graduate of the University of KwaZulu-Natal, in the field of theology and development. Her doctoral work is based on a gendered theology of work, giving attention to the experiences of Indian women.

Sibusiso Masondo (PhD) has taught religious studies at the University of Cape Town, and now is a senior lecturer in the School of Religion, Philosophy and Classics at the University of KwaZulu-Natal. His research and teaching is focused on African religion, African Christianity and indigenous meaning systems, African indigenous churches, African intellectual history, and comparative religion. His current research focus is on the challenges of African religion in contemporary South Africa.

Scott Everett Couper writes in his capacity as a senior honorary lecturer at the University of KwaZulu-Natal's School of Religion, Philosophy and Classics in Pietermaritzburg (South Africa). Couper is also the minister of Bethel Congregational Church (United Congregational Church of Southern Africa) in Sydenham (South Africa), the academic coordinator of the School for International Training (USA), Political and Social Transformation Programme in Durban (South Africa), an adjunct lecturer at the Seth Mokitimi Methodist Seminary in Pietermaritzburg, resident historian at Inanda Seminary in Inanda (South Africa), and long-term volunteer for Global Ministries in Indianapolis, Minnesota (USA).

Tahir Fuzile Sitoto is a lecturer in comparative religion and thought in the School of Religion, Philosophy and Classics, University of KwaZulu-Natal, Howard Campus. His research focus more recently is on the interface between Islam and Africana existential thought, Africana critical theory, black African Muslim identity and subjectivities, as well as on Islam as a spiritual category.

Vuyani S. Vellem is a professor in the Department of Dogmatics and Christian Ethics, University of Pretoria, South Africa. He is the director of the Centre for Public Theology. He focuses his research on liberation theology, including themes such as Christianity and democracy, Christianity and economics, and fields such as ecclesiology, public and liberation theologies, and spirituality.